W9-BLF-931

ALSO BY A. J. LANGGUTH

Driven West: Andrew Jackson and the Trail of Tears to the Civil War (2010)

*Union 1812: The Americans Who Fought the
Second War of Independence* (2006)

Our Vietnam: The War 1954–1975 (2000)

A Noise of War: Caesar, Pompey, Octavian and the Struggle for Rome (1994)

Patriots: The Men Who Started the American Revolution (1988)

Saki: A Life of Hector Hugh Munro (1981)

Hidden Terrors (1978)

Macumba: White and Black Magic in Brazil (1975)

Marksman (1974)

Wedlock (1972)

Jesus Christs (1968)

HOW THE NORTH WON THE CIVIL WAR AND LOST THE PEACE

AFTER LINCOLN

A. J. LANGGUTH

SIMON & SCHUSTER

NEW YORK   LONDON   TORONTO   SYDNEY   NEW DELHI

CONTENTS

CAST OF CHARACTERS

Benjamin Franklin Butler
November 5, 1818–January 11, 1893
The Union general occupying New Orleans. A Radical Republican, he argued for the impeachment of Andrew Johnson and wrote the anti-KKK Act of 1871.

Salmon Portland Chase
January 13, 1808–May 7, 1873
Ohio senator and governor and Lincoln's Treasury secretary. In December 1864, Lincoln named Chase to replace Roger B. Taney as U.S. Supreme Court Chief Justice.

Jefferson Finis Davis
June 3, 1808–December 6, 1889
A West Point graduate, U.S. senator from Mississippi, president of the Confederate States of America. Captured by Union troops in 1865 but never tried for treason, Davis retired to Biloxi to write his memoirs.

Nathan Bedford Forrest
July 13, 1821–October 29, 1877
Lieutenant general in the Confederate army, he was accused of—but never tried for—the slaughter of black Union troops at Fort Pillow, Tennessee, in 1864. Said to be the first Grand Wizard of the Ku Klux Klan in 1867.

Ulysses S. Grant

April 27, 1822–July 23, 1885

Commanded the Union army in victory over the Southern Confederacy. As the nation's eighteenth president (1869–1877), he oversaw Reconstruction efforts and opposed the Ku Klux Klan. While Grant was personally honest, his second term was marred by corruption within his administration.

Horace Greeley

February 3, 1811–November 29, 1872

Founder and editor of the *New York Tribune*, Greeley promoted the nation's expansion to the Pacific Coast and was widely quoted for advising, "Go West, young man." Greeley broke with the Radical Republicans to run for president against Grant in 1872 on the new Liberal Republican ticket.

Rutherford Birchard Hayes

October 4, 1822–January 17, 1893

Republican governor of Ohio, Hayes succeeded Grant in 1877 when he became the nineteenth U.S. president by one electoral vote. His supporters had agreed he would withdraw the last Federal troops from Louisiana and South Carolina, ending the twelve-year effort at Reconstruction.

Oliver Otis Howard

November 8, 1830–October 26, 1909

A Union general, he went on to head the Bureau of Refugees, Freedmen, and Abandoned Lands. His emphasis on education for the former slaves led to the founding of Howard University.

Andrew Johnson

December 29, 1808–July 31, 1875

A slave owner from Tennessee, Johnson became America's seventeenth president upon Lincoln's assassination. Clashing with Radical Republicans over Reconstruction policies, he became the first president to be impeached and was saved from conviction by one vote. Johnson was elected to the U.S. Senate in 1875, months before his death.

Pinckney Benton Stewart Pinchback

May 10, 1837–December 21, 1921

Son of a white plantation owner and his slave, he became the nation's first African American governor (Louisiana, December 9, 1872, to January 13, 1873). Elected to both the House and the Senate, he was denied his seat by Democrats.

Hiram Rhodes Revels

September 27, 1827–January 16, 1901

Born to free parents in North Carolina, he attended Union County Quaker Seminary in Indiana and was ordained as a minister in the African Methodist Episcopal Church. Elected to the U.S. Senate from Mississippi in 1870, Revels became the first African American to serve in the U.S. Senate.

William Henry Seward

May 16, 1801–October 10, 1872

Governor of New York and Lincoln's secretary of state, he survived an assassination attempt by the John Wilkes Booth cabal. Seward, who remained loyal to Andrew Johnson, bought Alaska from Russia in 1867.

Edwin McMasters Stanton

December 19, 1814–December 24, 1869

Lincoln's secretary of war, he refused Andrew Johnson's demand that he relinquish the office because of ties with the Radical Republicans. Stanton died days after Grant nominated him for the U.S. Supreme Court.

Thaddeus Stevens
April 4, 1792–August 11, 1868
A fierce abolitionist and member of the House from Pennsylvania, Stevens was a Radical Republican who drove the fight to impeach Andrew Johnson.

Charles Sumner
January 6, 1811–March 11, 1874
An uncompromising U.S. senator from Massachusetts, he was a leader of the Radical Republicans who first introduced civil rights legislation for former slaves.

Samuel Jones Tilden
February 9, 1814–August 4, 1886
A Democrat who stayed loyal to the Union, Tilden ran as New York's governor against Hayes in 1876 and lost the brokered election by one electoral vote.

William Magear Tweed
April 3, 1823–April 12, 1878
From a minor New York City job, "Boss" Tweed built a Tammany Hall political machine that controlled state legislators and judges. Tweed was the third-largest landowner in the city, after bribery and payoffs estimated at tens of millions. Convicted of corruption in 1877, he died in a New York jail.

Benjamin Franklin Wade
October 27, 1800–March 2, 1878
As a Radical senator from Ohio, he was highly critical of Lincoln's Reconstruction policies. Presiding over the U.S. Senate's impeachment trial, Wade would have replaced Andrew Johnson if he had been convicted.

Morrison Remick Waite
November 29, 1816–March 23, 1888
Waite was appointed by Grant in 1874 as Chief Justice of the U.S. Supreme Court. Despite his early antislavery position, he ruled

regularly against new legislation protecting the rights of the former slaves.

Thurlow Weed
November 15, 1797–November 22, 1882
New York newspaper publisher responsible for the political career of William Henry Seward.

Abraham Lincoln
March 6, 1865

APRIL 14, 1865

Lt. General Ulysses S. Grant begged off when the president invited Grant to join him and his wife later that evening at the theater. Julia Grant felt she had been snubbed recently by Mary Lincoln, and since Grant had just accepted Robert E. Lee's surrender at Appomattox five days earlier, he could offer the diplomatic excuse that he and his wife were eager to return to their home and children in Burlington, New Jersey.

The Grants boarded the 4 p.m. train to New York, which entered Philadelphia on Broad Street to let passengers be ferried across the Delaware River. Grant had not eaten since 9 a.m., and at a restaurant near the ferry landing he ordered a plate of oysters.

Before they could be served, an aide appeared with one telegram, and then a second and a third. "Is anything the matter?" his wife asked. "You look startled."

"Yes," Grant answered. "Something very serious has happened. Do not exclaim. Be quiet, and I will tell you."

President Lincoln had been assassinated at the Ford Theater. Secretary of State William Henry Seward and his son had also been shot at their home and might not survive. General Grant was requested to return to Washington immediately.

Grant was overcome with emotion. Like most of his relatives, he had supported Illinois Democratic senator Stephen A. Douglas against

Lincoln in the presidential election five years earlier. But before that, as a twenty-one-year-old soldier in 1842, Grant had shared Lincoln's opposition to war with Mexico.

By the time Grant was commanding troops during the Civil War, he had become the target of scurrilous reports to Lincoln in the White House. The editor of the *Cincinnati Commercial* summed him up as "a poor drunk imbecile." But Grant was winning battles, and Lincoln stood by him.

From their first meeting, they seemed to understand each other. Grant had listened sympathetically as the president admitted that he had no military expertise. What he wanted, Lincoln said, was a general who would take responsibility. And act. He would supply such a man with all the assistance at his command.

Grant promised to do his best.

Over time, the general had warmed to Lincoln's generous heart, and he shared the president's vision of a country reunited at the war's end.

Grant had concluded, however, that Vice President Andrew Johnson was a far different sort of man—vengeful toward the South and likely to set back the healing that would be required for a successful reconstruction.

With Burlington only an hour away, Grant decided to escort his wife home before he returned to the capital. By the time he disembarked in Washington once more, Grant saw that the news of Lincoln's death had spread rapidly. Where there had been joy in the streets over an end to the war, Grant now saw faces contorted with grief. All of Washington seemed to be in mourning.

He found that early rumors about the killings had been exaggerated. George Atzerodt, a German immigrant, had been assigned by the conspirators to kill Vice President Johnson but refused at the last minute to go through with it. Secretary of State Seward had been the target of a more determined attempt; he and his son were in critical condition but alive.

From those first reports, Grant did not learn that he had been another intended victim. Details of the conspiracy emerged only later, weeks after John Wilkes Booth, the actor who had killed Lincoln, was trapped in a tobacco barn in Virginia and shot to death by a Union army sergeant.

For the moment, Grant was forced to turn aside from the turmoil in official Washington and devote himself to winding down the war. Leaving Appomattox, he had ordered George Meade, the victorious general at Gettysburg, to take his armies back to camp and wait for Confederate general Joseph Johnston to respond to Lee's surrender.

Grant authorized another of his generals, William Tecumseh Sherman, to offer the same terms to Johnston that Grant had accorded Lee.

Grant remembered that Lincoln had set only two conditions for surrender: The Confederacy must agree to preserve the Union and to abolish slavery. If the rebels were willing to concede those two points, Lincoln had said, he was all but ready to sign his name to a blank piece of paper and let them fill out the balance of the terms.

In that spirit, Grant had accepted General Lee's surrender with the courtesies due a worthy adversary. He allowed Lee's officers to retain their sidearms and Lee to keep his ceremonial sword. Confederate officers and enlisted men could also hold on to their mules and horses, including Lee's famous Traveller. At General Lee's request, Grant provided rations for the rebel troops, who had been near starvation.

Grant suspected that Lincoln would have been relieved if Confederate president Jefferson Davis managed to escape across the Mississippi River and spared Lincoln from dealing with his punishment. "He thought," Grant recalled, "that enough blood had already been spilled to atone for our wickedness as a nation."

Looking toward the future, Grant did not believe that most Northerners were in favor of Negroes voting. They might expect that development eventually, but only after a period of probation during which the ex-slaves could—as Grant put it—"prepare themselves for the privileges of citizenship before the full right would be conferred."

And the rebellious Southerners "surely would not make good citizens if they felt they had a yoke around their neck."

Charles Sumner

CHAPTER I

CHARLES SUMNER (1865)

Charles Sumner disagreed, vehemently, with General Grant's vision of life after the Civil War ended. A fifty-four-year-old senator from Massachusetts, Sumner had already been a casualty of that war, four years before its first shot was fired.

Sumner's grandfather had fought in the American Revolution, but he had inherited his abiding fervor from his father, who opposed segregated schools and the law forbidding marriage between whites and blacks. A lifelong crusader, the elder Sumner was fond of saying, "The duties of life are more than life," and he passed on that philosophy to his twins, a boy and a girl, born in 1811. Although Matilda Sumner died at twenty-one, her brother Charles never forgot the lesson.

From Boston Latin Grammar School, Charles went on to Harvard, where he strongly impressed his law professor Joseph Story, who was also a justice on the U.S. Supreme Court.

But a trip to Washington soured Sumner on a political career. He developed a loathing for the theatrical airs of the Senate and for what he derided as "newspaper fame." Apart from Judge Story, he found the Court no better. Calling on Chief Justice Roger Taney, Sumner was disdainful of his "paltry collection of books, which seem to be very seldom used."

He chose instead to travel extensively throughout Europe, where he picked up fluency in German, Italian, French, and Spanish. Members of the British aristocracy were taken with this young Yankee's erudition and welcomed him into their circle for fox hunting at their country estates.

Sumner dined at the Garrick Club and took tea with Mary Shelley, the author of *Frankenstein*. His hostess forgot his nationality so completely that as they chatted she exclaimed, "Thank God, I have kept clear of those Americans!" Sumner pretended not to hear.

Invited by lawyers to Guildhall, London's administrative center, Sumner was pleased to find a marble bust of an early British abolitionist in a place of honor. At Windsor Castle, he toured the private rooms, where he found the royal dining hall unappealingly "showy and brilliant."

When Sumner went home after eighteen months, it was only because his money had run out.

Sumner's father had died during his travels. Back in Boston, he went to live with his mother on Hancock Street while he practiced law and oversaw the upbringing of his brothers and sisters. Friends decided that Europe had sent Charles home more portly but better tailored.

Sumner found that, at six-foot-four and with a powerful voice, he was becoming a popular speaker despite his weakness for fustian language. In the past, Boston's traditional Fourth of July oration had left John Adams unimpressed. By the time the nation's second president died in 1826, he was complaining that the event featured "young men of genius describing scenes they never saw" and professing "feelings they never felt."

When Sumner was chosen for the honor of delivering the oration in 1845, he resolved to do better. The familiar ritual at Tremont Temple began with a prayer, the reading of the Declaration of Independence, and music from a choir of a hundred girls. Then Sumner rose in a dress coat with gilt buttons and white trousers to face an audience of two thousand patriots. Barely referring to notes, he spoke for the next two hours.

Sumner began by denouncing the recent annexation of Texas be-

cause it would probably lead to war with Mexico. Amid murmurs of disapproval from supporters of President Polk's war policy, Sumner spelled
out his theme:

"In our age there can be no peace that is not honorable; there can be
no war that is not dishonorable."

Sumner lauded the glories of nearby Harvard University before
pointing out that after two centuries, the school had accumulated property worth only $703,175. In contrast, the warship *Ohio* docked in Bos-
ton Harbor had cost $834,845.

"War is known as the last reason of kings. Let it be no reason of our
republic. Let us renounce and throw off forever the yoke of a tyranny"—
war—"more oppressive than any in the annals of the world."

It was far from the thrilling martial rhetoric his audience had anticipated. Afterward, during the dinner at Faneuil Hall, Boston's politicians
and military officers angrily disavowed Sumner's sentiments. To restore a
semblance of good humor, the dinner chairman suggested that the problem with his friend Sumner was that since he was a bachelor, he knew
nothing of domestic strife and therefore nothing of war.

But at least one Boston general admired Sumner's reaction to the
discord he had aroused: He withstood "all these fusillades with the
most quiet good nature, and even with good-humored smiles," the man
reported. "No man could have behaved with more exact and refined
courtesy."

When Judge Story died two months later, Sumner debated whether
he wanted to succeed him as head of Harvard's law school. He worried
that taking the position would mean censoring his opinions; he would
"no longer be a free man." But after his Fourth of July oration, Harvard
settled the question for him, and the job was not offered.

Over the next two years, Sumner became appalled by the compro-
mises that Senator Daniel Webster and other Northern Whigs were
making to preserve the Union. In response, Sumner joined with a group
including Salmon P. Chase of Ohio to form a Free Soil Party.

As a Free Soiler, Sumner ran against a Whig congressman in 1848,
lost badly, and retreated to the practice of law. But when President Mil-

lard Fillmore appointed Webster as his secretary of state, the naming of Webster's replacement fell to the commonwealth's legislature.

Many of its members were put off by what they considered Sumner's arrogance and self-righteousness. These days, when he was invited to speak, Sumner insisted that he appear on a stage and not behind a pulpit, which he called "a devilish place." To heighten the insult, he added, "I do not wonder that people in it are dull."

That uncompromising spirit had closed the doors of most of Boston's first families to him. Even his closest friend from Harvard, Henry Wadsworth Longfellow, lamented Sumner's growing obsession. "Nothing but politics now. Oh, where are those genial days when literature was the topic of our conversation?"

Despite those misgivings, Sumner was sent to the U.S. Senate by the margin of a single vote. Once there, he became an unyielding champion of his father's ideals and took satisfaction in being described as the conscience of New England.

Sumner was unperturbed by his unpopularity. Ideas mattered to him, the men who held them hardly at all. When he had come across congenial spirits, they tended to be poets and writers—Longfellow, Ralph Waldo Emerson, John Greenleaf Whittier. And the circle was exclusively male. One friend observed that at any gathering, Sumner "would at once desert the most blooming beauty to talk to the plainest of men."

In the years leading to the war, Sumner had remained a bachelor.

If Charles Sumner was a product of the culture that had produced the stern John Quincy Adams, Representative Preston S. Brooks reflected—like Henry Clay—the more indulgent life of the South and West. By the time he graduated from village grammar schools, Brooks had become so devoted to local taverns that the faculty of South Carolina College felt compelled to tighten its disciplinary code. Even so, Brooks was expelled before he could graduate for what the college described as "riotous behavior."

Moving on to practice law in Edgefield, South Carolina, Brooks was twenty-one when he fought his first duel—turning a trifling affront into a point of honor. Because dueling was illegal in the state, he met his antagonist on a nearby Georgia island. Brooks took a bullet in his abdomen and thigh. The other man was also wounded, but both of them survived.

At six-foot, Brooks was nearly as tall and imposing as Sumner, but his life involved far more romance. When his first wife died after two years of marriage, Brooks married her sister. A supporter of the war with Mexico, he went off jauntily to fight. A fever soon sent him home again, but his service contributed to his military bearing.

As a Democrat who did not favor immediate secession, Brooks was rewarded for his moderation in 1852, with election to Congress from South Carolina. There he joined his cousin, the state's senator, Andrew Pickens Butler, and he was present in the Senate chambers on March 19, 1856, when Sumner of Massachusetts rose to argue that for Kansas to enter the Union, it must outlaw slavery.

Sumner had already annoyed fellow senators in 1852 by urging repeal of the Fugitive Slave Act at a time when both parties wanted to slip past that year's presidential election without debating the issue. Senate leaders did their best to stop Sumner from speaking, but he finally got the floor and introduced a motion to end the requirement that every citizen, North or South, join in apprehending runaway slaves. Sumner attracted three votes besides his own.

Although his crusade failed, Sumner's eloquence drew disaffected Whigs and Free Soilers to another new movement. In September 1854, they came together in Worcester, Massachusetts, to form a coalition they called the Republican Party.

Other Whigs, however, were still put off by Sumner's intemperance. For the time being, men like Abraham Lincoln of Illinois and Henry Seward of New York saw a brighter future with the Whigs than with the Republicans or another splinter group, the secretive and anti-immigrant Know Nothings.

And yet, the Know Nothings did much better than any other slate in the election for the Massachusetts legislature—377 Know Nothings won, against a single Whig, one Democrat, and one Republican.

Sumner responded with renewed passion. On a trip through Kentucky, he absorbed the lessons of his first extended exposure to slavery. In Lexington, he watched a slave auction and saw a coach driver whipping a Negro. At his hotel, a black child who was waiting on tables was knocked to the floor by a white man's blow to his head.

Back home, Sumner's speeches berated the Know Nothings—"I am not disposed to place any check upon the welcome of foreigners"—and stumped energetically for the Republicans. But within his new party, schisms were already arising. Men who shared Sumner's resolute politics—Senator Benjamin Wade of Ohio, Congressman Thaddeus Stevens of Pennsylvania—were being called radicals.

By the time Sumner rose for his next two-day oration, the label had become official: Sumner was a Radical Republican. Yet he considered his speech simply a historical review of slavery, and he had shown a draft to New York senator Henry Seward, also an abolitionist but far less impatient and outspoken than Sumner. Seward had not supported Sumner's repeal of the Fugitive Slave Act four years earlier, and now he urged Sumner to delete any personal attacks from his speech.

Henry Seward already knew, however, how stiff-necked Sumner could be. Once he had asked Sumner, as a personal favor, to support legislation that would benefit a New York steamship line. Sumner refused. He said that he had not been sent to the Senate to get Seward re-elected.

Seward had snapped, "Sumner, you're a damned fool."

Sumner ended up voting for the bill, but the two men did not speak for months. Their coolness thawed, partly because Seward's wife, Frances, had always been unstinting in her praise of Sumner's "clear moral perceptions" and his being "so fearless a champion of human rights." But even she had advised Sumner against denouncing his colleagues by name.

Sumner ignored her advice and shifted from a mild review of the Kansas affair to biting ridicule. He assailed President Franklin Pierce for bowing to slave owners and Illinois senator Stephen Douglas for supporting a proslavery community within the Kansas territory.

In the past, Sumner had enjoyed his place on the Senate floor next to Preston Brooks's cousin, Andrew Butler. In fact, Sumner had once paid him a high compliment: If only Butler had been born in New England, Sumner said, "he would have been a scholar or, at least, a well educated man."

But Sumner's opposition to the Fugitive Slave Act had destroyed any traces of friendship. Now Sumner claimed that there was nothing Butler touched "that he does not disfigure." The accusation was especially pointed since it could be taken as referring to the defect in Butler's lip that distorted his speech. Sumner went on to add that Butler "cannot open his mouth, but out there flies a blunder."

Butler was not in the chamber as Sumner mocked the way he had boasted about South Carolina's venerable traditions. "He cannot surely have forgotten its shameful imbecility from slavery, confessed throughout the Revolution, followed by its most shameful assumptions for slavery since."

The first Democrat to respond was Michigan's Senator Lewis Cass, his party's presidential candidate eight years earlier. Cass called Sumner's speech "the most un-American and unpatriotic that ever grated on the ears of the members of this high body."

Speaking next, Stephen Douglas charged that Sumner had shown "a display of malignity that issued from every sentence." Douglas asked, "Is it his object to provoke some of us to kick him ...?"

Answering Douglas, Sumner referred to him as a skunk or—as he put it euphemistically—"a noisome, squat and nameless animal" that was "not a proper model for an American Senator."

When newspapers published extracts from Sumner's oration, titled "The Crime Against Kansas," he received lavish congratulations from throughout the North. The *New York Tribune* praised his "inspiring eloquence and lofty moral tone." Sumner's friend Longfellow called the speech "the greatest voice on the greatest subject that has been uttered."

After listening to the first day of Sumner's speech, Preston Brooks had not returned for its conclusion, but Sumner's diatribe against South Carolina was being hashed over at every dinner party in the capital. A consensus was emerging that the tepid response by Southerners to Sumner's provocation had been unmanly.

Brooks realized that his cousin was expected to punish Sumner for his insults. Southerners agreed that a duel was out of the question since Sumner was no gentleman. He would have to be whipped like a dog or a slave.

And yet Senator Butler, a frail sixty-year-old, could not carry out that retribution against the powerfully built Sumner. Brooks decided that punishment fell to him, even though Sumner outweighed him by thirty pounds.

For two days, Brooks lay in wait for Sumner to leave the Senate, but each time Sumner got immediately into his carriage. After another sleepless night, Brooks was ready to change his tactic and run up the flights of stairs to confront Sumner as he entered the Capitol. But when he confided that plan to Congressman Henry Edmundson, the Virginian warned him that the exertion would exhaust him. Since Sumner was the stronger man, Brooks should conserve his strength.

On the third day of his vigil, Brooks went inside the Capitol to pass the time until the Senate adjourned. He then had to wait another hour until a group of women visitors finally left the lobby. Edmundson saw that Brooks had taken a seat on the largely vacant Senate floor and said lightly, "Are you a senator now?"

Brooks was in no mood for joking. "I will stand this thing no longer," he said.

Sumner had remained at his desk, franking copies of his "Crime Against Kansas" speech to mail to constituents. He did not rise when Brooks approached him.

"Mr. Sumner," Brooks began, "I have read your speech with care and as much impartiality as was possible, and I feel it my duty to tell you that you have libeled my State and slandered a relative who is aged and absent, and I am come to punish you for it."

With that, Brooks raised a cane that had been given to him a few months earlier. He had chosen it today because it was made from gutta-percha, a tropical wood that he thought would be less likely to splinter.

Brooks brought down his cane on Sumner's head, pleased to see each strike hitting home. He swung so rapidly that Sumner was soon blinded by his own blood and could not fight back. As the beating continued, however, Sumner made a desperate effort and pulled himself up with such force that he ripped the desk from its iron screws embedded in the floor.

He found, though, that by crouching he had made himself even more vulnerable. The unrelenting blows had splintered the cane, after all, but Brooks persisted, reveling in the sound of Sumner's pain. His victim was bellowing "like a calf," Brooks said afterward.

Sumner passed out and was about to fall. Brooks caught him with one hand while he kept beating him with the other. His cane was in shreds, but Brooks was still flailing when two congressmen heard the uproar and rushed to Sumner's aide. One of Brooks's friends, Representative Laurence Keitt, brandished his own cane to ward them off and shouted, "Let them alone, God damn you!"

But the two reached the scene and pulled Brooks away from Sumner just as a Kentucky senator was hurrying up the aisle to plead, "Don't kill him!"

Awakening from his frenzy, Brooks mumbled, "I did not intend to kill him." As he pocketed his cane's gold head, he added, "But I did intend to whip him."

With Brooks being led to a side room, Sumner slipped again toward the floor. Supported by a friendly congressman, he leaned against a chair while he regained consciousness. A Senate page brought him a glass of water.

Sumner's bleeding head was soaking his coat and trousers. He said he could walk to a sofa in the Senate anteroom but asked that someone recover his hat and the papers on his desk. A doctor arrived to stanch Sumner's wounds and sew four stitches in his scalp.

Soon afterward, he visited Sumner at his lodgings and warned Sumner's friends that he must have absolute quiet. As he drifted off to sleep, Sumner murmured, "I could not believe such a thing was possible."

The doctor was optimistic about Sumner's recovery. He described the beating as producing "nothing but flesh wounds" and predicted that

Sumner could take up his Senate duties within a few days. But when Sumner continued to run a high fever, his brother brought in specialists who found that Sumner's spinal cord had been injured, which made his walking erratic and painful.

As time passed and Sumner did not return to the Senate, his enemies accused him of cowardice. But it took many months at health spas before he could move about freely. In the meantime, Republican lawmakers in Massachusetts elected him to a second Senate term.

When Sumner finally returned to the Capitol, he found that the first day at his desk exhausted him and "a cloud began to gather over my brain." He decided that the most effective cure would be a return to Europe after twenty years.

During the next seven months on the continent, Sumner's hectic social calendar suggested a full recovery. In Paris, the young novelist Henry James, expecting stigmata from the abolitionist hero, was surprised to find Sumner's wounds "rather disappointingly healed."

But returning again to Congress for the new session in December 1857, Sumner discovered that he was still not ready. He could concentrate for only short periods, and he took no interest in the jousting over the status of Kansas between Stephen Douglas and the new president, James Buchanan. Sumner withdrew to Boston and diverted himself by examining a collection of engravings recently donated to Harvard College.

Preston Brooks's assault had made both men famous. From the time of the attack, crowds throughout the North cheered Sumner's name and groaned and hissed at any mention of Brooks. At an Indignation Meeting, Emerson spelled out the lesson of Sumner's beating: "I think we must get rid of slavery, or we must get rid of freedom."

In the South, acclaim and calumny were reversed. The *Herald* of Laurensville, South Carolina, described Brooks as "noble" and Sumner as "notorious." The merchants of Charleston took up a collection to buy Brooks a new cane inscribed "Hit Him Again."

That theme was taken up by the *Richmond Whig*, whose editors had argued in the past for civility. Now they regretted only that Sumner had not been horsewhipped and urged that "Seward and others should catch it next." Another Virginia newspaper, the *Petersburg Intelligencer*, went further in singling out Henry Seward of New York:

"It will be very well to give Seward a double dose at least every other day until it operates freely on his political bowels."

But North Carolina's *Wilmington Herald* spoke for other Southerners when it argued that although perhaps "Sumner deserved what he got," the editor could "not approve the conduct of Brooks" and found the entire episode "disgraceful."

Andrew Butler, his honor avenged, returned to the Senate in time to hear Sumner's friend Henry Wilson denounce Brooks's "brutal, murderous and cowardly assault."

At that, Butler shouted, "You are a liar!" and demanded a duel. Wilson turned away the challenge as a "lingering relic of a barbarous civilization."

The Senate appointed an investigative committee of two Southern Democrats and three Northerners considered moderate on the issue of slavery. They invited Brooks to offer his version of the incident. After he declined to appear, they concluded that he could be punished, if at all, only by his colleagues in the House.

While the House debated over expelling Brooks, a denunciation by one of Sumner's friends provoked Brooks to issue his own challenge to a duel. The other man agreed. But to avoid U.S. laws, he proposed a site on the Canadian side of Niagara Falls.

Brooks backed out, complaining that he could not be protected from Northern mobs. His enemies turned that refusal into a ditty:

> *"But he quickly answered, No, no, no.*
> *"For I'm afraid, afraid, afraid,*
> *"Bully Brooks's afraid."*

Nearly two months after Sumner was assaulted, the House motion to expel Brooks came to the floor. It passed 121 to 95, less than the required two-thirds vote. The following day, the House censured Laurence Keitt for his role but absolved Henry Edmundson.

In New York State, Frances Seward was resigned to the verdict. In the days after the hearing, she had been asked whether Brooks would hang if Sumner died from his wounds. No, she said cynically, only slaves were hanged in Washington, and then by men who thought it was too mild a punishment.

After a district court fined Brooks three hundred dollars, voters returned him to the House in the next election. When he died from a throat infection early in 1857, Sumner was visiting Longfellow in Boston and received the news calmly. He saw Brooks as "a mere tool of the slaveholders," Longfellow recalled.

To another friend, Sumner said, "The Almighty has settled this, better than you or I could have done."

When Sumner returned full-time to the Senate, however, his colleagues learned that any mildness had been fleeting. As a martyr, he had been spared criticism from Northern Whigs, even those who considered him insufferably self-righteous. They found that it was a trait his convalescence had not mitigated.

Sumner said he dreaded being again in Washington "amidst tobacco-spitting, swearing slave-drivers, abused by the press, insulted so far as it is possible, pained and ransacked by the insensibility . . . to human rights and the claims of human nature."

On their side, Southerners had forgiven nothing. They sent threatening letters promising "another pummeling."

Through an accident of history, Sumner was drawn into the debate over a raid of a Southern arsenal by the untamable abolitionist John Brown. After the attack by Preston Brooks, Brown had called on Sumner in Boston to ask if the senator still had the coat he had been wearing on the fateful day.

With effort, Sumner limped to a closet and brought out the coat, caked with his blood. Brown did not speak but held it with his lips pressed tight, while his eyes, Sumner recalled, "shone like polished steel."

Now with Brown about to be hanged for his failed raid at Harper's Ferry, Sumner granted that Brown must be punished, but he also recognized a kindred soul. Yes, he condemned Brown's actions and the bloodshed, Sumner said, "but how can I refuse admiration to many things in the *man*?"

That spirit was on display when President Buchanan invited Sumner to the White House to urge that he endorse recent Senate propositions aimed at warding off civil war.

Sumner heard Buchanan out, then replied that the people of Massachusetts "would see their state sink below the sea and become a sand bar" rather than acknowledge that a human being could be treated as property.

With the presidential election of 1860 approaching, many men in Sumner's Republican Party hoped to attract Northern Whigs and prevent Stephen Douglas from fanning emotions throughout the South. They certainly did not want Sumner's intransigence on public display.

He, in turn, was contemptuous of their caution. He was resigned to the prospect of Henry Seward being the Republican nominee. But Sumner had never fully trusted Seward's commitment to immediate and outright abolition.

When the Republicans met in Chicago, however, delegates passed over Seward to nominate a man who had served only one term in the Congress. Although Sumner did not know Abraham Lincoln, he decided to spell out the principles that Lincoln must embrace.

The result was a four-hour oration on June 4, 1860, titled "The Barbarism of Slavery." Sumner began mildly, alluding indirectly to the recent deaths of Preston Brooks and Senator Butler—"tombs that have been opened since I spoke."

After assuring his audience that he was not motivated by vindictiveness, Sumner laid into the slave-owning states, with special disdain for South Carolina. And, he argued, if the African race was indeed inferior, as the slave owners claimed, "then it is the unquestionable duty of a Christian Civilization to lift it from its degradation, not by the bludgeon and the chain," but by a "generous charity."

Republican politicians deplored Sumner's unrepentant diatribe. His friends began sleeping on his parlor floor to protect him against further retaliation. When Lincoln was sent a copy of the speech, he would not be drawn into the controversy. "I have not yet found time to peruse the speech," Lincoln wrote in his note of thanks, "but I anticipate much both of pleasure and instruction from it."

Although Sumner still had not met the Republican nominee and knew little about him, when the election returns were counted he celebrated Lincoln's victory with a partisan group called the Wide-Awake Club. Throughout the campaign, its members had been demonstrating for Lincoln in Northern cities by carrying torches on long poles to light up the night sky.

Even though they could not vote, the female Wide-Awakers at Mount Holyoke College were no less enthusiastic. The young women were described as "laughing and shouting and drinking lemonade" as they carried a banner that read, "PRESIDENT—ABRAHAM LIN-COLN. Behind a homely exterior, we recognize inner beauty."

When Wide-Awakers in Concord reached the home of Ralph Waldo Emerson, the exuberant crowd spotted Sumner and shouted to him for a speech. At that point, Sumner still hoped that South Carolina's threat to leave the Union would prove idle, but his remarks acknowledged that a cataclysm might be coming:

"A poet has said that the shot fired here was heard round the world, and I doubt not that this victory, which we have achieved in our country, will cause a reverberation that will be heard throughout the globe."

As the consequences of Lincoln's election became inevitable, Sumner could sound torn—never about abolition, but about the fate of the Union. "Much as I desire the extinction of Slavery," he wrote in a letter to an English correspondent, "I do not wish to see it go down in blood."

At other times, he seemed to take a fatalistic satisfaction in the crisis. When South Carolina became the first state to secede, Sumner predicted that "Virginia will go, and will carry with her Maryland and Kentucky. *They will all go.*"

At their first meeting, the president-elect managed to reassure Sumner that he would be steadfast. All the same, Sumner concluded that Lincoln lacked the social grace and dignity to lead the nation. But he had to admit that his conversation could flash with extraordinary insights.

Lincoln was also taking the measure of his guest. Commenting on Sumner's imposing height, he suggested that they stand back to back to see who was taller.

Sumner declined with a reproach: This was "the time for uniting our fronts against the enemy and not our backs."

Lincoln, who admired Sumner's idealism, took the rebuff in good part. He told the story afterward with the glint in his eye that his friends recognized. He had found Sumner's remark "very fine," Lincoln said. "But I reckon the truth was . . . he was afraid to measure!"

In the same teasing tone, Lincoln reminded listeners that he had "never had much to do with the bishops down where I live. But do you know, Sumner is just my idea of a bishop."

From that time on, Lincoln tried to shield Sumner's sensibilities. John Eaton, an army chaplain, recalled the day that Lincoln had been lolling comfortably with a long leg twisted over the arm of his chair. When Sumner was heard approaching, Lincoln instantly snapped to, rose to his feet, and prepared to return his visitor's bow.

Sumner had come to recommend a name for a consulship. Lincoln thanked him warmly and saw him out. Returning to Eaton, Lincoln sank back in his chair, resumed straddling its arm, and explained his hasty attempt at propriety:

"When with the Romans, we must do as the Romans do!"

Sumner's patronizing of the new president persisted to the day he was walking home from the inaugural. He had been pleased with Lincoln's address, and he observed to a Massachusetts colleague that the speech could best be described as "a hand of iron and a velvet glove."

But, Sumner added, Lincoln might not recognize Napoleon's famous phrase.

The president was soon to disappoint Sumner in a more substantial way. Sumner felt he could legitimately expect appointment as secretary of state, since few Americans matched his wealth of experience or his contacts overseas. And yet Lincoln chose Henry Seward, the man he had just defeated for the Republican nomination.

As Lincoln's term unfolded, however, the president and Sumner adjusted to each other. Mary Lincoln reported that she sometimes overheard them in her husband's office, where they would talk and "laugh together like two schoolboys."

When Lincoln struggled with the proclamation that would define his presidency, he did not turn to Charles Sumner for advice. Instead, the president called together his cabinet on July 22, 1862, and even then he confided the purpose of the meeting only to Secretary of State Seward and Secretary of the Navy Gideon Welles.

Overcoming his lingering reluctance, Lincoln was ready to declare that slaves within every state rebelling against the Union were free "thereforward and forever." The result would put an end to slavery for three and a half million black men, women, and children but not for the 425,000 within the states that had not rebelled, since they did not fall under the president's war powers authority.

First reading of the Emancipation Proclamation

Before reading his proclamation aloud, Lincoln announced that his mind was made up and that he "had not called them together to ask their advice."

When he had finished reading, most cabinet officers were stunned into silence or quietly indicated their support. Only Salmon Chase, despite his reputation as a fervent abolitionist, recommended caution. He would have preferred a more sweeping decree, Chase said, but he recommended that discretion be left to the generals on the ground to free the slaves within their occupied territory "as soon as practical."

Speaking last, Henry Seward raised one consequence that Lincoln admitted he had not considered: Given the reverses suffered lately by the Union army, Lincoln's action might look like a desperate last resort.

The list of the North's defeats was indeed sobering, beginning with the first major battle of the war at Bull Run in Northern Virginia. When the troops of Confederate general Thomas Jackson had stood fast and forced the Union army to retreat, both North and South had been shocked into accepting that the war would be a long one. From that day, the general had been called "Stonewall" Jackson, and now a second battle at Bull Run promised to go no better.

Seward recommended that the president wait for a battlefield success. Then, when "the eagle of victory takes flight," Seward said, Lincoln could "hang your proclamation about his neck."

Lincoln was persuaded. He returned the two foolscap pages to his pocket and hoped for a military success.

That moment was slow in coming. In mid-September 1862, General Lee made a daring decision to carry the war to the North. By invading Maryland, he intended to tie down the Union forces that were defending Washington.

Lee did not know that a letter outlining his tactics had been left behind when his army vacated an earlier camp at Frederick City. Recovered by a Union soldier, the letter had been sent to George McClellan, the thirty-six-year-old commander of the Army of the Potomac.

Although McClellan was admired for his meticulous planning, he was proving to be sluggish on the ground. But with Lee's strategy in his pocket, he moved to vanquish Lee's vastly outnumbered Confederate troops.

The battle was fought at Antietam Creek, near the town of Sharps-burg, Maryland. When fighting ended on September 17, 1862, the number of American casualties was greater than in any other single day in the nation's history.

Nearly 24,000 Union and Confederate soldiers had been killed or wounded or were missing in action. Despite the disparity in the num-ber of troops committed to battle, the losses on both sides proved to be close—about 12,500 of McClellan's men against 11,500 of Lee's.

But McClellan's critics pointed out that the general—always worried about being outnumbered—had held back from battle two corps of his reserves that totaled more than Lee's entire force. McClellan's caution had enabled Lee to withdraw to fight again.

Five days after the battle, Lincoln issued the first of a two-part procla-mation. He set a deadline of January 1, 1863, for freeing slaves in any state that did not return to the Union.

Lincoln's ultimatum infuriated the South. Jefferson Davis swore that if freed slaves were recruited as soldiers, he would never recognize them as legitimate combatants and would punish black troops harshly along with their white commanders.

The Union army responded by publishing a code of conduct that protected prisoners of war and forbade torture. The pamphlet warned against mistreating Negro troops and held that the rules of war allowed for "no distinction of color."

When Lincoln's deadline came and went, his second proclamation freed the slaves in the ten states of the Confederacy. But while invoking his authority under Article II of the Constitution, Lincoln exempted the border states that had not seceded—Kentucky, Missouri, Maryland, and Delaware. Also exempted were the state of Tennessee, back again under Union control, and the city of New Orleans, together with thirteen Louisiana parishes.

· · ·

Claiming victory at Antietam had not improved George McClellan's standing with Lincoln. On November 5, 1862, the president removed him from command of the Army of the Potomac and two days later appointed Ambrose Burnside to replace him.

Only two years older than McClellan, Burnside wanted to prove his eagerness to fight. On December 13, he provoked a battle at Fredericksburg, Virginia, where his casualties ran to 12,653 men, almost 1,300 of them killed. Lee's losses were less than half that number—5,377, with 608 dead.

The fiasco led Radical Republicans to step up their scornful criticism of the president's conduct of the war. Lincoln lamented, "If there is a worse place than hell, I am in it."

He sent Burnside to the Army of the Ohio to repair his reputation and, with severe misgivings, appointed Joseph Hooker, a major general approaching fifty but unflagging in his enthusiasm for liquor and for the women available at military encampments.

Further Union losses served to test the alliance between the president and Charles Sumner during the months leading to Lincoln's re-election campaign. Early in January 1864, during a second battle at Cold Harbor, northeast of Richmond, Virginia, Ulysses Grant had lost nearly 7,000 men to General Lee's 1,500.

Dispirited, Sumner became sympathetic to a movement by other Radicals to replace Lincoln, even after he had been nominated by the Republicans for a second term.

Sumner's rift with the president was repaired, however, during the intense debate over a constitutional amendment to outlaw slavery. Although abolition was the crusade of his lifetime, Sumner had not been leading the congressional charge. Instead, it was Missouri senator John Henderson who submitted a joint resolution for the amendment in January 1864. Henderson, no Radical Republican, was a Democrat who had stayed loyal to the Union.

As variations on the amendment were put forth, Sumner found all of them wanting. In a speech on April 8, 1864, he denounced his colleagues for their past inaction:

Since "nothing in the Constitution" supported slavery, Sumner said, no amendment had been necessary. Congress could have acted on its own. But because members had been too timid, he grudgingly acknowledged that an amendment might now be called for.

In the end, Sumner voted for a version cobbled together by the chairman of the Senate Judiciary Committee that would add the United States to the expanding list of nations that banned slavery.

France's revolution had ended slavery in 1794. England first abolished the slave trade in 1807, then outlawed slavery itself in 1832. As America was launching its civil war, Russia had freed its serfs in 1861, and the Netherlands ended slavery in its colonies two years later.

The pending amendment reversed the intention of an amendment offered by Congressman Thomas Corwin of Ohio that had passed Congress in the last days of the Buchanan administration. If ratified by the states, Corwin's proposal would have forbidden any future amendments to abolish or restrict slavery.

Corwin's Thirteenth Amendment would have been the first change in the Constitution in almost sixty years. It had passed both houses of Congress, and in his first inaugural address, Lincoln had seemed to endorse its sentiments.

By April 1864, however, the president had become committed to an amendment that would end slavery. With a vote of thirty-eight to six, the Senate approved the measure on April 8, 1864. When Democrats in the House blocked passage, Lincoln saw to it that the amendment was added to the Republican platform during his re-election campaign.

That election produced enough gains for the Republicans for Lincoln to predict its inevitable passage in the next Congress, but he pressed former Whigs who had become wavering Democrats to switch their votes even before that. He sent aides to lobby for the amendment with a stirring admonition:

"Remember that I am President of the United States, clothed with immense power, and I expect you to procure those votes."

On January 31, 1865, the amendment passed the House 119 to 56, and Lincoln signed it the next day, the final step on the path he had begun with the Emancipation Proclamation.

The president's home state of Illinois hastened to become the first to ratify the amendment on the day he signed it. By the night that Lincoln was shot, Arkansas had become the twenty-first state to ratify, and eight months later, with Georgia's ratification on December 6, 1865, the amendment became part of the U.S. Constitution.

A few states rejected or tabled the change and ratified it only later. The state of Mississippi did not add its approval until 1995 and neglected to notify Washington until February 2013.

The language of the amendment was terse:

1.   Neither slavery nor involuntary servitude, except as a punishment for crime whereof the party shall have been duly convicted, shall exist within the United States, or any place subject to their jurisdiction.
2.   Congress shall have power to enforce this article by appropriate legislation.

Charles Sumner had already moved on. He was preparing to confront the discrimination that he expected the newly freed slaves to face, and he protested a system in the District of Columbia that designated separate streetcars for black passengers. Sumner called it "a disgrace to the city, and a disgrace to the National Government, which permits it under its eyes."

He achieved only limited success—barring discrimination on a single railway—but he did win equal pay for the black soldiers who had been recruited since 1862.

Sumner's crusading continued to come at a price. One of his friends, a Polish translator in the Senate, lamented that he "is attacked by political enemies and is obnoxious, nay at times, nauseous, to men of the same party principles as his."

That same friend acknowledged that Sumner's manner was at least partly to blame—"his petty schoolmaster-like conceit, and by the everlasting pompous display of his rhetorical superiority and undigested erudition."

William Henry Seward

CHAPTER 2

WILLIAM HENRY SEWARD
(1865)

WILLIAM HENRY SEWARD—CALLED HARRY FROM BOYHOOD, HENRY afterward—had always scoffed at the threat of assassination. It was "so vicious and desperate" that it simply could not occur in the United States. "Assassination is not an American habit," Seward had chided a Parisian informant in 1862 who warned of a plot against Lincoln and his cabinet.

And when Seward was laid low three years later, the cause was not a bullet. He had been out for a carriage ride with his daughter Fanny and son Frederick when their coachman pulled to the side of the road to let Fred jump down and repair a broken door. At that point, their horse bolted.

The sixty-four-year-old Seward lunged for the reins. Instead, he fell out of the coach, fracturing his jaw, breaking his right arm, and wrenching his shoulder from its socket.

Seward had already dislocated a shoulder in a similar accident two decades earlier. At that time, a coach wheel had broken free, throwing him from the top of the carriage, where he had been riding so that his cigar smoke would not annoy other passengers.

This second time, he was carried unconscious to his house, where he awoke in great pain. His doctor pronounced his injuries serious and fitted his head with a metal frame to allow the broken jaw to knit.

Seward's wife, Frances, at home as usual at her father's house in Auburn, New York, was notified by wire and hurried to Washington. She wrote to her sister that, seeing him for the first time, "It makes my heart ache to look at him."

President Lincoln had gone to Virginia to wait outside Richmond until Lee's surrender was ensured. He had been informed of Seward's accident and, returning to Washington, walked across Lafayette Park to his bedside. The family had been turning away most well-wishers as Seward moved in and out of delirium, but the sight of the president roused him.

Barely able to speak, Seward whispered, "You are back from Richmond?"

"Yes," Lincoln replied, "and I think we are near the end at last."

As the nurse and family members withdrew, Lincoln stretched across the bed, resting on his elbow to get closer to Seward. For half an hour, he spoke of the situation on the war front. When Lincoln stepped back outside, he gestured to the family that Seward had fallen asleep.

The warm regard between the two men had not come easily. Grandson of a Revolutionary War officer, son of a successful land speculator, Henry Seward had been a small and frail child with a jutting nose, unruly red hair, and an unusually quick mind. At fifteen, he entered Union College in Schenectady, New York, but after two years he quarreled with his father over his meager allowance and ran away with a friend to Augusta, Georgia. In a newly opened academy, Seward set himself up as a teacher of Latin and Greek.

Eight weeks later, Henry's father read in a newspaper about his being hired and wrote to the headmaster that his "much-indulged son" had plunged his parents "into profound shame and grief."

Contrite, the boy returned home, but his escapade in the South—and what he had seen there—fortified a lifelong aversion to slavery.

Graduating from Union College at nineteen with highest honors, Henry went to New York to pursue the law and any willing young women. On being admitted to the bar, however, he settled down in Auburn, New

York, and married Frances Miller, the daughter of his law firm's senior partner. Because his high-strung bride felt secure only in her childhood home, the newlyweds moved in with her family.

As Henry became drawn to politics, he broke with New York state party leader Martin Van Buren and his Democrats because they supported slavery. In the 1824 presidential election, he declared publicly for John Quincy Adams.

During that campaign, Seward denounced the practice in New York State of a political party passing over the best-qualified applicants for public jobs to fill them instead with "supple and needy parasites of power." Seward was describing the spoils system that Van Buren and his candidate, Andrew Jackson, would introduce into the federal government four years later.

Seward found a home in the Anti-Masonic movement, the faction formed to protest the influence of Freemasonry in American life. The apparent murder of William Morgan, who disappeared after threatening to publish Masonic secrets, had ignited enough outrage that Seward was nominated for Congress by the Anti-Masons.

He withdrew, to avoid losing with John Quincy Adams in his re-election campaign. In defeat, Seward soured on politics but remained with the Anti-Masons. He found Adams's political heir, Henry Clay, unacceptable because Clay owned slaves.

As it happened, however, Seward's political career had just begun.

Four years earlier, he had been coming back from an excursion to Niagara Falls when his coach suffered another mishap and lost a wheel. As Seward struggled to get back on the road, he was grateful for help from a strapping newspaper editor from Rochester named Thurlow Weed.

At that first meeting, Weed detected in Seward—four years his junior—enough political promise that he resolved to know him better.

Edward Thurlow Weed, son of a father in and out of debtor's prison, had a passion for books that compensated for the few months of formal education he got in a family that was always obliged to move on.

Sixteen at the time of the War of 1812, Weed volunteered for the Fourteenth Regiment of the New York State Militia. He patrolled along Lake Ontario but saw no action. At war's end, Weed worked as an apprentice journalist, following the jobs from Auburn to Albany. His fledgling career was interrupted briefly in Cooperstown when he was arrested and charged with assault and battery.

According to the complaint, Weed had been with two other youths when one of them offered to assist a girl onto her wagon. She claimed that during the hoisting, he had been "guilty of some rudeness to her person."

With no money, Weed spent a night in jail as an accomplice. But the trial itself was brief. Jury members did not leave their seats before they acquitted all three defendants.

His reputation restored, Weed courted sixteen-year-old Catherine Ostrander, the daughter of his Cooperstown landlady. By the time they were allowed to marry, he had spent an interlude in New York City, where he printed political tracts and indulged his love of the theater. Only the offer of a foreman's job at the *Albany Register* lured him back to the state capital.

When a paper that had backed Martin Van Buren was put up for sale, Weed and a partner bought it and converted it to the *Republican Agriculturalist*, a four-page weekly dedicated to farm news. Very soon, however, politics proved irresistible, and Weed made his first endorsement; his candidate lost.

Moving on to Rochester, a flourishing mill town, Weed became an influential columnist with an intemperate style, attacking opponents as "Van Buren's pimps" or as mentally damaged. Weed drew the line at a candidate's family, however, and never joined in the scurrilous onslaught against Andrew Jackson's wife, Rachel.

Weed used the coach-wheel incident to foster an unlikely friendship— he, burly and aggressive, given to mispronouncing words and committing spelling errors that betrayed his spotty education; Seward, acknowledged to be brilliant but lacking Weed's sharp insights into human nature.

As they exchanged letters, Seward began to call on Weed whenever his legal practice took him to Rochester. Their wives swapped recipes;

the Seward children took to calling the bluff, generous editor "Uncle Weed."

Weed's notoriety had won him a seat in the state assembly, but after a term he had drifted home to his newspaper and his regular softball games. By 1830, however, Weed was confessing that he "liked the excitement of politics" and was ready to return to the state capital. He decided that Seward should join him as a member of the state senate, and by that time Weed could make it happen.

Seward's move to Albany set a pattern for his family. While he was mastering the intricacies of practical politics, Frances stayed behind in her father's house with their two small sons, Augustus and Frederick. In the capital, Seward developed a lifelong interest in the banking system and in transportation—the canals and railroads of New York State.

When Andrew Jackson assailed the Bank of the United States, Thurlow Weed saw it as a shrewd political maneuver on the president's part. Weed himself favored the bank as a necessary tool for conducting the nation's business. But he had also found it "easy to enlist the laboring classes against a 'monster bank' or 'moneyed aristocracy.'"

Other leaders of his party, including Seward, disdained that populist tactic. In 1834, he rose in the state senate to subject his colleagues, who were accustomed to folksy homilies, to a formal discourse on high finance.

The chamber was filled with Albany's prominent citizens, come to hear one of the state senate's youngest members. Driving home his central point, Seward did not disappoint them. If Jackson's Democrats were so afraid that a national bank would create an aristocracy, why did his administration want to charter state banks that would foster similar elites in every corner of the state?

His audience agreed that Seward's rhetoric had been impressive, even when delivered in his flat and uninflected voice. They came away feeling, in the words of one observer, "lost in admiration at the power of intellect."

• • •

In recent months, the Anti-Masons had joined with some Southern Democrats and the National Republicans of New England to form the Whig Party, which promised to speak for an emerging middle class. With his banking speech and others like it, Seward was becoming more than a one-note Anti-Mason spokesman.

His new stature led the Whigs to nominate him for governor. Jacksonians struck back by shaving eleven years off Seward's age and claiming that, at a mere twenty-two, Seward was far too young for a governor's responsibilities.

Their deceit had been unnecessary. Andrew Jackson's popularity was too strong to withstand, and his party's candidate beat Seward by twelve thousand votes.

Thurlow Weed granted that his "disappointment occasioned temporary depression." It certainly dampened Seward's normal ebullience. Then, at home, he found further cause for dismay.

While he had been traveling in Europe with his father, Frances had been courted by Seward's good friend, a state senator named Albert Tracy. Handsome, a few years older than Seward, and a better listener, Tracy's ardent letters had convinced Frances that she was in love with him.

And yet Frances was pious. Being unfaithful, even by mail, caused her such guilt that she confessed her temptation to her husband and handed him Tracy's letters. Seward burned the letters without reading them, but the marriage seemed ended.

Then, after he lost the governorship, Seward wrote his own letter to Frances at home in Auburn, to assure her that he had always loved her despite his being led astray by political ambition. He regretted that he could not share her Christian fervor, but he was ready to try to repair their marriage.

"My heart turns to you," Seward wrote, "possibly with less than its original force but still with all the energy . . . left to it."

Frances replied that she accepted the fact that she would always love him more deeply than he cared for her, but the flirtation with Tracy had convinced her that she could never love anyone but Henry.

• • •

As Seward was reconciling with his wife, his feelings toward Albert Tracy remained convoluted. He wrote to his former friend, pointing out that, except for Frances's virtue, Tracy would have destroyed Seward's peace, "if not my honor." He concluded, "I have long since forgiven you this wound, for weakness I knew it was, but I cannot forget it."

Tracy's enthusiasm for politics had declined, however, and he withdrew from public life just as Seward was returning to the fray with renewed vigor.

During the 1838 race for governor, Thurlow Weed professed to be impartial even as he went about burnishing Seward's reputation. Weed had calculated that Seward was the best choice for "awakening enthusiasm especially among the young men of the state." To mend fences, Weed assured Henry Clay's supporters that Seward had overcome his distaste for Clay as a slave owner and would support him for president in 1840.

Despite Weed's efforts, Seward's chances for the nomination were looking dim by the time the party met in Utica. Then, after a third ballot, Weed went to work. He took care not to offend delegates pledged to other candidates since he wanted to guarantee that "the nominee would be cheerfully and heartily accepted by the whole convention."

After Weed's night of strenuous lobbying, Seward was nominated, and his nomination made unanimous.

As the campaign progressed, Seward was cautious to a fault. Pressed by abolitionists to spell out his position in specific terms, he hedged so blatantly that Weed worried a backlash from antislavery voters might lose them the election.

Weed's own talents, however, were on constant display. He courted the growing Irish vote, and he oversaw the hiring in Philadelphia of laborers who worked and voted in New York. When Seward won by ten thousand votes, he knew whom to thank.

"God bless Thurlow Weed!" the new governor exclaimed. "I owe this result to him."

Weed made creative use of his victory. Lawmakers soon learned that Weed avidly collected information about their lives and was prepared to expose their secrets if he was crossed. Since Whigs now controlled the legislature, he immediately rewarded himself with the post of state printer, the most lucrative contract the legislature could bestow.

Very soon, Weed had established such sway over the appointment of judges and commissioners that he was being denounced as a dictator or, snidely, as "My Lord Thurlow."

While Governor Seward preferred to stay aloof from national politics, Weed continued to wield a potent influence. In 1840, he had considered Clay unelectable, managed to undercut him for the presidential nomination, and helped swing the party to William Henry Harrison.

During the campaign, Weed led the charge against President Van Buren by painting him as a luxury-addicted fop compared with honest, homespun General Harrison. To pursue that line of attack, Weed backed a partisan newspaper called *Log Cabin*, edited by one of his protégés, a fervent twenty-nine-year-old abolitionist, Horace Greeley.

Like Weed, Greeley was an early believer in gaudy trappings for a political campaign. Promoting the catchy "Tippecanoe and Tyler, too," he assured Weed that "our songs are doing more good than anything else." Greeley printed them on the back pages of his newspaper and wrote, "really, I think every song is good for five hundred new subscribers."

The campaign produced a landside vote for Harrison, and a jubilant Weed ran an editorial mocking those who had wagered against him in the election. To pay off their bets, he wrote, "please call one at a time, approaching our office from Washington Street and departing through Congress Street, keeping in line, so as not to block up the highway."

During the second of Seward's two-year terms as governor, he proved more liberal than other Whig leaders on the issues of improving public education and abolition. His call for a freer immigration policy made him popular with the Irish, even though many went on voting for the Democrats. As he declined to seek a third term, Seward addressed that paradox:

"My principles are too liberal, too philanthropic, if it be not vain to say so," Seward observed, with a degree of self-satisfaction. "My principles are very good and popular only for a man out of office."

At home in Auburn, the Sewards settled into a routine of limited intimacy. Frances's father had moved his bed into the cooler living room for the summer, and while Frances was visiting friends in Rochester, Seward installed his own parents in one of their parlors.

Frances had insisted that Seward refrain from conducting his law practice from home because of the unsavory men it would attract. But on one occasion former president John Quincy Adams, returning from a trip to Montreal, passed through Auburn, and Frances looked on aghast as his admirers led a torchlight parade to her yard, where they broke the gates and trampled her rosebushes.

As he practiced law in Auburn, politics were never far from Seward's thoughts. When President Harrison died after a month in office, his successor, John Tyler, tried to keep Thurlow Weed appeased with patronage, but as Tyler lost support, Weed drifted reluctantly to Henry Clay. Equally halfhearted, Seward put aside his earlier qualms and went on the campaign trail.

Since Clay was still waffling on slavery, Seward's speeches addressed the issue head-on: "You will say that Henry Clay is a slave owner. So he is. I regret it as deeply as you do." He went on to remind voters that Clay's rivals would be even less acceptable.

But the Democrats nominated James K. Polk, who ran on a popular promise to annex the state of Texas. Seward opposed the extension of slavery that Texas would bring and the war with Mexico that was sure to follow.

Clay lost narrowly to Polk, and war soon broke out. When their son, Augustus, graduated from West Point and was ordered immediately to fight in Mexico, Seward feared that Frances might not survive her forebodings.

Four years later, Seward was out stumping again for the Whig

Thurlow Weed

nominee, this time the victorious general of the Mexican war, Zachary Taylor. For his efforts, Taylor's brother had promised Thurlow Weed that Seward would be appointed secretary of state.

Sticking by the Whigs, Seward and Weed had resisted the appeal of another new party, the Free Soilers, which was more outspoken against slavery. Charles Sumner and the other Northern liberals who became Free Soilers nominated ex-president Martin Van Buren, even though he had been repudiated by his own Democrats.

The campaign provided Seward with his first look at Illinois congressman Abraham Lincoln. He deplored Lincoln's rambling speeches, which depended more on homespun stories than on a forthright denunciation of slavery. But Seward granted that Lincoln did excel at "putting the audience in good humor."

Twenty years later, Seward reminisced about one night on the campaign trail in Worcester, Massachusetts, when limited accommodations at an inn forced him to share a bed with Lincoln.

As they talked throughout much of the night, Seward exhorted Lincoln to speak out more boldly for abolition. Finally, in Seward's telling, Lincoln "admitted that I was right in my anti-slavery position and principles" and rolled over and went to sleep.

Zachary Taylor's election as president in 1848 encouraged Seward to seek a U.S. Senate seat, and on January 31, 1849, the New York legislature chose him by a four-to-one margin. The birth of their fifth child had left Frances Seward even more housebound, but since she regarded her husband's election as a victory for the forces of virtue, she was almost cheerful as she sent him off to Washington.

In debates over the Compromise of 1850—which excluded slavery from California and New Mexico but also included the Fugitive Slave provisions—Seward seemed to imply in one speech that the dictates of God overruled the U.S. Constitution.

Looking on, Thurlow Weed fretted that the ensuing outcry would be politically damaging. Seward remained unrepentant, however, even after Frances forwarded a packet of threatening letters from South Carolina.

Seward had grown close to President Taylor. Then in July, Taylor died and Millard Fillmore succeeded him. When Seward realized that Fillmore would not honor Taylor's Whig principles, he predicted doom:

"All is dark for him and for the country, and there is not a ray of light to enable me to see through it."

Although Weed was urging caution for political reasons, Seward had come to see himself as fervently antislavery. He remembered rejoicing "almost as heartily as the slaves themselves" after a law passed in New York State to provide for gradual emancipation.

Given that mood in the north, Weed's *Evening Journal* was finally prepared to throw down a challenge to the South: Rather than wrangling over the status of Kansas and Nebraska, those territories should be settled immediately by antislavery homesteaders.

Seward took up the cry in the Senate:

"Come on, then, gentlemen of the slave states! Since there is no escaping your challenge, I accept it in behalf of the cause of freedom. We will engage in a competition for the virgin soil of Kansas, and God give the victory to the side which is stronger in number, as it is in the right!"

When thousands of Northerners responded, the ensuing battles caused the territory to be called "Bloody Kansas," and Seward's wish to see Kansas enter the Union as a free state would go unrealized until January 21, 1861, the same day that Jefferson Davis resigned from the Senate to join the Confederacy.

For the present, Weed was directing his energies to fusing support from Northern Democrats and Whigs with the new Republican Party, aiming for a unity that would guarantee Seward the presidency in 1856. As for the anti-immigrant Know Nothings, Seward predicted that, despite their current strength, they would "inevitably disappear." He said, "The heart of the country is fixed on higher, nobler things. Do not distrust it."

Preparing for his campaign, Seward tried to lure Frances to Washington by taking a house on Twenty-first and G streets. When the pull of Auburn remained too great, Seward excused her absence to Charles Sumner on the grounds that life in the capital was raw and uncongenial: "She is too noble a woman to think of parting from and too frail to hope to keep long."

To inspire voters, Seward authorized the publication of a campaign biography and a three-volume collection of his letters. Weed began extolling him in the *Evening Journal* as heir to the lofty principles of John Quincy Adams.

But by the time the Republicans convened, Weed considered the timing premature and arranged that Seward's name not be entered. The nomination went instead to John C. Frémont, who proceeded to lose to the Democrat James Buchanan.

With Weed's tutoring, Seward had learned his way around the nation's financial centers at a time when New York, with the largest population, was also the wealthiest state. Leading the new Republicans, Seward was increasingly well regarded in the Senate, even by Democrats and Southerners. His easy amiability allowed him to count among his friends both Douglas of Illinois and Davis of Mississippi.

With Frances in Auburn, Seward's daughter-in-law acted as his hostess, providing a convivial background for lavish dinner parties and lively conversation. Soon after Mississippi's second senator, Henry "Hangman" Foote, had blistered Seward on the Senate floor, he was surprised to be invited to Seward's house for terrapin, fried oysters, and roast duck.

When Jefferson Davis's wife, Varina, came near death during child birth, Seward sent his carriage to brave a Washington blizzard and take the Davises' nurse to her side. Mrs. Davis later praised his genuine "earnest, tender interest."

As threats to the Union grew, Seward's advice was eagerly sought by Southern Whigs and antisecession Democrats. Above all, he was determined not to commit Charles Sumner's unforgivable sin: Seward never attacked his fellow senators by name.

Thirty years earlier, Van Buren, another New Yorker, had been considered a magician for his mastery of the art of politics. Now observers were regarding Seward as the same kind of sorcerer.

Carl Schurz, a young German-born journalist, saw past "the slim wiry figure, the thin, sallow face, the overhanging eyebrows, and the muffled voice" to glimpse "a sort of political wizard who knew all secrets and commanded political forces unknown to all the world, except himself and his bosom friend, Thurlow Weed, the most astute, skilful, and indefatigable political manager ever known."

By the time of the 1860 presidential election, Seward seemed headed inevitably to the Republican nomination. His competition included former congressman Lincoln, but Seward was eight years older and far more experienced. As for renown, Seward's speeches had been circulated across America in printings of fifty thousand copies while Lincoln had begun to build his national reputation only in 1858, through a series of debates with Stephen Douglas.

During the fourth debate in the central Illinois town of Charleston, Lincoln had reacted to Douglas's unyielding defense of slavery with a concession that distressed his Northern allies without winning him the Senate seat. "I am not," Lincoln had said, "nor ever have been, in favor of bringing about in any way the social and political equality of the white and black races."

Lincoln went on to insist that he did not favor Negroes voting, or Negroes serving on juries, or holding public office, or intermarrying with whites.

By 1860, the issue of race dominated the presidential campaign. The attack by John Brown at Harper's Ferry had churned up emotions to such a pitch that Seward's former Southern friends in the Senate stopped speaking to him. One of them warned the Republicans, "You may elect Seward to the presidency of the North. But of the South, never!"

Addressing again the admission of Kansas to the Union, Seward delivered a principled speech that was well received throughout the Northeast. But on February 27, 1860, Lincoln spoke in New York at a hall built by an industrialist and fervent abolitionist, Peter Cooper, for a new school that would offer free classes to workingmen.

Lincoln's message at Cooper Union was more equivocal than his audience may have expected. He argued that slavery should be prohibited in the future but not overturned where it already existed, and yet the elegance of Lincoln's language won over urbane Easterners who had questioned entrusting the presidency to a backwoods lawyer.

"Let us have faith that right makes might," Lincoln said, "and in that faith, let us, to the end, dare to do our duty as we understand it."

After counseling against Seward's run four years earlier, Thurlow Weed now counted on the division among Democrats to elect a Republican president. On the first ballot at the Republican convention in Chicago, Seward's vote far outstripped those of his challengers, and Weed's confidence seemed justified.

But Seward's delegate count still fell short, and by the third ballot, the Republicans had turned to Lincoln as more electable in the Middle West.

Despite his aching disappointment, Seward took his cue from Henry Clay, who had overcome his bitterness to campaign for William Henry

Harrison in 1840 and for Zachary Taylor eight years later. In defeat, Seward remained true to his nature—calm, wry, and detached, even fatalistic. He wrote back to one sympathizer, "Who can certainly know that what has been done in Chicago will not prove better" than if he had been the nominee?

Gamely, Seward campaigned throughout New York State for the Republicans and moved on by rail through the Middle West. His retinue had picked up Charles Francis Adams, Jr., grandson and great-grandson of presidents. The young man, four years out of Harvard, became a devotee of Seward's "really remarkable speeches," sometimes so elevated that Seward forgot to mention his party's ticket.

Charles's brother, Henry, three years younger, described an evening he spent with Seward:

"I sat and watched the old fellow with his big nose and his wire hair and grizzly eyebrows and miserable dress, and listened to him rolling out his grand, broad ideas that would inspire a cow with statesmanship if she understood our language."

To bolster Lincoln's prospects, Seward again tempered his antislavery jeremiads as he campaigned for the Republicans in fifteen states and territories. To a Detroit audience, he described Negroes as "a foreign and feeble element" that was "incapable of assimilation."

But Southerners were not placated. Twenty-three Southern representatives and seven senators were already urging the creation of a Southern Confederacy.

When the ballots were counted, Lincoln had won less than 40 percent of the popular vote, and Republicans took control of neither house of Congress.

At that, South Carolinians acted on the threats they had been making for more than twenty years. On December 20, 1860, the state withdrew from the Union. Laurence Keitt, who had cheered Preston Brooks's caning of Charles Sumner four years earlier, announced, "Loyalty to the Union will be treason to the South."

As president-elect, Lincoln invited Thurlow Weed to Springfield to spend two days reviewing the political landscape. When they said good-bye, Lincoln asked playfully whether Weed hadn't forgotten something.

Weed looked blank. Lincoln prompted him: "You have not asked for any office."

Weed hedged. Yes, he said, when the proper time arrived, "I should probably, like hosts of other friends, ask for such favors."

Lincoln said confidingly, "I was warned to be on my guard against you. And the joke of the matter is that those who gave the warning are after offices themselves, while you have avoided the subject."

Weed had merely retreated to his preferred role behind the scenes. He knew that Lincoln had asked his newly elected vice president, Maine senator Hannibal Hamlin, to sound out Seward about accepting the post of secretary of state. Weed had been furious since 1854, when Horace Greeley had defected from his ranks. He could finally revenge himself by blocking Greeley for the Senate seat that Seward might be vacating.

In contacting Seward about a cabinet position, Hamlin was not initially persuasive. Seward's loss of the nomination had deflated him, despite his soldiering on for Lincoln through the campaign. And at home, Frances Seward was plainly relieved by the outcome. She wrote to her husband, about to turn sixty, "You have earned the right to a peaceful old age."

But when Hamlin presented Seward with a note from Lincoln, its language touched Seward's heart. In formally tendering the offer, Lincoln expressed his "belief that your position in the public eye, your integrity, ability, learning and great experience" all testified to Seward's fitness for the position.

Problems arose almost immediately. During a second visit, Weed learned that Lincoln intended to appoint former Whigs and rival Democrats to his cabinet. Seward joined Weed in protesting, but reluctantly he had to accept the president's decision.

In the months before Lincoln arrived from Springfield to take office, leadership of the Republican Party in Washington fell to Seward, and he seized the chance to expand his portfolio beyond foreign affairs. Almost alone among Republican officials, Seward promoted further concessions to the South in hopes of staving off civil war. All the same, on January 9, 1861, Mississippi led the procession of states that followed South Carolina out of the Union.

By February, Lincoln's safety was in sufficient jeopardy that to assume the presidency he had to be smuggled into the capital. Inevitably, he then replaced Seward as the head of their party, and Seward resented his demotion. He particularly objected to Lincoln's choice of Salmon P. Chase as secretary of the Treasury since he distrusted Chase as one of the Radical Republicans who would insist on a hard line in dealing with the South.

Not that Seward was entirely without influence. At Lincoln's request, he went over a draft of the president's first inaugural address and struck out phrases he considered too partisan. Seward also offered a coda, which Lincoln refined into immortality when he invoked "the better angels of our nature."

On April 12, 1861, Jefferson Davis, acting as the Confederacy's president, ordered that his guns compel the surrender of a Union enclave at Fort Sumter, South Carolina. The skirmish confirmed Lincoln's doubts that the surrounding border states could ever be sufficiently appeased to keep them in the Union, and it silenced Seward's plea for concessions to the South.

The onset of the war in earnest provoked new restrictions from the Lincoln administration. For the first time, Washington began to censor reporters by stationing soldiers at the telegraph offices to prevent reports of early casualties.

Seward explained to the outraged journalists that releasing such information would make reconciliation more difficult later.

He also urged Lincoln to act when a secessionist mob in Baltimore threatened to disrupt Northern troop movements. To prevent them from tearing up the train tracks between Annapolis and Philadelphia, Lincoln suspended the writ of habeas corpus and ordered General Winfield Scott to arrest summarily anyone who threatened the public safety.

• • •

In the despairing days of reversals for the Union forces, Lincoln confronted an insurrection in the Senate. Recent evidence of military incompetence had provoked a growing movement in the North to end the war. The Confederate army had long been plagued by desertions; now two hundred Union soldiers were deserting every day.

Unwilling to attack the president directly, Radical Republicans looked for a scapegoat to explain a recent battlefield humiliation at Fredericksburg, Virginia, and settled on Henry Seward. They already viewed Seward with suspicion, and lately he had offended Charles Sumner and other Radicals by equating their stubborn insistence on ending slavery with that of the Confederates in defending it.

Led by Salmon Chase, the Radicals called for Seward's resignation, accusing him of being a "paralyzing influence" who dominated Lincoln's thinking. In the *Chicago Tribune*, Joseph Medill wryly explained Seward's dominance: He "has been President *de facto* and has kept a sponge saturated with chloroform to Uncle Abe's nose."

Informed on December 16, 1862, of an impending vote by his former colleagues, Seward wrote out a letter of resignation and sent his son, Fred, to deliver it at the White House along with Fred's note resigning as assistant secretary of state. Lincoln understood that he, not Seward, was the target and resolved not to part with the man he had come to consider his most valued adviser.

After their initial awkwardness in the days when Lincoln had felt the need to assert himself, the two men now found themselves united by their humor and by the pleasure they took in sitting together, apart from their wives, in easy camaraderie. Seward repeated to Fred what would become one of Lincoln's better-known jokes, even though Seward had been its butt.

Seward by then had the run of the White House, and one day he had come upon Lincoln polishing his boots.

Seward, the New Yorker, chastised the Midwesterner. In Washington, Seward chided the president, we do not blacken our own boots.

"Indeed?" Lincoln replied. "Then whose boots *do* you blacken, Mister Secretary?"

• • •

Before the Senate resolution attacking Seward could come up for a vote, a compromise was reached that called for a "reconstruction of the cabinet" but did not single out Seward by name. A Committee of Nine called on Lincoln at the White House to urge that he return to the practice of John Quincy Adams and submit his policies to a vote of the cabinet.

Lincoln received them warmly and promised to study their paper. But he had also invited to the meeting his full cabinet except for Seward, and he compelled Chase to state whether he was being regularly consulted. Reluctantly, Chase fibbed and assured them that the cabinet was working together without dissension.

When the five-hour session broke up at 1 a.m., not only had the senators backed down, but they had turned on Chase for misleading them about Seward's role.

Their denunciation was so harsh that Chase felt compelled to offer his own resignation. When he did, Lincoln received it with what Chase considered an unseemly eagerness. It turned out, however, that the president was simply relieved that he could now refuse to accept both resignations at the same time.

Mary Lincoln agreed with the Radical Republicans in deploring the decision to keep Seward in the cabinet. Since the election, she had worried that Seward would hog the credit for the administration's achievements, and she had found an excuse not to receive Frances Seward during a visit to Washington. But in fact, Mary Lincoln harbored misgivings about most of Seward's colleagues as well. To a friend, she complained that "there was not a member of the Cabinet who did not stab her husband & the country daily."

Navy Secretary Welles felt that he understood Lincoln's desire to keep both Seward and Chase at his side. The president deemed Chase a necessity for the marvels he was working at the Treasury. As for the secretary of state's role with Lincoln, Welles said simply, "Seward comforts him."

• • •

As the war ground on, however, dissension persisted in the cabinet. Secretary of War Edwin Stanton aligned himself with the Radical Republicans, who had become ever more hostile to Seward. Charles Sumner declined a dinner invitation rather than share a table with him, and Chase rebuffed Seward's overtures when, for the president's sake, he tried to heal their breach.

In his dealings with Europe, Seward had succeeded in reinforcing Britain's decision to stay out of the American war, and he had steered a course that kept France from acting on her sympathy with the South.

Seward had also adroitly resolved the *Trent* affair—a diplomatic flap that arose when a rash U.S. commander seized two Confederate commissioners headed for London. As secretary of state, Seward persuaded Lincoln to take the unpopular step of releasing the captives.

Whatever his opponents might think, Seward had suffered his own misgivings during the military defeats of the Army of the Potomac. But the battle at Gettysburg gave him heart, and when Vicksburg fell on July 4, 1863, Seward could believe that the end of the Confederacy was in sight.

Through the darkest months, his relations with the president had remained fraternal. Seward wrote the resolution with which Lincoln proclaimed the first national day of Thanksgiving, and he read and admired a draft of brief remarks that Lincoln intended to make at Gettysburg.

As victory for the North began to look inevitable, the mood in Washington relaxed, and a search resumed for pleasure and diversion. Seward was now spending twice his annual salary of eight thousand dollars on sumptuous dinner parties, and he joined the Lincolns at the theater for a sold-out performance of Edmund Booth as Richard III.

With the presidential election of 1864 approaching, Salmon Chase and other Radicals had been intriguing with no success to replace Lincoln as the Republican nominee. In New York, Seward worked to reconcile Thurlow Weed to Lincoln's second term despite Weed's dismay that the president these days was emphasizing the purpose of the war as ending slavery rather than preserving the Union.

As it became clear that strengthening the ticket meant replacing Hannibal Hamlin of Maine as Lincoln's vice president, Weed assisted in securing the nomination for Andrew Johnson of Tennessee. Johnson had been the only senator from a Confederate state to resist the call for secession.

Democrats who had stayed with the Union were denouncing the war as Lincoln's failure, and they nominated General McClellan to run against him. With four million men voting, the president won nationally by four hundred thousand, an electoral victory of 212 to 21.

When a celebration in Washington erupted in front of Seward's house, he stepped outside and compared Lincoln with the nation's heroes, from George Washington to Andrew Jackson. Seward assured the crowd that Lincoln's re-election had placed him "beyond the pale of human envy and human harm."

Just before his second inaugural, the president named Salmon Chase as U.S. Chief Justice. At his own swearing-in, Lincoln delivered what he considered to be his finest speech. He called on the citizens of the Union to finish the work ahead "with malice toward none, with charity for all."

It was only weeks later that Seward's carriage overturned. Then, on the evening of April 14, 1865, a few nights after Lincoln's visit to his bedside, a hulking young man dismounted at Seward's three-story brick house in Lafayette Park. He was calling himself Lewis Payne, an alias he had adopted earlier that year when he deserted the Confederate army and slipped into the North as a civilian.

Born Lewis Thornton Powell, he had achieved a military reputation as an expert horseman with a foul temper, and he had not changed in either regard. Staying at a boardinghouse in Baltimore, he insulted a black maid, who retaliated by refusing to clean his room. Powell knocked her to the floor, stamped on her body, and vowed to kill her. In his rage, he had forgotten that Maryland's slaves had been freed. As an aggrieved citizen, the maid could bring charges.

Powell was arrested, taken before a military court, and released only after he produced his written oath of allegiance to the Union.

Lewis Powell

Given the myths and confusion that would soon surround Powell, his meeting in Baltimore with John Wilkes Booth prompted differing later accounts. One report had a desperate and out-of-work Powell spotting a familiar face passing on the street.

Powell had attended the first stage play of his life in Richmond four years earlier and had been mesmerized by its star. As the curtain came down, Powell had pushed his way backstage and introduced himself to John Wilkes Booth.

The actor had been flattered by his adulation. Now in Baltimore he remembered Powell when the young man accosted him. "Booth," Powell said, "I want bread. I am starving."

At that moment, Booth was consumed by a daring plan he had been hatching. He immediately promised Powell money if the young man first swore allegiance to him and to Booth's new project. Powell readily agreed, then asked what they would be doing. Booth replied curtly that it would be in the "oil business."

During meetings over the next days, Booth reminded Powell of the many indignities being inflicted on the South and passed along rumors of rampaging Negroes and violated Southern maidens. In Booth's view, "the country was formed for the white man and not for the black." Nevertheless, he insisted that the South was not fighting to protect slavery but rather for the noble cause of freedom. Certainly, Booth saw no basis for denying any state the right to secede.

When Booth judged Powell primed, he confided that together they would avenge the North's crimes by kidnapping Abraham Lincoln. During a public appearance by the president in Washington, they would spirit him into Confederate territory and hold him there until the Yankee government agreed to release its prisoners.

To prepare for that bold action, Powell was directed to go to a boardinghouse at 541 H Street, run by a woman named Mary Surratt. Powell was to introduce himself as Mr. Wood. Booth explained that he had already recruited Mrs. Surratt's twenty-year-old son, John Harrison Surratt, for his plan.

At that address, Powell found a three-story brick building with its kitchen and dining room at street level. Greeting Powell amiably, Mrs. Surratt reported that her son was away, but she saw that Powell was ravenously hungry and prepared a meal for him. Powell returned a few days later, wearing a new suit, calling himself Mr. Payne and claiming to be a Baptist preacher.

When John Harrison Surratt appeared, he turned out to be a weedy youth with tentative chin whiskers. Powell learned that Surratt had been carrying messages about Northern troop movements to Confederate boats on the Potomac.

During his forays, Surratt had developed contempt for the Union detectives assigned to foil his spying. He had never come across a more stupid set of men, he said, and he simply hid the incriminating papers in his boots or between planks in his buggy.

Surratt said that a friend, Dr. Samuel Mudd, had introduced him to John Wilkes Booth. The two conspirators were a striking contrast—Booth, his pallor set off by glossy black curls and a thick mustache; Mudd, somewhat taller, fair-skinned, and balding. Surratt had been quickly won over to Booth's plot and brought the actor home to meet his mother.

Mary Surratt proved to be the better recruit. Past forty, with a straight back and ruddy cheeks, she was a Catholic convert and fierce secessionist. Damning every victory by the Northern forces, she swore that Abraham Lincoln should be sent straight to hell.

Most of Mrs. Surratt's boarders were family friends, but even they were disconcerted when they happened upon Lewis Powell and John Surratt inspecting a cache of revolvers and bowie knives. They complained to Mrs. Surratt about the weapons, but she said they should think nothing of it. Her son often rode far into the countryside at night and needed the protection.

When Booth began to call regularly at the house, the boarders found it inexplicable that a celebrated actor should befriend a youth as callow as John Surratt. But Booth fluttered pulses among the women of the house, treating them with extravagant courtesy while he let it be known that he was courting the daughter of a Republican senator.

Besides Powell and Surratt, the group of Booth's young male admirers who gathered at the boardinghouse now included George Atzerodt, who spoke broken English with an accent from his native Germany. Booth had promised him a large sum to supply a boat to ferry the captive Lincoln across the Potomac. Also meeting regularly were Samuel Arnold and twenty-four-year-old Michael O'Laughlen, who had served briefly in the Confederate army before returning to Baltimore. At thirty-five, Dr. Mudd was the oldest of the group.

On the afternoon of March 16, 1865, the seven conspirators set out for the Seventh Street Hospital, determined to kidnap Lincoln while he attended a show being staged for wounded soldiers. To their chagrin, the president did not show up.

• • •

A month later, when Lewis Powell knocked on Secretary Seward's door, Booth's cabal had become murderous. Powell pushed aside Seward's black servant, William Bell, and strode toward the staircase to the secretary's bedroom. Told that Seward was sleeping, Powell claimed to be bringing him medicine prescribed by Seward's doctor. "I must go up, must see him," Powell kept repeating. "Must see him."

At the top of the stairs, Powell was intercepted by Fred Seward, who said he would take the medicine to his father when he awoke. Repeating his mantra—"must see him, must see him"—Powell turned as though to go back downstairs, then wheeled abruptly, swore at Fred, and knocked him to the floor with the butt of his revolver.

Terrified, William Bell ran out the front door, shouting, "Murder! Murder!"

Hearing the uproar, Seward's male nurse came out of the bedroom. Powell struck him down with a bowie knife. The gas lights in Seward's room had been turned down, but Powell groped his way to Seward's side and began stabbing, opening a large gash on Seward's right cheek and a cut under his left ear. Another slash to Seward's throat bounced off the steel frame fitted to his jaw.

Awakened by the assault, Seward had the presence of mind to wrap himself in his blankets and roll off his bed to the floor.

Seward's daughter Fanny had been keeping a vigil in the shadows. Her scream awoke her brother, Augustus, who rushed in from the next room. But in the dim light, he thought the struggle by the bed was between his delirious father and the nurse trying to subdue him. When he grabbed at a figure, he found himself holding Powell, who broke free and ran down the stairs muttering, "I'm mad! I'm mad!"

Passing a State Department official who had come to call, Powell slashed him deeply down the right side of his body.

Frederick was left behind with a fractured skull, which required that a silver plate be embedded. His father lay on the floor, bleeding badly, as their assailant escaped on his horse.

Galloping away, Powell had no better plan than to stay out of sight until he could return to Mary Surratt's boardinghouse.

Jefferson Davis

CHAPTER 3

JEFFERSON DAVIS (1865)

ALTHOUGH HE SOON LEARNED OF GENERAL LEE'S SURRENDER, JEFferson Davis, president of the Confederate States of America, was not reconciled to defeat. Throughout his life, he had found it all but impossible to admit that he was wrong. On April 19, 1865, Davis was still developing plans for continued resistance as he rode into Charlotte, the North Carolina town he intended to make his temporary capital.

To find a house for Davis in Charlotte, his advisers had to win over even friendly citizens, who were afraid of the Yankee reprisals to come. But as Davis approached, several residents cheered loudly and clamored for a speech.

Pausing outside his new lodgings, Davis thanked them and promised to remain faithful to the Southern cause. While acknowledging that General Lee had surrendered, Davis added, "But we may still hope for success."

He was about to go inside when a telegraph operator raced up with a wire from a Davis ally, John Breckinridge: "President Lincoln assassinated in the theater in Washington." Breckinridge added that Henry Seward, who had been Davis's friend before the war, had been stabbed, probably fatally.

Davis read the wire without comment. When someone shouted for him to tell them what it said, Davis responded, "Here is a very extraordinary communication" and handed it to an aide to read aloud.

Hearing the news, a few men cheered. Most remained somber as they drifted away.

Alone with his aides inside the house, Davis said, "I certainly have no special regard for Mr. Lincoln. But there are a great many men of whose end I would much rather have heard than his."

The aides understood that if Davis mourned, it would be less for Lincoln himself than for the end to Lincoln's policy of reconciliation. They remembered the bitterness toward the South among Radical Republicans like Charles Sumner. In life, Lincoln had barely restrained those men. Now they would be free to demand from Andrew Johnson the harshest penalties for joining the Confederacy.

Long before secession, war had marked Jefferson Davis's life. Growing up in Kentucky, "Little Jeff" knew only that he had been born on the third of June but not which year. Only later did he calculate that he had been four years old when his three brothers went off to fight the British in 1812. What was never in doubt, however, was the depth of his family's devotion to the Union.

Davis's father, Samuel, an ambitious farmer on the Kentucky frontier, purchased slaves to raise his crops of tobacco, corn, and wheat. He took the family briefly to Louisiana, but when his property proved to be a mosquito-ridden swamp, he settled permanently in the territory that would become the state of Mississippi.

The Davis family flourished on the fertile land, and Jane Davis gave birth to four more of her ten children. She and her husband indicated their determination to make Jefferson their last child by giving him "Finis" as his middle name.

At age eight, Little Jeff was sent off to the St. Thomas Catholic school in Kentucky. On the way, he and his companions stopped at the Hermitage in Nashville, where Jeff played for a time with Andrew Jackson's adopted son.

Back home as a teenager, he tried to rebel against any further studies until his father put him to work picking cotton. After the boy spent two days stooping under the Mississippi sun, the classroom became more appealing.

Upon the death of their father, Jefferson's oldest brother arranged an appointment for him to the U.S. Military Academy at West Point. His commission was signed by John C. Calhoun, President James Monroe's secretary of war.

At West Point, the seventeen-year-old cadet was messy, forgetful, and rebellious. Three close friends were expelled for drinking, and Jefferson was arrested by his commanding officer after being caught at the raucous Benny Havens tavern. Edgar Allan Poe, who arrived at West Point a few years later as another reluctant cadet, described Benny Havens as the only sanctuary from the "Godforsaken" academy.

Poe lasted less than a year. Davis managed to scrape by and graduate but without distinction. His low standing relegated him to a commission as a second lieutenant in the infantry. He was sent off to the Michigan Territory, where he spent seven uneventful years.

Davis was accompanied by his father's slave, James Pemberton, who had been attending to him since Davis was fifteen. He explained that he always called Pemberton simply "James" because it would have shown "disrespect to give a nickname."

The tedium of army life was relieved when Colonel Zachary Taylor arrived in Wisconsin with his family to take command of Fort Crawford. Davis fell in love with one of the colonel's three daughters, eighteen-year-old Sarah. Because she had been born at Fort Knox in the Indiana Territory, the family called her "Knoxie."

Davis soon clashed with the girl's father. It was over a trivial matter, but when Davis's pride was wounded, any slight became epochal. He was talked out of challenging Taylor to a duel only after a fellow officer pointed out that dueling was hardly the way to ingratiate himself with a future father-in-law.

As their antagonism faded, Davis had to overcome Zachary Taylor's less personal objection to the match. The colonel did not want the life of an army wife for his daughters—too much traveling, too much separation. To a friend, Taylor lamented, "I scarcely knew my own children or they me."

Davis cleared that hurdle by resigning his commission in favor of a life raising cotton. He brought his new bride to acreage in Mississippi near his family's holdings at a curve in the river already called Davis Bend. Knoxie wrote to reassure her parents that "the country is quite healthy."

Very soon, however, both she and Davis were stricken with the malaria that swept over the region every summer. Knoxie Davis died on September 15, 1835, three months after her wedding.

With her died the spirit of the rollicking cadet from West Point. Davis developed a new rigidity and a readiness to find fault in others. Men meeting the twenty-seven-year-old widower often thought him older than his years, and cold.

Davis's choice of career seemed to foreclose ambition, and for eight years he withdrew to his plantation. During the leisurely days, he read widely in history and political theory. But by 1844, he had cast off his despondency and begun to court the granddaughter of a New Jersey governor.

His new romance sparked an interest in political service. In 1845, Davis married Varina Howell and took office as a Mississippi congressman. In time, the couple had six children, although only one would reach adulthood and marry.

With the outbreak of war with Mexico, Davis left Congress, recruited volunteers, and set himself up as commander of the Mississippi Rifles, making no secret of his intention to seek glory on the battlefield. Colonel Davis seldom won the affection of his men, but he gained their respect, and his regiment won praise for its military prowess.

At the Battle of Buena Vista, a musket ball shattered Davis's right foot near the ankle. He stayed in the saddle, stanched his wound with a handkerchief, and led his men in the charge that vanquished Antonio López de Santa Anna.

Zachary Taylor had been commanding the U.S. forces, and Davis had at last impressed his former father-in-law. In his official report, Taylor praised Davis for his "coolness and gallantry." When the general came by to visit the wounded man, Davis was touched to see "Old Rough and Ready" with "a mother's softness" in his eyes. A later account may have improved on their conversation by claiming that Taylor said, "My daughter, sir, was a better judge of men than I was."

With his new renown, Davis could weigh attractive options for his future. President James K. Polk offered to commission him as a brigadier general, but Davis declined. In an overtly political letter, he thanked the president but pointed out that, under his reading of the Constitution, only the states had the authority to bestow that commission, not the federal government.

Instead, in the fall of 1847, Davis accepted an appointment to the U.S. Senate from Mississippi and was elected the following year to the remainder of the term. Davis welcomed the escape to Washington as a way of avoiding his wife's complaints about being shunted off to live with the family of Davis's older brother.

Davis wrote to let her know that he could no longer bear her "constant harassment." But he professed to love her still and to want her with him if only she would be "kind and peaceful." As proof of his abiding affection, he sent home several tokens, including a bracelet with a cameo of his face.

In 1850, Davis opposed Henry Clay's compromise on slavery and resigned from the Senate to run for his state's governorship. Losing narrowly, Davis embraced the cause of states' rights and campaigned actively for Franklin Pierce, the Yankee nominated for president by Davis's fellow Democrats. When Pierce won, he rewarded Davis by appointing him secretary of war.

In that post, Davis clashed often with Winfield Scott. Not only had Scott been Pierce's rival for the White House, he had also contested in the past with Davis's former father-in-law, Zachary Taylor. In long, angry screeds, Davis denounced Scott for his vanity and his falsehoods.

Winfield Scott could match Davis's capacity for invective and had been perfecting it for two decades longer. He accused Davis of trying "to crush me into servile obedience to your self-will." After many more volleys, Scott shut down his side of their feud: "Compassion is always due to an enraged imbecile."

Fellow officers in the army sided with General Scott and found the secretary of war far too imperious. Pierce tried to resolve the problem by suggesting that Scott, as the army's general-in-chief, move his New York headquarters to Washington. That solution did end their correspondence, but once Scott was based in the same city, Davis simply ignored and bypassed him.

When the Democrats split over extending slavery in Kansas, James Buchanan defeated Pierce for their party's nomination in 1856 and won the presidency. Davis returned to the Senate. In the summer of 1858, he took an extended leave in New England to treat an ailment that threatened to blind his left eye.

At that year's July Fourth celebration and again the next October, Davis gave passionate speeches on the importance of the Union. He still claimed that states had a legal right to secede, but he predicted that the North would never let them go peaceably.

At the Democrats' nominating convention in 1860, Davis was one of eight men to challenge Stephen Douglas but drew almost no support.

Events then took command. Lincoln was elected president. South Carolina seceded from the Union. And, on January 9, 1861, Mississippi joined the Confederacy.

At that, Jefferson Davis bade a formal farewell to the United States Senate and rode home to Mississippi.

Even though Davis had resolved not to take a prominent role in the looming crisis, a constitutional convention of the new Confederacy unanimously voted him its provisional president. In accepting the position, Davis carefully avoided any mention of slavery. He repeated instead the traditional Southern claim that the rebellion was motivated solely by concern for states' rights.

By withdrawing from the Union, the South had "merely asserted a right which the Declaration of Independence of 1776 had defined as inalienable."

But his vice president, Alexander H. Stephens of Georgia, dismissed the constitutional argument and cut to the quick: Thomas Jefferson and other Founders had believed "that the enslavement of the African was a violation of the laws of nature," Stephens told a rally in Savannah, "that it was wrong in principle, socially, morally and politically."

But that idea was itself "fundamentally wrong," since it "rested upon the assumption of equality of races."

Stephens explained, "Our new Government is founded upon exactly the opposite idea; its foundations are laid, its cornerstone rests, upon the great truth that the negro is not equal to the white man; that slavery, subordination to the superior race, is his natural and moral condition."

President Davis was disturbed by Stephens's political tactlessness, but he also called a reunion with the North "neither practical or desirable." He did, however, appoint a commission to negotiate with Washington over the fate of Fort Sumter, a Union army base in the Charleston, South Carolina, harbor.

Hearing of secession, Union major Robert Anderson had moved his garrison to Sumter from its more vulnerable position at Fort Moultrie. Davis had known Anderson as a fellow cadet at West Point and sympathized with his dilemma. He was sure that Anderson, as a Kentucky slave owner, was suffering from divided loyalties.

In early January, with James Buchanan still in the White House, South Carolinians had fired on a merchant ship arriving to reinforce Sumter. A showdown had been averted then only because the ship sailed off without returning fire.

At that time, Davis had called in person on Buchanan to urge that they find a "peaceful solution." Buchanan had declined, but Davis's new delegation to Abraham Lincoln fared worse. Lincoln refused to receive them.

From the outset, Davis had hoped that it would not be the South that fired the first shot in the impending war. But he found that South Carolinians would no longer tolerate a Yankee military post on Confederate soil.

At 3:20 on the morning of April 12, 1861, Major Anderson received a formal message from aides to Pierre G. T. Beauregard, who had been Anderson's student at West Point. Six weeks earlier, Beauregard had been awarded his rank of brigadier general in the Confederate army.

"We have the honor to inform you," the aides wrote, "that he will open the fire of his batteries on Fort Sumter one hour from this time."

At 4:30 a.m., General Beauregard made good on his threat, and the shooting war began.

Over the next months, enthusiasm for the war rose and fell throughout the South with reports from the battlefield. Morale initially ran high when Fort Sumter was evacuated with the death of only one soldier—and that death accidental. Surrender of the fort was followed by the first major confrontation, at Manassas, Virginia—called the Battle of Bull Run by the Union and Manassas by the Confederates. Davis had been severely ill before the battle, and its strategy was devised at his sickbed.

Again, the South prevailed. On July 21, 1861, General Beauregard saw his raw troops inflict 2,890 casualties on the Union troops, a thousand more than his own men suffered.

But the South's political maneuvering was less successful. Adroit gambits by Henry Seward were preventing Britain and France from allying themselves with the Confederacy, while Davis was confronted by the same bureaucratic infighting that was plaguing Lincoln in Washington. By the end of 1864, after William Tecumseh Sherman had devastated Georgia, the tide against the Confederacy seemed unlikely to turn.

Within Davis's cabinet, his secretary of state, Judah Benjamin, recommended that Davis issue his own emancipation proclamation. Benjamin suggested that it might stimulate belated European support and induce newly freed black men to join the Confederate cause. Throughout much of the South, Benjamin was disdained as a Jew, but he had Davis's confidence, and General Lee also saw advantages to the idea.

When the Confederate Congress met, however, the proposal was greeted by bitter outcries from the slave owners who made up its membership. The Senate's president demanded, What did we go to war for, but to protect our property?

The measure finally passed the Senate but too late to demonstrate its effectiveness, since few blacks took up arms for the South.

As Confederate hopes spiraled downward, an influential Virginia congressman went to ask Robert E. Lee if he would wrest control of the administration from Davis and proclaim martial law. The men who had rebelled against domination by the North now pronounced themselves ready for a dictator.

Lee refused the suggestion, but he warned Davis that his starving army was no longer fit to carry on the war. In response, Davis asked his Congress for authority to suspend habeas corpus, the desperate measure that Lincoln had taken in 1861.

Although Davis could not accept the Confederacy's inevitable col lapse, he had begun on April 3 the long evacuation from Richmond that brought him to Charlotte.

As Davis called together the Confederate troops scattered around his new headquarters, some advisers headed home instead. Others debated whether to urge their president to prepare himself for exile in Europe.

When Varina Davis wrote from a town in Georgia to assure her husband that she and their children were well, Davis responded that he now distrusted his own troops. Since he had no confidence that they would protect her, Davis set off to meet his family. His security escort was down to ten men.

It galled Davis to learn later that Andrew Johnson, the newly installed president of the United States, had charged him with being part of the conspiracy to assassinate Lincoln and had announced a $100,000 reward for his capture.

When Davis caught up with his wife's party, she was adamant that they must separate. She urged Davis to ride off alone, rally the surviving troops, and carry on the fight. She would take their older children to England, enroll them in school there, and return with the two younger children to join him in Texas.

Davis agreed that his family would be safer without him at their side. But there were reports of nearby marauders, and his horses were too exhausted to go farther. And the rain was unrelenting. Davis would stay one more night. Stripping off his coat and boots, he tried to sleep.

Then, before dawn, a former slave who had remained loyal to Davis came to report hearing rifle fire nearby. Looking to the horizon, Davis saw a mass of Yankee cavalry bearing down on his encampment. His wife warned him that he had only moments to escape through a swamp a hundred yards away.

Davis hesitated long enough that the approaching troops cut off the road between him and his horse. In the darkness, he snatched up a light overcoat against the rain, and his wife threw a shawl over his head and shoulders.

He had gone no more than twenty yards when a soldier rode up and ordered him to surrender. To the last, Davis had a plan: He would put his hand under the man's boot and tip him over the far side of his horse. While he was struggling to get to his feet, Davis would leap onto the man's saddle and race off.

But seeing the carbine pointed at her husband, Varina Davis ran to his side and tried to protect him by throwing her arms around his chest. The moment for a final rebellion was lost, and the president of the Confederate States of America was taken prisoner.

As cavalrymen drew close, they mistook other troops from their own ranks for Southerners. In the confusion of cross fire, two of Davis's aides were able to walk away. Watching them slip off, Davis endorsed their decision. But left behind, he suffered an unexpected slur on his honor.

In the gloom, Davis found that he had picked up his wife's coat by mistake, and he had not waved her away when she wrapped him in her shawl.

His captors were pleased to tell the world that Jefferson Davis had tried to escape from them by dressing as a woman.

Pinckney Pinchback

CHAPTER 4

PINCKNEY BENTON STEWART PINCHBACK (1865)

On New Year's Day, 1863, a company of escaped slaves was being led through a military drill to prepare them for serving in the Union army's First South Carolina Volunteers. The exercise ended abruptly when they were herded together with white soldiers to hear a clergyman read President Lincoln's order that they were "henceforth free."

When the speaker finished, the white commander, Colonel Thomas W. Higginson, grabbed up the American flag by its standard and was waving it over the crowd when he heard a man begin to sing:

"My country 'tis of thee—"

The former slave's powerful voice was joined by two black women harmonizing with him: "Sweet land of liberty, of thee I sing!"

Higginson had never experienced a moment so electric. It was "the choked voice of a race at last unloosed," he recalled. Their singing "made all the other words seem cheap."

The celebration was not confined to Southern slaves. At Tremont Temple in Boston, a mass of white and black abolitionists stood waiting until near midnight to hear confirmation that the majority of the nation's slaves were now free.

And in Washington, a fugitive slave told a crowd that his daughter had once been sold away from him. At last, those days were over, and he blessed the Lord that white slave owners "can't sell my wife and child any more."

The *New York Times* joined in the rejoicing. The newspaper hailed the dawn of a new era in the history of "this country and the world."

In Louisiana, a handsome twenty-five-year-old nicknamed "Pinch" regarded the jubilation sardonically. As a quadroon—one-quarter black—Pinckney Benton Stewart Pinchback had learned long ago that good intentions alone did not change men's hearts.

Throughout Pinchback's early life, he had hardly been a slave at all. His father, Major William Pinchback, was a typical Virginia plantation owner in every respect but one: When he first spied beautiful, light-skinned Eliza Stewart, he did not see one more slave but rather the love of his life. She moved into his house, bore his children, and prepared to move with him to his expansive new estate in Holmes County, Mississippi.

First, though, Pinchback took Eliza to Philadelphia and officially set her free.

On their way back to Mississippi, the couple was forced to stop in Macon, Georgia, on May 10, 1837, when Pinckney, their eighth child, was born prematurely. Until then, only two of their children had survived—a daughter, Mary, and a son who had been named Napoleon before his mental weakness became apparent.

In Mississippi, Major Pinchback and his family settled into a life of ease, its comforts provided from the slave quarters. Lighter even than his mother, Pinckney might have passed for white, but he preferred to spend his time among his father's slaves, listening to their African songs and stories.

When he was nine and Napoleon seven years older, the boys were sent to study at Gilmore's High School in Cincinnati. For different reasons, neither of them took to formal education. Pinckney found his way to the city's waterfront along the Ohio River, where riverboat gamblers adopted him as a mascot and taught him to shoot craps and play poker.

After eighteen months, his agreeable truancy ended when their father fell ill and summoned the boys home. They were back in Mississippi when Major Pinchback died, shattering their world.

• • •

Eliza Stewart learned from the major's executor that Pinchback's East Coast relatives were disregarding his wishes and claiming his estate. Worse, she and her children had become so vulnerable in Mississippi that she gathered them up and headed for safety in Cincinnati.

The danger that they could all be seized as slaves unhinged Napoleon's fragile mind, and at twelve Pinckney Pinchback became the man of the family. Part of his new role meant talking enough like the black men around him that he aroused no resentment among the white citizens.

Pinckney hired out as a cabin boy on canal boats running from Cincinnati to the other towns on the Ohio. For five years, earning eight dollars a month, he sent home what he could. Then in 1854, at seventeen, he graduated to a more lucrative occupation. Landing a job on a riverboat, he caught the eye of a well-known gambler named George Devol.

As Devol's servant, the young man learned the tricks of his trade, including how to fleece the other passengers with games of three-card monte. Devol worked with three partners, including a grifter notorious as "Canada Bill," and they were pocketing tens of thousands of dollars.

Although the partners praised Pinckney's aptitude for their scams, he could not play against the wealthy white men. He was restricted to belowdecks with the ship's barber and the other black crew. But he rose to the position of steward, and he could tell time with his solid gold pocket watch.

Stories circulated later about the risks to his lucrative life: How he had to hide whenever angry deckhands chased after him until he could bribe a ship's pilot to steer close enough to shore that he could jump to safety. How he had once killed a man in a shootout. How he was forced to marry a pregnant girl but then was stabbed by her brother when Pinckney paid to have the marriage annulled.

By 1860, at twenty-three, Pinchback was trailed by a swirl of rumors and scandal. But after many affairs, he fell in love with a sixteen-year-old white girl named Nina Hawthorne and married her.

At first, the impending war seemed ready-made for a brave and reckless young man, but blacks were not serving in the Union army. Pinchback made his way to the federal troops who were occupying New Orleans, and by mid-May 1862 he had persuaded other freed black men to petition the commander of the Department of the Gulf to allow them to fight for the Union.

Before a decision was made, however, Pinchback was attacked on the street by John Keppard, his sister's husband, who slashed at him with a knife. Caught by surprise, Pinchback said afterward that he had never learned the reason for the assault. He struck back, and Keppard collapsed with a minor wound.

It was Pinchback, however, who was taken before a military court. Receiving bad advice, he pleaded guilty to assault with intent to kill. The provost judge sentenced him to two years in the city's workhouse.

"I nearly fainted in court," Pinchback told friends. He claimed that lawyers and the court staff had been trying to extort money from him that he refused to pay.

Prison records listed Pinckney Pinchback as educated but with "intemperate habits." He eased his imprisonment by having the money to buy his own bed and better food.

Money also may have bought the prompt pardon that he received from a military commander. As soon as the Lincoln administration decreed that "persons of African descent" could join the army or navy, Pinchback was accepted into a volunteer unit. Its commander was Major General Benjamin Franklin Butler, named for the sage of the American Revolution.

Butler, now forty-five, had been born in Deerfield, New Hampshire, but had a family tie to Louisiana since his father had fought there in 1815 with Andrew Jackson at the Battle of New Orleans. The elder Butler died when the boy was two, and his mother sent Ben to school at Exeter and then applied for him to enter the U.S. Military Academy at West Point.

But the family lacked the political sway for Ben to be selected, and he went instead to Colby College in Maine, which was then a Baptist institution called Waterville.

After a hitch on a fishing ship and an apprenticeship in a Lowell, Massachusetts, law office, Ben Butler grew his thinning hair long, joined

Benjamin Butler

the state bar, and courted an actress named Sarah Hildreth. Butler won her heart but not her hand. It took four years before his prospects satisfied her parents and they allowed the marriage.

Butler made his first foray into politics on the losing side, backing Martin Van Buren in his failed campaign for re-election in 1840. Butler was convinced that the U.S. Constitution gave each state the right to set its own policy on slavery, and he remained a Jacksonian Democrat.

At the same time, however, Butler joined a campaign to shorten the working day at the textile mills in Lowell to ten hours. His stand provoked the wrath of the mill owners, and the *Lowell Courier* denounced him as a "notorious demagogue and political scoundrel." Butler responded by accusing the editor of having picked up a venereal disease from a prostitute during the U.S. war with Mexico.

Exploiting the divisions among both political parties, Butler formed a faction pledged to the shorter mill hours. One large plant, Hamilton Mills, retaliated by posting a notice: "Whoever employed by this corporation votes the Ben Butler ticket on Monday next will be discharged."

Over the years, Butler had been rising in the state militia, and his gift for command was on display when he addressed a throng at the Lowell City Hall:

"As God lives and I live, by the living Jehovah! If one man is driven from his employment by these men because of his vote, I will lead you to make Lowell what it was twenty-five years ago—a sheep-pasture and a fishing place. And I will commence by applying the torch to my own house!"

The Whig owners backed down, the *Lowell Courier* printed their pledge not to fire anyone, and every candidate on Butler's slate won election. The ten-hour law fared less well. It took several legislative sessions to pass, and then the limit was set at eleven hours, fifteen minutes.

Running as a Democrat, Butler won election to the Massachusetts House of Representatives at age thirty-five. During the presidential nominating convention of 1860, Butler hoped to block the nomination of Stephen Douglas, whom he considered unelectable, and stuck with Jefferson Davis through fifty-seven unavailing ballots.

But by the time war was declared, Butler had concluded that no state had the right to leave the Union, and he led his militia into battle for the North.

When a Confederate mob in Baltimore killed twelve men, including four from Massachusetts, Butler's war was officially launched in blood. He ignored pleas from Maryland's governor, who hoped to remain neutral, and seized Annapolis. That action ensured control in the coming months over the gateway for supplying Union troops.

Butler wrote to his wife, "I think no man has won more in ten days than I have."

Then Butler ignored orders from General Scott, his superior in Washington, and invaded Baltimore. Outraged, Scott summoned Butler to his headquarters and lectured him like a truant for the unacceptable risks he had taken. Scott concluded, "You can be trusted with nothing in this army again."

Butler answered with angry words of his own, but when he returned to his billet, he sank down on a couch and wept. Although he submitted his resignation, Lincoln's secretary of war reminded him that Scott was in his midseventies and so doddering that he would soon be replaced.

The affair ended when Lincoln met personally with Butler and offered him a commission as a major general in the U.S. Army. Accepting, Butler spelled out one condition: If he were ordered to do anything he could not support, he would return the commission.

"That is frank, that is fair," Lincoln agreed. "But I want to add one thing. When you see me doing anything that for the good of the country ought not to be done, come and tell me so, and why you think so, and then perhaps you will not have any chance to resign your commission."

Back in command, Butler became the first commander to flout the Fugitive Slave Law of 1850 and refuse to return to their owners the slaves who reached his army's lines.

By April 1862, Butler's troops had captured New Orleans. With a population approaching 150,000, it was the largest city in the South; its citizens, mostly white, included many Northern merchants and bankers and also the South's largest number of free black citizens. Lightskinned, often wealthy, more at ease speaking French than English, they had arrived from Haiti or were the mulatto children of French settlers and black women.

In New Orleans, Butler was a whirlwind propelled by his New England values. He ordered a reeking canal cleansed of dead mules and rotting dogs and cats, and he closed down the outdoor food stalls in order to scrape filth from their stone floors. Butler tackled widespread unemployment by paying men fifty cents a day, plus a soldier's rations; in return, he expected every house to be repainted or whitewashed. Littering was punishable by three months in jail.

With strict surveillance, Butler broke up a burglary ring, and he censored or shut down the city's newspapers. He prevented churches from offering a day of prayer for the Confederacy, but he ordered his troops to arrest clergymen who refused to pray for Abraham Lincoln.

In that same spirit, he took on a morale problem among his troops. Rebel women were showing their contempt by getting off a streetcar if a Union soldier boarded or by holding a handkerchief to their nostrils when they passed a Yankee on the street.

At first, Butler had laughed off the insults. When a group of city matrons ostentatiously turned their backs on him, Butler said loudly to his aides, "Well, these ladies certainly know which end of them looks best."

As the snubs got more aggressive, however, with women spitting or making retching noises, Butler issued what became known as the Woman Order. It concluded: " . . . When any female shall, by word, gesture, or movement, insult or show contempt for any officer or soldier of the United States, she shall be regarded and held liable to be treated as a woman of the town plying her avocation."

The punishment for streetwalking was a night in jail and a five-dollar fine.

The uproar that followed raised new questions about Butler's fitness to command.

Southerners next accused him of confiscating the silverware of those Confederate supporters he had driven out of New Orleans, and they took to calling him "Spoons."

But there had been nothing frivolous about Butler's response when a New Orleans resident, William B. Mumford, faced execution for desecrating the Stars and Stripes.

The incident had occurred during the five days while Union navy ships had waited at the port for Butler to take control of New Orleans. As a gesture in the meantime, their commander had sent an armed squad to fly the American flag over the building that housed the city's mint.

Mumford, a local gambler, hauled down the flag, ripped it to shreds, and sported a remnant in his buttonhole. When he was caught, tried, and convicted of treason, New Orleans rebels sent Butler anonymous letters warning that if Mumford was hanged, Butler would pay with his life.

Butler admitted later that he had been frightened. He put in a sleepless night before the execution, then allowed Mumford's wife and small children to visit him during his last hours.

With that hanging, Butler became detested throughout the South. Jefferson Davis branded him "an outlaw." If Butler was captured, Davis decreed that he should be executed "in expatiation of his crimes." Throughout the Confederacy, he was reviled as "Beast Butler."

As New Orleans commander, Butler set no color bar for men volunteering for his army. He followed up his flouting of the Fugitive Slave Law by sheltering thousands of runaway slaves in New Orleans, and when Washington rejected his call for white reinforcements, Butler set out to raise three full Negro regiments on his own initiative.

Pinckney Pinchback opened an office at the corner of Bienville and Villere streets and quickly rounded up an entire company for Butler's new Corps d'Afrique. Along with the regiment's other black officers, Pinchback became a temporary captain, pending a qualification examination.

When those tests were completed, however, every other black candidate failed. They were discharged and replaced by white officers who did not hide their contempt for the one surviving black captain in their midst. Pinchback struck back with a symbolic protest. He refused to abide by the rules of the local streetcar company, which painted a large star on the only streetcars open to black passengers. When Pinchback boarded a whites-only car, however, employees closed its doors so that no whites would get aboard by mistake.

The military authorities ignored Pinchback's infraction, but when he was passed over a second time for what should have been an automatic promotion, he resigned his commission. The other officers were "inimical to me," Pinchback wrote, which made "my position very disagreeable indeed."

No effort was made to dissuade him. He received $521.95 for his service.

Two months later, Pinchback addressed a crowd at a "Meeting of Free Colored Citizens" at the New Orleans Economy Hall, called to seek the rights of free black men to vote. He appealed to a basic sense of fairness: If colored people were citizens, they had a right to cast ballots.

His army experience had embittered him but had not quenched his desire to serve in the war. Spending his own money, he rented a headquarters and printed advertisements for a new company of black men, this time in the cavalry.

He soon found that discrimination was not limited to the army's lower echelons. His application was quashed by an adjutant general less willing than Butler to ignore the letter of the law, which held that awarding commissions to Negroes was illegal.

Pinchback took up his protest with a vengeance. In speeches, he praised Benjamin Butler—although he noted that the general had "hesitated for a long time" before he had authorized the commission of black officers. Now, he added, after "it was proven beyond a doubt that colored men were as brave and trusty as any other man and would make just as good soldiers," they were removed from their posts because "white men alone are fit to command."

Troubling then to Pinchback—but no surprise—was President Lincoln's Proclamation of Amnesty and Reconstruction late in 1863. With the North's victory in sight, the president was turning his attention to post-war reconciliation. White backers of the Confederacy were offered the right to vote again after they took an oath to support the Constitution and the Union. When the number of those repentant rebels in any state reached 10 percent of the votes cast in the 1860 presidential election, the president would recognize their state government, and they could proceed to draft a new state constitution so long as it abolished slavery.

Called the Ten Percent Plan, Lincoln's proposal was designed to discourage Southerners from persisting in their rebellion. But to the dismay of Louisiana's black population, Lincoln's terms still prohibited them from voting or holding office.

Lincoln's leniency to the Confederates infuriated the Radical Republicans in Congress. To meet the administration's challenge, Senator B. F. Wade of Ohio—named, like General Butler, for Benjamin Franklin—joined with Henry Winter Davis, his counterpart in the House.

The Wade-Davis bill of July 1864 called for far more than the abolition of slavery. Confederate states would be required to repudiate their war debt. The bill required the appointing of military governors, who would then administer to all citizens an oath of loyalty to the United States. Only when a majority—not simply 10 percent—had sworn to the oath could they establish their government.

Benjamin Wade also tried to strike the word "white" from the section that restored voting rights. Charles Sumner's was one of the five votes to support him.

When the legislation reached the White House in the closing moments of the congressional session, Lincoln turned to a tactic first employed by Andrew Jackson, the pocket veto. When he did not sign the bill, it died.

Lincoln explained that since governments in Arkansas and Louisiana had already been installed under his plan, he would not reject them. He was "sincerely hoping and expecting that a constitutional amendment abolishing slavery throughout the nation may be adopted," but meanwhile he was satisfied with his own approach.

Although Wade was criticized for his inflexible party loyalty, he had made it clear for years that Lincoln, as a man, did not impress him. As long ago as 1861, Wade had written to a friend that Lincoln's recent evasions on the issue of race "could only come of one, born of poor white trash and educated in a slave state."

Half amused, Lincoln had put up with Wade's insolence and struck back with his own weapon of choice. Ben Wade may not have been the senator most devoid of humor—that distinction remained with Charles Sumner—but neither was he equipped for bantering with the president.

Lincoln described to a friend one of their run-ins, which may have made Wade "my enemy for life."

In response to something Wade said, Lincoln had remarked, "Senator, that reminds me of a story."

Wade interrupted "in a petulant way: 'It is with you, sir, all story, story! You are the father of every military blunder that has been made during the war. You are on your road to hell, sir, with this government, by your obstinacy, and you are not a mile off this minute.'"

Lincoln replied—"good-naturedly," he was sure—that the mile to hell that Wade had mentioned "is just about from here to the Capitol, is it not?"

Wade "was very angry, grabbed up his hat and cane, and went away."

Lincoln was prepared, then, for the Wade-Davis Manifesto, which appeared in the New York Tribune on August 5, 1864. It began, "We have seen without surprise, but not without indignation, the proclamation of the President of the 8th of July."

Their statement went on to uphold the supremacy of Congress over the executive branch, an argument that would persist long after Lincoln was removed from the debate.

The congressmen concluded that Lincoln's action had been motivated by his desire for electoral votes in the coming presidential election. But he "must understand that our support is of a cause, not a man."

. . .

At that disheartening moment for the Negroes of New Orleans, they seemed to be about to lose their staunch white advocate. For weeks, Ben Butler had been hearing rumors that Secretary of State Seward was calling for his recall from New Orleans. Butler's offense was said to be the high-handed way he had treated those foreigners he considered sympathetic to the Confederacy. Protests from embassies in Washington had forced Seward to defuse their bitterness at the same time that he was working to undercut European support for the South.

Butler's enemies had also tainted his success in stabilizing the New Orleans banking system by accusing him and his brother of reaping large personal profits from his changes.

In December 1863, General Nathaniel Banks arrived in New Orleans and handed Butler orders from the secretary of war that named Banks as the new military chief. Humiliated, Butler put up a brave front. He briefed Banks on the challenges he would face and then, ignoring the latest threats against his life, announced that he would be attending a performance at a local theater.

That night, to Butler's great surprise, the audience gave him a tumultuous standing ovation.

In Washington, Ben Butler pressed Lincoln successfully for a new posting, but he would be reporting to Ulysses Grant, who had taken command of all Union armies, and Grant considered Butler an amateur who held his rank only because he was supporting Lincoln's re-election.

Grant's misgivings seemed confirmed when Butler's troops were defeated outside Richmond, Virginia, in May 1864, by Confederate general Pierre Gustave Toutant Beauregard. Butler, however, could point to the fact that Grant had diverted seventeen thousand of Butler's troops to reinforce his own men.

Grant's hesitation and the relentless bureaucratic infighting may indeed have contributed to the defeat. But blame for the humiliation fell to Butler.

Butler himself brought on his own final disaster. He insisted on taking command for an attack on an unusually well-defended fort, although Grant wanted to put another officer in charge.

Fort Fisher was a critical gateway between the Cape Fear River in North Carolina and the Atlantic Ocean, and Butler proposed a daring idea for breaching its ramparts: A Union ship crammed with gunpowder would sail directly at the fort, then ground troops would follow up with an assault. Grant went along with the scheme and allocated sixty-five hundred men.

Bad weather, poor communication, and failed technology combined to produce an epic failure. Butler arrived on the scene to find that Admiral David Porter had already launched his ship, but its muted explosion had done little damage to the fort.

Acting on his own, Butler withdrew his landing forces. During the planning stages, he had already alienated Porter. Now the admiral was quick to report to Washington that Butler could have proceeded with the attack and easily overwhelmed the fort's defenders.

"If this temporary failure succeeds in sending General Butler into private life," Porter wrote, "it is not to be regretted."

Grant took that cue and relieved Butler of command. Some two weeks later, Butler's replacement, General Adelbert Ames, took Fort Fisher. Ben Butler returned to private life.

Much later, Grant would make a halfhearted attempt at being fair: "General Butler certainly gave his very earnest support to the war," Grant wrote in his memoirs, "and he gave his own best efforts personally to the suppression of the rebellion."

Secretary of the Navy Gideon Welles offered a different judgment, one that was never widely shared: "Butler's greater intellect overshadowed Grant, and annoyed and embarrassed the General-in-Chief."

In New Orleans, Nathaniel Banks was pursuing a policy different from Butler's in dealing with the city's black residents. General Banks, who saw himself as a presidential possibility for 1868, worried that giving the vote to freed black men would undercut his popularity with white voters.

After President Lincoln had met privately with two wealthy black businessmen from Louisiana who argued for black voting rights, Lincoln raised the possibility with the state's civilian governor. But he also made clear that it was "only a suggestion, not to the public but to you alone."

Pinckney Pinchback was dissatisfied with the tenor of the postwar planning. He calculated that since the Emancipation Proclamation, black regiments totaling 180,000 men had been fighting for the Union, and he went north early in 1865 to appeal directly to Lincoln for permission to raise more of the all-black regiments in Ohio and Indiana and speed the war to its end.

Before he could apply for an interview at the White House, Pinchback learned that Lincoln had been shot.

He traveled on to Cincinnati to see his wife and mother. Pinchback was now twenty-seven, as tall as his father had been, with a fashionable beard but untamable hair. He intended to wait in the North to see what direction Vice President Andrew Johnson would take once he was installed as Lincoln's successor.

By autumn, however, Pinchback's impatience overcame him, and he and Nina headed south to assess his future.

In Washington, debate was under way on the problems certain to arise once the last shot was fired. Charles Sumner worried that time was running out for the major changes in society that only wartime could advance. He was gratified when Lincoln appointed his ally Salmon Chase as U.S. Chief Justice, and he looked to the Court to overturn the Dred Scott decision. Sumner attacked that decision—a ruling that Negroes were not citizens—as "more thoroughly abominable than anything of the kind in the history of the court."

On February 1, 1865, with the Thirteenth Amendment pending before Congress, Sumner introduced a motion to permit John Sweat Rock to become the first black attorney to address the Supreme Court. That milestone would be a vindication for the forty-year-old Rock, born in New Jersey to parents who fostered his talents and encouraged his ambition. Denied entrance to medical schools because of his race, Rock had turned to law and had been admitted to the Massachusetts bar.

Sumner fretted over the fate of Southern slaves who lacked Rock's early advantages. Without federal protection, Sumner saw them being kept in peonage by their former owners, who would establish "slavery under an alias."

Secretary of War Stanton had formed the American Freedmen's Inquiry Commission to recommend means to help the former slaves support themselves. But Sumner found the commission sluggish in producing its report, and other Radical Republicans objected to leaving the effort under the control of the War Department. They pointed out that the Treasury already managed the land that should be parceled out when the war ended.

Division over the issue ran deep. Did the majority of the Congress believe that Washington should guarantee Negroes land, jobs, and education? Or, along with many Northerners, were they convinced that the result would be a dangerous incursion of federal power into private life?

Republican senator James Grimes of Wisconsin framed the fate of the former slaves starkly: "Are they free men or are they not? If they are free, then why not let them stand as free men?"

After legislative jockeying and concessions by the Sumner camp, a bill created a Bureau of Refugees, Freedmen, and Abandoned Land within the War Department.

On March 3, 1865, President Lincoln signed legislation that stipulated that the life of the bureau was limited to last "during the present War of Rebellion and one year thereafter." The bureau's commissioner could provide applicants with no more than forty acres of land, for which the tenants would pay low rent for three years. After that, they could buy the property at its appraised market value.

Up to the final vote, Senator Sumner's opponents were protesting that the bureau would favor black farmers over white. Samuel Pomeroy of Kansas sounded their rallying cry: "I do not believe it is necessary to secure the property of one race that another shall be destroyed."

To head a new bureau already beset by controversy, Lincoln intended to name a Northern graduate of West Point, Major General Oliver Otis Howard.

Andrew Johnson

CHAPTER 5

ANDREW JOHNSON (1865)

When Andrew Johnson took the presidential oath of office on the morning of April 15, 1865, the occasion was clouded by more than the murder of the man he was replacing. Six weeks earlier, Johnson had disgraced himself at Abraham Lincoln's second inaugural ceremony in ways he was still trying to live down.

For entirely political motives, Lincoln's advisers had settled on Johnson, the fifty-six-year-old senator from East Tennessee, as their vice presidential candidate. With Hannibal Hamlin of Maine on the ticket in 1860, Lincoln had not won a majority of the vote—39.8 percent. Stephen Douglas and his Democrats had taken slightly less than 30 percent, and the remainder split between John Breckenridge's Southern Democrats and John Bell's Constitutional Union Party.

For re-election, Lincoln needed a stronger running mate. Right up to Election Day, he had been apprehensive about the outcome, and he told a friend, "I wish I were certain."

Although the votes would not be counted from either Louisiana or Johnson's Tennessee, the new vice presidential nominee brought in support from Democrats in other states, and the ticket won by four hundred thousand votes. That was 55 percent of the total vote, to 45 percent for General McClellan, running as a peace candidate.

Andrew Johnson had first won acclaim in the North as the sole

Southern Democrat in the Senate to commit himself to the Union. While voters in his state were deciding whether to secede, Johnson stumped the countryside trying to separate the issue of slavery from the question of loyalty to the country:

"Damn the Negroes," Johnson said. "I am fighting those traitorous aristocrats, their masters."

When Northern troops took control of Tennessee, Lincoln appointed Johnson as the state's military governor. He moved forcefully against the secessionists who cited the U.S. Constitution to justify their right to withdraw from the Union. "Whenever you hear a man prating about the Constitution," Johnson said, "spot him for a traitor."

He freed his own slaves and argued for giving black men the vote. "A loyal Negro," Johnson said, "is worth more than a disloyal white man."

Andrew Johnson's contribution was not the only factor in Lincoln's re-election. For the first time, most army troops had been allowed to vote by absentee ballot, and news from the battlefield had continued to be heartening.

On the morning of Lincoln's second inaugural, on March 4, 1865, Johnson was in no condition to attend. His friends later claimed that he had been recovering from typhoid fever or malaria. They pointed out that Johnson had asked to stay on in Tennessee and delay his own swearing-in until April but that Lincoln had insisted he come to Washington.

In any event, on the night before the inaugural Johnson had indulged himself at a reception given by his friend John Forney, the secretary of the Senate. On the cold and rainy morning of the most important day of his life, he showed up at the Capitol looking ashen and weak.

The ceremony had been moved inside to the overheated and muggy Senate chamber. In the vice president's office, Johnson prevailed on his outgoing predecessor to fetch him a whiskey. "I'm not well," Johnson complained, "and need a stimulant."

Hannibal Hamlin did not drink, but to oblige Johnson, he sent out for a bottle of whiskey, then watched with dismay as Johnson quickly filled and downed three tumblers.

The Senate was crowded and noisy when Johnson entered arm in arm with Hamlin and took a seat while Hamlin made his brief remarks. In the visitors gallery, women observed that as Johnson began to speak without notes he was flushed and unsteady.

For seventeen agonizing minutes, a lifetime of bitterness spewed out across the chamber, even though not many in his appalled audience could appreciate the background for Johnson's tirade.

As a boy named for Andrew Jackson, he had been three when his father, a tavern waiter, died in Raleigh, North Carolina. The boy was told that he had been trying to rescue two drunken patrons from a nearby swollen river. Andrew's mother struggled for the next ten years. When she could no longer support him and his brother William, she apprenticed them to a tailor.

After a scrape with the law, the two young men ran away. Eventually, they rejoined their mother and her new husband and made their way to Greenville, Tennessee.

With no formal education, Andrew opened a tailor shop. At nineteen, he married an orphan, Eliza McCardle, who encouraged his efforts to read and write. A hard worker, Andrew amassed modest holdings, including a few slaves. Short, always well-dressed, but often glowering, Johnson entered politics as an alderman in 1829 and as the mayor of Greenville five years later.

Elected to the Tennessee legislature, Johnson introduced a bill to give indigent men 160 acres of public land if they would live on it. He promoted that measure when he reached the U.S. Congress in 1843 and finally saw it become law during the Civil War's second year.

As a populist, Johnson opposed Congress accepting the bequest of James Smithson to create a museum because, he said, taxpayers would soon have to support the institution. In a highly charged era, Johnson's opposition to secession was marked by its fiery language. He denounced Jefferson Davis as one of the South's "illegitimate, swaggering, bastard, scrub aristocrats."

Johnson's ingrained sense of victimhood never left him. "Some day," he vowed, "I will show the stuck-up aristocrats who is running the country." Like Andrew Jackson before him, he found the wealthy and educated "not half as good as the man who earns his bread by the sweat of his brow."

His resentments were on full display as Johnson singled out Lincoln's cabinet appointees to upbraid them by name and remind them that they owed "what you are or ever will be to the people." Gideon Welles was nearly spared when Johnson could not remember his name, but he leaned over to ask John Forney, "Who is the Secretary of the Navy?"

Finished with his domestic insults, he railed against the diplomats in the chamber for "all your fine feathers and geegaws."

Johnson was determined to set himself apart from the wealthy and well-born: "Today, one who claims no high descent, one who comes from the ranks of the people, stands, by the choice of a free constituency, in the second place of this Government." Gleefully, he observed that "there may be those to whom things are not pleasing."

Lincoln had entered the hall and taken his place at the center of the notables. He listened impassively, head bowed and sometimes closing his eyes. His response was impossible to read. Charles Sumner first sat with an ironic smile until he covered his face with his hands and rested his head on his desk.

Gideon Welles murmured to Secretary of War Stanton, "The man is either drunk or crazy." Not visibly disturbed, Henry Seward seemed prepared to hear Johnson out, but Hannibal Hamlin leaned forward to pull on Johnson's coattails, and the oath of office was finally administered.

At its conclusion, Johnson brought the Bible to his lips. To general mystification, he announced, "I kiss this book in the face of my nation of the United States."

Other years, the vice president would then swear in the new senators, but since Johnson could not perform that task, the duty was turned over to a clerk.

• • •

It fell to Lincoln to redeem the day. The skies had cleared, and the audience moved outdoors for his oration. As the president mounted the platform to deliver what he would consider his best speech, the sun appeared and gave hope to those looking for a better omen.

Where Johnson had been intent on settling scores, Lincoln sought to heal the nation's wounds. The solemnity of the occasion brought forth a scriptural tone from a man who resisted religious cant. With a lofty impartiality, he surveyed both sides in a conflict nearing its end.

"Both read the same Bible," Lincoln said, "and pray to the same God, and each invokes His aid against the other." That was not to say that the president was neutral about slavery. "It may seem strange that any men should ask a just God's assistance in wringing their bread from the sweat of other men's faces." But "let us judge not that we be not judged."

Lincoln said that he prayed fervently for the war to end, and yet in the righteous judgment of the Lord 250 years of slavery might require that the wealth accrued from slavery be lost and that "every drop of blood drawn with the lash shall be paid by another drawn with the sword."

But from this day forward, Lincoln concluded, "With malice toward none, with charity for all; with firmness in the right, as God gives us to see the right, let us strive on to finish the work we are in; to bind up the nation's wounds, to care for him who shall have borne the battle, and for his widow, and his orphan—to do all which may achieve and cherish a just, and lasting peace, among ourselves and with all nations."

That evening, five thousand people swarmed the White House, and the president shook every hand. Mary Lincoln, not always the most obliging political wife, promised "to remain till morning, rather than have the door closed on a single visitor."

Two days after Johnson's performance at his swearing-in, he appeared briefly at the Capitol again and then left town for the remainder of a special congressional session that ended on March 11. But if he was gone, the vice president was hardly forgotten. Around Washington, people were quoting a verse that concluded:

> *"O, was it not a glorious sight*
> *To see the crowd of black and white*
> *As well as Andy Johnson tight*
> *At the Inauguration."*

Charles Sumner lamented the "frightful" behavior of the vice president and would have pushed for his impeachment except that the House adjourned and could not hear the charges.

Johnson's letter to the Senate's recorder made it clear that he himself did not remember just what he had said in his speech except that it was provoking "some criticism." He asked for "an accurate copy of your report of what I said on that occasion." In time, his seventeen minutes were edited down for publication to a decorous six.

At the White House, Lincoln was calming fears about Johnson as best he could. To the comptroller of the currency, the president said, "I have known Andy Johnson for many years. He made a bad slip the other day, but you need not be scared. Andy ain't a drunkard."

Circumstance delayed the two men from meeting until the afternoon of April 14, when Johnson called on the president. His memory of Lincoln's inaugural remarks seemed as sketchy as his memory of his own, since he urged an unforgiving reception for the Southerners who had betrayed the Union. Genial but noncommittal, Lincoln shook his hand warmly and called him "Andy."

Henry Seward had survived Lewis Powell's murderous attack, although the family was troubled by the slow recovery of his son Fred.

By May 9, 1865, the secretary of state was able to move downstairs to his parlor and receive Andrew Johnson and Seward's fellow cabinet officers when they came to call.

Frances Seward had stayed in Washington to nurse her husband back to health, but by the end of the month she had fallen ill with a fever, and she became the patient. When she died on June 21, Thurlow Weed blamed the distress she had suffered over Seward's ordeal.

As Seward grew stronger and could return to his duties at the State Department, he was finding, like Charles Sumner, that being attacked had won him a new popularity nationally. In Washington, however, the earlier protests against his policies were reignited, and some Radical Republicans were urging President Johnson to replace Seward with General Benjamin Butler, whom they saw as a martyr to the political intrigue in New Orleans.

While Johnson was resisting their pressure, Seward was warning France against trying to exploit the Civil War by installing its own ruler in Mexico. Bowing to Seward's pressure, Napoleon III withdrew his French troops, and Seward found Great Britain ready to repair the strains with Washington that had arisen from its dealing with the Confederacy.

As those foreign complications were being resolved, the nation soon learned that domestic healing would not come so easily. Traveling through the South, one writer from Massachusetts spoke with a South Carolina innkeeper who had been ruined by the war. The Yankees had left him "one inestimable privilege," the man said, and that was "to hate 'em. I get up at half past four in the morning, and sit up till twelve midnight, to hate 'em."

That was the mood in the South on May 29, 1865, some six weeks after he had been sworn in as president, when Andrew Johnson revealed his vision for uniting America.

Johnson issued a sweeping amnesty so "that peace, order and freedom may be established." His decree would restore all property—except slaves—to the rebels so long as they took an oath to "support, protect and defend the Constitution and all laws and proclamations issued during the existing rebellion with reference to the emancipation of the slaves." The oath would end with the traditional "So help me God."

Johnson went on to list the categories of men who were not to receive that amnesty. He barred those who had assumed an office in the Confederacy or had left Congress or their Union judgeships to join the rebellion. Also excluded were those who resigned their army or navy commissions to hold a rank above that of colonel in the "pretended Confederate government" or its military.

The several other exemptions involved participants in the rebellion whose taxable property was worth more than twenty thousand dollars and anyone who had mistreated Union prisoners of war.

But even those men denied the general amnesty could apply directly to the president "and such clemency will be liberally extended as may be consistent with the facts of the case and the peace and dignity of the United States."

Since Johnson's terms for amnesty were not significantly different from those Lincoln had proposed at the end of 1863, the Congress seemed prepared to endorse them.

But when Johnson appointed William Holden, who had stayed loyal to the Union, as provisional governor of North Carolina, the president did not act jointly with Congress but rather made the appointment in his capacity as commander-in-chief.

Within six weeks, Johnson had issued similar proclamations naming governors for Mississippi, Georgia, Texas, Alabama, South Carolina, and Florida. He considered reconstruction far enough advanced in the other four Confederate states—Virginia, Arkansas, Tennessee, and Louisiana—that he need not provide a provisional governor.

As federal control was re-established, Johnson directed his appointed governors to select officials in their state who had remained loyal to the Union. To establish qualifications for voting, the rebel states themselves would be responsible, either through a convention or through their re-instituted legislatures.

For Charles Sumner, the question of voting for blacks was "the essence, the great essential" of Reconstruction, and his conversations with the new president were reassuring. In fact, he considered Johnson more sympathetic to Negro suffrage than Lincoln had been. "There is no difference between us," the president had assured him.

In the week following Johnson's proclamation, he was besieged with individual requests for amnesty. None was more poignant than the handwritten submission of June 13, 1865, on plain ruled paper:

Asking for full restoration of his rights, Robert E. Lee concluded, "I

Robert E. Lee

graduated at the Mil: Academy at W. Point in June 1829. Resigned from the U.S. Army April '61. Was a General in the Confederate Army, & included in the surrender of the Army of N. Va: 9 April '65.

"I have the honour to be Very respt. your obt. Servt. R. E. Lee."

Bureaucratic requirements and confusion held up Lee's petition. His pardon was not issued until it was included in a broad category on Christmas Day, 1868.

Through all the delays, General Lee's request seemed likely to be granted since he had never been linked in any way to Lincoln's assassination.

During the weeks after the murder, investigators had been filling in details of the president's last night while Booth was being tracked down.

They concluded that the actor's familiarity with the play *Our American Cousin* had allowed him to fire his shot during a bit of dialogue in the third act guaranteed to provoke gales of laughter. During an intermission, Booth had taken a drink at a saloon next to the Ford Theater, then returned to a stairway to the dress circle to await his moment.

He heard the actress playing the pretentious Mrs. Mountchessington insult her rustic foil, Asa Trenchard, and stalk offstage. Watching her go, Trenchard grinned and delivered the last words Lincoln would hear:

"Don't know the manners of good society, eh? Well, I guess I know enough to turn you inside out, old gal—you sockdologising old man-trap."

Booth put his .44-caliber Derringer to the back of Lincoln's head and pulled the trigger. With a knife, he fought off a young army major invited by Mary Lincoln to the box with his fiancée as substitutes for the Grants.

Booth's leap from the president's box was broken when his boot nicked a portrait of George Washington and his spur got caught in a display of regimental colors. Once on the stage, Booth confronted the horrified audience and shouted, "Sic semper tyrannis!"—thus always to tyrants! Long before it became the motto of the Commonwealth of Virginia in 1776, the cry had been attributed to Brutus as he struck down Julius Caesar.

Brandishing his knife, Booth hobbled past the actor playing Trenchard and stumbled down a back corridor to the alley, where a stagehand called "Peanut" was holding Booth's rented horse.

As a dragnet spread across Maryland, Lincoln's murder revived the career of Lafayette Baker, a Union army operative. Baker had once headed the War Department's intelligence unit until he was caught intercepting Secretary Stanton's wires and banished to New York.

Called back to hunt down the assassin, Baker sent men along the trail Booth had ridden in the company of David Herold. Booth's leg was painful, but they were young and fit—Herold twenty-three, Booth twenty-six. They rode nine miles to a tavern that Mary Surratt had once owned and then another nineteen miles to reach the house of Dr. Samuel Mudd. There, on the afternoon of April 15, they learned that Secretary Stanton had posted a hundred-thousand-dollar reward for Booth's capture.

On April 18, Lincoln's open casket went on display in the East Room of the White House before his body would be sent off by rail for burial in Illinois. Tens of thousands of mourners lined the train's route, and Booth was aggrieved to learn from the newspapers that even in the South not everyone saw his deed as heroic.

In Washington, a young actress named Ella Starr was appalled by the stories of Lincoln's murder. Although she was pregnant with Booth's child, she had not been his only lover. As Baker's men closed in on him, she tried, and failed, to kill herself with chloroform.

On April 25, Booth's pursuers had finally trapped Booth and Herold in a tobacco barn on the farm of Richard Garrett, six miles south of the Rappahannock River. The fugitives had told Garrett's family that they were Confederate officers heading for Mexico.

When Union troops demanded that the men come out of the barn, David Herold emerged and tried to separate himself from the man still inside. "He told me that his name was Boyd," Herold said.

The barn was set on fire. In the confusion, a soldier named Boston Corbett claimed that Booth had fired and Corbett fired back. Booth died three hours later. Some witnesses said his last words were "Useless, useless."

Booth's body was identified by the initials "JWB" tattooed on his left hand. He had left a journal justifying his action. One entry read, "I can never repent it, though we hated to kill."

In addition to David Herold, six of the other nine defendants were in custody. Booth had been identified quickly and then John Surratt, since the two men had not tried to disguise their unlikely intimacy.

In fact, a warning about the Surratt boardinghouse had been received by army officers from Louis Weichmann, who had studied for the ministry with Surratt in Maryland at the College of St. Charles Borromeo. While living at Mary Surratt's establishment, Weichmann had become alarmed and reported what he had overheard there, but no one in authority had acted on his vague suspicions.

The next break in the investigation came when officials from the War Department seized Booth's effects from the National Hotel and found the handcuffs Booth had intended for Lincoln in the days when he had hoped to kidnap him.

They also uncovered a letter from Samuel Arnold and traced him to his job in a store at Fort Monroe. Arnold promptly named the rest of the conspirators, including George Atzerodt and Michael O'Laughlen, but he could supply only their aliases for Lewis Powell and David Herold.

O'Laughlen was quickly picked up in Baltimore. Herold had been assigned to stand guard outside Seward's house while Powell murdered him, but at the sounds of a struggle, he had ridden off to join Booth.

Disoriented, Powell had taken refuge in a crypt at a cemetery near the Capitol. On Easter Sunday, he crept out to retrieve a newspaper that nearby mourners had left behind and learned that his mission had failed and Seward lived. By Monday, suffering from hunger, Powell stumbled to Mary Surratt's house.

He arrived a minute after an army officer had arrested her, her daughter Anna, and two other women in the house. Questioned by the soldiers, Powell concocted an alibi. Mrs. Surratt had engaged him, he said, to dig a gutter. The commander took Mary Surratt into the hall and asked whether she knew the man.

Looking back at him steadily, she raised her right hand and swore, "Before God, I do not know this man and have never seen him before, and I did not hire him to dig a gutter for me."

She then asked for permission to pray, which was granted. As she rose again from her knees, Mrs. Surratt seemed satisfied with her performance. "I am so glad you officers came here tonight," she said, "for this man came here with a pickaxe to kill us."

Powell was taken to army headquarters along with the women from the house, and Seward's servant, William Bell, was called to identify

Mary Surratt

him. Ushered into a room of prisoners, Bell went directly to Powell. "I know you," Bell exclaimed. "You are the man."

A knottier problem concerned the fate of Jefferson Davis. New York senator Edwin Morgan, who had been governor of his state during the rebellion, assured Andrew Johnson that to court-martial Davis for his "complicity with the assassination plots" would meet "with the approval of the world."

It was while Davis was being taken in custody to Macon, Georgia, that he learned of a hundred-thousand-dollar reward posted for his arrest on the charge of conspiring with Booth to murder Lincoln. Davis regarded the charge as false on its face. He and Andrew Johnson had been personal and political foes since they served in the House of Representatives in 1845. He would have done nothing to make Johnson president.

Davis was transported with his wife and their youngest children from Macon to Augusta, Georgia, and reunited with another captive, his vice president, Alexander Stephens. They were next sent by ship to Norfolk, Virginia, and on to a primitive cell at Fort Monroe on Hampton Roads.

Since Secretary of War Stanton had left Davis's treatment to his jailers, Brigadier General Nelson A. Miles ordered Davis put in leg irons. When Davis resisted, a shamefaced officer directed several privates to lock the irons in place forcibly. Within five days, word of Davis's ordeal had outraged even Northerners, and Stanton ordered the shackles removed.

But the rumor that Davis had tried to escape capture in his wife's clothes proved harder to shake off. As the story swept Washington, Stanton's representative called on Varina Davis. Without telling her the reason, he took away the gray raglan cloak she had thrown over her husband's shoulders. The following day, he returned for her shawl.

Stanton had been pleased to see Northern editors accusing Davis of cowardice. As one newspaper put it, "a peal of inextinguishable laughter" was being directed at Davis for "cowering under a petticoat."

When Stanton saw the garments, however, he realized that the cloak was hardly different from a male raincoat and that many men, including Lincoln, commonly wore a shawl for warmth. The story of bonnets and hoopskirts was too good to debunk, however, and Stanton locked away the garments in a War Department safe.

The ridicule had reached Davis in captivity and contributed to his decline. He had long suffered from insomnia, and now a light was kept burning in his cell throughout the night while a guard checked on him every fifteen minutes.

The prison doctor detected a deterioration in Davis's sight and hearing. Learning that he had trouble eating and had lost weight, President Johnson sent an emissary to the prison to monitor Davis's condition and surroundings. By August, the prisoner's health had improved, although the doctor described his mood as "dull and depressed."

In October, Davis was moved to dry and brighter quarters being vacated by a Union artillery officer. By that time, he was permitted visits from his family, and his reading material included Washington Irving's life of George Washington and a Bible from which Davis drew consolation as he waited for the Johnson administration to decide what to do with him.

Davis thought of himself as a martyr to the Confederate cause. If he were released eventually, he was determined never to submit to Yankee rule. Instead, he might join the ten thousand Confederate soldiers who had gone to live abroad or in Mexico.

Several from Davis's cabinet had already made that decision. His secretary of state, Judah Benjamin, regarded as the smartest man in the Confederacy, had escaped to Florida and then to the Bahamas before reaching a haven in England. John C. Breckinridge, James Buchanan's vice president, was taking a different route to the same sanctuary—first Cuba and Canada and on to London. Davis's attorney general and his secretary of the Treasury had disappeared altogether.

After President Johnson asked his attorney general whether the defendants should be tried in civilian court or by a military tribunal, the responsibility fell to Joseph Holt, a fifty-eight-year-old Kentucky lawyer and former postmaster general.

Four years of Civil War had provided ample precedent for tribunals. More than 4,270 of them had already been held, even though most of the thirteen thousand defendants were civilians. Attorney General James Speed characterized the accused assassins as secret belligerents whose previous spying for the Confederacy disqualified them for civilian trials.

Hearing that the proceedings would be conducted by the military, Secretary of War Stanton wrote a quick note to his staff confirming Holt as the judge advocate general: "You should be governed by the opinions of Judge Holt. You will consider yourself under his direction."

On April 29, Stanton ordered six prisoners transferred from ships anchored in the Potomac to the military prison at Washington's arsenal.

Samuel Mudd and Mary Surratt, who had been held at the Old Capitol Prison, were also taken there.

Indicted were David Herold, brought back from the Garrett farm; Samuel Arnold, implicated in the kidnapping plot; Michael O'Laughlen, named by Arnold in his confession; George Atzerodt, who also confessed freely but stressed that he had not carried out Booth's orders to kill Andrew Johnson; and Edward Spangler, a scenery mover at the Ford Theater, who was accused of aiding Booth's escape.

Lewis Powell was indicted under his long-standing alias, Lewis Payne. Indications from the government suggested that Jefferson Davis would be tried separately on other charges in a civil court.

As for John Surratt, he had been traveling to Elmira, New York, on Confederate business when he learned that Booth had carried out their plot. Managing to slip into Canada, he eluded the attempts to capture him there. By the time of the trial, he had found refuge in a small town outside Montreal.

When the tribunal opened on May 11, 1865, the proceedings captivated the nation. Twelve-year-old Thomas Lincoln, called "Tad" by his parents, showed up to listen solemnly to the testimony as a crowd of reporters strained to convey the scene. Each male defendant was scrutinized and appraised, although during their first appearance in court they were wearing hoods.

In a punitive spirit, Secretary Stanton had ordered the hoods made of heavy canvas and padded with cotton for maximum discomfort. With only a small hole at the mouth, they had none at all for the eyes or ears. Mary Surratt was spared a hood, but the men could not remove them nor were they permitted to bathe during the proceedings.

Only after the prison doctor protested were guards allowed to remove the hoods, although Lewis Powell remained in his. The brawniest of the prisoners, he did not seem to be suffering.

Powell was also the male defendant who most fascinated the observers; one spoke of his "massive robustness of animal manhood." But journalists also accepted claims by Powell's attorney that he was a weak-willed and illiterate man led astray by Booth.

Samuel Arnold and Michael O'Laughlen came off better—Arnold with his "intelligent face, curly brown hair and restless dark eyes," and O'Laughlen, "a small, delicate-looking man with pleasant features" that were composed in "a sad, remorseful look."

George Atzerodt, as a German foreigner, became "short, thick-set, round-shouldered" or, to another journalist, "crafty, cowardly and mercenary."

Observers were puzzled by Dr. Samuel Mudd, who seemed too high-born to be mixing with rabble like Atzerodt. With his hairline receding from an imposing brow and his "astute blue eyes," Mudd was termed "the most inoffensive and decent in appearance of all of the prisoners."

And yet Mudd had looked nervous when investigators came to question him about the men seen at his house soon after the assassination. Mudd claimed that they were strangers to him but that medical ethics had obligated him to set the broken leg of one of them.

But Mudd had also lent the man a razor to shave his mustache and had directed him and David Herold to an escape path through a nearby swamp. Since his patient was proved to be John Wilkes Booth, Mudd's conviction seemed ensured.

None of the men in the courtroom, however, captured the spectators' attention like Mary Surratt. Gallant reporters described her regularly as a devoted mother, and one account noted that as a former Southern belle, she still had "pleasing features." To those journalists, Mrs. Surratt seemed entirely deserving of the testimonials to her good character from her several Catholic advisers.

As the trial proceeded, a grand jury in the District of Columbia indicted Jefferson Davis and John Breckinridge for high treason. Prosecutors announced that they would try Davis instead for his involvement in a July 1864 attack on Washington. But as delays mounted, critics wondered whether the government was trying to avoid a debate over the legality of secession. As Davis waited in prison through the many months, Breckinridge remained at large in England.

During the forty-eight days of testimony in the assassination trial, prosecution and defense called a total of 366 witnesses. The charges did not distinguish between the four men linked directly to the plot to kill Lincoln and the six involved in the earlier kidnapping scheme. The prosecutors argued that even if they had balked at the assassinations, none of the five men or Mary Surratt had come forward to prevent them.

Despite the outrage provoked by their crime, the defendants attracted several prominent attorneys. Reverdy Johnson, a Maryland senator, agreed to represent Mrs. Surratt on grounds that she and her fellow prisoners had been entitled to a civil trial. He demanded to know whether constitutional rights existed only in peacetime.

Despite Reverdy Johnson's maneuvering, he could not erase the damning evidence against Mary Surratt offered by Louis Weichmann, the boarder who had once studied with her son. Weichmann was desperate to convince the authorities that he had not been involved in the plot, and he testified to the many times that Booth beckoned John Surratt upstairs for talks that might last two or three hours. He added that when her son was away, Mrs. Surratt and Booth held similar long private conversations.

Gratefully, Weichmann took up hints from Judge Holt to keep his answers consistent with what he had already told government detectives. In his final questioning, Holt drew from Weichmann an account of a meeting between Booth and Mrs. Surratt eight hours before the murder. It came soon after the actor learned that Lincoln would be attending the Ford Theater that evening.

Reverdy Johnson seemed to have given up on proving his client innocent. Instead, he tried and failed to tie Weichmann into the conspiracy.

An hour before noon on June 29, 1865, Judge Holt and the nine commissioners voted on the charges against the defendants. David Herold was the first to be sentenced—"to be hanged by the neck until he be dead." The same verdict was reached for Atzerodt and Powell, convicted under the name Lewis Payne.

The court decreed life sentences for Michael O'Laughlen and Samuel Arnold. The evidence against Edward Spangler, the stagehand accused of helping Booth escape from the Ford Theater, had been only thinly corroborated. He was sentenced to a six-year prison term.

Last to be announced were the verdicts against Mary Surratt and Dr. Mudd. Mrs. Surratt was sentenced to be hanged for her "traitorous conspiracy," which the commission deemed to have begun on March 6.

Because those deliberations had taken the full day, Mudd's case was held over to the next morning. His testimony about not knowing Booth had been contradicted by witnesses who had seen them together and yet, by a vote of five to four, Mudd was spared the gallows. Hanging required a two-thirds vote, and Mudd was sentenced instead to life in prison.

The prospect of hanging a woman for the first time in U.S. history provoked five of the commissioners to urge clemency, and they attached their recommendation to the court's findings that were sent to President Johnson. They did not argue for her innocence but instead on behalf of her sex and her age, which they established was forty-two. Throughout the trial, reporters had estimated that Mrs. Surratt was between forty-five and sixty.

Andrew Johnson had not stirred from the White House since he had moved in earlier in the month. Rumors spread that he feared another round of assassinations, but in fact he was swamped with visitors and paperwork, and his health was suffering.

When Johnson received the verdicts, the commissioners' petition for clemency for Mrs. Surratt was somehow omitted. In any case, the new president might have balked at commuting her death sentence, since he was insisting that everyone must understand that "if women committed crimes they would be punished" like men. Johnson added that if he agreed to the request for clemency, "hereafter conspirators and assassins would use women as their instruments."

By his reasoning, Johnson was protecting the rest of Mrs. Surratt's gender by letting her hang. He concluded, "It would be a mercy to womankind to let Mrs. Surratt suffer the penalty of her crime."

• • •

When all last-minute appeals failed, families of the condemned prisoners were allowed to pay their final visits. David Herold's bevy of six
sisters were sobbing, seemingly more unnerved by his fate than Herold
himself, with his cultivated air of indifference. Lewis Powell, who had
lost two brothers fighting for the Confederacy, also had six sisters, but
none came to visit.

One heavily veiled woman asking for George Atzerodt set off speculation in the press that she was either his mother or his sister. The trial
had not disclosed that Atzerodt had fathered a child with a common-
law wife.

John Surratt, unwilling to jeopardize his sanctuary in Canada, never
saw his mother again.

On July 7, 1865, a thousand spectators showed up at Washington
Arsenal, where scaffolding had been erected. Its platform had been
measured to ensure that the prisoners would climb the traditional thirteen steps before reaching the four hangman's nooses that dangled in
a row.

At 1 p.m., the four prisoners were led to chairs on the platform.
Lewis Powell wore a straw sailor's hat, tilted at a rakish angle.

An official read out the death warrants, and a clergyman offered a
prayer. When the prisoners were summoned forward, George Atzerodt
was trembling so violently that his hands and legs had to be tied. Mary
Surratt's arms were also bound but she complained that the tight knot
was uncomfortable, and it was loosened.

Given his height, Powell had to bend his head to let the rope be
slipped over his neck. The officer doing the fitting explained that because
Powell's neck was so thick, a looser noose would make his dying less
painful. Powell said, "You know best, Captain."

The four prisoners were draped with white cloth, and soldiers kicked
away the wood blocks beneath the trapdoors. The four bodies fell about
six feet before the ropes jerked them back again for an instant.

When all four bodies were motionless, surgeons examined them and
soldiers cut them down. The scaffolding would remain in place for days,
a reminder for Samuel Arnold, Edward Spangler, Michael O'Laughlen,

and Samuel Mudd when they were brought out to exercise in the court-yard.

With the spectacle ended, the crowd moved out of the hot noonday sun and headed for makeshift stands selling lemonade and cakes. Some in the audience loitered in the shadow of the gallows throughout the afternoon until officers shooed them away.

Oliver O. Howard

CHAPTER 6

OLIVER OTIS HOWARD (1865)

Abraham Lincoln's selection of Major General Oliver Otis Howard to head the Freedmen's Bureau was quickly proving to be a mixed mark of favor. Howard had welcomed the appointment as a way of extricating himself from a posting in the army's Western Theater. But almost at once he found that no job in the rebuilding of the United States was subject to harsher criticism.

Howard's reputation had made Lincoln's settling on him easy to understand. Born in Leeds, Maine, Howard attended Bowdoin College and then, at twenty, was offered in 1850 an appointment to the U.S. Military Academy. He accepted even though four years at West Point would delay his marriage to Elizabeth Ann Waite, his attractive young fiancée, who approached life seriously.

Lizzie Waite's sober manner suited Howard. Bearded and with a full head of brown hair, he cut a dignified figure as he stubbornly attended the Bible classes that were unfashionable among his fellow cadets.

Although Howard did well in his studies, he found that his mild support for abolition, combined with his religiosity, made him something of a pariah. Custis Lee—whose father, Robert E. Lee, was soon to be named West Point's new superintendent—told Howard, with consummate politeness, to stop coming to his room without an invitation.

For his part, Howard's Christian tolerance did not extend to Southern members of the academy's debating society. He described them as "full of gas, seldom ever speaking to the point, but have a great flow of language."

Graduating near the top of his class, Oliver Howard married Lizzie Waite, fathered a son, and left as a second lieutenant to fight in Florida against the Seminoles.

At a Methodist revival meeting near Tampa, Howard had an experience that changed his life. When the preacher called for sinners, Howard stepped forward, and very soon he was wondering whether he should resign from the army and devote his life to the ministry. But at home, awaiting their second child, Lizzie Howard was not sure that she wanted the life of a clergyman's wife.

Howard was still debating his future—possibly applying for a six-month leave to study at Bangor Theological Seminary—when Fort Sumter fell to Southern forces, and he felt committed to the Union army for the war's duration.

Commanding a brigade, Howard first saw the carnage of war at the Battle of Bull Run, and the sight caused his legs to tremble but confirmed his determination to protect civilians and minimize casualties. Together with his diligence and sense of fairness, that spirit raised him rapidly to the rank of brigadier general and led to a nickname, "the Christian General."

In late May 1862, Howard's right arm was badly shot up in fighting outside Richmond and was amputated between his elbow and his shoulder. When Major General Phil Kearny, who had lost his left arm in the war with Mexico, visited Howard's camp, the new amputee offered a money-saving suggestion: Henceforth, the two of them should buy their gloves together.

After a brief period of recovery in Maine, Howard returned to battle but with dismal results.

His errors in judgment in May 1863 contributed to a rout of Union forces by Confederate general Thomas "Stonewall" Jackson. That public embarrassment was followed two months later by Howard's disorganized retreat at Gettysburg.

The Eleventh Corps that Howard commanded was made up largely of German immigrants, and they were humiliated to learn that within the Army of the Potomac, his two debacles had sullied the reputation of their entire unit.

Then, in an unexpected reversal, Howard's name was included in a congressional resolution praising the Union command at Gettysburg. Although the gesture of rehabilitation gratified Howard, he wanted his family and friends to know that to get it he had not engaged in any unworthy political chicanery.

When Howard learned of President Lincoln's assassination, he shared his grief with his mother. "I anticipated a real pleasure in serving under his administration after the war was over," Howard wrote, and he said he had felt the "complete confidence in Mr. Lincoln that I would in my own father and knowing that he would sustain me in every right course."

Within the month, Howard was summoned to Washington, where Secretary of War Stanton told him that Lincoln had intended to appoint him as the new commissioner of the Bureau of Refugees, Freedmen, and Abandoned Lands. Stanton added that President Johnson desired to carry out Lincoln's wish.

Howard had considered buying a farm in Maine and retiring from public life. But the chance to do good was too tempting to refuse. Howard rolled up his sleeve and set to work.

Howard could expect that Southerners would be hostile to his assignment, but elsewhere the choice was hailed. The *New York Times* praised the selection "of this Christian patriot." In New Orleans, the French-language *Tribune* took heart from Howard's history as an abolitionist. And Secretary of War Stanton received a fervent endorsement from a man with a unique perspective. Henry Ward Beecher's daughter, Harriet, had written *Uncle Tom's Cabin.* On meeting her, Lincoln was quoted as saying, "So you're the little woman who started this great war."

Now her father described Howard as "of all men yet mentioned, the *very one.*" Beecher envisioned Howard carrying "a wax candle lighted and signifying the word of God and the spirit of Love."

On May 24, 1865, Howard received his nation's thanks in person as he rode through Washington in the capital's Grand Review. Spectators who had learned of Howard's appointment called out his name during the victory parade, but at his side, William Tecumseh Sherman was less enthusiastic. Sherman had already warned Howard against letting "the theorists of New England" force upon the South the right of the Negro to vote and perhaps provoke a second civil war. Given the expectations for the bureau, Sherman added, "I fear you have Hercules' task."

Sherman was like other Union generals who had been unsure about how to deal with the former slaves who swarmed to their camps. In the war's earliest days, when Ulysses Grant was trying to prevent slavery from becoming the central issue in the conflict, he had ordered his officers to "turn the negro out of your camp as you would any other vagrant."

But within months Grant had come to believe that he had no choice but to supply sustenance for the dispossessed blacks.

As thousands of former slaves followed Sherman during his march from Atlanta to Savannah, he had written, "It is hard to tell in what sense I am most appreciated by Sambo—in saving him from his master" or in protecting him from politicians who were scrambling for his vote, if black men were allowed to cast it.

Sherman explained his misgivings to Howard: "I have realized in our country," he said, "that one class of men makes war, and leaves another to fight it out. I am," William Sherman concluded, "tired of fighting."

Howard saw his mission as assisting the former slaves, not as shielding the property or sensibilities of their former owners. To his wife, Howard wrote that "the negroes must be employed, instructed, cloaked, and fed, borne with and kindly treated as well as emancipated."

He was also mindful of the limits to his authority and its duration.

He expected enlightened Southerners to commit to fair play for the former slaves and to extend to them full equal rights, although he recognized that the former owners were a "people claiming to be superior."

When a state fulfilled its legal obligations, Howard was prepared to withdraw his bureau. He often repeated that he did not intend to perpetuate a permanent occupation.

And yet, if Howard succeeded, his Bureau would transform the lives of the former slaves—through land policy, education, voting rights, and even marriage practices—more surely than an occupation by Union troops.

Howard expected his assistant commissioners to share his optimism that "all good men" would recognize former slaves as "free laborers." But the assistants were also pragmatic. To guide the blacks of Kentucky and Tennessee, Major General Clinton Fisk issued a brochure he called "Plain Counsel."

Fisk cautioned black men from marrying hastily as a reaction against the laws that had prohibited marriage between slaves. Once they took a wife, however, the bureau expected them to respect their vows, even though few assistant commissioners went as far as Rufus Saxton, Howard's longtime friend in South Carolina.

Saxton decreed that a wife who left her husband because of his adultery would be entitled to exclusive control of their children and "one-half of his real and personal property, and all household effects."

In appointing his first ten assistants, Howard had drawn most of them from the ranks of the Union army and described them as "men of integrity with Christian hearts."

He made an occasional blunder. One appointee, an army chaplain in New Orleans, seemed more concerned with his salary than with the work to be done, and Howard replaced him.

In other instances, Howard had first considered candidates for his team who were hostile to their black clientele. Major General George Hartsuff had been a cadet with Oliver Howard at West Point, but Howard found that he was lecturing Negroes around his army command that they better get to work because their former owners owed them nothing.

Howard passed him over as head of the bureau in Virginia in favor of Colonel Orlando Brown, a protégé of Ben Butler.

More to Howard's liking was Colonel John Eaton, to whom General Grant had turned over the seven hundred thousand Negroes emancipated along the Mississippi River. Eaton had commandeered the estate of Jefferson Davis at Davis Bend, Mississippi, and turned it into what was described as a "Negro Paradise" with all white people banished from the area. Howard named Eaton his assistant for the District of Columbia.

They would be working out of a Washington townhouse on the northeast corner of I and Nineteenth Streets, taken over four years earlier, when the Southern congressman who owned it had gone home.

Given his limited budget, Howard could afford to to hire only nine hundred staff members for the entire South. At his office, he amassed stacks of the petitions flooding into the War Department, fresh evidence of the epic casualties from the war.

Although 360,000 Union troops had died during the four years, the North had been spared widespread devastation, and its industries were flourishing.

The Confederacy's losses were numerically less—a hundred thousand fewer soldiers killed and wounded than the North. But that represented a higher percentage of its eligible men. The future for the South's nine million white residents and four million former slaves looked dire.

From Richmond to Atlanta, ruined neighborhoods were disfigured by burnt-out stores and warehouses. Miles of streets were overrun with weeds. Thousands of widows had no support at all. Destitute blacks and whites were living in shelters thrown together on the cities' outskirts while hordes of black men roamed the desolate landscape looking for wives and children who had been sold into other states.

Former slaves were often at the mercy of the Black Codes, the state laws passed soon after Johnson became president.

White lawmakers in South Carolina decreed that if a black man aspired to any work except as a farmer or a servant, he must apply for a license from a judge and pay an annual tax that ranged from ten dollars to one hundred dollars.

Mississippi demanded that a black man present proof to the white mayor of his city that he had a home and a job.

Louisiana representatives modified their law to require that all heads of working families must sign contracts within the first ten days of each year that committed them and their children to work on a plantation.

In North Carolina, orphans were sent to work for the former masters of their families rather than allowing them to live with grandparents or other relatives. Violating an owner's rules would be considered "disobedience" and punished with a dollar fine for each infraction.

In Kentucky, all contracts had to be approved by a white citizen.

Florida law made either disobedience or "impudence" a form of vagrancy, and a vagrant could be whipped.

And a more subtle maltreatment: For months, some slaves had gone on working at their plantations because their owners had kept the news from them that they had been set free.

Their sponsors often justified the Black Codes as protection for the former slaves. Inflexible contracts were required, they claimed, because rootless black men could not survive a free competition for jobs. One South Carolinian predicted that they would perish because they would fail in the "struggle for life with a superior race."

In the fall of 1865, General Grant went south at President Johnson's request to check on the operations of the Freedmen's Bureau. Grant's report admitted that his tour had been hurried and that he could not give the bureau the attention he would have preferred.

But Grant said that conversations with bureau officials had convinced him that "in some states its affairs had not been conducted with good judgment or economy." Grant praised Howard as "the able head of the bureau" who "made friends by the just and fair instructions he gave." He added, however, that many on Howard's staff were encouraging unrealistic expectations among the former slaves.

Overall, Grant found that since Southerners were accepting the new realities, extending the life of the bureau would be unnecessary, even harmful.

• • •

The president had to weigh Grant's judgment against a contradictory report from Carl Schurz, the thirty-six-year-old German-American journalist.

After studying at the University of Bonn, Schurz had become caught up in the revolution sweeping through Germany. When the uprising failed, he escaped through European capitals, coming to rest by the mid-1850s in Milwaukee. In 1860, he campaigned in German for Lincoln, who sent him as ambassador to Spain to prevent the country from siding with the Confederacy.

Schurz returned to become a brigadier general of volunteers, and at the Battle of Chancellorville, he had quarreled over strategy with General Howard in the hours before Stonewall Jackson's decisive victory. For Howard, the president's choosing Schurz to assess the Freedmen's Bureau did not seem auspicious.

Meeting with Andrew Johnson before he left Washington, Schurz became another Radical lulled by the president's credo: "Arson is a crime, robbery is a crime, murder is a crime, and treason is a crime worse than them all."

Schurz was persuaded that Johnson intended to break up the South's plantations and parcel out their land as small farms. He thought he also detected vague hints from the president that "colored people should have some part in the reconstruction of their states."

Initially, Johnson's request that Schurz inspect conditions throughout the former Confederacy was unapplealing to him, partly because he would be traveling during July and August, the hottest months of the year. But at the War Department, Edwin Stanton was urging him to accept the assignment because the president was getting all kinds of advice and needed to hear from someone who would tell him the truth.

Although Stanton sent a captain from the New York Volunteers as an escort to his first stop in South Carolina, Schurz's education began on the steamer trip to the town of Hilton Head.

He had struck up a conversation with a well-spoken former Confederate army officer, like Schurz in his midthirties. The fellow described his prewar life as a prosperous plantation owner with ninety slaves on four thousand acres of land near Savannah.

He was returning home after a prolonged stay in a Northern hospital, and he anticipated that General Sherman's march through Georgia had left him destitute. Since he seemed utterly without hope for the future, Schurz tried to brighten his spirits by suggesting that he could contact his former slaves and invite them back to work as free laborers under a fair contract.

Schurz saw the man grow animated, even excited. "What? Contract with those niggers? It would never work."

Schurz persisted, but the man was adamant: Why, was not President Johnson a Southerner, and did he not know equally well that the nigger would not work without compulsion?

Schurz tried a different tack. The man could sell off part of his land and farm the rest for himself. As Schurz recalled, the response was equally disbelieving: "The idea that he should work with his hands as a farmer seemed to strike him as ludicrously absurd. He told me with a smile that he had never done a day's work of that kind in his life.

"He mused for a while in sad silence, and said at last, 'No, I can't sell my plantation. We must make the nigger work somehow.'"

It was the conclusion Schurz would hear dozens of times over the next three months: To get a Negro to work required physical compulsion.

Schurz was disturbed as well by the way Southern whites were venting their anger at losing the war. He detected throughout the former Confederacy "an entire absence of that national spirit, which forms the basis of true loyalty and patriotism."

In hospitals, Schurz found black women as well as men whose bodies had been beaten and their ears cut off. "Dead Negroes were found in considerable numbers in the country roads or on the fields, shot to death, or strung on the limbs of trees."

Schurz was appalled by evidence of the "almost insane state of irritation" among Southern whites. He recommended continued control of the South by the federal government. Anything less "may result in bloody collisions and will certainly plunge Southern society into restless fluctuations and anarchical confusions."

Blacks throughout the South already knew they could not expect relief from the reports of Grant or Schurz, however well meant. They were collecting accounts of fellow Negroes being whipped and killed, and no one being punished.

Much as Oliver Howard wanted to end that injustice, he was hindered by the patchwork nature of his assignment. Each of the eleven Confederate states had its own leaders, needs, and responses to its defeat. Abuses had cropped up in Louisiana even before Lincoln was assassinated, and yet Charles Sumner in Washington had gone along reluctantly with a plan to readmit the state. Under the direction of Nathaniel Banks, the state's constitutional convention had met the principal requirement by voting to abolish slavery by seventy-two to thirteen.

His service in Louisiana had brought Banks's thinking closer to that of Ben Butler, the man he replaced. When the convention appeared ready to restrict voting to white citizens, Banks intervened. Overnight, working with the civilian governor, he persuaded forty delegates to change their votes.

The result was a resolution that opened the way to Negro suffrage. Its language had been kept deliberately cloudy, but many white delegates agreed with the New Orleans man who denounced it as "a nigger resolution." They vowed to continue their fight, and the Freedmen's Bureau would become their battleground.

Oliver Howard considered education to be the major answer to his challenge and welcomed donations for schools from the North. As he waited for Congress to appropriate funds, the $770,000 that came in would be Howard's chief source of revenue.

Many officers from his staff resigned from the bureau to return home as soon as they were mustered out, leaving Howard with little money to pay their civilian replacements. And even when local white men could be hired, Howard might decide that a candidate was not equipped for the job. He thought that members of the Georgia staff, for example, "shamefully abused" their powers.

Howard was also learning that his crusade to enroll blacks in public schools was meeting as much resistance as the campaign for voting rights. Typical was the white legislator in New Orleans who got his first look at a school opened by the Freedmen's Bureau.

"What? For niggers?" he demanded. "Well, well, I have seen many an absurdity in my lifetime, but this is the climax!"

In fact, black parents were embracing education for their children after generations in a society that had prohibited teaching slaves to read and write. Nat Turner's slave uprising in 1831 had made those laws even stricter. At the war's end, fewer than 150,000 of the four million slaves were literate.

Southern white children had fared only somewhat better. Leading up to the war, fewer than half of the poor white children in Virginia had been enrolled in any school. Thomas Jefferson had once tried to set a minimum school term of eleven weeks a year. He found that plantation owners decreed that poor children did not need an education, and they refused to tax themselves for the expense.

Notable exceptions to that attitude had arisen in the Carolinas. Even before the war, North Carolina had embraced public schools, and in Charleston, South Carolina, residents celebrated Andrew Johnson's inauguration by opening public schools to children of every race. The *New York Tribune* sent a reporter to assess the result.

He noted that the races were still segregated in the classroom but mingled freely on the playground. He also observed a number of students in the Negro classrooms with blue eyes and "pure white skin," the legacy from "very old families" who "aided in obliterating all the complexional distinctions by merging their blood with that of their slaves."

But in Mississippi, black men who donated money for a school were then forbidden to send their children to it. One white teacher arriving in Adams County was targeted for murder by four young white men but instead was only roughed up "somewhat barbarously."

Thomas Conway, Oliver Howard's appointee in Louisiana, warned that if Union soldiers were withdrawn from his state, whites had made it clear that the Negroes "shall not own one acre of land or have any schools." In fact, "they are more hostile to the existence of schools than they are to owning land."

From the outset, Howard had approached the bureau's land policy with concern that he was acting legally. When a dispute arose between his agent, Rufus Saxton, and a Union army commander, Howard wanted reassurance from the Johnson administration before he made his ruling.

As the bureau's assistant for South Carolina, Georgia, and Florida, Saxton was enforcing a civilian order that allotted 485,000 acres of land along the Atlantic coast to forty thousand former slaves, but Major General Quincy Adams Gillmore intended to return the land to its white owners.

Both men enjoyed a military reputation. Gillmore was acclaimed for his 1862 artillery victory at Fort Pulaski near Savannah. Saxton's equally high standing resulted from his skillful defense of Harper's Ferry that same year.

Secretary Stanton left the arbitration to Howard, whose first compromise pleased no one: Black farmers would own the land while white families would be allowed to live on it. To resolve the dispute more satisfactorily, Howard asked for a ruling from Attorney General James Speed. But Speed refused to be trapped between congressional support for the bureau and Andrew Johnson's own approach to reconstruction, and he bucked the decision back to Howard.

Howard bought time by requiring his staff to make title searches for all the land they intended to allocate to freedmen in their states. While that was under way, Rufus Saxton went to Washington to lobby Howard in person for policies that he already knew Howard favored. Saxton reminded him of the time the two of them had toured the Sea Islands together.

The plantations on those Atlantic islands between Charleston and Savannah had been farmed since 1861 by former slaves working for wages paid by their Northern landowners. Their children attended schools staffed by Northern teachers.

At the time when Howard had visited the island of Port Royal, Brigadier General Saxton was making his headquarters there, and the two of them invited Secretary of War Stanton for an inspection.

Sharing their enthusiasm, Stanton had promoted Saxton to major general on the spot, and in Washington, President Lincoln had agreed that Port Royal might serve as a postwar model.

Now even after Saxton pointed to the Sea Islands success, Howard hesitated to act. To prod him further, Saxton returned home and issued a circular throughout his territory that promised its freedmen their forty-acre farms on abandoned lands. Saxton wrote to Howard that the former slaves were owed no less for "two hundred years of unrequited toil."

Saxton's goading worked. In late July 1865 Howard issued Circular 13, his own directive on land distribution. Emboldened by his interpretation of Attorney General Speed's ruling, Howard quoted directly from the congressional act of March 3, 1865.

Forty acres would be leased for three years to the male head of a family; the rent would be no more than 6 percent of the land's value as appraised in 1860.

Howard foresaw the potential conflict with President Johnson that Speed had ducked. He did not intend to clear his circular with the White House, and it would be unequivocal:

"The pardon of the President will not be understood to extend to the surrender of abandoned or confiscated property."

Thaddeus Stevens

CHAPTER 7

THADDEUS STEVENS
(1865–1866)

CHARLES SUMNER HAD WANTED TO BELIEVE IN ANDREW JOHNSON. His relations with Lincoln had never been easy, despite their surface amiability and their determination to avoid a public break. During the long debate over readmitting Louisiana, Sumner had opposed the president's policy. Yet a few days later, Lincoln pointedly invited him to escort Mrs. Lincoln to his second inaugural ball.

At the core of their dispute, Lincoln had seemed to have more faith than Sumner did in the South's ability to reorganize its postwar society. On one issue, however, they were united. They worried that in future elections rebellious whites might end up outvoting Southerners who had stayed loyal to the Union. For Sumner, apart from simple justice, that concern was reason enough to give the ballot to former slaves.

When Sumner heard of Lincoln's assassination on the night of April 14, he knew where he must be. He went to the house where the president had been taken and sat at his bedside sobbing from midnight until seven o'clock the next morning. Sumner was still holding Lincoln's hand when Mary Lincoln entered the room with her son for a final look at her husband. Todd Lincoln began to cry, and Sumner offered the boy his shoulder for support.

Yet, one day later, Sumner contrived an excuse to call on Lincoln's successor. Both men were aware that Sumner had tried to force Andrew

Johnson from office because of his behavior at the inaugural. But the meeting went well, and the next day, Johnson won over Sumner completely when he declared, "There is no difference between us."

Sumner's euphoria continued for months. He applauded when the new president spoke of sending the Confederate leaders into exile, and he withdrew his objection to an early recognition of Virginia that brought the state back into the Union.

During their meetings, Sumner pressed Johnson to support the right of freedmen to vote. In return, he received the president's assurances that "you and I are alike." Given their new fellowship, Sumner was no longer insisting that Congress, not the president, must oversee Reconstruction.

But when Sumner returned to Washington in the late spring from a vacation in Boston, he was shocked to find that Johnson intended to reorganize the Southern states exclusively with white men.

The president had appointed as governor in North Carolina a reluctant rebel named William Woods Holden, who had run as a peace candidate in 1864. Johnson required of Holden simply that he call a convention of Union loyalists to ratify the Thirteenth Amendment and repudiate the debt run up during the war.

Since Johnson had stipulated that only those who had been eligible to vote in 1861 could vote now, his decree guaranteed that black men would be excluded.

This was "inconsistent with what he said to me, and to others," Sumner complained to Carl Schurz. It was as though Johnson were suffering from some "strange hallucination."

Despite Andrew Johnson's resentment of entrenched privilege, the Radicals feared that a man who had owned slaves would have more urgent priorities than justice for Oliver Howard's freedmen.

They knew the president was besieged by appeals for pardons from former rebels, which he was granting at a rapid rate. To meet the demand, Johnson was at work by nine each morning and, stopping only for meals, receiving petitions far into the evening. Men alert for any signs of heavy drinking reported that he was taking only tea and crackers.

From June to August 1865, the president awarded more than five thousand pardons in three states alone—Virginia, North Carolina, and Alabama. Johnson regarded each application for pardon as the same as a rebel's confession. He said privately that he did not expect to deny many of them.

Typical of the Southern pleading was a letter from Charles McLean, who owned a plantation near Memphis. McLean pronounced his white neighbors "well satisfied" with Johnson's record so far, although he thought the current problems could have been eased with "gradual emancipation."

Instead, McLean wrote, his "family Negroes," who had been worth one hundred thousand dollars in 1860, were now a liability—composed as they were of underage children and workers who refused to take responsibility for their aging fellow blacks.

McLean warned the president that in Tennessee "the regulations of the 'Freedman's Bureau' are a perfect failure. The Northern People do not understand managing 'Sambo.'"

McLean assured Johnson that he felt "a deep solicitude" for his slaves. But he was seventy years old and was "at a loss to do them justice, for they have little self-reliance and no management, unless directed by some person of experience, and having a correct knowledge of their *character.*"

Months before Johnson's State of the Union address, Pennsylvania congressman Thaddeus Stevens had become alarmed by the president's emerging policies. Stevens regarded the Southern states as conquered property to be confiscated. If Johnson treated them instead as legitimate entities that could be quickly resuscitated, Southern Democrats might combine with fellow party members in the North. Johnson might then build a new coalition of unified Democrats and the more conservative congressional Republicans. That strategy would relegate Radicals like Stevens and Charles Sumner to the margins.

In a meeting with Johnson early in May, Stevens recommended that the president take no action until Congress could meet—if necessary, during a special session. The election of 1864 had given the Republicans a majority of 42 seats in the Senate to 10 for the Democrats and 149 Republicans to 42 Democrats in the House.

But Stevens knew that his Radicals did not control their own Republican Party and, in fact, represented only a third of the Congress. And the fact that Johnson had been elected on the Republican ticket seemed to be counting with him for less and less.

Johnson heard Stevens out, but he appeared to regard his request as a challenge and ignored it.

With Congress still in recess, the president not only reinstated the leadership in Virginia, he went on to restore the governments of other rebel states on his own authority. Stevens could only look on aghast.

"I write," he confided to a friend, "merely to vent my mortification."

In early July, Stevens tried again to dissuade the president from acting, this time by letter. "I am sure you will pardon me for speaking to you with a candor to which men in high places are seldom accustomed," Stevens began.

He wrote that among all of the prominent men of the North with whom Stevens had spoken, "I do not find one who approves of your policy." They thought Johnson's "restoration" would destroy the Republican Party "(which is of little consequence)" but would also "greatly injure the country."

Stevens asked Johnson to let the military commanders continue to govern the rebel states until Congress could take action. He also called on the president to end his "profuse pardons," which will "greatly embarrass Congress if they should wish to make the enemy pay the expense of the war or a part of it."

Again, Johnson ignored the Radicals' pleas, but Southerners took them seriously. At the war's end, prominent Confederates could hope for little more than to be spared hanging as traitors and having their property confiscated. Acknowledging defeat, they neither waged guerrilla war nor challenged the law that had freed their slaves.

But with Andrew Johnson standing up to the Radicals and showing unexpected sympathy for the rebels, Southerners went on the offensive.

Johnson had to beg the governor of South Carolina to cajole his legislature into ratifying the Thirteenth Amendment, and Mississippi held firm against it.

As a delegate to the Thirty-ninth Congress, Georgia elected the Confederacy's vice president, Alexander Stephens, who had been released from prison in Boston Harbor after Johnson pardoned him. Once seated, Stephens would be joined in Congress by four Confederate generals, five colonels, six rebel cabinet officers, and fifty-eight former representatives.

By December 2, 1865, when Charles Sumner went to the White House to confront Johnson in person, he already knew that his earlier impression of him had been an illusion.

For two and a half hours, the president sidestepped the chasm emerging between them. At last, Sumner accused Johnson of throwing away the Union victory.

How? Johnson asked.

Sumner said that "the poor freedmen in Georgia and Alabama were frequently insulted by rebels."

Johnson was no longer concerned with Sumner's good opinion. Unlike Lincoln, he was not amused by Sumner's superior manner. Pointedly, he asked, "Mr. Sumner, do murders ever occur in Massachusetts?"

Sumner replied, "Unhappily yes, Mr. President."

"Do people ever knock each other down in Boston?"

"Unhappily yes, Mr. President, sometimes."

"Would you consent that Massachusetts should be excluded from the Union on this account?"

"No, Mr. President, surely not."

Sumner had always written out his orations and practiced them in front of a mirror. Now he was reminded that he had never mastered the cut-and-thrust of debate.

Yet Sumner's discomfort was not over. Preparing to leave, he reached down for his silk top hat resting on the floor and found that the president—perhaps inadvertently—had been using it as a spittoon.

• • •

A man less optimistic—or self-involved—than Sumner might have detected much earlier signals that he and Andrew Johnson were not alike, after all.

He would have understood that Johnson was trying to mollify several warring factions: Sumner and his Radicals; Seward and Thurlow Weed, who wanted to unify the moderates of both parties in a new coalition; and the Democrats who hoped to reclaim Johnson as their own.

Such a balancing act did not come gracefully to a man as tactless as Johnson. At one point, he told Southern allies that he might "disarm the adversary"—whom Johnson identified as "the radicals who are wild upon negro franchise"—by extending the vote to a small number of educated black men.

To Sumner's chagrin, he had discovered that Johnson's spontaneous ranting at Lincoln's second inaugural was a more accurate guide to his thinking than any sober remarks at the White House. In his frenzy that day, Johnson had exposed how bitterly he despised the South's plantation owners—not for owning slaves, but for maintaining a stranglehold over the economy that had kept him poor so long.

As December approached and Johnson prepared to send to Congress his first State of the Union message, Thaddeus Stevens and the other Radical Republicans were poised to examine his policies far more critically than Charles Sumner had been inclined to do. Lately, Stevens had asked Sumner to recommend a history—in English—that described how Russia's twenty-three million serfs had been emancipated in 1861.

But his temperament did not equip Stevens for passive research. He devised his own plan for dealing with the rebellious states. Revealing it on September 6, 1865, Stevens became infamous throughout the South as America's Robespierre.

• • •

From birth, Thaddeus Stevens had been stigmatized. When he was born on April 4, 1792, with a disfigured foot, superstitious townspeople in his family's remote Vermont village took it as confirming the judgment of God; two years earlier, his brother, Joshua, had been born with two clubfeet.

Their father, a failed farmer and part-time shoemaker, turned first to whiskey, then vanished entirely, leaving his wife with two handicapped sons and two younger children born without their affliction.

Thaddeus had been named for Tadeusz Kosciuszko, the Polish hero of the American Revolution, and he was barely past adolescence when word came that his father had been killed during America's second war with England in 1812.

Throughout his life, Stevens praised his mother, Sonia, for her determination to make his education compensate for the misshapen foot he dragged behind him. She enrolled her sons in an academy in the town of Peacham and worked as a maid and nurse to keep them there.

Schoolmates taunted both brothers; Joshua responded by taking up their father's trade and moving west as a shoemaker. The more truculent Thaddeus propelled himself to Dartmouth College, where he did well but was passed over for membership in Phi Beta Kappa. He tried to dismiss the affront as blithely as he ignored jeering about his foot.

After a year of teaching and reading law in York, Pennsylvania, Stevens crossed into Maryland, where there was no residency requirement. Treating his examiners to rounds of liquor, he passed the bar and returned to set up practice in Gettysburg.

His first client, a defendant in a sensational murder case, was hanged, a defeat that left Stevens a lifelong opponent of capital punishment. Despite the setback, his quick mind and daring courtroom strategies quickly made Stevens prominent throughout the area.

He became expert at calibrating how far he could indulge his wit. To a judge who warned him against "manifest contempt of court," Stevens felt safe in answering, "Manifest contempt, Your Honor? Sir, I am doing my best to conceal it."

Except for his foot, Stevens had become a conventionally handsome young man, almost six feet tall and admired for his luxuriant brown hair. He scorned marriage, however, and his friends speculated that he might believe that his deformity would repulse a bride. Then, before he was forty, illness left him entirely bald. He bought a wig, which, as he well knew, fooled no one.

With slavery outlawed in Vermont since 1777, Stevens had grown up knowing few black people, but Gettysburg was only eight miles from a flourishing slave trade across the Mason-Dixon Line. Stevens was approached by a slave owner who had slipped into Pennsylvania to kidnap his former slave, Charity Butler, and her two children. He wanted Stevens to establish his ownership, and Stevens took the case.

That decision said little about his politics. At the same time, Stevens was representing three slaves who were suing for their freedom.

When the judge ruled against Charity Butler, her husband, Henry, appealed the decision to the Pennsylvania State Supreme Court. Stevens prevailed again there, but afterward he never took the side of a slave owner. And within two years, Stevens was offering a public Fourth of July toast that was politically risky, even in Pennsylvania:

"The next president," Stevens said, raising his glass. "May he be a freeman, who never riveted fetters on a human slave."

Violent events seemed to provoke in Stevens equally extreme responses. One night, his guests at dinner included a local bank cashier who drank too much to get home by himself. Other guests helped him to his door and left him there, trusting he would get inside.

The next day, the man's body was found frozen on his doorstep. Neighbors in Gettysburg heard that Stevens took a hatchet to every bottle in his wine cellar and vowed never to drink again. He also briefly joined the temperance crusade until he decided that legislation could not prevent drunkenness.

In time, his remorse eased sufficiently for Stevens to buy both a tavern and a brewery and to argue for low liquor taxes.

. . .

Stevens passed his middle years aloof from even those closest to him. He won more than a thousand cases, earned a comfortable living, and was elected director of the Bank of Gettysburg. All the while, he kept a note to himself: "He is a happy man who has one true friend, but he is more truly happy who never had need of a friend."

Stevens endorsed that sentiment even after his renown won him election to Pennsylvania's House of Representatives at the age of forty-one. His reputation included stories of a sharp tongue, which were relished by everyone but their targets.

One favorite had Stevens confronting a political opponent on a narrow footpath. The man refused to give way, muttering, "I never stand aside for a skunk." Stevens bowed and moved off the path. "I always do," he said.

Stevens visited his mother in Peacham every year but otherwise kept in touch with his family mostly with gifts of money and hectoring letters to his nephews, warning them against rum and indolence.

Thaddeus, Jr., reacted by flunking out of the University of Vermont and being expelled four times from Dartmouth. Another nephew, Alanson Stevens, saw his uncle's unforgiving side when he fathered a child with a fourteen-year-old girl named Mary Primm.

The infant died at nine weeks, and by the time the couple had another child, they claimed to be married. As a public man, Stevens had cultivated a reputation for protecting the poor and friendless. Yet when Alanson was killed during the Battle of Chickamauga in 1863, Stevens disavowed both mother and child and prevented Mary Primm from collecting the twenty-four hundred dollars that her husband had bequeathed to her.

Another widow brought out Stevens's softer side. Lydia Smith, born in Gettysburg to a black servant and a white father, had married a free black man, a barber, and they had two sons. When he died in 1848, she went to work as the latest in Stevens's succession of housekeepers.

She was attractive, light-skinned, and thirty-five. Stevens was fifty-six. Whatever their relationship became—and rumors persisted past the grave—Stevens treated her in public with unfailing courtesy.

He demanded that every visitor, including his family, address her as "Mrs. Smith," never as "Lydia."

As a prominent bachelor, Stevens had learned to ignore town gossip. One scandal had arisen when a young black servant was found facedown in a shallow well, with an eye badly bruised and unmistakably pregnant. Even though the dead woman, known simply as Dinah, had a lover, unsigned letters tried to shift the blame to Stevens.

As president of the local borough council, Stevens did not respond to the accusations, but when the anonymous campaign resumed in the press after another murder three years later, Stevens sued for criminal libel. He won the suit, and the editor was sentenced to three months in the county jail before being pardoned by Pennsylvania's governor.

Since Stevens was also awarded eighteen hundred dollars in damages, the editor had to sell his house to satisfy the judgment. Steven bought the property and, in a show of humanity or scorn, signed it back to its owner.

Such experiences had inured Stevens to the speculation over Lydia Smith until late in life, when another hostile editor seized on their relationship to deplore the hypocrisy of the "ultra-gadfly, super-sanctified saint of the African ascendancy." Even then, Stevens did not respond directly. But he mused with a friend about his predecessors in politics.

He was not so lewd as Henry Clay, Stevens said, and "less vicious" in his personal habits than Daniel Webster. His hostility to Webster dated from 1850, when Stevens had listened in the Senate gallery while Webster spoke in favor of the Fugitive Slave Law and described abolitionists as fanatics "leading silly women and sillier men." Hearing those words, Stevens said, "I could have cut his damned heart out."

Stevens rejected any comparison with Martin Van Buren's vice president, Richard M. Johnson of Kentucky, who had proudly fathered two daughters with his mulatto housekeeper. What galled Stevens was that he himself "with three times" Richard Johnson's ability and "a thousand times his honesty" had been denied his place on a national ticket.

• • •

On his limited stage, however, Stevens played a prominent role. He had first joined the Anti-Mason Party as a member of Pennsylvania's legislature. He enlisted in that cause partly because of the murder of a renegade Mason but also because of his distrust of every form of organized religion. To a young seminary student, Stevens once offered avuncular advice: "Preach the Gospel," he said, "but don't attempt to prove it."

When the Anti-Mason Party dissolved, Stevens turned to the Whigs. In 1844, he campaigned for Henry Clay, who lost Pennsylvania and the presidency.

Four years later, Stevens stood for Congress. As a candidate, he received a letter from Representative Abraham Lincoln soliciting Stevens's "experienced and sagacious" opinion about the likely outcome of their coming elections. Stevens's reply was cautiously pessimistic, but he won his seat easily, and Lincoln lost his.

In the House, Stevens became a fiery orator against slavery, basing his argument less on morality than on the crippling effect of slavery on economic growth. He contrasted New York and Pennsylvania with Virginia and claimed that since Virginia lacked a middle class, it had become no more than an incubator for "selecting and growing the most lusty sires and most fruitful wenches" to supply slave masters throughout the South.

On the House floor, Stevens backed the admission to the Union of California as a free state and rejected all compromise. He swore that he would never vote to admit another slave state; he presented petitions to repeal the Fugitive Slave Law; and he spoke eloquently about the need for public education.

His boldness put Stevens out of step with his fellow Whigs, and he was not nominated for re-election. Casting about, Stevens fastened on the Know Nothing splinter party as his instrument for returning to politics. He chose to ignore any inconsistency in supporting a secret society after his years of attacking the Masons.

By 1856, Stevens was a delegate to a convention made up of Whigs, Know Nothings, and the fledgling Republicans. He offered only tepid support to the presidential nominee, John C. Frémont, but he tore gleefully into Frémont's opponent, the Democrat James Buchanan. "A bloated mass of political putridity," Stevens called him.

Buchanan won the presidency but with a divided party that left him and his Democrats vulnerable. When Stevens was nominated for Congress as a Republican, his success was denounced by the *Lancaster* (Pennsylvania) *Intelligencer* as "Niggerism triumphant."

Stevens had stubbornly supported a different candidate before the Republicans nominated Abraham Lincoln in 1860, which explained why he did not join his colleagues in a pilgrimage to Illinois to congratulate the president-elect. Lincoln returned Stevens's distrust, but both men knew Lincoln would need his support, and Stevens briefly entertained hopes of a cabinet position.

With secession looming, Stevens attacked the South's position on the House floor so bitingly that an observer reported, "Nearly fifty Southern members rose to their feet and rushed toward him with curses and threats of personal violence."

But Stevens was more concerned with his Northern allies. He was especially wary of Henry Seward for his willingness to admit new slave states in order to keep the Union intact. Stevens worried that Lincoln might be won over to that fatal compromise rather than show the mettle to stand fast.

When war burst upon the nation, Stevens was appointed chairman of the Committee on Ways and Means. In that post, he was both highly effective and unyielding. Should it turn out, Stevens said, that the entire South "must be laid waste and made a desert to save the Union from destruction, so let it be." Better, he added, to let the whole region be repopulated with free men than to assist Southerners in the destruction of their slaves.

Throughout the war, Stevens met with the president only when their positions required it. He could resist Lincoln's warm personal appeal, and humor was not a bridge between them. Lincoln laughed heartily as he recounted stories from his vast fund; Stevens had kept a straight face when he once remarked in the House, "I yield to the gentleman for a few feeble remarks."

And when Lincoln asked Stevens whether his fellow Pennsylvanian Simon Cameron was honest, Stevens answered judiciously, "I don't think he would steal a red-hot stove."

Relishing the remark, Lincoln told it widely, even repeating it to Cameron. Stevens had demanded to know why.

"I thought it was a good joke," Lincoln said, perhaps disingenuously, "and didn't think it would make him mad."

Stevens replied that Cameron was in fact very mad, and since he was demanding a retraction, Stevens was prepared to oblige him. "I believe I told you," Stevens said to Lincoln, "he would not steal a red-hot stove. I will now take that back."

Although Stevens chided the president for not being sufficiently committed to the antislavery cause, in Lincoln's view they shared the same goals but Lincoln was simply more adroit in reaching them. Although Lincoln had overruled the generals who had freed slaves on their own authority, he signed Stevens's bill in March 1862 forbidding any member of the armed forces to return fugitive slaves to their masters.

When the president announced that emancipation would take effect on January 1, 1863, Stevens wrote to his constituents, "Lincoln's proclamation contained precisely the principles which I had advocated."

Even so, Stevens went far beyond Abraham Lincoln in his determination to punish the rebels. Lincoln had permitted the confiscating of rice plantations around Port Royal in the Sea Islands, the experiment that had so impressed Oliver Howard. But the president backed away from supporting Stevens when the senator said, "I would seize every foot of land, and every dollar of their property" from the Southerners who were trying to destroy the Union.

Uncompromising as he could sound, Stevens's position was not restricted to his fellow Radicals in Congress. On a trip to England, Thurlow Weed predicted that the North would give the South's plantations "to well-deserving officers and men." And as military governor of Tennessee, Andrew Johnson had seemed determined to see the rebels "impoverished." Even after he entered the White House, Johnson had

pledged to a delegation of Radical Republicans: "Treason must be made infamous, and traitors punished."

But as Johnson moved further into his presidency, that unity of purpose seemed lost.

In the looming battle over reconstruction, Stevens could expect little effective support from Charles Sumner. Always tentative, Sumner's standing with his colleagues appeared to be headed toward its nadir. When he tried to convert cabinet officers to his own disillusionment with Johnson's policies, Sumner had been rebuffed.

Navy Secretary Gideon Welles assured him that Southerners were "patriotic" and not "irreclaimable." At the Treasury, Hugh McCulloch was chafing under a requirement that Sumner had forced through Congress that all federal employees swear an oath to the Union. Unable to find enough qualified agents, McCulloch was ignoring the law and hiring former rebels.

Sumner was often disappointed as well by the Northern press. He considered *The Nation*, a fledgling New York weekly, too timid in supporting Negro voting rights, and he wrote to one of the magazine's backers, "Suspend the *Nation*. It does more harm than good."

Amid his flailing, Sumner got an angry letter from a fellow Radical, Ohio senator Benjamin Wade, who could sound like John Brown. Letting his imagination run free, Wade conjured up a bloody scenario:

If "the colored people of the South" staged an insurrection and managed to slay half of their oppressors, Wade wrote, "the other half would hold them in the highest respect and no doubt treat them with justice."

Sumner was not shocked. Two years earlier, he had worried that the North might win the war but Henry Seward would insist on an amnesty for the South that left slavery intact. To a British friend, Sumner wrote that before the war's end, he wished for "two hundred thousand Negroes with muskets in their hands, and then I shall not fear compromise."

• • •

In New York, the historian George Bancroft had been working in secret for a month on Johnson's first message to Congress. But, like Sumner, Thaddeus Stevens was suspicious of Henry Seward, and he surmised that it would be Seward who drafted the president's address. Stevens was determined to set out his own vision for Reconstruction first.

Voting rights for the newly freed blacks were not on Stevens's agenda. He worried that former slaves, deprived of education all their lives, would simply vote the way their prewar owners told them. "The infernal laws of slavery," Stevens concluded, "have prevented them from acquiring the education, understanding of the commonest laws of contract or of managing the ordinary business of life."

If he was not ready to bestow the vote, Stevens had devised a formula for compensating the slaves in more material ways. In early September 1865 he laid out his incendiary ideas in a speech in Lancaster, Pennsylvania.

Stevens would treat Southerners as a conquered people, and he had devised a mathematical formula for punishing them:

He calculated the total property owned by the wealthiest slave owners at 394 million acres. From that figure, he proposed allotting land to the South's former slave families—forty acres for each of the one million adult males. That would dispose of forty million acres.

Stevens claimed that his plan would leave another 354 million acres for sale to the highest bidder. Predicting that an average acre would sell for ten dollars, the result would deliver to the U.S. government $3.54 billion. Some of that money could be used to pay for veterans' benefits and for damages to Southerners who had remained loyal to the Union.

But speaking as chairman of the Ways and Means Committee, Stevens recommended that the bulk of the funds go toward paying down the national debt.

Anticipating his critics, Stevens assured them that his plan would confiscate land from only the wealthiest seventy thousand plantation owners and would not affect nine-tenths of all Southerners. As for that seventy thousand—former plantation owners who would indeed lose their property—let those "proud, bloated and defiant rebels" go into exile. Better that than trying to repatriate four million former slaves to Africa.

As the Congress prepared to convene, Stevens acknowledged that, at seventy-three, he was finding the duties of the Ways and Means Committee too strenuous, and he agreed instead to head a new committee on appropriations. But no member doubted that, whatever title Stevens might hold, when he caught the Speaker's eye, he would be heard.

Although Stevens's step might be slower, his mind still raced ahead of most colleagues. Because he was reading Darwin's *On the Origin of Species*, he would answer ironically when asked about his health: "Growing weaker and weaker every day, thank God."

The Thirteenth Amendment, near ratification, promised to change America's electoral mathematics. Ever since the queasy compromise of 1787, slaves had been counted politically as three-fifths of a citizen. In electoral voting, one hundred slaves counted as sixty persons. But if blacks were now counted as whole votes, the rebel states would gain twenty-eight more congressmen.

To prevent that calamity, the Republican leadership accepted Stevens's plan to bar all new Southern representatives approved by President Johnson from taking their seats. To enforce that strategy, Stevens could count on the connivance of his former law student Edward McPherson, who was now clerk of the House of Representatives.

As he read the roll, McPherson omitted the Southerners' names. When he finished, a Tennessean who had been left out demanded to speak. Thaddeus Stevens replied smoothly that he would not yield the floor "to any gentleman who does not belong to this body."

The president's address read to Congress on December 6, 1865, began with ritual praise for the Founding Fathers and then sounded a more recent note of the triumph. Looking ahead twelve days to the expected ratification of the Thirteenth Amendment, Johnson praised it as "one of the greatest acts on record, to have brought four millions of people into freedom."

The president segued into the same stern warning that had cost George Hartsuff a job in the Freedmen's Bureau. The former slaves' "future prosperity and condition must, after all, rest mainly on themselves." Johnson added a chilling afterthought. "If they fail, and so perish away, let us be careful that the failure shall not be attributable to any denial of justice."

In Johnson's view, the black man's hopes must not rest with Washington but with the Southern states. "When the tumult of emotions that have been raised by the suddenness of the social change shall have subsided, it may prove that they will receive the kindest usage from some of those on whom they have heretofore most closely depended."

He made no reference to the Black Codes that were pending in state legislatures or the version that had been passed in Mississippi two days before his address. Mississippi had also defiantly elected as its governor Benjamin G. Humphreys, a Confederate general, and its convention delegates had rejected Johnson's demand that they ratify the Thirteenth Amendment.

On this day, Johnson's target was the Southern aristocracy. He argued that by closing their fields to white laborers and foreign workers, they had kept such men in a different, but very real, bondage. Now at last, he predicted, the Confederate South, with "soil of an exuberant fertility, a climate friendly to long life," could absorb the Northern laborer and men "from the most cultivated nations in Europe."

The reasonable tone of Johnson's address was favorably received in the North, nowhere more approvingly than in New York by George Bancroft, who said that everyone he spoke with—"all sorts of people"— endorsed the president's message, especially its "total want of *asperity* and passion."

The historian ventured a prediction: "In less than twenty days, the extreme radical opposition will be over."

Bancroft followed up his letter with praise culled from British and French journals. In Paris, *La Presse* had hailed the address as a model "of intelligence, of moderation, of wisdom."

Maryland senator Reverdy Johnson extolled Johnson's message as he interpreted it: "The moment the insurrection was terminated, there was no power whatsoever left in the Congress of the United States over those states."

Lulled by their sense of relief, Republicans in Congress drafted an extension of the Freedmen's Bureau and expected Johnson to sign it. But the mild tone of Johnson's ghostwritten address had been as misleading as his equivocal conversations with Charles Sumner.

Johnson's low expectations for the freedmen had been revealed two months earlier when he addressed a black regiment returning to the District of Columbia after serving in the South. Johnson had praised their patience and had urged them to be peaceful at home before he began to sound like one of the Southern plantation owners who were petitioning his office:

"Freedom is not simply the principle to live in idleness," he said. "Liberty does not mean merely to resort to the low saloons and other places of disreputable character."

Now Johnson, facing the first test of his commitment to Reconstruction, was being asked to guarantee assistance to men who, not long ago, had been his slaves.

The terms of the bureau's extension were straightforward: It would continue until Congress abolished it. Bureau authority would be expanded throughout the country wherever there were freedmen. The president was authorized to reserve three million acres of unoccupied public land to be rented in forty-acre parcels to freedmen and to Union loyalists dispossessed by the war. They would have the option of buying that land.

Penalties for depriving citizens of their rights included a thousand-dollar fine, a year in jail, or both. The president was charged with enforcement.

Critics complained that the bureau was unconstitutional, that it was on the way to becoming permanent, and that it was too expensive—Oliver Howard had requested $11,745,050. One Delaware senator used the debate for a belated challenge to abolition itself, claiming that even though three-fourths of the states might agree to the Thirteenth Amendment, Congress had no right to outlaw slavery.

Other senators noted that the bill was premature since the Freedmen's Bureau would continue to operate for several months under the existing legislation.

Although some conservative Republicans shared those misgivings about the bill, the Senate passed it in January 1866, by a vote of thirty-seven to ten.

In the House, Stevens wanted to strengthen its terms along the lines of his Lancaster speech. He tried to add the "forfeited estates of the enemy" to the federal acreage, but his amendment failed. As reported out by the House Judiciary Committee the following month, the bill passed, 136 to 33.

Southern protests, which continued loud and unrelenting, were receiving a sympathetic hearing at the State Department. When Henry Seward took his family to the Caribbean in January, he announced that the trip was part of his protracted convalescence.

At the Navy Department, however, Gideon Welles concluded that Seward wanted to duck the rupture over Reconstruction until "the way is clear for him which course to take." Welles assured his diary, "The talk about his health is ridiculous."

If evasion had been Seward's intention, it failed. He was back in Washington for the House vote on the Freedmen's Bureau, and he agreed with Johnson that the bureau should not be expanded until the Southern states were represented again in Congress.

Seward wrote a veto message for the president that termed the bill not only unconstitutional but unnecessary because the current condition of a freedman was "not so bad." The message explained that "his labor is in demand, and he can change his dwelling place if one community or state does not please him. The laws that regulate supply and demand will regulate his wages."

Johnson also rejected a provision that would continue to permit Union military officers to serve as judges in the South for cases involving civil rights. The president wrote the final salvo himself, claiming that he could legitimately criticize Congress since he was the only official "chosen by the people of all of the states."

The implication that Congress had no right to interfere in a state's affairs stung Stevens into action. But in trying to override the veto, he found that six members from his own party were siding with the Democrats. He could not muster the required two-thirds vote needed to override the veto. The president was upheld, thirty to eighteen.

Consulting with General Howard, the Republican leadership set to work. Members drew up a new bill to extend and strengthen the Freedmen's Bureau, and they soon got an unexpected boost from the White House.

Andrew Johnson was showing himself to be a sore winner. He intended to demonstrate that while Thaddeus Stevens might hold forth on the House floor, the president could dominate the hustings.

Johnson had convinced himself that Stevens was a dangerous adversary, a schemer who planned to seize control of the nation and exile Johnson to Tennessee. His suspicions seemed confirmed when Stevens brought to the House a resolution from its powerful Joint Committee of Fifteen that only Congress could declare a state entitled to representation.

The timing suggested to Johnson that the Radicals were bent on denying Tennessee's readmission, even though Radical sympathizers were firmly in charge of the state. To the president, it looked as though the delay was part of the strategy to depose him.

Johnson's view was endorsed by his allies, who protested that Stevens was ramming through the resolution without debate. Stevens said his opponents were simply fighting the prewar battles of 1861 all over again. Back then, Stevens said, he had waited them out, and now "I am ready to sit for forty hours."

• • •

Three days after his Freedmen's veto, Johnson was scheduled to speak before a huge celebration to honor George Washington's birthday. Advisers who remembered his disastrous ad-libbing urged him to prepare written remarks. But Johnson, feeling both beleaguered and virtuous, wanted the nation to know how badly he was being treated.

The ceremonies began with a hundred-gun salute in New York City and praise for Andrew Johnson as even greater than his famous namesake from the Hermitage. The most unlikely tribute used bookbinding as a metaphor: Johnson "was a modern edition of Andrew Jackson bound in calf."

Speaking at Cooper Union, Seward dismissed the conflict over the Freedmen's Bureau as "comparatively unimportant." He added, however, that it did point up the difference between the president and his "nervous" critics in the House. Johnson had the courage to see that "in this troublesome world of ours," no one can always have his own way.

"The nervous men, on the other hand, hesitate, delay, debate and agonize"—not because the war did not end as it should, "but because they have not individually had their own way in bringing it to a happy termination."

Returning for extemporaneous remarks in Washington, President Johnson ignored Seward's example of criticizing his opponents in generalities. Instead, the president listed several of his Confederate enemies, beginning with Jefferson Davis, although he went on to say that he had extended "the right hand of fellowship" to Southerners who had renewed their loyalty to the Union.

But, Johnson said, there were other men "opposed to the fundamental principles of this Government, and now laboring to destroy them."

When voices from the crowd demanded names, Johnson yielded to the provocation.

"You ask me who they are," Johnson cried. "I say Thaddeus Stevens of Pennsylvania! I say Mr. Sumner of the Senate is another!" Rounding out his list, the president added a crusading Massachusetts abolitionist. "And Wendell Phillips is another!"

The loud cheers emboldened the crowd as well as the president. One man called on Johnson to excoriate his former friend, secretary of the Senate John Forney.

"Give it to Forney!" the man shouted.

"In reply to that," Johnson replied, striving for a moment of dignity, "I will simply say that I do not waste my time upon dead ducks."

The exchange had unleashed a torrent of self-pity. Before his hour-long harangue was done, Johnson had referred to himself more than two hundred times.

Describing his tormentors, the president asked, "Are they not satisfied with one martyr? Does not the blood of Lincoln appease the vengeance and wrath of the opponents of this government? Is the thirst still unslaked? Do they want more blood?"

He had no doubt, Johnson went on, that the men he had named intended to incite his assassination. Grieving prematurely over his own martyrdom, the president said that "when I am beheaded, I want the American people to be the witness." His body should be laid out on an altar dedicated to the Union. That way, "the blood that now warms and animates my existence shall be poured as a fit libation to the union of these States."

Johnson's speech accomplished what had seemed impossible. For many conservative Republicans, the president confirmed Charles Sumner's warnings that Johnson, not the Radicals, constituted the true threat to the country.

Senator William Fessenden of Maine had been able to work with Thaddeus Stevens but considered Charles Sumner "a malignant fool." His detestation became so great that he left his seat ostentatiously whenever Sumner rose to speak. Sumner professed not to understand why Fessenden should take offense when Sumner described the bills he introduced as "shocking to all morals" or as reeking with the "loathsome stench of bad mutton" or as "disgusting ordure."

After Johnson's speech, even Fessenden wrote to an ally that the president "has broken the faith, betrayed his trust and must sink from detestation into contempt."

Such conservative Republican senators as Edwin D. Morgan of New York and William Stewart of Nevada now regretted upholding the president's veto of the Freedmen's Bureau. And, except for Sumner's unbending nature, the bureau could have picked up another two votes by admitting Colorado to the Union.

Sumner, however, objected to a clause in Colorado's state constitution that limited voting to white men. When frustrated fellow Radicals pointed out that there were only ninety black men in the entire territory, Sumner was unmoved. He wanted to establish a precedent, he said. *"No more states with inequality of rights!"*

Colleagues made the mistake of suggesting that it would be expedient for him to back down. To that, Sumner had a pat answer: "Nothing can be expedient that is not right."

Besides putting forth the Freedmen's Bureau bill, the Committee of Fifteen had been sifting through 140 proposals for legislation, nearly half of them aimed at guaranteeing political rights for black men.

Senator Lyman Trumbull of Illinois, once a close friend of Abraham Lincoln, had not broken with his successor. He went to the White House as a conservative Republican to consult with Johnson about a civil rights bill that would rectify the wrongs of the Dred Scott decision. Its central provision would make it a criminal offense to deny a black man his civil rights, although those rights would not extend to allowing him to vote.

Charles Sumner likened the current debate to the fight over Kansas with its near-fatal consequences for him. "Congress must dare to be brave! It must dare to be just!"

Sumner rejected the argument that civil rights were an issue best left to the states. Freedom for the Negroes cannot "be entrusted to the old slave-masters embittered against their slaves. It must be performed by the national Government."

At the White House, Trumbull was pleased by Johnson's seeming support for his bill, but within the president's cabinet, response was mixed. Henry Seward and Secretary of War Stanton were among those who thought that some legislation was necessary but that sections of the bill, as written, might be unconstitutional. Only Navy Secretary Welles flatly opposed it.

To his diary, Welles acknowledged his feeling about the black man: "I do not want him at my table, nor do I care to have him in the jury-box or in the legislative halls, or on the bench."

When Trumbull's bill reached him on March 26, 1866, Johnson sided with Gideon Welles and vetoed it.

Trumbull complained loudly that he had been deceived. Other conservative Republicans, recalling that Johnson had raised no objections to the bill in their private meetings, shared Trumbull's sense of betrayal and made futile trips to the White House.

Illinois representative Shelby Cullom urged the president to smooth over his differences with those congressmen who wanted to remain loyal to him. "I will never forget that interview," Cullom said later. Johnson "gave us to understand that we were on a fool's errand, and that he would not yield."

Cullom returned to the Capitol, joined reluctantly with the Radicals, and reconciled himself to voting with them from that point forward.

As a result, when an attempt was made to override Johnson's veto, Thaddeus Stevens could count on votes that had shifted since Congress failed with the Freedmen's Bureau six weeks earlier.

Democrats tried to postpone the vote because two senators who supported Johnson were ailing, but Ben Wade scoffed at their appeal:

"I will tell the President and everyone else, that if God Almighty has stricken one member so that he cannot be here to uphold the dictation of a despot, I thank Him for His interposition, and I will take advantage of it if I can."

One of those absent members was brought to the Senate floor on a stretcher, an exertion that was unavailing. With one senator absent, Johnson's veto of the civil rights bill was overturned thirty-three to fifteen.

Julia Grant

CHAPTER 8

THE FOURTEENTH AMENDMENT (1866)

ON THE FIRST DAY OF MAY 1866, SEVERAL HUNDRED BLACK SOLDIERS recently released from service were waiting at a fort outside Memphis for their back pay before they headed home. They had already turned in their weapons, and that evening many of them were singing as they went toward the taverns on South Street.

They knew that the city's heart remained with the Confederacy. A friend of Thaddeus Stevens had sent him an item from the *Memphis Avalanche* that protested the Radicals' proposal "to give a greasy, filthy stinking negro" the right to vote. And since the largely Irish police force seemed to share that opinion, the soldiers were alert for signs of trouble.

Speculating about reasons for the hostility, Tennessee's governor had concluded that for Southern white men, a black soldier "constantly reminds them of their defeat, and of what they call 'a just but lost cause.' And the sight of him in enjoyment of freedom is a constant source of irritation."

When a collision of horse-drawn carts gave police officers a reason to arrest two black drivers but let the white drivers go free, loud protests broke out among the soldiers. One shouted the inflammatory words: "Abe Lincoln!"

A police officer shouted back, "Your old father, Abe Lincoln, is dead and damned."

Facts afterward were hard to come by. Several black soldiers had apparently kept their weapons. They shot at the police, who fired back. When the gun smoke cleared, four soldiers and two policemen were dead.

By the time police reinforcements could arrive, the soldiers had run back to their barracks at Fort Pickering. Outraged, the police surrounded the fort, spurred on by John C. Creighton, a city judge. Witnesses quoted him as calling, "Boys, I want you to go ahead and kill the last damned one of the nigger race, and burn up the cradle!"

Storming the surrounding black neighborhood, police and their accomplices set fire to ninety cabins and twelve schoolhouses. A gang of seven, including two Memphis policemen, broke into the house of Frances Thompson, a Negro washerwoman, and a sixteen-year-old girl, Lucy, who lived with her. They demanded supper, and after they had finished the eggs, ham, and biscuits she prepared for them, they said they wanted a woman to sleep with.

"I said we were not that sort of women," Frances Thompson testified later. "They said that 'didn't make a damned bit of difference.' One of them hit me on the side of my face and, holding my throat, choked me."

The men drew their pistols and said that if the women resisted, they would shoot them and set fire to their house. Four men raped Frances Thompson, and the others raped Lucy.

Reports from the scene indicated that another three black women were raped that night during a shooting spree that wounded at least seventy Negroes. Forty-six black men, three women, and two children were murdered outright.

In Washington, Thaddeus Stevens called for a full investigation. But apologists for the Memphis police pointed out that wartime New York had seen far worse mayhem on July 13, 1863, when mobs of white workingmen had rioted to protest being called up for service in the Union army. They had complained then that wealthy young men could pay a three-hundred-dollar "commutation fee" that would exempt them.

White workers already resented having to compete for jobs with emancipated blacks, and they had become convinced that the war was being fought to free the slaves, not to preserve the Union.

At that time, Lincoln had dispatched several regiments of militia and volunteers to New York, but before order could be restored at least 120 persons had been killed and 2,000 wounded—possibly more. A black orphanage had been burned to the ground, although the children escaped.

Senate Republicans rejected the New York comparison since the authorities there had suppressed the riot, while in Memphis the police had instigated it.

Two weeks after the bloodshed, the Tennessee legislature moved to prevent a repetition by transferring control of the police in Memphis, Nashville, and Chattanooga to three commissioners appointed by the governor. Anyone interfering with that chain of command would face criminal charges.

Much as Stevens might deplore the loss of life, he hoped to use Northern outrage to toughen a proposed Fourteenth Amendment currently being debated. In an early version, the amendment would forbid discrimination based on race and forbid any bar to Negroes voting—but only after July 4, 1876.

The proposal would also outlaw paying the Confederate debt, and it authorized Congress to enforce its terms. But William Fessenden, as chairman of the Committee of Fifteen, was absent due to varioloid, a mild form of smallpox, and other committee members were resisting the suffrage clause, even though it was to be deferred for ten years.

Stevens upbraided them—"Damn their cowardice"—but he went along with the deletions.

Charles Sumner again promised to resist compromise. He had already warned the amendment's author, Robert Dale Owen of Indiana, "I must do my duty, without looking to the consequences."

In this case, however, Sumner's call to duty was somewhat muted. Because of political rivalries at home in Massachusetts, he had found himself backed into opposing the amendment. Since he had introduced very similar legislation himself, Sumner's reasoning was convoluted, and when his bill died, even fellow Radicals had mocked his failure to pass any legislation at all after more than two decades in the Senate.

And yet Sumner could not be ignored. During the fight for the civil rights bill, Sumner had lobbied for it incessantly and could share in the credit for repudiating President Johnson.

As the Fourteenth Amendment headed for a showdown, Sumner was prepared to vote for it, but he covered his backtracking with a florid speech:

"Show me a creature, with lifted countenance looking to heaven, made in the image of God, and I show you a MAN, who, of whatever country or race, whether browned by equatorial sun or blanched by northern cold, is with you a child of the Heavenly Father, and equal with you in all the rights of Human Nature."

Sumner also might have pointed out an inconsistency that his fellow Radicals were willing to overlook. They demanded that the Southern states ratify the amendment in order to qualify for admission to the Union, even though only members of the Union could ratify a constitutional amendment.

Sumner's vote on June 8, 1866, for adopting the Fourteenth Amendment was one of the thirty-three ayes to eleven nays, more than the required two-thirds vote.

In the House, Thaddeus Stevens deplored the weakened language but also voted for the amendment, which passed 120 to 32, with 32 abstentions. Stevens took consolation in reminding himself that he was living among men, not angels.

While Congress struggled with its amendment, black men in New Orleans were moving their cause forward in the local arena. They had been included in organizing the Union Republican Party of Louisiana, and once the state had its legitimacy restored, they hurried to elect a representative before the reconstructed legislature backed by Johnson could take its own action.

To send to the House, pragmatic black leaders sacrificed the symbolism of sending one of their number and supported instead a sympathetic white man named Henry Clay Warmoth.

Glib, charming, and only twenty-three, Warmoth was one of those impoverished Union army officers who were migrating from the North. Coming to make their fortunes in the new South, they expected a grateful welcome from the Negroes they had helped free.

White Southerners watched with contempt and envy as men arrived with everything they owned in suitcases stitched from cut-up rugs. As the interlopers began a steady ascent in business and politics, the defeated rebels could only sneer at them as "carpetbaggers." Equally despicable to them were the white turncoats who were cooperating with these Northern scavengers in undermining the foundations of the Old South. Such men were "scalawags."

Warmoth had arrived in Louisiana only the previous year, but black voters were content to test their power by electing him, carpetbagger or not. Warmoth received nearly twice as many votes as Lincoln had stipulated were needed to legitimize a state's government.

Once in Washington, he was seated promptly in the House of Representatives at the same time that Thaddeus Stevens and his Radicals were blocking the entry of men from President Johnson's legislatures.

Louisiana's governor, J. Madison Wells, was torn between his past loyalty to the Union—he had opposed secession—and the plantation owners who were as hostile as he was to Negro suffrage. Those former slave owners were embracing the Black Codes and pressing Wells to restore the state constitution as it had existed before the war.

To chart the future, the governor called a convention for July 30, 1866, at Mechanics' Institute in New Orleans. Perhaps delegates could reach a compromise: Voting rights might be extended to Negroes, but only those who were deemed intelligent and who owned property.

Governor Wells got no backing for the idea from New Orleans officials. Mayor John Monroe told the local Union army commander that he intended to prevent the assembly, and the police chief was known to be arming men from his secret society, "The Southern Cross Association."

The association harked back to a prewar New Orleans group formed by the Know-Nothing Party and known simply as "Thugs." In disguises and carrying brass knuckles, Thugs had stormed into immigrant neighborhoods to scare off potential voters.

Wells was enough alarmed by the threats of violence to warn the president about the sort of "diabolical outrages" once perpetrated by the Thugs. But Johnson was taking advice from a former rebel and declined to recommend action.

The organizers of the convention heard about the widespread threats and moved their opening session from nighttime to noon. Even so, the city's police force was lying in wait, listening for the signal of a pistol shot. Hearing it, they marched down Dryades Street, burst into the hall, and took aim directly at the delegates.

Anthony Dostie, a dentist from New York, tried to reassure the audience by taking up an American flag and shouting, "Keep quiet! We have here the emblem of the United States. They cannot fire upon us when we have this emblem!"

But a policeman cried, "Damn that dirty rag!" A woman with the police called out, "Those dirty Yankees were sent down here to destroy us! And those niggers! Kill them! Don't let one of them get away!"

Dostie had delivered a fiery speech to a black audience three days earlier, and he was one of the first to die, shot in the spine, then run through with a sword.

The Reverend J. W. Horton, a New England clergyman, pulled out his white handkerchief and waved it at the uniformed police charging toward him. "Gentlemen!" he cried. "I beseech you to stop firing! We are non-combatants!"

As the gunfire intensified, Horton pleaded, "Make any arrests you please. We are not prepared to defend ourselves."

A survivor reported that a man with the police answered, "God damn you! Not one of you will escape from here alive!"

Horton was shot and killed. Around the hall, the 150 delegates, most of them black, grabbed up chairs and tables to barricade themselves as they forced the police outside. Each time, the police broke through again with their pistols firing. The few black men who escaped from the hall were chased as they ran and gunned down in the street.

By the time Union troops reached the scene, 48 men were dead, all but one of them Negroes. Another 116 were wounded. Ten of those were police officers.

A white spectator told later of a young white man holding aloft a bludgeon covered with blood and black hair and boasting, "I have just killed a nigger with that."

He scoffed when the other man warned him that he might be punished: "Oh, hell! Haven't you seen the papers? Johnson is with us!"

So it could seem. The president received a copy of the wire sent by General Philip Sheridan to his commander, General Grant. Sheridan wrote that while he was out of the city, Mayor Monroe "suppressed the convention by use of their police force, and in doing so attacked the members of the convention and a party of two hundred negroes, and with firearms, clubs, and knives, in a manner so unnecessary and atrocious as to compel me to say that it was murder."

When the White House leaked Sheridan's cable to the *New York Times*, that paragraph was omitted.

Johnson had received other reports from Mayor Monroe and Louisiana's lieutenant governor, who assured him that forty-two policemen had been killed and only twenty-seven Negroes. They identified the convention delegates as rioters who had been inflamed by white radicals to rise up against state and local authorities.

After Johnson read their telegrams at a cabinet meeting, Gideon Welles was convinced. "There is little doubt," he wrote in his diary, "that the New Orleans riots had their origins with the Radical members of Congress in Washington." To Welles, it was the first in a series of riots that the Radicals were planning throughout the South.

The president seemed to agree. He charged that the convention in New Orleans had been "illegal" and that its "revolutionary proceedings" had set off the riots.

But the massacre had horrified the country, and for once Andrew Johnson was criticized for not being passionate enough. Many citizens believed with the *Nation* magazine that "perhaps the most alarming incident in this sad affair" was Johnson's response, "the coolness with which he refrained from expressing one word of honest indignation at the slaughter, in an American city, of unarmed men by a mob of their political opponents for political reasons."

In New Orleans, the only men arrested for the bloodshed were a few survivors of the aborted convention.

Throughout the spring of 1866, Charles Sumner had suffered from an illness so severe that his alarmed friends wrote for reassurance that he would survive. When his mother died in June, they wrote again. And yet Sumner's response was curiously buoyant.

"My experience," he wrote, trying to buck up a constituent, "admonishes me not to despair."

Andrew Johnson's political missteps may have contributed to Sumner's good cheer, but the reason for his high spirits was more personal. He gave a hint in a letter to Henry Longfellow. Sumner wrote that he had "come to an epoch in my life. My mother is dead. I have a moderate competency. What next?"

Sumner added mysteriously that when they met again, "I may have something to tell you."

His hesitancy suggested that his news was as startling to Sumner himself as it would be to his friends. Fifty-five years old, stiff-necked, and proud of his reputation for never compromising, Charles Sumner was considering marriage.

Even more astonishing, Sumner was courting one of the most eligible women in Washington. Beautiful Alice Mason was the granddaughter of a conservative Massachusetts senator who had developed the residential enclave on Beacon Hill where Alice was raised. In 1857, at the age of nineteen, she had married William Sturgis Hooper, whose father, Samuel, was both her Massachusetts congressman and a fervent supporter of emancipation.

At that time, her acquaintance with Sumner had been slight, but she was demonstrating the same fierce commitment to a cause. Encountering a Boston man who favored compromising with the South, Alice cut him dead when he extended his hand. "I don't know you, sir," she said.

At the outbreak of war, William Hooper was sent to Louisiana as a military aide to General Nathaniel Banks. He took sick there and died in September 1863. Alice Hooper was left a widow with a young daughter, Isabella, she called Bell.

Grief-stricken, Alice began to visit Washington regularly to work as a volunteer nurse among the Union wounded. As her mourning deepened into depression, her in-laws prevailed on her to join them in Washington for the capital's 1866 social season.

By the time her period of mourning ended, Alice Hooper had become sufficiently fascinating to local males that William Fessenden stopped dropping by for games of bezique. Alice was simply looking "prettier than ever," he explained, and he was a married man.

But Indiana congressman Schuyler Colfax, the Speaker of the House, was a bachelor and continued to call regularly. Colfax seemed to be a logical match for Alice. Forty-two and considered handsome, he had lost his wife in the same year that Alice was widowed.

And for a woman passionate about abolition, his politics could not be faulted. The day that the Thirteenth Amendment had come up for a vote expected to be close, Speaker Colfax had broken with precedent to ask that he be recorded as "aye." The amendment passed, and a visitor to the Capitol recalled that the "cheering in the hall and densely packed galleries exceeded anything I ever saw before and beggared description."

Another rival to Colfax had appeared, however. Senator Fessenden watched with disbelief at the gallantry Charles Sumner displayed whenever Alice and her companions visited the Congress—"a most unusual thing for him."

In the past, any flirtation would have ended when Sumner reviewed his finances. Since he rejected all political donations and gifts, he was living on his annual salary of three thousand dollars, plus travel expenses. Although he indulged himself with fine rented rooms in Washington and bespoke suits from London tailors, Sumner lived frugally and had amassed a small savings account.

But five thousand dollars would not support an elegant young bride. Then, thanks to his mother's bequest, Sumner's circumstances changed. He inherited sixty-five thousand dollars to be split with his sister and a three-story house on Hancock Street valued at $10,500.

During Sumner's illness, Alice Hooper had called often at his Washington rooms, bringing the comforts of her experience as a nurse. Now Sumner could entertain the idea of marriage, and Alice Hooper was ready for a proposal.

Washington gossips were appalled at the prospect of a beautiful woman of twenty-eight throwing herself away on a man nearly twice as old. No matter that he was still a fine-looking man—for his age. He was notoriously difficult as a colleague and impossible to imagine as a husband.

Julia Ward, a red-haired young writer, had once accompanied Sumner and Henry Longfellow on an excursion during which she met Samuel Howe. After they married and she had come to deplore Howe's pompous rigidity, she told him, "Sumner ought to have been a woman, and you ought to have married her."

With Alice Hooper, money could not explain the attraction. Her father was wealthy, her father-in-law was richer still, and her husband had left her and their daughter more than Sumner's mother had bequeathed to him.

Distasteful as it might be around the capital, Alice seemed as attracted to Sumner's strict principles as Julia Howe was impatient with them. He was flattered by her attentions, and they had convinced themselves that their mutual high regard would lead to contentment. Sumner did, however, warn his fiancée that "unless we are both satisfied that this union is to be a happy one, we had better separate now."

In September, Sumner wrote to tell an old friend that he was engaged to a "beautiful lady of 28." He added, "I write this gaily, & yet I cannot withhold from an early friend the solicitude which I feel at this great change in my life. I am an idealist & I now hope to live my idea. But I cannot forget that I am on the earth where there is so much of disappointment & sorrow. But I have said enough."

Alice Hooper ignored Sumner's jitters and the dismay of her relatives and went ahead planning for her wedding. The ceremony was to be performed by the Episcopal bishop of Boston in the house of Alice's late brother-in-law, who had been one of Sumner's most unsparing political enemies.

By October 17, 1866, Sumner had thrown off his doubts. "Today at 3 o'clock, and at the age of 55," he wrote to John Greenleaf Whittier, "I begin to live."

An hour and a half later, Sumner, his bride, her daughter, Bell, and her dog Ty left Boston for Newport and a three-week honeymoon.

When President Johnson planned a trip out of Washington for late August 1866, his stated destination was Chicago and the dedication of a memorial to Stephen A. Douglas, Abraham Lincoln's debating partner. Douglas had rallied support for the Union when the Civil War began but died soon afterward. The dwindling Northern faction of the nation's Democrats intended to honor his memory.

Even though Johnson would not be on the ballot, his intemperate remarks were turning the coming congressional elections into a referendum on his presidency. Friends, worried that his emotions had been rubbed raw, urged him not to give speeches along his route. Johnson overruled them and launched a two-and-a-half-week tour from Washington to Chicago and back again that became known as the "Swing Around the Circle."

In Philadelphia, the campaign season had produced competing political conventions. Radical Republicans denounced a session expected by the president to build support for his new Union Party as the "Jefferson Davis and Andrew Johnson convention."

As the party's patron, the president was making creative use of the spoils system Andrew Jackson had introduced to Washington. Throughout the spring of 1866, Johnson had warned the nation's tax collectors, postmasters, and other federal employees that they would be fired if they did not join his Union Party.

Republicans who refused were replaced by Democrats from the party they had defeated in the last election. Fifty-two postmasters and more than sixteen hundred other officials lost their jobs.

William Fessenden, surveying the result in his home state of Maine, complained, using the slang term for those Democrats who had wanted to go on negotiating with Southerners rather than go to war against them. Fessenden said that Johnson had handed Maine over to "Copperheads and flunkies."

At their competing convention, the Republicans nominated Thaddeus Stevens for re-election to the House, even though he had not shown up for the event. No one could doubt Stevens's dedication to voting rights for blacks. But he was also realistic enough to deplore the sight of Frederick Douglass, the celebrated former slave, arm in arm at the convention with Theodore Tilton, a white editor.

"It does not become radicals like us to particularly object," Stevens acknowledged to an ally. "But it was certainly unfortunate at this time. The old prejudice, now revived, will lose us some votes. Why it was done I cannot see except as foolish bravado."

As he headed for Chicago, Andrew Johnson confirmed Stevens's misgivings by playing to the underlying apprehensions of Southern white males. The president announced that he did not want the South to rejoin the Union as "a degraded and debased people." Rather, "I want them to come back with all their manhood."

Johnson would be traveling with cabinet officers, including Gideon Welles and Henry Seward, who shared his policy on reconstruction. Seward, in fact, had become actively hostile to the campaign of the Radical Republicans for Negro rights. Privately, he said that he expected to see the former slaves voting eventually but that "the North must get over this notion of interference with the affairs of the South."

As for the blacks themselves, Seward did not pretend to have sympathy. "I have no more concern for them than I have for the Hottentots," he said. "They are God's poor; they always have been and always will be so everywhere. They are not of our race. They will find their place. They must take their level."

Seward understood the political price he was paying for standing by the president. Thaddeus Stevens, for one, scorned him as the "malign force" who was responsible for Johnson's defection from the Republicans who had elected him. These days, Seward saw himself as a man "who has faith in everybody and enjoys the confidences of nobody."

The president was also taking along Wisconsin senator James Doolittle, and he intended to enhance his stature by appearing with the nation's victorious military commanders. A reluctant General Grant had agreed to make the trip, along with several other officers. One, George Armstrong Custer, was a twenty-seven-year-old captain who had graduated last in his West Point class but redeemed himself at the battles of Bull Run in 1861 and Appomattox four years later.

Also on the train would be sixty-five-year-old Admiral David Farragut, who had secured his place in naval history at the Battle of Mobile Bay in 1864. When Southern forces hemmed him in during the battle, Farragut's supposed response was widely quoted: "Damn the torpedoes! Full speed ahead!"

With those popular figures at his side, the president would now make publicly the charges that Welles had confided only to his diary. In St. Louis, Johnson assured the crowd that "every drop of blood that was shed" in New Orleans was the responsibility of "the Radical Congress."

At first, the president's off-the-cuff remarks about the Civil War and its aftermath were met with cries of "Hang Jeff Davis!" But as he once again compared himself to Jesus and named his trio of Judases—Thaddeus Stevens, Charles Sumner, and Wendell Phillips—the crowd began to chant, "Hang Thad Stevens!"

The president seemed to be mulling it over before he asked, Why not? and then pledged that, since the South had been whipped, he was now "prepared to fight traitors at the North."

As each repetition of the president's stump speech reached the Northern press, Johnson outraged more readers with his hysteria and sacrilege. A loyal friend, Henry J. Raymond, both a New York congressman and the editor of the *New York Times*, wrote that he greatly regretted Johnson's behavior: "The President of the United States cannot enter upon an exchange of epithets with the brawling of a mob."

As the tour moved north, the brawling continued, but the crowd's response had soured. Aboard the train, Senator Doolittle fretted that the president's outbursts were costing his political allies two hundred thousand votes.

A reporter from the *New York Herald* recorded the scene in Indianapolis when Johnson tried to speak above the din of protesters.

Appealing for "your attention for five minutes," the president was shouted down: "No, no! We want nothing to do with traitors!"

Johnson tried again. "I would like to say to this crowd here tonight . . ." Men yelled, "Shut up! We don't want to hear from you!"

Supporters who continued to chant, "Johnson!" were drowned out by louder calls for "Grant! Grant!"

After a few more minutes, the president gave up and retreated from the train's platform.

General Grant's own warm reception from the crowds did not temper his irritation with the president's performance. One journalist got Grant's sentiments almost right when he quoted him as telling friends, "I am disgusted at hearing a man make speeches on his way to his own funeral."

What Grant had said privately to General John Rawlins was that he "did not choose to accompany a man who was deliberating digging his own grave."

Grant had other reasons to regret the tour. In Seward's home town of Auburn, Grant's carriage ran over a boy whose leg had to be amputated. In Niles, Ohio, he was thrown to the ground when the speakers' platform collapsed.

And Grant was drinking again. Accompanying the tour was Sylvanus Cadwallader, who had reported from Grant's headquarters during the war and had come to revere the general as being "pure in speech and heart." But Cadwallader also joined regularly with General Rawlins in efforts to protect Grant from himself.

When subordinates refused to intervene, Cadwallader was not afraid to take a stern line with the general, once locking him in a stateroom of a riverboat when he was drunk and throwing his whiskey bottles overboard.

His esteem for Grant prevented the reporter from filing stories about his binges. Rawlins told him of Grant's repeated promises to stop drinking, and Cadwallader observed that Grant often went without a drink for months at a time.

Rawlins made it clear to junior officers that any attempt to lure Grant into drinking would end their career, and when Grant's Negro servant named Bill yielded to Grant's entreaties and supplied him with liquor, Rawlins threatened to burn him alive if he did it again.

Only Julia Grant required no warnings or threats. Whenever she turned up in camp, Cadwallader marveled at her "quiet, firm control" as long as she was at Grant's side.

At the war's end, grateful citizens of Philadelphia presented Grant with an expensive town house furnished down to a wine cellar stocked with the finest vintages. Mrs. Grant had consulted Rawlins about her options but found him reluctant to get involved now that a lapse by Grant would not lead to battlefield casualties.

At last, Rawlins advised her to engage a reputable broker, sell the entire stock, and put the money in her own pocket. Cadwallader heard that she had done as Rawlins suggested and that her husband never knew about the sale.

On this tour with Andrew Johnson, Grant was confirming Cadwallader's judgment that he "could not drink moderately." The reporter, now chief of the *New York Herald*'s Washington bureau, foresaw trouble when he spotted a table of refreshments furnished by the Cleveland reception committee.

Grant could not resist the waiters who passed through his car urging passengers to eat and drink. Very soon, Cadwallader and John Rawlins had to lead Grant to the baggage car and cajole him into sleeping on a pile of rubbish and empty sacks. They took turns standing guard to keep witnesses away until the train reached Cleveland.

There, Gideon Welles's son, Edgar, helped carry Grant and his drinking companion, the nation's surgeon general, to a chartered boat that ferried them to Detroit. Grant waited there for the tour, but in St. Louis he left Johnson's entourage for good.

Along the route, reporters had been studying Secretary Seward for any signs of disapproval of the president's speeches, but he sat through them all, chewing on a cigar and applauding on cue. To some degree, Seward owed his impassive expression to Lewis Powell's bowie knife, which had severed the nerves on one side of his face.

Although there was no evidence of a split, Seward's influence on Johnson had become limited. He had agreed with the president that the Fourteenth Amendment exceeded Congress's authority but recommended Johnson's support since it was bound to pass. Johnson disregarded his advice. When Seward fulfilled the obligation of his office by forwarding the amendment to the states for ratification, Johnson had seemed annoyed with him.

At the same time, with the enthusiastic urging of Thurlow Weed, Seward had endorsed Johnson's idea for the new Union Party, a fusion of Democrats and conservative Republicans. But when a Philadelphia convention was scheduled, Seward became wary and chose to spend the week at home.

Seward's distancing of himself did not mean he would join Johnson's attorney general, postmaster general, and secretary of the interior in resigning. Instead, he soon found a dramatic occasion for reaffirming his loyalty.

On the train back to Washington, Seward was struck down by cholera. Seward's daughter Fanny, twenty-one and herself suffering from tuberculosis, became convinced that her father was near death once again and traveled to Harrisburg to be at his side.

But when Johnson also arrived at his bedside, Seward roused himself to assure the president that "if my life is spared," Johnson would continue to have his support.

Once back in Washington, Seward recovered just as his daughter died. Losing Fanny, he said, he felt "a sorrow that only God himself can heal."

Thaddeus Stevens, also ailing, made only two campaign speeches. But addressing a crowd in Bedford, Pennsylvania, on September 4, 1866, Stevens outdid Andrew Johnson in passion and plain speaking. Gone was the wary politician concerned with white and black men being seen arm in arm.

Stevens predicted for voters what they would be hearing "ten thousand times" from his opponents: " 'The Radicals would thrust the Negro into your parlors, your bedrooms, and the bosoms of your wives and daughters. They would even make your reluctant daughters marry black men.' And then they will send up the grand chorus from every foul throat, 'nigger,' 'nigger,' 'nigger!' 'Down with the nigger party, we're for the white man's party.'

"These unanswerable arguments will ring in every low bar room, and be printed in every blackguard sheet throughout the land whose fundamental maxim is 'all men are created equal....'

"A deep seated prejudice against races has disfigured the human mind for ages," Stevens concluded. And so the doctrine of Negro rights "may be unpopular with besotted ignorance. But popular or unpopular, I shall stand by it until I am relieved of the unprofitable labors of earth."

For the nation's voters, the election of 1866 had become a choice between the president's plan for reorganizing the South and the congressional plan, and they decisively rejected Johnson's approach. Republicans

picked up 37 House seats to boost their total to 173. Northern Democrats lost 9 votes, giving them 47 seats and ending Johnson's hope for a
national realignment.

The Democrats' votes came from the border states of Delaware,
Maryland, and Kentucky. Tennessee had been the only one of the Confederate states allowed to vote.

Johnson could no longer look to the major New York newspapers for
comfort. The editor of the daily with the country's largest circulation,
James Gordon Bennett of the *New York Herald*, was unfettered these
days by both propriety and party loyalty. The scourge of Radical Republicans, Bennett had headed a story about their recent assembly, "First
Grand National Convention of Nigger Worshipers at Philadelphia."

But after Johnson's campaigning, *Herald* readers no longer were
treated to that slant on the news. Bennett began to write publicly—and
in a private letter to the president—that he should heal his breach with
Congress and accept the Fourteenth Amendment.

Johnson preferred to believe those of his friends who dismissed Bennett as an unprincipled opportunist, a man whose endorsements always
went to the strongest political party.

Harder to explain away was the disaffection of Henry Raymond at
the *New York Times*. Since Raymond enjoyed an agreement with the
Times owner that guaranteed him complete editorial freedom, he was
not obliged to change course because circulation began to fall. And yet
as he backed away from supporting Johnson, Raymond watched reader-
ship rise again.

Despite the unmistakable warnings from the public, the president
was no more able than Charles Sumner to compromise, but it was Sumner and his allies who held the upper hand. During a campaign stopover
in St. Louis, struggling through a barely coherent thicket of self-pity,
Johnson had shared his presentiment of what might lie ahead:

"Yes, yes, they are ready to impeach. And if they were satisfied they
had the next Congress by as decided a majority as this, upon some pretext or other they would vacate the Executive department of the United
States."

As Congress prepared to meet again in December, the question became whether Johnson would give the Radicals that pretext.

Edwin Stanton

CHAPTER 9

EDWIN STANTON (1867–1868)

When Edwin McMasters Stanton first met Abraham Lincoln in 1855, he had looked him over and whispered to the friend who introduced them, "Why did you bring that damned long-armed ape here?"

Ten years later, as Lincoln's secretary of war, Stanton stood by the president's bed when he died and pronounced his first epitaph: "Now he belongs to the ages."

The transformation had been slow in coming. From childhood, Stanton had suffered asthma attacks severe enough to provoke seizures. He had lost his father to apoplexy at age thirteen and had worked his way through his freshman year at Kenyon College in Ohio before his mother required that he drop out and return to Steubenville to support their family. Stanton had survived the cholera epidemic of 1833, then studied law informally until he passed the Ohio bar examination at twenty, too young to practice.

Those early struggles had left Stanton immune to any glorification of Abraham Lincoln's rise from adversity on the frontier.

As soon as he turned twenty-one in 1835, Stanton moved the twenty-three miles down the road from Steubenville to Cadiz, Ohio, where he gained a reputation for being both shrewd and passionate in the courtroom. Short and husky, with a cheerful expression behind thick eyeglasses, he courted Mary Lamson, a clergyman's bookish daughter. With marriage, Edwin bowed to his bride's wishes, gave up alcohol, and cut back on the number of his daily cigars.

Intrigued by politics, Stanton became a strict party man, moving up in the ranks of the state's Jacksonian Democrats. During campaigns, he was free with insults for his opponents and derided Whig president William Henry Harrison as "an old imbecile."

Stanton also fell into a habit of passing along to his allies whatever confidential information he could glean from an enemy's camp.

After four years of marriage he and Mary were grateful for the birth of a daughter, Lucy, and then heartsick when the infant died the following year. The birth of a son and namesake, Edwin Lamson Stanton, helped revive his father's spirits, but the solace was fleeting.

In February 1844, Mary Stanton fell ill with what was described as a "bilious fever." Despite her husband's constant prayers, she died three weeks later. Stanton wrote to a friend that the "calamity has overwhelmed me."

Grief, in fact, seemed to unhinge him. Nights, he would carry a lamp through the house, wailing, "Where is Mary?"

The blows had not ended. For years, he had stinted on his own expenses in order to send his brother Darwin to study medicine at Harvard University. When war with Mexico broke out in May 1846, both brothers tried to enlist. His asthma kept Edwin at home; a fever of the brain was blamed when Darwin cut his throat.

Hearing of the suicide, Stanton ran distraught into a nearby woods. Friends chased after him, afraid that he, too, would kill himself.

Stanton brought his brother's widow and her three children into his house and promised to provide for her and raise her children with his own adored son. But even with his house filled again with life, Stanton was aware that he had changed. From the jovial man whose high spirits had drawn others to him, he had become dour and brooding.

"Events of the past summer," Stanton began one letter, "have broken my spirits, crushed my hopes, and without energy or purpose in life, I feel indifferent to the present, careless of the future—"

For months, Stanton never willingly left his house. But to make a living meant going back to court and being immersed again in politics. When legal matters first took him to Washington, Stanton found the same gloom hanging over the capital that had descended on him. He pronounced the city boring and everyone worn out from the debates over slavery. He lamented that the Library of Congress, burned down during the War of 1812, still had not been restored forty years later.

But one observation suggested that his grief over Mary's death might be abating. "There are not many pretty faces on the avenue to look at— handsome women are very scarce here," Stanton complained. He added that "stupid lectures are delivered at the Smithsonian."

Friends introduced him to Charles Sumner. Hearing Sumner speak on the Senate floor, Stanton came away impressed with his uncompromising ethics but not foreseeing their near-fatal consequences.

As Stanton's fortunes improved, he moved to Pittsburgh. Although his mother had gone to live in Virginia, he paid workmen and a gardener to keep up her house in Steubenville should she care to return.

Stanton's son seemed to be weathering the crises in his family, including an accident that had blinded him in one eye. Seeing father and son together, people remarked on the obvious devotion the gruff elder Stanton showed for the boy.

A dozen years had passed since his wife's death, and Stanton had turned forty-one when he became smitten with Ellen Hutchinson. Tall, fair-skinned, and quick to laugh, Ellen defied her mother, who objected that Stanton was too old for her twenty-six-year-old daughter. They were married in June 1856 and moved to Washington.

In the capital, Stanton's growing involvement in government lawsuits gave him the air of an assistant attorney general. But the trial that extended his reputation was a squalid tale of adultery and murder.

Stanton's scapegrace friend, New York congressman Daniel Sickles, had shot and killed Philip Barton Key, the son of Francis Scott Key, author of the popular patriotic lyric. Sickles believed Philip Key had been having an affair with his young wife.

Stanton not only got Sickles acquitted, but in the process he introduced into American jurisprudence the concept of not guilty by reason of temporary insanity.

In 1860, President Buchanan recruited Stanton to serve as attorney general in the last days of his flailing administration. Stanton did not discourage rumors that he had stiffened Buchanan's backbone to the point that the president finally denounced secession.

With the onset of the war, Edwin Stanton was still among the skeptics who referred to Lincoln as "the original gorilla." But if his ridicule was unchanged, Stanton's appreciation of Lincoln's politics had evolved. From his position in the Buchanan cabinet, he began to feed privileged information to Henry Seward, who was representing the incoming administration until Lincoln could arrive from Illinois.

Stanton reaped no immediate reward from his indiscretion. When the new president formed his cabinet, Lincoln's priority was resolving a touchy matter with Pennsylvania senator Simon Cameron, who believed that his help in delivering his state for Lincoln had earned him the position of secretary of the Treasury.

Thaddeus Stevens's joke about a red-hot stove had confirmed Cameron's dubious reputation for Lincoln. And he considered Salmon Chase, the Ohio governor who had vied with him for the Republican presidential nomination, to be far better qualified for the Treasury.

When the president at last persuaded Cameron to accept instead the post of secretary of war, Cameron found that he had inherited a department with fewer than two hundred employees and sorely ill equipped for waging war. The North lacked guns, bullets, horses, medical supplies—even uniforms and food for the volunteers who were overrunning the capital. Worst of all, much of official Washington was staffed by agents and clerks loyal to the Confederacy.

Cameron turned to private contractors only to watch discipline suffer and money evaporate. Within months, Congress was scrutinizing bloated wartime profits, and Northern newspapers were excoriating

Cameron's political cronies for getting rich from selling blind horses, rotting food, and carbines that jammed on the battlefield. Cameron had once seemed indifferent to slavery. Now he tried to fend off the attacks by aligning himself with the Radicals.

He decided to give weapons to those slaves who had taken refuge behind Union army lines. It would be a daring strategy, and Cameron asked Edwin Stanton for his judgment. He claimed afterward that Stanton had been enthusiastic.

But when Cameron announced his policy without clearing it with Lincoln, the president was distressed. He anticipated the anger it would arouse among his conservative supporters, and Lincoln himself was clinging to a postwar vision of sending the emancipated slaves back to a place with "a climate congenial to them."

Cameron would have to go. Lincoln shunted him off to St. Petersburg as ambassador to Russia while Congress was preparing its report on his derelictions. To replace him, Lincoln wanted a Northern Democrat to demonstrate that the war transcended party affiliations. Whatever Edwin Stanton might be saying behind his back, Lincoln knew of his energy and his mastery of detail.

To a friend, the president said that Stanton's great abilities had "made up my mind to sit down on all my pride" and "maybe a portion of my self-respect" and nominate him.

From retirement, James Buchanan regarded the appointment sourly. He granted to his niece that Stanton was "a perfectly honest man and in that respect differs from his immediate predecessor." But the ex-president thought Stanton was unqualified for "the greatest and most responsible office in the world." He did note, however, that Stanton "was always at my side and flattered me *ad nauseam*."

Equally flummoxed by the president's choice, the Radicals warned Lincoln that Stanton was gruff and undiplomatic. The president responded with the story of a Methodist clergyman he claimed to have met out West. "He gets wrought to so high a pitch of excitement in his prayers and exhortations," Lincoln recalled, "that they are obliged to put bricks in his pockets to keep him down.

"We may be obliged to serve Stanton in the same way, but I guess we'll let him jump a while first. Besides, bricks in his pockets would be better than bricks in his hat."

Once confirmed in office, Secretary Stanton inaugurated an open-door policy at the War Department. Every Monday at 11 a.m., he stood behind a tall desk and surveyed contractors, office seekers, suspended military officers, and impractical inventors. From each, he demanded, "What brings you here?"

In a few moments, he had disposed of one petitioner and—ferocious or kindly, as the case might require—turned to the next. When Lincoln had a free hour, he walked over to the War Department and watched from the back of the room. The president called it "Going to see Old Mars quell disturbances."

But the most daunting challenge Stanton faced could not be resolved with the snap of his fingers. General George McClellan, whose reluctance to do battle had become Lincoln's greatest frustration, found comfort in casting Stanton as an enemy who was always plotting against him. The general's allies in the press took up his charges, with the *New York World* especially harsh in pitting a meddlesome middle-aged civilian against the dashing thirty-six-year-old McClellan.

Stanton regularly complained of his anguish at being unable to get McClellan to move, and their telegrams leading up to the disastrous battles of late June 1862 revealed the general offering one excuse after another for his delay. First the timing was wrong, then his forces were inadequate to challenge Robert E. Lee and march on the Confederate capital in Richmond.

When he was forced to retreat instead, McClellan blamed Stanton and wired him angrily, "If I save this day now, I owe no thanks to you or to any other person in Washington.

"You have done your best to sacrifice this army."

Stanton did not need to respond to the accusation. A clerk in the War Department's telegraph office decided that those sentences bordered on treason and deleted them before he handed over the wire.

McClellan's language had been mild, however, compared with what he was writing home to his wife: "Stanton is the most unmitigated scoundrel, the most depraved hypocrite and villain."

It may have reassured the general to think that the secretary of war was acting alone, but when he was finally relieved of command, Lincoln himself wrote out the order.

McClellan had gone on to run as a Democrat against Lincoln in the 1864 election, campaigning on a promise to end the war through negotiations with the Confederacy. His party won 45 percent of the vote, Lincoln's Republicans 55 percent.

Long after the war ended, men were still debating McClellan's behavior. General Grant had no explanation for it. "McClellan," he acknowledged, "is one of the mysteries of the war."

But in writing to his wife, McClellan may have provided an explanation. His letter also demonstrated why, to the end, he remained popular with his men.

"I am tired of the sickening sight of the battlefield, with its mangled corpses and poor suffering wounded!" McClellan wrote. "Victory has no charms for me when purchased at such cost. I shall be only too glad when it is all over and I can return where I best love to be."

Through the failures and successes on the battlefield, the president and Stanton remained united, although Lincoln sometimes had to rein in his high-jumping secretary. After reviewing strategy, Stanton commanded one general, "Go ahead, begin now!" To which the president said mildly, "Mr. Secretary, I have not yet given my consent."

Lincoln's need to cope with the temperaments within his cabinet had drawn sympathy from a young Ohio reporter who served briefly as the president's bodyguard. William Coggeshall observed the president's attempts to cobble together his policy from various rival philosophies and likened Lincoln to a boy carrying a big basket of eggs when he faced an urgent dilemma:

"Couldn't let go his basket to unbutton his breeches—was in sore distress from a necessity to urinate—& stood dancing, crying—What shall I do?"

The individuals of the cabinet might be sharp and even positive,

Coggeshall concluded, "but thrown together neutralize each other & the result is an inspid mess."

While he lived, Lincoln would listen to the contending voices and often trust events to guide him to his goals. After the assassination, each survivor could claim to be following the path Lincoln had marked out for the country. Much as it outraged the Radicals, Andrew Johnson was able to cite decisions and quote casual remarks that proved his fidelity to Lincoln's vision.

Johnson had entered the presidency with high regard for Stanton's effectiveness at the War Department. But as the breach developed with the Radical Republicans, Stanton turned to a tactic that had served him in the past: He opened a channel with the Speaker of the House so that each of them would have advance information on matters involving the army and the Congress.

The arrangement served to bond Stanton with Johnson's congressional critics, and Navy Secretary Welles was suspicious enough to urge that the new president remove Stanton from his cabinet.

Johnson refused. He had come to appreciate the fact that Stanton might argue against his policies—as when he opposed a presidential veto of the civil rights bill—but once he saw that Johnson had made a decision, Stanton withdrew his objections.

The secretary could not always move so nimbly. When he was forced to state his position on the Fourteenth Amendment to a crowd of Johnson loyalists, Stanton admitted that he had endorsed its original provisions, except for denying voting rights for five years to House members who had supported the Confederacy.

Gradually, however, Johnson was coming to prefer a secretary of war more attuned to his thinking. He had held off replacing Stanton before the congressional campaign of 1866, and as the campaign grew bitter, Stanton became convinced that a higher duty required him to cling to his position.

Ellen Stanton rejected her husband's definition of duty and urged him to resign. Stanton was clearly tired and sick, and she herself was coughing in a way that suggested pneumonia.

Stanton responded by quoting to her Lincoln's words from a time when Stanton had been tempted to leave his post: "Reconstruction is more difficult than construction or destruction," Lincoln had said. "You have been our main reliance. You must help us through the final act. It is my wish and the country's that you remain."

With the Radicals' decisive victory at the polls and with Ellen Stanton's health improving, Stanton felt more than ever that it was his patriotic obligation to fight on.

At the White House, Generals Grant and Sherman were letting Johnson know that if the president did dismiss Stanton, they would refuse to replace him. Johnson understood that a move was under way to draft Grant for the presidency in two years' time and hesitated to cross him.

As the president prepared his second December message to Congress, he continued to ignore Stanton's suggestion that he temper Radical hostility by accepting the inevitability of the Fourteenth Amendment, advice that Grant was seconding.

Johnson preferred a last-ditch effort to scuttle the amendment. Speaking to officials from Alabama, the president called for them to stand firm because the amendment would "change the whole character of our government."

To the president's satisfaction, all but one of the Confederate states rejected the amendment. The exception was Tennessee, and Congress rewarded that state by seating its senators and representatives.

Johnson learned just how outraged congressmen were by his rigidity when Representative James Ashley of Ohio introduced a bill that he claimed sprang from his feeling of "a painful but, nevertheless, to me, an imperative duty." Ashley called on the House to impeach Andrew Johnson on the grounds of high crimes and misdemeanors.

Ashley's indictment accused Johnson of usurpation of power, violations of the law, and corruptly using his powers of appointment, pardon, and the veto. Ashley added that Johnson had also "corruptly disposed of public property" and "corruptly interfered in elections."

On January 7, 1867, the House voted 107 to 39—with 45 members not voting—to authorize its Judiciary Committee to pursue an inquiry into the president's conduct.

With Stanton staying on, Johnson knew he could not yet withdraw the troops from the Southern states, but he might find ways to curtail the army's power. The president's hand had been strengthened by decisions from the U.S. Supreme Court, which had ruled, by a five-to-four vote, against loyalty oaths, but which upheld the president's right to issue pardons over the objections of Congress.

The Court also outlawed martial law in those Southern states with functioning civil courts. As a result, Southern courthouses could punish the Northern soldiers charged with keeping the peace. The Radicals found a mocking irony in the idea of the vanquished passing judgment on the victors.

And if a Northern military commander challenged Southern justice, he got no support from the White House. Brigadier General Daniel Sickles, deemed to have recovered from his insanity in killing Philip Key, had gone on to command troops at Gettysburg, where he lost a leg in battle. Sent to the Carolinas after the war, Sickles was appalled by Negroes' often being whipped for trivial offenses, and he banned all public whipping.

The civilian governor traveled to Washington to intervene with the president. Johnson countermanded Sickles's order and the whippings went on.

As the investigation proceeded on James Ashley's call for impeachment, his Ohio colleague, Senator John Sherman, introduced a series of reconstruction bills that would undo the effects of the Supreme Court's rulings. Before they were enacted, however, the Radicals cast an early vote that demonstrated they could override any veto.

Their test was a bill to extend voting rights in the District of Columbia to any male twenty-one years old. The exceptions included spies and men on welfare or convicted of major crimes or guilty of having sheltered Confederate troops. But those exceptions did not prohibit black men from voting. Alone among the cabinet members, Stanton recommended that Johnson sign the bill.

Instead, the president vetoed it on January 5, 1867, noting that white voters in the District had rejected Negro suffrage two years earlier. Three days after the veto, Congress approved it—the first bill in U.S. history to give the vote to black men. The margins were 112 to 38 in the House, 29 to 10 in the Senate.

Johnson had also given notice that he would veto statehood for Nebraska and Colorado, since their territories were too sparsely populated to entitle them to even one representative. Over his objections, Nebraska was accepted into the Union as the thirty-seventh state on March 1, 1867. The congressional session ended before Colorado statehood could be reintroduced.

Senator Sherman's proposals represented Congress's most determined effort to take control of the South. Provisions of his Military Reconstruction Bill divided the former Confederacy into five military districts, replacing the civilian governments that Congress had declared void.

U.S. Army generals would administer each district under martial law. Local governments were to be "provisional" until they were set up under new state constitutions. Delegates to those assemblies would be of "whatever race, color or previous condition" so long as they had resided in the state for one year and were not disqualified under the Fourteenth Amendment.

The effect would be to qualify former slaves for public office while excluding the most prominent white slave owners.

The president was ready to fight. Meeting in private with Charles Nordhoff of the *New York Evening News*, Johnson was angry and unguarded. He denounced the Reconstruction laws as promising only anarchy and chaos, and he called the people of the South poor, quiet, unoffending, and harmless people who were to be trodden underfoot "to protect niggers."

When Nordhoff protested, the president used the reasoning with which he had silenced Charles Sumner. He began by telling of a rape case in New York he had read about. He claimed that if it had taken place in the South and the victim had been black, there would be na-

tional public outrage. The president concluded, "It's all damned prejudice."

Like Carl Schurz, Nordhoff was a German immigrant who sympathized with the former slaves. He left the White House that day
convinced that Johnson was "a pig-headed man." The president seemed
opposed to voting rights for blacks and, Nordhoff concluded, with "a
determination to secure the political ascendancy of the old Southern
leaders."

Nordhoff had summed up the president's transformation in office.
Throughout his political life, Johnson had been outraged at being denied
power and respect by the South's aristocracy. Over the last two years,
however, those plantation owners had knelt before him to receive his
pardon. These days he was despised instead by the Northern Radicals
with their commitment to the nation's former slaves.

For Johnson, race now mattered more than social class, and he had
chosen to side with his fellow white men.

At a cabinet meeting, Secretary Stanton once more spoke on behalf of
the reconstruction bill, knowing very well that it was offensive to the
president. Once more, Stanton's arguing was futile. Johnson vetoed
the bill. On March 2, 1867, Congress passed it over his veto.

The Radicals rallied to protect Stanton's job. Their Tenure of Office
Act represented the most sweeping challenge ever attempted by Congress to limit presidential powers. Under the Senate draft, if the approval
of Congress had been required for a presidential appointment, the president could not then remove that man unless Congress also approved the
dismissal.

The Senate bill had exempted the president's cabinet. In the House,
Thaddeus Stevens's version not only included cabinet appointees but applied the protection to them even if, like Stanton, they had been named
by a previous president.

And for section six of his House bill, Stevens crafted language that
warned a president that violating the act could cost him his job.

Eighty years earlier, the framers of the U.S. Constitution had modeled the entire impeachment process on British tradition. From the end of the Middle Ages to more recent times, Parliament had prosecuted errant nobles through charges in the House of Commons followed by a trial in the House of Lords.

When the American constitutional convention struggled with how and why to remove a bad president, bribery and treason had been obvious justifications. But for less easily identifiable offenses, George Mason of Virginia had first proposed "maladministration" and, when that was rejected as too vague, had come up with the more high-flown but equally murky "high crimes and misdemeanors."

To give his Tenure of Office bill unmistakable heft, Stevens condensed the charge to "high misdemeanors."

Stanton called the bill unnecessary and spoke publicly against it. His enemies took that opposition as another proof of Stanton's habitual deceit—professing one position, maneuvering behind the scenes for another.

He soon gave them new reason for distrust. Stanton had learned that the president was issuing private orders to friendly Southern commanders that he did not share with either the War Department or General Grant.

Stanton worked quietly with members of the House to make it a misdemeanor for a president to issue such orders and for an officer to act on them. Thaddeus Stevens then attached that language as an amendment to the Army Appropriations Bill.

Johnson fumed over the insult, but he signed the bill since he considered it vital for maintaining the army.

In the field, the military commanders were generating their own controversies. While still in his thirties, General Philip Sheridan, who was now commanding Texas and Louisiana, had become a hero in the North by razing Virginia's breadbasket in the Shenandoah Valley and by blocking General Lee's retreat at Appomattox.

As he had demonstrated after the New Orleans riot, Sheridan was not courting popularity in his territory. Newspapers quoted him saying, "If I owned Texas and Hell, I would rent Texas and live in Hell."

Sheridan had involved himself again in the riot's aftermath by removing Major J. S. Monroe and other officials who refused to prosecute the white men responsible for the bloodshed.

However much Radicals might endorse those specific actions, conservative Republicans were troubled by the questions Sheridan presented about the limit to military power. Congress had set no date for ending military rule, and Thaddeus Stevens had defused any attempt to impose one.

When Stanton again stood alone in asserting that Sheridan's authority in Louisiana exceeded even the president's, Johnson was determined at last to purge him from his cabinet.

With Congress passing its first Reconstruction Act and Louisiana again a political maelstrom, Pinckney Pinchback decided it was time to end his two-year rustication in Alabama. He moved his family to a large frame house on Derbigny Street and plunged into renewing alliances from the war years.

His time away had given Pinchback a perspective that he thought other black leaders lacked. He ridiculed their grandiose talk of running white Democrats out of the state and warned that a working government had to include white men. Pinchback added frankly that most former slaves were not ready to take over the state legislature.

But as Philip Sheridan waited for specific instructions from General Grant about how to proceed with military reconstruction, Pinchback set about organizing the Fourth Ward Republican Club. Given that base, he then claimed a seat at a new constitutional convention, which had been called to accomplish what the rioting had blocked.

To many delegates on the convention floor, Pinchback was a new face, and his speech had been relegated to the ninth day when everyone would be surfeited with oratory. But Pinchback was intent on impressing the state's Republican leadership and counting on his street-corner rallies in Alabama to have honed his gifts.

His speech was a calculated blend of settling scores and generous forgiveness. Pinchback accused the Southern aristocracy of having worked to "feed the prejudices of the whites against the blacks," and he warned his fellow black men to guard against "the hissing of the serpent" that would infect their hearts with the same "damnable jealousy and prejudice."

Looking to the future, Pinchback concluded, "No more will our people be killed by mobs, no more will our women be exposed to the violence of a privileged class. No more will our cries and supplications be treated with contempt, no more will our demands for justice be disregarded and answered by the lash.

"But peace, blessed peace, will again bless the land."

Pinchback had fallen into the cadences of the pulpit. When he finished, silence was followed by an ovation, and Pinchback was elected to the Republican Party's executive committee.

Elections for the drafting of Louisiana's state constitution resulted in Republicans winning ninety-eight of the hundred places, with delegates equally divided between white and black.

Pinchback had been taken up by Henry Clay Warmoth, the suave carpetbagger popular with black voters. Warmoth was now only twenty-six and preparing a bid to become one of the nation's youngest governors. Although Warmoth had backed Pinchback to be a delegate, his protégé was following no party line.

Pinchback attacked a measure to strip several categories of white Southerners of their votes in retaliation for their backing the Confederacy. He lost that debate by a vote of forty-four to thirty. When he rewrote another civil rights bill until it satisfied him, his version was rejected as too extreme.

Pinckney Pinchback had been defeated on two major issues, but throughout Louisiana his eloquence had established his reputation.

As Congress prepared to adjourn on March 2, 1867, the House Judiciary Committee reported itself unable to conclude its investigation into the charges against Andrew Johnson.

Committee members had heard eighty-nine witnesses, several of them called back two and three times. General Lafayette Baker from the War Department offered the sort of dubious testimony that proved typical.

Baker was remembered as the compromised head of the Union Intelligence Service, and his reputation had suffered further from his claim that the journal of John Wilkes Booth proved that Edwin Stanton had been part of the conspiracy to kill Lincoln. When the journal was produced and proved nothing of the sort, Baker insisted that eighteen damning pages had been removed.

Testifying at the impeachment hearings, Baker's evidence against Andrew Johnson was equally tainted. He claimed to have heard about a letter that Johnson was said to have written to Jefferson Davis early in 1864, when Johnson was the acting governor of Tennessee, in which Johnson had sought a position in the Confederacy.

Baker was asked, Where was the letter now?

He said it had been stolen from Johnson's writing table and never sent.

As the investigation skittered off into irrelevant inquiries about Johnson's business dealings, Secretary Stanton put an end to the attempt to prove corruption by testifying that he—not the president—had overseen the disposal of railroad tracks and rolling stock. When practical, it had all been sold as conquered property belonging to the United States. What could not be sold within the rebel states was transferred back to its original owners. In no way had Johnson profited from the transactions.

After sessions like that one, Thaddeus Stevens was heard to demand in frustration, "Well, have you got *anything*, anyhow?"

As Congress justified its attempt to impeach the president, two unexpected complications arose to distract Charles Sumner. He was urged to expand the borders of the United States, but at the same time his new marriage was unraveling.

His public dilemma was thrust on Sumner the evening of March 29, 1867, when he responded to Henry Seward's urgent invitation to come to his house. By the time Sumner was ushered in, Seward had already left for the State Department but had delegated his son Frederick to explain the emergency.

Before the war, Tsar Alexander II had hoped to bolster his faltering economy with a sale of Russia's Alaska territory to the United States. Now that the Union had won, Russia's minister to Washington, Eduard de Stoeckl, had entered into secret negotiations with Seward.

On the next day, the secretary of state intended to buy for $7.2 million all of Russia's holdings in North America, land that measured 591,000 square miles, or twice the size of Texas. The price worked out to about two cents an acre.

Stoeckl was on hand to assure Sumner that his government was prepared to act. He found a sympathetic listener, although Sumner had assumed that when the country's boundaries were moved north, it would be by absorbing Canada.

As chairman of the Senate's Foreign Relations Committee, however, Sumner's sense of propriety was offended at having the deal sprung on him at the same moment that Seward was having ceremonial copies of the treaty prepared for the next day.

Leaving that night, Sumner made no promises, but he scheduled a special session of his committee for April 1. President Johnson had called Congress back for the same day.

As word leaked out, newspaper opinion was mixed. Instead of "Alaska"—an Aleut word for "mainland"—editors were branding the territory "Walrussia" and "Seward's Folly." The *New York World* called Alaska a "sucked-dry orange" with one resource—the fur of seals, which had already been hunted to near extinction. *Harper's Weekly* joked that Alaska's cattle sat cross-legged on the frozen tundra and produced ice cream instead of milk.

Sumner's committee members were unimpressed with the acquisition, but over the next few days Seward lobbied them intensely. His loyalty to the president rankled Republicans, however, and William Fessenden remained opposed, with one facetious condition: He would change his mind if "the Secretary of State be compelled to live there, and the Russian government be required to keep him there."

When it fell to Sumner to take a stand, he announced, "I regret very much to go for this treaty."

On domestic issues, his colleagues often found Sumner rash and in-temperate, but they did not question his authority in foreign affairs. He carried the majority of his committee with him, and on April 4, 1867, the Senate voted to annex Alaska, thirty-seven to two.

The respect Sumner was accorded in the Senate was not being reflected at home. From the day they left Washington in their honeymoon car-riage, Alice Hooper Sumner had not turned out to be the gentle nurse and admiring acolyte Sumner believed he was marrying. Her close friends already knew the force of her temper, which she unleashed at the smallest provocation.

At first, Sumner had overlooked the warning signs and took pleasure in showing off his glamorous wife. But soon he was confiding to din-ner companions that he should be home working on legislation and not dragged out every night to balls and banquets.

Salmon Chase's daughter, Kate, recalled that her father had twit-ted Sumner before his marriage about the perils of prominent men with much younger wives. Kate considered Alice Sumner a "flutterfly" and was pained for Sumner—not a charming man, she granted, but warmhearted and a brilliant talker—that people should be gossiping about him.

One midnight at a dance, guests heard Sumner say mildly to his wife, "My dear, is it not time to go home?" And they heard her snap, "You may go when you like. I shall stay."

By the time of the debate over Alaska, Washington society was whis-pering that Sumner rarely accompanied his wife at all. These nights, she was often on the arm of an attaché from the Prussian delegation, Baron Friedrich von Holstein.

Because the good-looking young man showed no urgent interest in women, Alice Sumner seemed to expect that no one would question his constant presence at her side. One shrewd Washington matron thought that Alice was seeing Holstein only "as a catspaw to annoy her husband."

These days, conversation between the Sumners ran along the lines of the exchange when Sumner found Alice getting into a carriage with Holstein and another young couple.

He asked, "Where are you going, Alice?"

"I am going to enjoy myself."

"But where are you going?"

"That does not concern you."

Sumner retreated into his house alone and wept.

When Holstein gave Alice a costly amber necklace to replace her artificial stones, Sumner insisted on paying for it, even though he was badly strapped by the grand house they were building at the corner of H Street and Vermont Avenue.

The situation had become unbearable. Sumner agreed to spare her reputation by sending Alice on a cruise and letting it be understood that their separation was only temporary.

Their truce ended in April 1867, when Holstein was ordered home by his government, and Alice was convinced that her husband was behind the recall. As Sumner protested in vain, she cursed him and with a final "God damn you!" locked the door to her bedroom and prepared to live apart with her daughter, Bell.

Alice was not prepared, however, for the condemnation she received from women like Kate Chase. Alice struck back by overseeing a campaign by her friends to reclaim her honor. She let it be known that she had left her husband because—in the words of one rumormonger—"he could not perform the functions of a husband."

Alice Sumner had handed her husband's enemies a weapon as lethal in its way as Preston Brooks's guttapercha cane. Around Washington, Charles Sumner became "The Great Impotent."

All but forgotten during the stormy sessions in Congress, Jefferson Davis was wasting away in Virginia at Fortress Monroe, at the junction of the James River and Chesapeake Bay. Varina Davis overcame her contempt for Andrew Johnson and went in person to plead her husband's case. The president assured her that the unrelenting hostility of Thaddeus Stevens and his Radicals were to blame for Davis's suffering.

Since no evidence could be found connecting Davis to Lincoln's assassination, he was eligible for habeas corpus proceedings. To charge him with treason, however, required that he be tried in federal district court before the local Virginia judge and Salmon Chase as the U.S. Chief Justice. But Chase refused to lend his authority to any court in the Confederacy, and his critics suggested that his chief concern was not damaging his presidential chances for the following year.

As the months ground on, Davis's circumstance troubled a number of influential Northerners who joined in the protests—Cornelius Vanderbilt, the railroad millionaire; Gerrit Smith, a wealthy New York abolitionist; and Horace Greeley, now editor of the Republican *New York Tribune*. Smith offered to put up bail for Davis and lectured Johnson that holding the Confederate president without a trial dishonored his administration and the nation.

As attorneys for Davis wrangled over his case, they blamed Seward, as a victim of the assassination attempt, for his "most venomous influence" in keeping Davis confined.

At last, bail was approved, and on Saturday, May 11, 1867, Jefferson Davis walked out of Fortress Monroe with Varina at his side to board a steamer for Richmond. Women passengers recognized him and flocked around with embraces and kisses.

Once landed at Richmond, the Davises rode along a carriage route lined with well-wishers from the dock to the Spotswood Hotel. Men raised their hats; women waved handkerchiefs; no one made a sound.

In court on Monday, the district judge set bail at one hundred thousand dollars. Vanderbilt, Greeley, and Smith each put up twenty-five thousand dollars; ten other men guaranteed the rest. The government's lawyer told the court that no prosecution was planned, and the judge instructed the marshal to discharge the prisoner.

That same night, Davis and his wife left for New York on their way to an impoverished exile. Among the letters Davis received was a note from Robert E. Lee, now the president of Washington College in Lexington, Kentucky.

Lee assured his former president that Davis's release "has lifted a load from my heart, which I have not the words to tell" and wished for Davis "that peace which the world cannot take away."

• • •

At the White House, it was not a peace Andrew Johnson could enjoy. He had already decided to remove Edwin Stanton from the War Department when he discovered a new cause for firing him: Johnson had never been shown the petition for clemency for Mary Surratt, although it had been signed by five of the nine officers at her trial. Her son had been captured after two years in hiding, and it was during his trial that the petition had come to light.

Johnson was convinced that Stanton had tricked him to get his signature on Mrs. Surratt's death warrant. He immediately dictated a note to Stanton that his resignation would be accepted.

Stanton ignored the note. With Congress just adjourned, Johnson suspended Stanton and appointed Grant as interim secretary of war. To underscore his point, the president also removed Philip Sheridan and turned his command over to General Winfield Scott Hancock, a credible wartime leader but without Sheridan's following throughout the North.

Grant believed that the Tenure of Office Act made the president's action illegal, and he cautioned Johnson that loyal people of the country—North and South—might object if he dismissed from government "the very man of all others" in whom they had confidence. But, Grant concluded, he was a soldier first and would obey orders.

At home, Grant confided his ambivalence to his wife. The president had worked himself up to a white heat of indignation, Grant reported, and he had agreed to the interim appointment "as I think it most important that someone should be there who cannot be used."

Grant added that he did not share the Radicals' high opinion of Stanton. "He was very offensive," Grant said, "voting 'nay' to every suggestion made by the president."

If anything, Johnson had been too lenient with him: "Stanton would have gone and on the double-quick if I had been president."

Over lunch, Grant brooded about recent developments, and in the afternoon, he rode with his wife to alert Stanton to his dismissal. They caught up with the secretary of war in his carriage on Seventh Street. Grant got out, stood on the step of the carriage, and told Stanton what Johnson had done.

"I thought, Mr. Stanton, it was but just to inform you so that you might not be unprepared and might arrange your actions, your papers, et cetera."

"Ah," Stanton replied, "I expected it. He could do nothing else and keep his self-respect."

Stanton indicated that he would accept Grant as his interim replacement but agreed that the Tenure of Office Act prevented Johnson from removing him outright. Exhausted, low in spirits, and short of funds, Stanton went home to Ohio for his first vacation in five years.

The same wrangling that had depleted him, however, had recharged Andrew Johnson. The president told the faithful Gideon Welles, "If Congress can bring themselves to impeach me, because in my judgment a turbulent and unfit man should be removed, let them do it."

And in his third annual message to Congress on December 7, 1867, Johnson flaunted his contempt for the Radicals' quest for universal voting rights. He railed against the prospect of "negro domination" and charged that "negroes have shown less capacity for government than any other race of people."

Giving black men the vote would have cataclysmic results: "All order will be subverted, all industry cease, and the fertile fields of the South will grow up into a wilderness."

The president had reason for his bravado. Congress had moved its Fortieth Session forward to prevent Johnson from taking advantage of its customary long adjournment, but when Congress returned to Washington in early July, the spirit for impeachment had flagged. Finding he could not revive it, Thaddeus Stevens was disheartened enough to agree that the motion should be tabled.

The chairman of the Judiciary Committee, Iowa congressman James Wilson, argued for ending the effort entirely. He complained that the anti-Johnson forces were trying to convict the president for actions that he might take someday. For example, he might station soldiers in Southern states "to overawe the loyal people of those states, especially the colored vote."

Wilson asked, "Are we to impeach the President for what he may do in the future?"

Undeterred, the Radicals called for a vote on impeachment. On December 7, 1867, they lost almost two to one—57 yeas to 108 nays. For Stevens, Sumner, and their Radicals, the defeat was the more galling since membership in the House was now two-thirds Republican.

Salmon Chase

CHAPTER 10

SALMON PORTLAND CHASE
(1868)

T**HE DAY AFTER THEIR EMBARRASSING DEFEAT,** R**ADICAL** R**EPUBLI**-cans met at Thaddeus Stevens's house on B Street to plot their next step. They agreed to keep up their campaign for impeachment by seizing on any political setback for Andrew Johnson or any slip he might make.

General Grant guaranteed that they would not have to wait long. From the first, he had been uncomfortable as interim secretary of war, given his approval of the congressional Reconstruction Acts. In mid-January 1868 he abruptly left the cabinet, turning the keys to the War Department back to Edwin Stanton and returning to his office at army headquarters.

By now, Grant's disillusion with civilian politics was complete. He wrote to William Sherman, "All the romance of feeling that men in high places are above personal considerations, and act only from motives of pure patriotism, and for the general good of the public has been destroyed. An inside view proves too truly very much the reverse."

Johnson felt betrayed. In front of the cabinet, he claimed that Grant had pledged to stay on until the Court could rule on the Tenure of Office Act. Grant denied making that promise. When a Washington newspaper sided with Johnson and suggested that Grant had deceived the president, Grant controlled his temper, called at the White House, and explained how their rift could be repaired.

Johnson ignored his advice, and the attacks on Grant by Democratic newspapers intensified. The angry correspondence ended with Grant writing, "And now, Mr. President, where my honor as a soldier and integrity as a man have been so violently assailed, pardon me for saying that I can regard this whole matter, from the beginning to the end, as an attempt to involve me in the resistance of law, for which you have hesitated to assume the responsibility in orders, and thus to destroy my character before the country."

When their letters were read in the Senate, Thaddeus Stevens offered Grant his backhanded praise: "He is a bolder man than I thought him."

The initiative now passed to Edwin Stanton. The president and Henry Seward were convinced that he had to resign. But with the conflict between the legislative and executive branches of government thrown into sharp relief, Congress was insisting that Stanton stay.

Fifty congressmen led by Speaker Schuyler Colfax called on Stanton in person, bringing with them an appeal signed by another sixty House members. The president's defiance guaranteed that the delegation was not limited to the Radicals. William Fessenden, despite his regular clashes with Charles Sumner, was among the voices urging Stanton to stand fast against the "renegade White House."

Seeing his chance, Thaddeus Stevens transferred the impeachment issue from the reluctant Judiciary Committee to his own Committee on Reconstruction. He was counting on the acrimony between Johnson and Grant to expose the president as a liar, although Stevens admitted that Grant might have misrepresented what he had told Johnson about accepting the cabinet post. But, Stevens concluded, "Grant isn't on trial; it's Johnson."

Even on his own committee, however, Stevens faced opposition. Six members rejected a new motion to impeach. Only two sided with their chairman.

Once again, Andrew Johnson ignored his friends' face-saving advice, refusing to ride out his term with Stanton at the War Department. Even knowing the risks, Johnson went ahead with his plan to name a replacement.

His first choice was John Potts, the War Department's chief clerk, but Potts refused to be thrust into the fray. Johnson then turned to Adjutant General Lorenzo Thomas, a sixty-three-year-old West Point graduate who delighted in his dress uniform, even though he tended to drink more enthusiastically than he fought.

Put in charge of abandoned plantations in the Mississippi Valley during the war, Thomas had sided with white plantation owners against the newly freed slaves until he was overruled in Washington. Thomas revealed an obvious nostalgia for the sluggish pace at the War Department under Simon Cameron, and Stanton felt only contempt for him.

Describing Thomas as "only fit for presiding over a crypt of Egyptian mummies like himself," Stanton had once threatened to "pick Lorenzo Thomas up with a pair of tongs and drop him from the nearest window."

For his part, Thomas was either more forgiving or well lubricated. He confessed that "Stanton is an enigma to me. He has no manners, and treats persons rudely, and yet he appears kind."

President Johnson understood that Thomas was no scrapper, but he promised to be a docile interim appointment until Johnson could prevail on General William Sherman to sign on as secretary. As Stanton sensed, it had come down to a matter of respect: Andrew Johnson's self-respect demanded that Stanton be fired. And Johnson expected that "the nation would entertain sufficient respect for the Chief Magistrate to uphold him."

At 9 a.m. on Friday, February 21, 1868, Johnson summoned Lorenzo Thomas for his next defiant move. Inadvertently, however, Thomas had deprived the president of the advantage of surprise. On Wednesday, while looking up the text of the tenure law, he had confided Johnson's scheme to a colleague.

As a result, Stanton was prepared when Thomas knocked on the door of the war secretary's office. Told to enter, Thomas came into the room as Stanton rose from his couch to receive him. Formally, Thomas said, "I am directed by the President to hand you this."

Stanton accepted the order dismissing him and seemed to study it intently. With no change of expression, he said, "Do you wish me to vacate at once, or am I to be permitted to stay long enough to remove my property?"

Relieved at Stanton's mild reaction, Thomas said, "Certainly, at your pleasure." He handed over Johnson's second directive, naming Thomas as secretary, and suspected nothing when Stanton requested a copy.

But while Thomas left to have the copy made, Stanton huddled with General Grant, who agreed that Stanton should not vacate the office.

Returning with the copy, Thomas found a different reception. "I want some little time for reflection," Stanton now said sharply. "I don't know whether I shall obey your order or not." He added that until he made up his mind, Thomas was forbidden to issue any orders.

That was not a message Thomas wanted to carry back to the White House. Meeting with Johnson in the early afternoon, he let the president believe that all had gone well. Johnson told him to occupy the secretary's office the next day.

Johnson went to report to his cabinet that he had prevailed and that "Stanton seemed calm and submissive." In that jubilant mood, he sent to the Senate an account of what he had done.

But Stanton had already informed his allies, and a Radical Pennsylvania congressman, John Covode, had introduced a resolution to impeach. By the time Johnson's message arrived, the Senate was meeting in executive session to weigh its course of action.

Stanton sent his son to the Capitol to monitor events, and at 3 p.m. Edwin reported that the prevailing sentiment was that "you ought to hold on to the point of expulsion" until the Senate could act. Senators were sending their own messages of support, and Charles Sumner condensed his advice to one terse word: "Stick!"

Emboldened, Stanton wrote out an order for Grant, as head of the army, to arrest Thomas "for disobedience to superior authority in refusing to obey my orders as Secretary of War."

Grant hurried to Stanton's office, drew him away from the men gathered there, and spoke with him in private for half an hour. Stanton had assumed that Grant respected him, but he was asking the nation's premier soldier to flout the president of the United States.

Stanton got his answer when Grant tore up the directive and went back to his own office. Night was approaching, and Stanton was prepared to sleep on his office couch, as he had done for many wartime nights as he awaited news from the battlefield.

Since his conversation with Stanton, Grant was refusing to receive calls, but he agreed to meet with Charles Sumner and a delegation of flustered Republican senators. Sumner said afterward that the general had reassured them by asking, How or when would the president get the soldiers to remove Stanton? From his question, the senators inferred that Grant would refuse to issue any order to evict Stanton by force.

All the same, reports circulated that Thomas was ready to pounce during the weekend commemorating George Washington's birthday. Stanton told his Senate callers that "Thomas is boasting that he intends to take possession of the war office at 9 tomorrow morning."

How could he continue to resist, Stanton asked, if the Senate had not backed him up? Within an hour of his plea, the Senate decreed, on a straight party-line vote, that Johnson could neither remove Stanton nor replace him with Lorenzo Thomas.

Buoyed by that assurance, Stanton vowed to occupy the war office night and day until the issue was resolved. Two congressmen gathered together a hundred fellow members to protect him, and Grant invested a guard unit with authority to summon every soldier to the War Department.

If Andrew Johnson intended to launch a second civil war, Stanton and the Congress would be ready.

At 8 a.m. on Washington's birthday, Lorenzo Thomas was awakened by an assistant United States marshal and a local policeman. Thomas learned that David Carter, a District of Columbia judge, was standing by to take the actions that Grant had refused.

Judge Carter had accepted Stanton's affidavit that Thomas violated the tenure law by trying to take control of the War Department, and Carter issued a warrant for Thomas's arrest.

While Stanton was barricaded in his office the previous night, Thomas had gone to a masked ball. After many drinks, he had boasted to the other guests that if Stanton should refuse to open his door, he would break it down.

The next morning, Thomas was suffering the effects of his revelry when the two arresting officials showed up before he had breakfast. They agreed to let him stop by the White House on his way to court and alert the president about his arrest. Impatient to get the issue before the courts, Johnson refused to intervene.

Two friendly tradesmen were on hand when Judge Carter heard the charges, and they put up Thomas's five-thousand-dollar bail. Thomas notified the president that he was free and set off for the War Department with a new resolve.

And yet, unlike his brash talk the previous night, Thomas was subdued when he confronted Stanton. The two men exchanged good mornings. Thomas indicated the group around Stanton and said he did not want to interrupt. "Nothing private here," Stanton said briskly. "What do you want?"

Among the onlookers was a Republican congressman with an ear for dialogue and a knowledge of shorthand. His notes allowed the *New York Times* to present the scene as political theater:

"Thomas: I am Secretary of War *ad interim*, and am ordered by the president of the United States to take charge of this office.

"Stanton: I deny your authority to act and order you to repair to your room and exercise your functions as adjutant-general of the army.

"Thomas: I am Secretary of War *ad interim*, and I shall not obey your orders, but I shall stand here. I want no unpleasantness in the presence of these gentlemen.

"Stanton: You can stand there if you please, but you cannot act as Secretary of War. I am Secretary of War. I order you to repair to your office as adjutant-general.

"Thomas: I refuse to do so, and will stand here.

"Stanton: You shall not, and I order you, as your superior, back to your own office.

"Thomas: I refuse to do so and will stand here.

"Stanton: How are you to get possession? Do you intend to use force?

"Thomas: I do not care to use force, but my mind is made up as to what I shall do. I want no unpleasantness, though I shall stay here and act as Secretary of War."

They repeated the gist of that exchange, and then Thomas crossed the hall to demand to be given the department's mail. As Stanton followed after him, the absurdity of the situation struck them. Thomas reported later that he told Stanton, "The next time you have me arrested, please do not do it before I get something to eat."

At that, Stanton reverted to his usual patronizing tone with Thomas, laying his hand on the nape of Thomas's neck and running his fingers through his hair. Turning to an aide, General Edmund Schriver, Stanton said, "Schriver, you have got a bottle here. Bring it out."

Schriver's bottle turned out to be nearly empty. Stanton sent out for another. As he poured out their drinks, Stanton said, "Now this, at least, is neutral ground."

Courage restored, Thomas returned to the White House for the harder task of reporting that Stanton would not budge.

The congeniality at the War Department had not reached to the Capitol. Hundreds of spectators had to be turned away from the House galleries, avid for the next act in the constitutional drama. The *New York Times* reporter was convinced that "if any one believes what he sees with his own eyes and hears with his own ears, Mr. Johnson's term of office is likely soon to come to a miserable, mortifying and ignominious end."

One Democrat loyal to Johnson tried to buy time by calling on the House to listen to a reading of Washington's Farewell Address and then adjourn. Republicans beat back that motion.

At 2 p.m., journalists reported "a buzz of excitement" as members of Thaddeus Stevens's Reconstruction Committee filed onto the House floor. The Speaker admonished House members and the crammed galleries to show neither approval nor disapproval during the debate.

From the gas lamps glowing in the early dusk, Stevens appeared trembling and weak as he rose to speak. That morning, his committee had met at his house, where they overrode the protests of their two Democratic members and voted for impeachment.

Stevens had sent for certified copies of Johnson's order removing Stanton and directing Lorenzo Thomas to assume the duties of the secretary of war. Those orders constituted the proof the Republicans would present to support the resolution for impeachment that Stevens had crafted months before.

With his committee's report read, Stevens yielded the floor but re-served the right to offer closing arguments. New York's Senator James Brooks, the Democratic leader in the House, sounded the alarm that had been circulating throughout the city, even though the president had let it be understood that he wanted to resolve the impasse in the courts, not by force. Brooks called Stanton's refusal to resign "arrogant, imperti-nent and insolent" and claimed that 80 percent of the army were fellow Democrats who would remain loyal to Johnson. If the president were to be impeached, Brooks vowed, "We will never, never—so help me, God!—never, never submit!"

Another New York Democrat took up his theme that Americans were approaching the French Revolution and would be "baptized in blood." He claimed that "Robespierre, Marat and Danton were less vindictive" than the Radicals—"and the bloody rule of the Jacobins was mild compared to that which is sought."

The chamber echoed with accusations until 11:15 p.m., when the House adjourned until ten o'clock on Monday morning.

At the White House, Washington's birthday had begun with Gideon Welles showing up to say that his son had heard that army officers had been ordered to their barracks and might be sent to stage a coup d'etat and take Johnson prisoner.

Johnson found the threat sufficiently real to call in the commander of the Washington garrison, who assured him that no plot was under way. In the course of the day, Johnson told a friendly reporter that he was untroubled by the prospect of impeachment. At the same time, he was dispatching messengers to the Capitol for fresh news of the debate.

At one point, Johnson became enough distressed to take the ad-vice of Attorney General Henry Stanbery and nominate a man more plausible than Lorenzo Thomas as secretary of war. Johnson sent to the Senate the name of Thomas Ewing, a conservative Ohio Republican of seventy-eight. But most senators were in the House chamber, listening to the impeachment debate, and Ewing's nomination went undelivered.

As congressmen were preparing to adjourn until Monday, the presi-dent was mulling over other strategies for saving his job. At a late hour, he left a dinner for the diplomatic corps and received Sam Ward, a pro-Southern Democrat. Notorious as "king of the lobby," Ward exerted his influence on behalf of bankers and gold traders. Now he advised Johnson to begin putting together a legal defense team—half Republicans, half Democrats.

The next evening, with Congress in its Sunday recess, Johnson's caller was Perry Fuller, a Kansan who was widely understood to have made his fortune at the expense of Indian tribes. Fuller had already bribed enough clerks to control the department of Indian Affairs, but he was angling for the lucrative office of commissioner of internal revenue. Now he volunteered his services in the showdown ahead. Fuller could boast political friendships with a number of congressmen, including Kansas senator Edmund Ross.

By 4:30 p.m. on Monday, February 24, 1868, with passions spent on both sides, Thaddeus Stevens rose to deliver the coup de grace. He began his remarks in a low, unsteady voice but quickly surrendered his speech to be read by the clerk of the House. Stevens assured his listeners unconvincingly that the impeachment was not motivated by personal animus, although he added that by shirking its obligation, the Congress guaranteed that the continent would be "a nest of shrinking, cowardly slaves."

As for the president, Stevens charged that Johnson had undertaken to rule alone over "the conquered country" of "the so-called Confederate States of America." When Congress had admonished him directly, "he disregarded the warning and continued his lawless usurpation."

Stevens concluded, "If Andrew Johnson escapes with bare removal from office, if he be not fined and incarcerated in the penitentiary afterward under criminal proceedings, he may thank the weakness or the clemency of Congress, and not his own innocence."

The party-line vote on adopting the impeachment resolution was foreordained: 126 to 47. The Republicans chose Stevens and Ohio representative John A. Bingham, leader of the House conservative faction, to deliver official notice of impeachment to the Senate. The two men would also serve on a House committee of seven managers and prepare the formal charges.

Stevens was carried in an armchair to the Senate. Once there, he rose to his feet, leaning for support on Bingham on one side and his cane on the other, and delivered the House indictment in a firm voice that reached through the chamber.

When the case against Andrew Johnson was ready, the president would be tried before a frankly political jury of senators. Presiding would be another political enemy, U.S. Chief Justice Salmon P. Chase.

For Chase, his high rank represented a consolation prize. During his last turbulent year as Lincoln's secretary of the Treasury, Chase had tried to bully the president once too often and wound up losing his cabinet position.

The way Lincoln resolved their latest dispute recalled his approach when Chase had led the congressional charge against Henry Seward. This time, the immediate cause of their standoff had been fairly trivial. Chase had insisted on a promotion for a lightly qualified protégé against the opposition of powerful New Yorkers, including Seward and Thurlow Weed.

Sure that he could assert himself and force the president to back down, Chase submitted his fourth letter of resignation. But Lincoln did not forget that Chase had conspired to replace him as the 1864 Republican nominee for president. Finding limited support at the time, Chase had withdrawn his name and seemed to expect that his behavior would not disturb his relations with Lincoln.

In that, he was wrong. The president bided his time, waited for Chase's next letter of resignation, and accepted it. Lincoln explained privately that the Treasury secretary had "fallen into two bad habits. He thinks he has become indispensable to the country. He also thinks he ought to be President. He has no doubt whatsoever about that."

Nor was it unreasonable for Salmon Chase to believe that the presidency should cap a distinguished career. Born in 1808, he had graduated from Dartmouth College and gone on to study law in Washington with Attorney General William Wirt. Chase had been attracted to Wirt's daughter, Elizabeth, but he had been convinced that his uncertain prospects made it futile to court her.

He returned to Cincinnati to live with his widowed mother and her nine other children while he explored his opportunities as a lawyer. As his income rose in Ohio, Chase began to entertain thoughts of marriage again.

When he was introduced to the eligible Catherine Garniss, the young woman did not race his pulse. He found "her features large and her face plain." On her side, Catherine considered Chase presentable enough but uncouth and in need of social polishing.

In time, they looked past appearances and discovered first friendship, then love. They were married in March 1834 by the Reverend Lyman Beecher. Chase knew the clergyman's daughter, Harriet, as a fellow member of Cincinnati's literary society, the Semi-Colon Club.

Within twenty months of the wedding, Kitty Chase had given birth to a daughter and was dead from infection. During the next eleven years, Chase lost that daughter, along with his second wife, Eliza Ann Smith, and two of the three daughters she gave him. Chase soon married a third time. Sarah Belle Ludlow Chase bore two daughters, but only one of them survived during the six years before Sarah died of tuberculosis. At forty-four, Chase had been grieving half his life.

Chase turned for solace to the Episcopal Church and to Ohio politics. He became a committed abolitionist as he rose through a succession of political parties—Whig, Free Soil, Liberty, Republican. Opposing slavery did not ensure popularity. Since early in the century, Ohio had been inhospitable to blacks, even requiring them to post a five-hundred-dollar bond before they could enter the state. Allowed in, they could neither vote nor hold office.

Yet as a lawyer, Chase took up the cause of so many slaves escaping to Ohio from their owners in neighboring Kentucky that he became known as "the attorney general for runaway slaves."

Chase was elected U.S. senator from Ohio in 1849 as a Free Soiler and the state's governor six years later as a Republican. In Congress, Chase found common ground with Charles Sumner in abolition and literature, but their friendship did not prevent him from seeing a bright side to the drubbing that nearly killed Sumner: It would do more to show "the true character of the men" who supported slavery "than ten thousand speeches" would do.

During an uneventful term as a governor pressing for teacher training and prison reform, Chase expected his standing in the new Republican Party to make him a national figure. But when a political bulletin listed the leading presidential candidates for 1860, Chase was not among them. At the Baltimore convention, he got only forty votes.

Two days after Lincoln's inauguration, Chase was away from Washington when, without consulting him, the new president nominated him as secretary of the Treasury. By the time Chase returned to the capital, the Senate had already confirmed him.

After trying in vain to decline the job, Chase turned out to be a shrewd and innovative choice. Citing the wartime emergency, Chase expanded the list of tariffs to boost revenue, and he successfully assumed for the federal government those taxing powers that had been left to the states.

With support from Jay Cooke, the Philadelphia banker, Chase raised $500 million in new federal bonds. He overcame his own antipathy to paper money and, with the support of Thaddeus Stevens, oversaw the first printing of federal bills, called "greenbacks." Looking toward future campaigning, he designed them with an etching of himself. When he ordered U.S. coins stamped "In God We Trust," Chase was acknowledging a religious faith strengthened by his many bereavements.

Along the way, Chase aroused bitter hostility from the conservative Blair family. Lincoln was turning often for advice to Francis P. Blair, a Jacksonian Democrat living in Maryland, whose son and namesake, Francis, Jr., had labored to keep Missouri in the Union. A brother, Montgomery Blair, was Lincoln's postmaster general and had defended Henry Seward against Chase's attempts to oust him.

The Blairs accused Chase of corruption, but since they could not prove the charge, Lincoln maintained an adroit balance between the two camps. With the death of the eighty-seven-year-old Chief Justice Taney, Lincoln was resolved to placate Chase's Radical friends by naming him to replace Tancy, even though Montgomery Blair pressed aggressively for the position. When Chase was chosen, Frank Blair told his brother that the appointment "shakes my confidence in the president's integrity."

Lincoln had misgivings of his own. He worried that Chase might use his position on the Court to promote one last try for the presidency. If Chase would finally give up that ambition, Lincoln said, he was sure that he would be "a great judge," and he would rule dependably for the newly freed black men during the looming struggle over reconstruction. Finally, Lincoln concluded that he "would despise myself if I allowed personal differences to affect my judgment of his fitness for the office."

In the Senate, Charles Sumner called Taney's death "a victory of Liberty and the Constitution" and praised Chase's appointment. The one Radical not celebrating was Chase's daughter from his second marriage. Catherine Jane Sprague had grown up to be free-spending and socially ambitious, and when she married William Sprague, a wealthy cotton merchant and senator from Rhode Island, Kate had envisioned herself presiding over the White House one day as her widowed father's hostess. Chase's friends speculated that he had pursued the presidency so fervently in order not to disappoint her.

When a jubilant Sumner hurried to tell Chase that he had been confirmed for the Court, he was confronted by an outraged Kate. She snapped, "You too, in this business of shelving Papa?"

Despite his daughter's dismay, Chase was sworn in as Chief Justice on December 6, 1864. Now, three years later, if the Radicals prevailed, Salmon Chase might never become president. But he might oversee the deposing of one.

Benjamin Wade

CHAPTER II

BENJAMIN FRANKLIN WADE
(1868)

Now that removing Andrew Johnson from the presidency had become more than a Radical dream, national attention was turning to his replacement. At the beginning of the Fortieth Congress, the Senate had elected Benjamin Wade over William Fessenden as its president pro tempore. If Johnson were convicted, rough-edged Ben Wade, with his impressive command of profanity, would inherit the White House.

It was not his cursing that made Wade an anathema to all Democrats and many conservative Republicans; it was his lifelong fight for the rights of blacks, women, and working-class men.

Born in 1800 on a farm outside Springfield, Massachusetts, as one of eleven children, Wade received little formal education but developed an early antipathy to all formal religion. And yet, observing him later in life, his critics blamed his unyielding sense of right and wrong on a Puritan upbringing.

At twenty-one, Wade went by wagon to Ashtabula County, Ohio, to join three older brothers on a farm they had hacked out on cheap Western land. Restless and ambitious, he left within two years to work as a drover, taking herds of cattle to the lucrative market in Philadelphia. With the threat of a stampede to keep them alert, drovers were known for their coarse invective in spurring on their livestock. The young man mastered the art, which contributed to his becoming known as "Bluff" Ben Wade.

He kicked around the frontier, laboring with immigrants to build the Erie Canal but all the while envying a brother who had become a lawyer. When a retired congressman agreed to tutor Wade in the law, he threw himself into the challenge, although he found the studies daunting, and addressing any audience but cattle left him tongue-tied.

By twenty-eight, however, Wade had been confirmed by an Ohio county court as an attorney. He joined forces with an eloquent abolitionist named Joshua Giddings, and together they prospered.

Like Andrew Johnson and Andrew Jackson before him, Wade had grown up resenting being poor and exploited. Unlike them, however, Wade drew on that resentment to champion equality for every race and gender.

Wade made his first tentative steps into local government when the financial panic of 1837 forced him and his partner to seek the steady pay of public office. Wade won a seat in the state senate as a Whig; Giddings moved to the U.S. Congress.

In Columbus, Wade crusaded against Ohio's early version of the Black Codes, which denied Negroes the ballot, jury service, and entrance to public schools, but he lost his campaign to repeal them. During a debate over a local fugitive slave law, Wade's remarks were shunted to a late hour, much as Pinckney Pinchback's had been in New Orleans. But when he finally rose from his seat at 2 a.m., ineloquent Ben Wade showed that he had found his voice:

"Until the laws of nature and of nature's God are changed," Wade said, "I will never recognize the right of one man to hold his fellow man a slave. I loathe and abhor the cursed system; nor shall my tongue belie the prompting of my heart."

And if Southerners could not see the festering misery of slavery, "Then away with your hypocritical cant and twaddle about equality and democracy!"

Wade concluded, "Mr. Speaker, it is because I love and venerate my country that I wish to wipe away this, her deepest and foulest stain. To be blind to her faults would be weakness, to be indifferent to them, unpatriotic."

Democrats in the chamber did not bother to respond. When they prevailed in an 8 a.m. vote, they adjourned to a nearby restaurant with slave owners from Kentucky to celebrate with champagne. And they defeated Wade in the next election.

Through an era of political parties splitting and dissolving, Wade held to his principles. When the Whigs managed to send him back to the state legislature, he defended Oberlin College from attacks by parents who accused its abolitionist faculty of promoting treason and loose morals.

Like Charles Sumner, Wade was past forty when he surprised friends by taking a wife. Caroline Rosekrans, the daughter of a prosperous New York merchant, had been edging toward spinsterhood before a trip to Ohio introduced her to Wade—tall, heavy, swarthy, and ready for marriage—and she accepted his proposal.

Although "Cad" Wade shared her husband's passion for politics, after she had given birth to two sons, she endorsed his decision to withdraw for a few years to build up their savings. It troubled Wade that the older boy, James, showed signs of inheriting his own early diffidence. "As the world goes," he wrote to his wife, "brass is more valuable than gold."

Eleven years had passed by the time a federal Fugitive Slave Law was enacted, harsher than the version Wade had protested in Ohio. As he explained, "I cannot and will not swallow that accursed slave bill. It is a disgrace to the nation and to the age in which we live."

His former law partner, Joshua Giddings, was running for the Senate on the Free Soil ticket, hoping to join Senator Salmon Chase, who had been sent to Washington from Ohio in 1849 as an antislavery Democrat.

But a deadlock in the state legislature forced politicians to look for a compromise candidate. On the twenty-eighth ballot, they settled for uncompromising Ben Wade and elected him Ohio's junior senator. Giddings, although he had come to dislike Wade, was gracious in defeat and endorsed him. Salmon Chase, who had supported Giddings, worried that Wade might waver in his opposition to slavery.

His misgivings reached Charles Sumner, who could only hope that Wade would "be true to the inspirations of his early life." In New York, Henry Seward got encouraging word about Wade's politics but no clue that their very different temperaments would make friendship impossible.

In Washington, Wade enjoyed being a senator, even when his exposure to a wider world left him befuddled. He was ill at ease at formal dinners hosted by ambassadors he considered "generally fools or cowards." At the theater, the former cattle driver professed to be shocked to hear the language of *Othello* spoken in mixed company. "And then," Wade complained, "after the obscenity, they must all be butchered before your eyes in a manner as rude as the butcher shops in Cincinnati."

Wade's summing up: "I think Shakespeare was a coarse vulgar barbarian with very little wit."

Throughout the decade before the war, Wade was one of a handful of senators—along with Sumner, Seward, Chase, and John Hale of New Hampshire—who were committed to ending slavery. Theirs was a radical position, but they were not yet called Radicals.

In the Senate, where Wade was in daily contact with Southerners, he offended one of them to the point of being challenged to a duel. Wade turned him away by saying that as a man he was ready, but as a senator he opposed dueling.

By the time of Wade's re-election in 1856, he had concluded that trying to appease the South was futile. Despite his earlier rejection of dueling, when Preston Brooks attacked Sumner, Wade challenged all of Brooks's allies: "I am here to meet you." As a product of the frontier, Wade was believed to be an excellent shot, a reputation enhanced by rumors that he had showed up in the Senate with two pistols to display on his desk.

Before the 1860 election, Wade was mentioned as the Republican presidential nominee, a possibility that upset Salmon Chase, who wrote to Cad Wade to suggest that her husband stand aside. Chase assured her that only his concern for Wade's health prompted him to write.

When Wade did not go to the Chicago convention, the New York editor Horace Greeley was among those pleased that he had stayed away. Greeley admitted that Wade was "a good soul" but deplored his speeches and his lack of religion. "I know it isn't as bad to have no religion as to be even suspected of Catholicism," Greeley wrote, "but better to avoid the issue entirely."

On the third ballot, it was Wade's friend David Carter who broke with Chase and guaranteed the nomination for Lincoln.

When war came, Wade pushed for daring moves by the military. He admired Ben Butler's rash occupation of Baltimore and matched him in nerve when he traveled out of Washington by carriage to inspect the battlefield at Bull Run. As Wade arrived, the ranks of Union soldiers were breaking and running.

Wade pulled his carriage across the route for their retreat, grabbed up his rifle, and shouted to his companions, "Boys, we'll stop this damned runaway!"

They held off the defectors until the Second New York Regiment arrived to force the men back to battle.

The experience left Wade soured on the army's leadership and ready to support a challenge to Lincoln in the next election. He had summed up Henry Seward as "by nature a coward and a sneak" and Lincoln simply as "a fool."

But he applauded vigorously when Lincoln replaced Simon Cameron as secretary of war with Edwin Stanton, another Ohio lawyer. Sharing Stanton's frustration at George McClellan's inertia, Wade used his position as a senator to bully the officers under McClellan's command. Once, faced with the prospect of another Union retreat, Wade objected to providing an escape route. "If any of them come back," he said, "let them come back in coffins."

Wade no longer made a pretense of being convivial. Invited to a ball at the White House, he returned his invitation with a note: "Are the President and Mrs. Lincoln aware that there is a civil war? If they are not, Mr. and Mrs. Wade are, and for that reason decline to participate in feasting and dancing."

Wade may have withdrawn from the social circuit, but within the Senate his influence was rising. Colleagues had come to understand that his rhetoric might be as radical as Charles Sumner's but he could be considerably more pragmatic. After the assassination, Wade shared in the brief Radical optimism about the new president. He considered Johnson's stated approach to Southern reconstruction superior to Lincoln's 10 percent policy and was even slower than Sumner to grasp that Johnson's intentions were different from his private assurances.

Wade was home in Ohio, recovering from a bout of ill health, when newspapers reported on Johnson's flood of pardons. He read that Southern politicians were lamenting publicly that secession had failed and were openly opposing voting rights for Negroes. Wade deplored the impact of those developments on the nation but also on his party. Their Republican allies throughout the South would be restoring the rights of "those traitors we have just conquered in the field. It is nothing less than political suicide."

Instead, Wade called on Northerners to treat the South in the same spirit that the Southerners were prepared to treat their former slaves.

By now, many of his fellow senators saw Wade as their version of Thaddeus Stevens in the House. He had won praise for his chairmanship of the Committee on the Conduct of the War, and no one doubted his integrity. Looking ahead to a showdown with Johnson, Wade's unvarnished language could be an asset. Already in his midsixties, Wade threw himself into combat with the president so violently that the *New York Tribune* described even his hair as "pugnacious."

After the president vetoed the Civil Rights Act, Wade led the movement to increase the Republican majority in Congress by admitting the territory of Nebraska as a state. His stand led to a temporary break with Sumner because Nebraska's constitution barred from voting any man who was not white. Putting aside his own disapproval, Wade guided the bill successfully through the Senate. The president undid his efforts with a pocket veto, but Wade's flexibility had impressed the conservatives in his party.

He soon riled them again when he became one of nine senators to brave the prevailing sniggering and apathy to endorse allowing women to vote in the District of Columbia. Writing to Susan B. Anthony in November 1866, Wade pledged himself to equal suffrage "without any distinction on account of race, color or sex."

Speaking on that point to a crowd in Lawrence, Kansas, he invoked his wife, Cad: If he had not believed she had sense enough to vote, Wade said, he would never have married her.

That quip was less incendiary than the next vow he made—to fight

for a redistribution of wealth between workingmen and their employers. Congress "cannot quietly regard the terrible distinction which
exists between the man that labors and him that does not," Wade said.
Then, tying together the two strands of his impromptu remarks: "If
you dullheads can't see this, the women will, and they will act accord-
ingly."

But Democrats won the Ohio legislature, and the voting amendment
lost badly. Political observers agreed that Wade had guaranteed he would
never be president. Unlike Salmon Chase, Wade did not seem to care.

Yet on March 4, 1867, the Radicals lined up the votes to install him
as president pro tem of the Senate. In the absence of a vice president,
Wade was now waiting in the wings, ready to assume the presidency if
his party could proceed from impeachment to conviction.

Wade promised to make himself familiar with Senate rules "at the
earliest period" and to administer them "with promptness and impartiality."

As the date of Andrew Johnson's trial approached, Salmon Chase, like
Charles Sumner, was distracted by tumult at home. The Chief Justice
shared his house with his daughter and Senator Sprague, and Kate made
no secret of wanting to see Johnson vindicated. Reporters were watching
guests arrive at Sixth and E Street for signs that Chase was attempting
to influence the senators for acquittal.

Inside the house, William Sprague seemed torn, convinced that
Johnson should be removed but unwilling to sacrifice his political future
if the tide turned. Kate's anger with his vacillation alarmed her doting
father, who wrote to remind her that "the happiness of a wife is most
certainly secured by being submissive."

Kate was having none of that. She planned to attend the trial each
day in fashionable dresses that guaranteed her presence could not be
ignored.

At 1 p.m. on March 8, 1868, Chief Justice Chase entered the Senate chamber, and an associate judge, Samuel Nelson, administered an

oath of impartiality. Since the U.S. Constitution provided only a vague fourteen words on the subject, Chase had imposed his own rules on the Senate committee overseeing the trial, including his right to cast tie-breaking votes.

The Senate's secretary, John Forney, then read the roll as each senator swore to the same oath. Johnson's son-in-law, David Patterson of Tennessee, duly took his turn, but when Forney called Ben Wade's name, he was challenged by Thomas Hendricks, a Democrat from Indiana. Not only would Wade benefit from a guilty vote, but the Radicals were known to be trying to influence votes by circulating a list of the cabinet appointments Wade would make if he advanced to the presidency.

They had even tested the loyalty of Henry Seward by promising that if he would withdraw his support for Johnson, Wade would retain him as secretary of state. As the author of the Tenure of Office veto message, Seward responded predictably: "I'll see you damned first. The impeachment of the president is the impeachment of his cabinet."

The Senate debate over Wade's role went on for two days before Hendricks dropped his objection.

Once the Senate had approved rules for the trial, the seven managers of the House impeachment committee were admitted to the chamber. Ohio Republican John Bingham, their chairman, understood, as did Salmon Chase, that when control of their state legislature had passed lately to the Democrats, Ben Wade's future options had diminished. If Wade failed to inherit the presidency from this trial, Ohio would not be sending him back to the Senate.

News was no better elsewhere for Chase's presidential hopes. Alabama had refused to ratify a constitution acceptable to Congress. Radicals had lost the governorship of Connecticut, and Michigan had rejected the vote for Negroes. An editor in Mississippi was challenging the right of the Reconstruction Acts to establish a military tribunal.

Among the House managers, Ben Butler was pressing to take the lead. Since throwing in his lot with the Radicals, Butler's postwar years had been a time of drift and frustration. Meeting in 1865 with President Lincoln, he had presented himself as a replacement for Seward at the

State Department, and he thought the interview had gone well. Three days later, Lincoln was shot.

Butler conferred next with Andrew Johnson to recommend that Jefferson Davis be tried in a military court with Butler as the presiding general. Johnson ignored the idea. Two years had passed before Butler learned that all charges against Davis were being dropped.

After a period of idling in Massachusetts at his beachfront home near Gloucester, Butler easily won a seat in Congress. Now, being chosen to lead the impeachment trial gave him an outlet for his energies. He worked around the clock for three days on his remarks for the March 20 opening.

Butler had wanted to see Andrew Johnson forced to stand in the dock, and he complained when his fellow managers were "too weak in the knees" to oblige him. Butler did not know that only strenuous protests from Johnson's defense team had prevented the president from showing up on his own at the Capitol.

If Johnson's advisers could keep him away from the Senate, they could not keep him out of the newspapers. The night before Butler was to deliver his opening address, the president granted an interview with a favorite reporter from the *Cincinnati Commercial* to settle old scores.

When the subject turned to heavy drinking, Johnson claimed that Lorenzo Thomas had been a bit "elated" when he made statements that Johnson had not authorized. As for Grant, the president was coy at first, hinting at the general's excesses without naming him. But Johnson added that during his Swing around the Circle two years earlier, he could guarantee that Thomas "didn't drink half as much as one or two others, about whose condition nobody dares to say a word."

The reporter pressed him to acknowledge that he meant Grant, and Johnson allowed that the general had been in his office "so drunk that he couldn't stand."

When the interview was published, Johnson claimed to have been misquoted.

At the Senate, visitors getting their first look at Ben Butler were disconcerted by his appearance. He was almost entirely bald, and a cocked eye gave him a devilish aspect. But Butler's opening statement was not at all sulfurous, and he disappointed the galleries with his lawyerly restraint.

Butler's most provocative remark was reminding the senators that they did not have to consider statutes or common law since the case was without precedent. They were bound only by "the natural principles of equity and justice."

Stressing the point that Johnson had been elected president by an assassin, not by the people, Butler blamed him for a wave of murders throughout the South. He claimed that thousands of freed Negroes were being killed, along with whites who had supported the Union.

During the next five days of prosecution testimony in an unseasonably hot chamber, the number of spectators declined until by Saturday, April 4, fewer than fifty House members were on hand. Butler had become increasingly aggressive, an approach that now seemed to offend some listeners.

At one point, he praised the Constitution for offering the people a lawful way to change leaders, while in the kingdoms of Europe, a monarch who "becomes a buffoon, or a jester or a tyrant can only be displaced through revolution, bloodshed and civil war."

But under Andrew Johnson, he added, violence was rife here at home. Butler picked up from his desk a bloodstained shirt and waved it before the chamber. The shirt, he claimed, had belonged to a Northerner from Ohio who had been denounced in Mississippi as a carpetbagger and killed by Johnson supporters.

Butler's theatrics could not substitute for the absence of the trial's star witness. The impeachment managers worried that if they brought Edwin Stanton to the Capitol, Lorenzo Thomas would rush to the War Department and change the locks.

On their side, the president's team had suffered a damaging loss when Henry Stanbery took ill midway through the proceedings and had to withdraw. Stanbery had resigned from the cabinet to lead the defense, and no one enjoyed Johnson's confidence more than his former attorney general.

He was replaced by William Evarts, who had been recommended by

Henry Seward for his quick wit. Seward had hesitated to defend John-son publicly to avoid complicating his negotiations with Stevens and Butler over the Alaska appropriation. But Seward joined with Thurlow Weed in raising eleven thousand dollars in New York for the president's defense fund.

And when Seward happened to encounter William Fessenden, Seward chided him as being "too good a lawyer" not to see the weakness of the case for impeachment. Fessenden responded with an anecdote: The majority feeling in the Senate, he said, was like "that of the jury that said they couldn't find the prisoner guilty of the crime he was in-dicted for, but they would like, if they could, to convict him of 'general cussedness.'"

Evarts intended to ignore Johnson's cussedness and elevate his mo-tives beyond mere pique and a spiteful flouting of Congress. The defense intended to show that the president was protecting the powers of his office against an unconstitutional assault. By that interpretation, Johnson had removed Stanton simply to test the Tenure Act in the courts.

Defense lawyers wanted to buttress that argument by calling on General William Sherman and Gideon Welles, and Chase ruled that they could be heard. Sherman was permitted to report that Johnson had said to him about the Tenure Act, "If we can bring the case to court, it would not stand half an hour." But in party-line votes, the Radicals blocked most other supporting testimony.

Being hectored by the Radicals nettled Chase, but he hoped they were creating a backlash that would damage their cause. As the days rolled on, Evarts also took to challenging Butler on every procedural point, with no purpose but to slow the trial and underscore its absurdity.

One leading instigator of impeachment had been largely sidelined. As the certainty of conviction became murky, Charles Sumner tried to prevent Chase from casting tie-breaking votes. Sumner contended that since Chase was not a senator, he had no authority to vote on any issue. A majority ruled, however, that their chamber now constituted a court, not simply another Senate session, and Sumner's motion was defeated.

Thaddeus Stevens also was taking little part in the day-to-day pro-ceedings despite being one of the seven House managers. A Philadel-phia journalist reported that Stevens kept his eyes shut for long intervals and that his dry voice suggested "the rattle in the throat of a dying man." Then he would rouse himself to wave "majestically toward some one of his colleagues and make a scarcely audible suggestion." A *New York World* reporter likened him to a ghost haunting the courtroom. Even as mundane a gesture as Stevens ordering crackers and tea appeared to astonish the galleries.

Stevens was even sicker than anyone knew. It took immense effort for him simply to leave his rooms for the Capitol, and one morning he had not recognized his own servant.

But when his turn came on April 27, Stevens managed to rise and stand at the speaker's desk. He began his remarks by promising to be brief since experience had taught him that "nothing is as prolix as ignorance."

Soon, however, Stevens asked for permission to sit. Then, after half an hour, his voice became too weak to be heard, and he passed his pages to Ben Butler to finish reading.

Stevens had said he would discuss the charges "in no mean spirit of malignity." Yet he concluded by demanding that if the president would not execute the laws passed by Congress, "let him resign the office which was thrust upon him by a horrible convulsion and retire to his village obscurity."

On Monday, May 11, the senators met in executive session to assess their progress. Outside the chamber, reporters, groups of partisans, and even the House managers were poised to question any senator who excused himself to step outside. The president's observers included Perry Fuller with his extensive Indian contacts and Charles Woolley, a Cincinnati lawyer for a cartel called the Whiskey Ring, liquor distillers who bribed tax collectors to overlook their profits.

Thurlow Weed had met with Woolley and the New York lobbyist Sam Ward to raise money for bribing any senator who would vote for acquittal. For public consumption, Weed protested that the funds were designated only for paying the president's lawyers.

But Weed no longer dominated New York politics. His influence had been overtaken by agents from Tammany Hall, led by William

M. Tweed, and the politics of Weed's latest paper, the *New York Commercial Advertiser*, were the opposite of Ben Wade's. Weed advocated delaying the vote for Negroes and strict separation of the races. His columns satirized feminists Susan B. Anthony and Elizabeth Cady Stanton, and he advised workingmen against strikes or agitating for an eight-hour day.

The Radicals were engaged in their own campaign of inducements and intimidation, and Ben Butler was receiving discarded documents from Executive Mansion trash from Negro servants more loyal to their cause than to their employer. With no apparent irony, Butler also was offering a bribe to expose bribery. He promised a hundred thousand dollars to any member of the president's team who would reveal the payoffs.

Three Republicans had declared outright that they were voting for acquittal—James Grimes of Iowa was the first, followed by Lyman Trumbull of Illinois and, no surprise to Charles Sumner, William Fessenden. When Sumner had complained to a friend about "senators calling themselves Republicans who are Johnsonite in sentiments," he identified Fessenden as the worst offender. The Maine senator "has opposed every measure by which this country has been saved," Sumner concluded. It would have been better "had he openly joined the enemy several years ago."

Four other votes looked lost for conviction. Joseph Fowler of Tennessee had called for impeachment, but during the trial he had begun sitting with the Democrats. George Edmunds of Vermont would vote to convict only on the relatively minor first three articles of impeachment but not on the crucial eleventh. John Sherman of Ohio also declared himself against the eleventh article, and John Henderson of Missouri seemed dubious about it.

Tallying up the prospects, Radicals left the Capitol that night anxious and gloomy. They needed thirty-six votes to convict Johnson, and their most optimistic projections left them short. Throughout the night, they sought out the wavering senators to bolster their resolve, paying particular attention to Frederick Frelinghuysen of New Jersey, Waitman Willey of West Virginia, and Henry Anthony of Rhode Island.

But they did find it possible to influence some of the senators leaning toward Johnson. Henderson of Missouri said that, after all, he might be able to vote to convict on article eleven. Or he could resign from the Senate and let his governor appoint a more reliable anti-Johnson vote. Resigning might simplify life for the forty-two-year-old Henderson. He had just announced his engagement to the daughter of a leading New York Democrat.

In the end, however, he decided to stay in the Senate and vote for acquittal.

When Frelinghuysen, Anthony, and Willey were cajoled back into the anti-Johnson camp, estimates of the balloting stood at thirty-five to eighteen. One vote would determine Andrew Johnson's fate, and it might be cast by Edmund Ross, a forty-two-year-old newcomer from Kansas who was refusing to reveal his decision.

After a day and night of growing tension, the vote scheduled for May 12 was postponed. Radical Jacob Howard had fallen ill, and his allies got the vote delayed until May 16.

Both sides might have preferred a further delay, but the calendar was inexorable. In four days, the Republican National Convention would open in Chicago. To meet the deadline, Howard would have to be brought to the Capitol on a stretcher. Two days earlier, James Grimes had suffered a stroke that left him partially paralyzed, and he, too, would be carried onto the Senate floor.

With a verdict definitely set for May 16, crowds again converged on the Capitol. As Salmon Chase put on his robe, he assured himself that his conduct had been impartial. Although he still favored acquittal, Chase expected that Johnson would be forced from office, and he was braced for administering the oath of office to a man he loathed.

But how long Ben Wade would serve as president was unclear. The relevant statute could be interpreted to mean that he might serve until the normal installation of a president on the following March 4. Or only until a special election was held within the thirty-four days before the first Wednesday in December.

The initial roll call concerned the eleventh article of impeachment, the comprehensive article considered most likely to remove Johnson.

Lesser articles would be dealt with later since the vote on them was unlikely to be different. Anticipation in the chamber had been growing steadily during the roll. With every Democrat committed to acquittal, attention continued to focus on the Republican who could supply the thirty-sixth guilty vote.

The difference between the conservative Republicans in Congress and the Radicals had come down to this: Both factions wanted to uphold the powers of the legislative branch against overreaching by the chief executive. But how should a proper balance be struck?

Johnson's vetoes had deeply angered Illinois senator Lyman Trumbull, who had drafted substantial portions of the Reconstruction Acts. But like other conservatives, Trumbull worried that if Johnson were convicted, "no future president will be safe who happens to differ with a majority of the House and two thirds of the Senate."

In that case, Trumbull asked, "What has become of the checks and balances of the Constitution?"

Trumbull's misgivings more than outweighed his personal antagonism toward Johnson. But the Radicals had no doubt about the threat—real and potential—that Johnson posed for the country and for the Republican Party. When they compared his current actions against possible future harm to the Constitution, they had no doubt which was the greater danger.

For many days, the Radicals had been resigned to losing Turnbull; Fessenden of Maine; Henderson of Missouri; Joseph Fowler of Tennessee; and James Grimes of Iowa. Peter Van Winkle of West Virginia would be called upon after Ross, but the House managers held no hope for him. The verdict would depend on Edmund Ross.

Chief Justice Chase addressed him: "Mr. Senator Ross, how say you? Is the respondent, Andrew Johnson, president of the United States, guilty or not guilty of a 'high' misdemeanor, as charged in this article?"

In a Senate of bustling energy, Edmund Gibson Ross had been easy to overlook. Born so tiny that his mother could cover his face with a teacup, Edmund had grown up in the Midwest, left high school before graduating, and seemed content to marry Fanny Lathrop, a girl from his

Edmund Ross

Congregational church, and live out his life working for a newspaper in Sandusky, Ohio.

But a cholera epidemic uprooted his family and sent them to healthier surroundings in Milwaukee, and by 1859, the lure of expanding opportunities in Kansas had drawn Ross and his brother William to found the *Kansas State Record* in Topeka. An ardent abolitionist, Ross sold the paper three years later to answer President Lincoln's call for volunteers in the Union army. Major Ross survived but only after two horses had been shot out from under him in October 1864, at what became known as Missouri's Battle of Little Blue River.

When his superior officer, Colonel Samuel Crawford, was elected governor of Kansas, he sent a note to Ross asking him to come to Topeka. Senator James Lane had voted against overriding Andrew Johnson's veto of the Civil Rights Bill, and when he committed suicide soon afterward, his family blamed the outpouring of abuse from his constituents.

Crawford intended to appoint Ross to the seat. The governor told him, "We need a man with backbone in the Senate."

• • •

Up until the minute that Chief Justice Chase called his name, Ross had refused to divulge his decision, but clues abounded. Ross had endorsed Lincoln's policies toward the South and saw Johnson as carrying them out. Even though he had not declared himself, his mail from Kansas had been as vituperative as any Senator Lane had received.

How high the stakes had become was demonstrated by an offer of twenty thousand dollars to William Ross if he would reveal how his brother would vote. When Ross persisted in his silence, Ben Butler was quoted—accurately or not—as exclaiming, "There is a bushel of money! How much does the damned scoundrel want?"

One bizarre tactic to win Ross's vote was the threat to evict his nineteen-year-old protégée from her basement studio in the Capitol. A precocious sculptor, Lavinia Ream had been contracted for a full-length statue of Lincoln, and because Ross was living in a room at her parents' house, the anti-Johnson forces tried to frighten Vinnie Ream into appealing to Ross to vote for conviction. But the young woman was the sister of Perry Fuller's wife, and Fuller had sworn allegiance to Johnson before the trial began.

As another point of attack, Ben Butler forwarded to Ross a letter accusing him of "being infatuated to the point of foolishness with Miss Vinnie Ream."

The pressure got only worse on the night before the Senate vote. General Daniel Sickles, removed by Johnson and looking for revenge, waited until 4 a.m. at the Reams' house for a chance to argue for conviction. But Ross was out, pacing the streets of Washington as he weighed his decision.

For breakfast on the morning of the vote, Ross chose to go to the nearby house of Perry Fuller. Then, just before leaving for the Capitol, Ross dictated a response to a telegram from Kansas sent by D. R. Anthony, a brother of Susan B. Anthony. An editor in Leavenworth, he claimed to represent a thousand voters who were demanding conviction.

Ross replied, "I do not recognize your right to demand that I vote either for or against conviction. I have taken an oath to do impartial justice according to the Constitution and laws, and trust that I shall have the courage to vote according to the dictates of my judgment and for the highest good of the country."

On the threshold of the Senate chamber, Ross was warned that if he voted for acquittal, he would be investigated on a charge of bribery. He moved inside and waited at his desk while Chase called the roll alphabetically. When his name was reached, Ross gave his verdict so faintly that senators across the hall called for him to repeat it. The second time, firmly and audibly, Ross said, "Not guilty."

A telegram from D. R. Anthony was waiting when Ross returned to his room in the Reams' house. "Your motives were Indian contracts and greenbacks," the wire read. "Kansas repudiates you as she does all perjurers and skunks."

Men and women who had not received a ticket of admission to the galleries were waiting outside the Capitol, impatient for news. When they spotted Thaddeus Stevens being helped to his carriage, they called, "What was the verdict?"

In a recent interview with a Scottish journalist, Stevens had already revealed the fury that he had restrained during the trial. If Congress did not remove Johnson, Stevens had said, "we are damned to all eternity."

Now bitterness and frustration gave Stevens the strength to shout, "The country is going to the devil!"

President Johnson had sent an aide to Willard's Hotel near the Capitol to wire the verdict to him even before jubilant friends and appointees descended on the White House. Former Tennessee representative Thomas Nelson, a member of Johnson's defense team, rushed to Johnson's side, exclaiming, "Well, thank God, Mr. President, you are free again."

To a *New York Times* reporter, Johnson predicted correctly that the votes on the lesser charges would not change before the next balloting. "Men's consciences are not to be made harder or softer," the president said philosophically. The Senate would not "know any more about the law and the evidence on the 26th instant than they do today."

Before the Senate took up the trial again, the Republican National Convention met in Chicago and nominated Ulysses Grant on a moderate platform that did not call for universal voting rights. The disappointing acquittal had killed the prospect of Ben Wade as vice president. The convention turned instead to House Speaker Schuyler Colfax.

On May 26, the second and third articles of impeachment—limited charges about Stanton's dismissal—met the same result as the vote ten days earlier. With the Radicals routed, the Senate adjourned, acknowledging that the remaining articles would not be resurrected.

As Salmon Chase left the Capitol, he was aware that his rulings had permanently alienated his fellow Republicans. But Chase was also hearing from Democrats who saw him as their party's nominee in a few weeks. The idea had its attractions. General Grant was clearly the Republican choice, and Andrew Johnson appeared to have no support in either of the two existing parties and little prospect of starting a third one. There were dim stirrings for Johnson in the grateful South, but in the North, the *New York Sun* was describing Johnson as "insane and an opium addict."

Publicly, Chase claimed that "the subject of the presidency has become distasteful to me." His three years of serving with conservative justices on the Supreme Court seemed to have tempered his philosophy. At the Treasury, Chase had shown that he could bend his principles to meet a crisis. But to pursue the Democratic nomination would mean yielding on a lifelong commitment to equal voting rights. At home, his daughter saw no conflict. For Kate, to have Chase in the White House outweighed any scruples about universal suffrage.

As Charles Sumner surveyed the Radical wreckage around him, he knew where the blame lay: "Bribery and personal vindictiveness toward Mr. Wade have been the decisive influences."

Bribery, however, was harder to prove than Wade's unpopularity. It was widely suspected that James Legate, a postal official from Kansas, spent his days raising money to pay off those who voted for acquittal. Pliant senators were offered fifty thousand dollars—twenty-five thousand dollars down, the rest when the verdict was announced. On the

advice of Perry Fuller, Legate disguised his slush fund as money for un-
derwriting a possible presidential campaign by Salmon Chase.

Early on, the Johnson team had hoped to provide cover for Edmund
Ross in strongly Republican Kansas by enlisting a fellow senator, Samuel
Pomeroy. But Pomeroy was among the most Radical senators and no
inducement would change his vote.

For the six weeks after the vote on May 16, Ben Butler's investigative committee took testimony about possible corruption. Committee
members often did not show up, and Butler acted alone in questioning
the witnesses, who included Thurlow Weed, Perry Fuller, and Sam Ward.
Unrepentant, Weed admitted to conversations about bribery but denied
he had followed up on them.

By the time Butler issued his report, he had to admit that he could
provide no proof of corruption. Charles Woolley was arrested, however,
for contempt after he refused to testify. He was locked up with his family in the Foreign Affairs committee room and then in Vinnie Ream's
basement studio.

With no conclusive evidence produced against him, Woolley was
released. Butler did no better with Perry Fuller or Sam Ward. And although he developed promising leads against several senators, they had
all ended up voting Johnson guilty.

When an enterprising reporter for the *Cincinnati Gazette* took up
the trail, he found more evidence than Butler had, but Henry Seward
and others had taken care to insulate Johnson from any illegality on his
behalf, and public interest evaporated.

All the same, John Henderson could announce at his wedding that
President Johnson was naming his new father-in-law the commissioner
of patents. Presidential appointments also went to other men being promoted by Van Winkle of West Virginia and Fowler of Tennessee.

Along with routine patronage, Grimes of Iowa got a less tangible
reward. Before the vote, the president had promised him that if he were
acquitted, he would name General John Schofield to replace Stanton. A
thirty-seven-year-old West Point graduate, Schofield was enforcing Reconstruction laws too diligently in the South to please Johnson, but the
president kept his word.

Edmund Ross wrote to Johnson urging that he gratify Perry Fuller's long-held desire to enrich himself as commissioner of internal revenue. Within three days of receiving Ross's letter, Johnson had nominated Fuller, but public outcry over so blatant a payoff forced him to withdraw Fuller's name, wait two months, and appoint him as tax collector at the Port of New Orleans.

Because the Senate was in recess, Fuller could assume the office, travel to New Orleans, and replace sixty-five Republican employees with 150 men beholden to him. Fuller also looked after the father of Vinnie Ream, making him superintendent of a porous warehouse system that leaked tax money. By the time Fuller was arrested seven months later, he was accused of bilking the government out of $3 million.

Senator Ross put up the bond to release Fuller, who fled from New Orleans. The case against him was dropped.

During Johnson's last months in office, Ross presented him with a number of other demands for patronage. In case the president might forget his obligation, Ross did not hesitate to remind him. Pressing for one applicant, Ross wrote that the appointment was "vital" especially because of "my activities on the impeachment."

Nathan Bedford Forrest

CHAPTER 12

NATHAN BEDFORD FORREST
(1868)

FORMER REBELS THROUGHOUT THE SOUTH CELEBRATED ANDREW Johnson's acquittal by pouring into the streets to set off fireworks and jubilant gunfire. Johnson's Southern friends wrote to him of a new day dawning. They expected that the president would now be free to proclaim a general amnesty, one that would—in the words of a letter from Memphis—"relieve us of the miserable Negro rule under which we groan in despair of any improvement in affairs."

White Southerners who had supported the Union throughout the war were apprehensive. One such man, condemned by his neighbors as a scalawag, reported to an equally downhearted friend that "the eyes of the rebels sparkle like those of fiery serpents."

Half a dozen young Confederate officers would have disputed his description. Ever since their army had been disbanded, those well-born sons of Pulaski, Tennessee, had been gathering at a friend's law office to complain about the boredom of small-town life and to look for something that would replace the excitement of war.

Their town had been named for Casimir Pulaski, a European count who had come to fight in the American Revolution. The count had never visited Tennessee before he was killed in battle at the age of thirty-one, but residents of this settlement in Giles County near the Alabama border had wanted to honor his sacrifice. Its population of two thousand was almost equally white and black.

Beginning early in 1866, the restless young men, all under the age of thirty, had been making a mild splash by showing up in costume at local fairs and public events. They wore white masks, long robes, and conical hats made of white cloth molded over cardboard. To communicate in a private code, they blew on a child's whistle that each of them carried. Their first pranks were limited to hazing other eager recruits by blind-folding them and clapping on skullcaps with donkey's ears pinned to them.

As an oath, candidates were required only to recite Robert Burns's lines from "To a Louse": "O wad some power the giftie gie us/To see oursels as ithers see us."

In choosing Greek letters for their name, the members upheld an American tradition that dated from the formation of the academic hon-ors society, Phi Beta Kappa, in 1776. They settled on *kuklos*—or circle, anglicized to Ku Klux. When they added "Klan," it was for its sound— "like bones rattling together." One of the six founders pointed out that *klan* was especially apt because "we are all of Scotch-Irish descent."

As membership grew, the group moved its headquarters outside town to a house half destroyed by a cyclone. The Pulaski Klan was only one of the postwar clandestine clubs springing up throughout the South—the Constitutional Guards, the White Brotherhood, the Society of Pale Faces. To sound more impressive, Klan members invented fanci-ful names for their leaders. Their president became the Grand Cyclops, his vice president the Grand Magi. They called their meeting place the Den.

By early 1867, a night's amusement for the Klan meant riding in white hoods through Negro neighborhoods, claiming to be the risen spirits of slain Confederate soldiers. A Klan member might carry a skel-eton's arm up his sleeve, offer to shake hands with a black man, and ride away laughing as the horrified Negro was left holding the bones.

With early reports out of Tennessee about the abuse and murder of Negroes not yet linked to the Klan, the pastime could seem foolish or degrading but not ominous. Southern newspapers enjoyed printing the stories, and even some Northern editors saw only humor in the attempt to terrify superstitious darkies.

But to others familiar with Tennessee's recent history, the night-riding could already have a sinister aspect. During Andrew Johnson's term as governor, he had managed to protect those farmers in eastern Tennessee who remained loyal to the Union. But after Johnson went off to Washington, he was followed by Governor William Brownlow, a Methodist preacher from Knoxville who had once been imprisoned by the Confederacy for his Northern sympathies.

Facing re-election in 1867, Brownlow needed votes to offset the Confederate majorities in central and west Tennessee. He and his allies—with no enthusiasm except for staying in office—pushed through a state law giving Negroes the right to vote.

Captain George Judd, the Freedmen's Bureau agent in Pulaski, understood the odds against peaceful elections. He wrote that white people "do all they can to degrade the Negroes and keep them down to what they see fit to call their proper place."

Pulaski began to attract violent white men who were assaulting blacks and any known Union supporter. Sheriff Bryant Peden still listed his former slaves as his personal property and boasted of whipping them as he deemed necessary. A young white man, widely known to be guilty of murdering a Negro, went free after his white jury acquitted him.

As those crimes became too flagrant to ignore, Governor Brownlow struck back by sending in his state militia and requesting a squad of federal troops from Louisiana. Former Confederates claimed that Brownlow was plotting to manipulate the new black voters and perpetuate his power with military force.

As Republican Reconstruction policy replaced President Johnson's state governments, any lingering prankishness died away within the Klan. Members became determined to reverse the South's defeat and safeguard the white man's future.

In April 1867, men from various supremacist groups scheduled a meeting at a Nashville hotel called Maxwell House to draw up a blueprint for subverting a state government increasingly hateful to them.

Security was intense as they debated an agenda drawn up by George

W. Gordon to reorganize the Klan and redefine its purpose. Gordon came to the task with his own grievances. As a young brigadier general with the Confederacy, he had been captured and imprisoned by the Union army.

With Klan goals expanding, their titles were rapidly inflating. The South became the Empire, presided over by a Grand Wizard, elected for a term of two years and assisted by ten Genii. Individual states were Realms, each with its own Grand Dragon and eight Hydras. The organizational chart included a "Council of Yahoos," its name taken from military manuals, not from the satire of Jonathan Swift.

The official pennant featured a flying dragon with a Latin phrase that translated as "What Always, What Everywhere, What by All Is Held to be True."

The Klan's penchant for secrecy extended to designating the months of the year only by eerie adjectives—Dark, Dismal, Furious. For newspaper notices of future meetings, days of the week were indicated by colors.

The Klan creed rang with nobility. "This is an institution of Chivalry, Humanity, Mercy and Patriotism," with its object "to protect the weak, the innocent and the defenseless from the indignities, wrongs and outrages of the lawless, the violent and the brutal." The Klan promised special care for the widows and orphans of Confederate soldiers.

But prospective recruits had to answer ten questions, including whether they had ever belonged to, or endorsed, the principles of the Radical Republican Party. They were also asked whether they opposed Negro equality—both social and political—and whether they advocated restoring the vote for white Southerners.

To lead this ambitious white resistance, the members named as their first Grand Wizard a forty-six-year-old Confederate lieutenant general, Nathan Bedford Forrest, who had joined the Pale Faces the previous year.

The oldest of twelve children born to the wife of a poor Tennessee blacksmith, Forrest grew to be a burly—and hot-tempered—six-foot-two. Despite only six months in school, he became a successful cotton planter. Devoted to gambling and horse racing, Forrest invested shrewdly and turned a profit as a slave trader, although it was a business usually considered unworthy of a Southern gentleman.

By the time Forrest enlisted in the war, he was one of the South's wealthier men. He joined as a fellow private with his fifteen-year-old son, but since Forrest's extensive property would have exempted him from service, the governor quickly commissioned him as a lieutenant colonel.

Forrest set up his own regiment, advertising for five hundred men with their own horses and weapons who wanted "a chance for active service." He also offered to free forty-five of his own slaves if they would act as teamsters for his troops, and they agreed.

Forrest won a reputation for a brawling courage. Sounding like Ben Wade in the North, Forrest once sent into battle those soldiers whose normal duty was to hold the regiment's horses. "If we are whipped," Forrest told them, "we'll not need any horses."

At Shiloh in April 1862, a musket ball struck his spine, but Forrest managed to elude the Union troops who pursued him. As he recovered from surgery, Forrest prepared for his next campaign by publishing a challenge in the *Memphis Appeal*: "Come on, boys, if you want a heap of fun, and to kill some Yankees."

Promoted to brigadier general despite the primitive spelling in his dispatches, Forrest won fresh praise for his skill as a cavalry officer and for his unsparing demands on his men. Disciplining a junior officer, he once had been struck when Lieutenant A. W. Gould's pistol discharged. Lunging from his chair, Forrest stabbed Gould with the pocketknife he had been using to clean his teeth.

Gould ran off. Forrest brushed aside a doctor rushing to his side. "Get out of my way!" he shouted. "I am mortally wounded and will kill the man who shot me!"

Forrest tracked Gould to a tailor shop where his wound was being treated and shot him. When Gould died, however, it was from the stabbing. Forrest's injury turned out to be a flesh wound, and he was back on his horse twelve days later.

Forrest fought his most famous battle in the spring of 1864 and never lived down his victory. Fort Pillow sat high on a bluff overlooking the Mississippi River near Henning, Tennessee. It had been evacuated by Confederate troops two years earlier, and since then about six hundred Union troops had occupied the fort. Many were former slaves, others were white Tennesseans. Some of the white soldiers had deserted from Forrest's ranks.

While Forrest was riding around the fort to reconnoiter, Union gunfire shot his horse out from under him, and Forrest took a severe fall. But he was satisfied that his men could overwhelm the fort, and he sent a flag of truce with a demand for surrender. Forrest promised the defenders that they would be treated as prisoners of war.

The Union commander sent back a note: "General: I will not surrender."

Forrest's men scaled the earthworks, took the fort, and tried to stop the Union troops from escaping to the river. In the confusion, the defeated soldiers threw down their weapons and raised their arms in surrender. Some waved white handkerchiefs.

It was no use. A Confederate soldier wrote to his sister that "the poor deluded negroes would run up to our men, fall upon their knees and with uplifted hands scream for mercy but they were ordered to their feet and then shot down. The white men fared but little better. The fort turned out to be a great slaughter pen. Blood, human blood stood about in pools, and brains could have been gathered up in any quantity. I with several others tried to stop the butchery and at one time had partially succeeded but Gen. Forrest ordered them shot down like dogs, and the carnage continued."

Even though other officers would testify that Forrest had, in fact, ordered the killing to stop, he could not shake off the accusations against him. Charles Fitch, a Union doctor from Iowa, was among those who absolved Forrest of instigating the bloodbath. But their exchange offered an insight into the general's emotions after the battle.

When Fitch requested the protection that was due a prisoner, Forrest said, "You are surgeon of a damn Nigger regiment."

Fitch replied, "No, I am not."

"You are a damn Tennessee Yankee, then."

Fitch told him he was from Iowa.

"Well, what the hell are you down here for?" Forrest demanded. "I have a great mind to have you killed for being down here. If the Northwest had stayed home, the war would have been over long ago."

Forrest turned Fitch over to a soldier, but with instructions that he was not to be harmed.

In his official report to Jefferson Davis, Forrest exaggerated Union losses and underestimated his own. He made no mention of a massacre but did add that he hoped that his troops' overpowering of the black recruits "will demonstrate to the Northern people that negro soldiers cannot cope with the Southerners."

In its account of the battle, the *Chicago Tribune* described Forrest as "tall, gaunt and sallow-visaged, with a big nose, deep-set black, snaky eyes." The paper reminded readers that the general and his brothers had been slave traders but that only Nathan Forrest with his "cowardly butchery" had run up "such a record of infamy." According to the *Tribune*, bribery had won Forrest his high rank in "the women whipping, baby-stealing rebel Confederacy."

When the scandal reached the White House, Lincoln's cabinet agreed not to take any "extreme" action in the case. With the impending 1864 election in doubt, Republicans preferred not to launch an investigation that might disturb undecided voters.

General Forrest went on to victory at the battle of Brice's Crossroads in June 1864. A month later, he was defeated by General William Sherman's men in the Battle of Tupelo. Although shot in the foot, Forrest was able to lead his surviving men in retreat.

Later that same year, Forrest and two brothers were among eighty residents of Memphis indicted for treason against the United States. Forrest posted a ten-thousand-dollar bond, and the quixotic indictment was never pursued.

At the war's end, Forrest won praise for the tenor of his farewell address to his troops. He acknowledged that civil war engendered "feelings of animosity, hatred and revenge." But, he added, "It is our duty to divest ourselves of all such feelings."

When Forrest returned to Memphis, he found that without slave labor, his plantations could not turn a profit. As he cast about for ways to restore his fortune, Forrest was often called upon to defend his role in the massacre at Fort Pillow. His reputation worked against him when he returned to court in 1866, charged with killing a former slave working on his property.

Forrest's defense claimed that the victim, Charles Edwards, had been a brute who regularly whipped his wife; Edwards's wife denied that he had ever abused her. Testimony developed that Forrest had become outraged at Edwards's "impudence" and struck him down with an axe.

Former slaves on Forrest's plantation built fires around its perimeters to prevent him from escaping before the sheriff could arrive. When a deputy showed up, he assured the Negroes that justice would be done. But the judge hearing the case instructed the all-white jury that if Forrest acted in self-defense, he should be acquitted, and that was their verdict.

On November 25, 1866, Forrest wrote directly to Andrew Johnson asking that he be pardoned for his role in secession. Forrest acknowledged that "I am at this moment regarded in large communities in the North with abhorrence, as a detestable monster, ruthless and swift to take life, and guilty of unpardonable crimes in connection with the capture of Fort Pillow on the 12th of April, 1864."

When Johnson approved his pardon, a survivor of the battle protested futilely to Ben Wade in the Senate that "a foul fiend in human shape" like Forrest had received a speedy pardon rather than "the punishment which his atrocious crimes richly deserved."

Joining the Pale Faces, Forrest described them as being much like the Masons in their dedication to preserving society's highest values. Although Forrest would become skittish about his membership in the Klan, witnesses claimed that during the 1867 conference, he became Grand Wizard in Room 10 at the Maxwell House.

The Klan was depending upon a tactic called night-riding, although an early example had occurred on a bright Christmas morning in the town of Columbia, north of Pulaski, in 1867. Police had told a group of parading Negroes to muffle their drums. When they protested, two Klansmen in red robes rode off amid rumors that they were rounding up men to enforce the order and that three hundred Klansmen would soon be on their way.

The Negroes prudently ended their parade. The local newspaper hailed the incident as proof that white men would not permit Negro disobedience.

By the following spring, the Klan was running notices in the *Pulaski Citizen*, defending the reputation of an organization still unknown to most of the nation. One early announcement carried a hint of threats to come: "This is no joke either. This is cold, hard, earnest; time will fully develop the objects of the Kuklux Klan!" Until then, members requested that the public "please be patient."

The wait was brief. On June 5, 1868, seventy-five Klansmen paraded through Pulaski. A *Citizen* reporter wrote that the leader was "gorgeously caparisoned" and "his toot, toot, toot on a very graveyard-ish sounding instrument seemed to be perfectly understood by every ku kluxer."

That flamboyant pageantry was attracting recruits from far beyond Pulaski. Dens were being set up in small towns throughout the piedmont, although less often in the larger cities. By the time the dens came together for a secret convention in Nashville, their leaders were bracing for political war against the congressional Republicans and the state governments of men who had opposed secession.

Officials of the Democratic Party remained hostile to Negroes voting. If it were inevitable, however, they hoped the emancipated slaves would follow the lead of their former owners. In South Carolina, where Negroes constituted a majority of the state's population, Democrats refashioned themselves into the Union Reform Party and ran black candidates for local offices.

But when black voters stayed loyal to the Republicans who had fought for their freedom, the former Confederates turned to the Klan. Persuasion had failed. Intimidation would not.

The effect in Pulaski's home county was immediate. Captain Judd of the Freedmen's Bureau no longer believed assurances from "the best citizens" that the Klan had been established "by the young men merely for fun."

"Unless something is done immediately by the governor to protect the colored citizens of the county," Judd wrote, "the cities will be flooded by poor, helpless creatures who will have to be supported by the State or United States government."

The Klan's defenders pointed to the Union League—sometimes called the Loyal League—a Northern patriotic group that had come South with the victorious army. It, too, was a secret society, but speakers at its rallies and barbecues openly defended the Republicans and courted black voters for their party. Although there were no signs that the league promoted violence, Klan members claimed to find its secrecy threatening, and both groups began to carry guns to their meetings. Captain Judd was accused of running the League, a charge that succeeded in evicting his family from their boardinghouse.

Advertisements in local newspapers were becoming a potent Klan recruiting tool. Typical was one headed "KKK":

"Speak in whispers and we hear you. . . . Hovering over your bed we gather your sleeping thoughts while our daggers are at your throats. . . . Unholy blacks, cursed of God, take warning and fly."

By the end of 1868, the Klan controlled several counties in mid-Tennessee. Republicans who had expected Klan activity to abate after that year's elections found instead that it was becoming more random and more brutal.

In later testimony, General Forrest estimated that the Klan had grown to fifty thousand in Tennessee, "and I believe the organization is stronger in other states." In North Carolina, the Klan was reaching its peak of thirty to forty thousand members and the total throughout the South was estimated at five hundred thousand.

A Methodist elder on a fact-finding trip through northern Alabama was invited to stay overnight with the state's leading families, and everywhere he heard the same refrain: "That they would never submit, that they would never yield; they had lost their property, their reputations; and last and worst of all, their slaves were made their equals, or were likely to be, and perhaps their superiors, to rule over them."

They were counting on the Klan to multiply throughout the South and "rid them of this terrible calamity."

In Washington, President Johnson was more concerned with the 1868 national elections than with the hooded terrorists in his home state. He believed that the people would ultimately appreciate his courage and took heart in early June from a victory by Oregon Democrats in their state elections.

In his few remaining months, the president waited for the Democrats to turn to him as their nominee. But Johnson had left too many scars on the party—by running with Lincoln as a Republican, by appealing at first to moderates and by not staffing his government exclusively with Democratic appointees. And he was pitted for the nomination not only against stalwart party loyalists but against Salmon Chase.

At the Democratic convention in July, delegates repaid any obligation to Johnson with flowery tributes—"entitled to the gratitude of the whole American people"—but on the first vote he placed only second and by the twenty-second ballot, far lower. Johnson had been braced for failure: "I have experienced ingratitude so often," he said, "that any result will not surprise me."

Horatio Seymour, a former governor of New York, was promoting Salmon Chase, abetted by Chase's daughter Kate and by the son of former president Martin Van Buren. Their strategy had been to avoid entering Chase's name too early in the balloting, but as they hesitated, their moment slipped away.

Realistic about the long odds, Chase had been concerned about damage to his reputation as Chief Justice. "Have a care," he instructed his daughter. "Don't do or say anything which may not be proclaimed from the housetops."

By the time the Democrats turned to Governor Seymour, Andrew Johnson's delegate count had sunk to four men from Tennessee. Despite his claim that he would not be disappointed, Johnson threatened to sit out the election until Sam Ward brokered a truce with Seymour.

As he filled out his term, Johnson not only paid off his political debts to men like Ross of Kansas, but he kept his word to the other conservative Republicans that he would no longer try to subvert the Reconstruction Acts or interfere with the army's chain of command. In William Fessenden's view, "Andy has behaved very well so far."

Although Johnson was not yet fully informed about the Klan, he had become more forthright about his views on race. In his final message to Congress, he wrote that even if a state constitution gave Negroes the right to vote, "it is well-known that a large portion of the electorate in all the States, if not a large majority of all of them, do not believe in or accept the political equality of Indians, Mongolians, or Negroes with the race to which they belong."

Over Johnson's veto, Congress passed an omnibus bill to admit back into the Union all Southern states except Virginia, Texas, and Missouri; Arkansas had already qualified with its new constitution. Upon the admission of those states, the Fourteenth Amendment was ratified on June 25, 1868. Johnson balked for three weeks but finally had no choice but to proclaim the legality of a measure he detested.

The president could not be dissuaded, though, from pressing for constitutional amendments to alter the terms of federal offices. Over the advice of Henry Seward and much of his cabinet, Johnson recommended one six-year term for the president and the elimination of the electoral college. He proposed direct elections for the Senate, rather than having senators chosen by their state legislatures, and he called for U.S. Supreme Court justices to be elected for one term of twelve years.

As those measures were being defeated, Johnson lost his most implacable enemy. Thaddeus Stevens died on August 11, 1868, ten weeks after the president's acquittal.

Much as Stevens had hated Johnson, he reserved a measure of scorn for the men who were drafting the Republican platform in Chicago. Stevens favored a new constitutional amendment—the Fifteenth—that would assure every American male the right to vote. To Stevens, that safeguard was the only way "you and I and every man can protect himself against injustice and inhumanity."

The convention backed away from his challenge. The Republican platform endorsed suffrage for black men in the former Confederate states but allowed Northern and border states to set their own policies.

Stevens called that evasion "tame and cowardly," but he predicted that the Democrats "from instinct and long practice will make a more villainous platform." He felt vindicated when the Democratic platform denounced "Negro supremacy" and avoided the issue of voting altogether.

Stevens recognized a disturbing trend in the recent Republican congressional victories around the country. Of the forty-four men elected from the newly enfranchised Southern states, twenty-six were Northerners—the hated Carpetbaggers. In the North, Stevens's home state of Pennsylvania had voted down Negro suffrage. Despite its Republican majority, Michigan had done the same.

And yet, Stevens was confident that a Fifteenth Amendment would eventually pass the Congress. With little enthusiasm he was also predicting the election of Ulysses Grant over Democrat Horatio Seymour, who had called the Emancipation Proclamation "a proposal for the butchery of women and children." Seymour's running mate, the abrasive Frank Blair, Jr., was promising to nullify the Reconstruction Acts.

In his last weeks, Stevens fretted that the Democrats might win and then refight the late war. "My life has been a failure," Stevens complained to a friend. "I see little hope for the Republic."

Stevens turned away the clergymen who descended on him hoping for a deathbed conversion. But for a spiritist who claimed to have made contact with Henry Clay, Daniel Webster, and Stephen Douglas, Stevens offered a message: "Especially present my compliments to Douglas," he said, "and tell him I think he was the greatest political humbug on the face of the Earth."

Stevens died at a charity hospital for colored people that he had supported. On his last night, Thaddeus Stevens—nephew and namesake—gave two nuns permission to baptize his uncle. Ten minutes afterward, Stevens died peacefully.

Stevens's will left five hundred dollars a year for life to Lydia Smith. Thaddeus would get most of his estate, but only if he gave up drinking. If that proved impossible, proceeds from the estate were to endow an orphanage that would be open to children of all races.

Stevens's body lay in state in the Capitol rotunda, watched over by a black honor guard from Massachusetts. As a final note of respect, his local Republican Party nominated Stevens for Congress one last time, and he was elected overwhelmingly.

The memory of Stevens did not die with his burial. New York newspapers acknowledged the sweep of his influence, but the *Times*, which had opposed him on Reconstruction, called him "the Evil Genius of the Republican Party," and the editor of the *Herald*, while granting that his friends had found Stevens genial and courteous in private, concluded equivocally, "Publicly, he was an evil, but a necessary evil."

Despite his lifetime of disbelief, it was Thaddeus Stevens's fate to be reincarnated. In 1905, an evangelist and writer named Thomas Dixon, Jr., dedicated his new novel, *The Clansman,* to the memory of "a Scotch-Irish leader of the South, my uncle, Colonel Leroy McAtee, Grand Titan of the Ku Klux Klan."

Born in North Carolina during the war's last year, Dixon drew upon real-life figures for his novel but changed some names; Thaddeus Stevens became Austin Stoneman. Otherwise, Dixon denied "taking liberty with any essential historical fact."

Dixon gave Stoneman a heavy brown wig too small for his enormous forehead and a left leg that "ended in a mere bunch of flesh, resembling more closely an elephant's hoof than the foot of a man."

Dixon said that his purpose was to celebrate the way the Klan had gone forth "against overwhelming odds, daring exile, imprisonment, and a felon's death, and saved the life of a people." His story, Dixon concluded, "forms one of the most dramatic chapters in the history of the Aryan race."

In Dixon's telling, Abraham Lincoln becomes heroic for reasons his Northern admirers might not have recognized. Not only is he saintly in his forgiveness for the conquered South, Lincoln is an outspoken opponent of white men being forced to live among their former slaves.

Dixon's Lincoln assures Stoneman that there can be no room in America for two distinct races of white and black. "We must assimilate or expel," the president says, and his choice is to return the former slaves to Africa: "I can conceive of no greater calamity than the assimilation of the Negro into our social and political life as our equal."

To that, Stoneman responds by "snapping his great jaws together and pursing his lips with contempt" as he says, "Words have no power to express my contempt for such twaddle!"

Dixon's novel, appearing at a time of heightened racial tensions, sold well throughout the South. But Thaddeus Stevens, as Austin Stoneman, would reach even greater posthumous fame in 1915, when D. W. Griffith, a forty-year-old film director, bought Dixon's novel, cast white actors in blackface as brutal and menacing Negroes, and called the result *The Birth of a Nation*.

Ulysses S. Grant

CHAPTER 13

ULYSSES S. GRANT (1869)

Julia Grant had been relieved when Andrew Johnson escaped conviction in the Senate. She sympathized with those who thought Johnson's light punishment of the Southern states seemed to condone their rebellion, but she also felt that his trial "savored of per secution" and set "a dangerous precedent." By that time, Mrs. Grant realized that her husband would very likely be the next president, and she did not want him hamstrung by Congress or defied by a cabinet secretary like Edwin Stanton.

Nor did she share Grant's ambivalence about the presidency. She had gloried in being the wife of the general-in-chief, alert to any slights or snubs and able to avenge them. It had given her satisfaction to decline somewhat curtly the White House invitation to attend the theater on the night Lincoln was shot.

Now, as the Republicans departed for their nominating convention in Chicago, she asked Grant directly, "Ulys, do you want to be president?" His answer was fatalistic. "No, but I do not see that I have anything to say about it. The convention is about to assemble, and from all I hear, they will nominate me. And I suppose if I am nominated, I will be elected."

Grant knew the job. With no feigned modesty, he thought he could handle it better than anyone else, and he was sure that Southerners would see him as a fair-minded president who enforced the law without prejudice against them.

Grant also understood that his wife, devoted but willful, required a combination of tact and firmness and might be unnerved by the full glare of a presidential campaign. William Sherman, Grant's friend and fellow general, tried to warn her:

"Mrs. Grant, you must now be prepared to have your husband's character thoroughly sifted."

Julia Grant responded with fervent praise for her husband that made Sherman smile. "Oh, my dear lady," he said, "it is not what he has done, but what they will say he has done, and they will prove, too, that Grant is a very bad man indeed. The fact is, you will be astonished to find what a bad man you have for a husband."

Partisan abuse had been familiar to Grant as he was growing up along the Ohio River. His father, Jesse, was working as a tanner on April 27, 1822, when his first child—Hiram Ulysses Grant—was born in a one-room shack.

But Jesse Grant's shrewd business sense—which was not to be his son's inheritance—had led to his becoming a man of substantial property who could move his wife, Hiram, and their next five children to a two-story brick house in Georgetown, Ohio.

A loud and ornery voice at town meetings, Grant would proclaim that he had left Kentucky because he "would not live where there were slaves and would not own them." That led to his being reviled by neighbors who depended on slave labor for their lucrative tobacco trade.

Addicted to reading, Jesse Grant consumed the local newspapers and the books that came his way. He regretted his own lack of formal education, and he was determined to avoid that fate for his children.

Since there was no public school, Grant paid for Hiram at subscription schools. Between terms, he put the boy to work on the family farm, where he enjoyed tending horses as much as he detested the tanning business.

His father intended Hiram to study at West Point, where he could receive a free education as an engineer, but his contentious views had alienated the local congressman. Rather than approach him, Jesse Grant wrote to Ohio senator Thomas Morris and got the appointment.

Young Grant had never considered defying his father, but military life held no attraction. Getting ready to leave for New York, he learned that Congress was debating whether to abolish West Point and read the papers eagerly, hoping he would be spared enrolling.

Registration day arrived, however, and a clerk at the academy entered Hiram's name as "Ulysses S"—the "S" for Simpson, his mother's side of the family. The new cadet adopted the error for life.

He was determined not to stay in the army past his eight-year commitment. The only allure of West Point had been the chance it gave him to see the country's two great cities—Philadelphia and New York—and perhaps one day to teach mathematics at a college. In a letter to a cousin, Grant showed an early concern for security: "If a man graduates here, he is safe fer life, let him go where he will."

During his years at West Point, Grant proved to be a mediocre student but superb on horseback. His good friend James "Pete" Longstreet described him as "the most daring horseman at the Academy."

Somewhat shy, Grant could not match the swagger of a brawny Georgian like Longstreet. He disdained the popular practice of dueling, and he was seldom moved to swear. Longstreet considered that Grant's marked reluctance to boast was due to a "girlish modesty," but he appreciated Grant for a "noble, generous heart, a loveable character, and sense of honor" that Longstreet found "perfect."

At graduation in 1843, Grant ranked twenty-first in a class of thirty-nine. He was six inches taller than when he entered West Point, but a racking cough had held his weight to the same 117 pounds. Given a family history of consumption, Ulysses considered himself a likely victim one day.

Posted to the Fourth Infantry in St. Louis, the twenty-one-year-old second lieutenant met Pete Longstreet's cousin, seventeen-year-old Julia

Dent. A merchant's daughter pampered by four indulgent brothers and a host of male slaves she called her "uncles," Julia was plain-featured, and a childhood ailment had left her eyes with a slight squint. But she had carried herself like a belle until she became one.

Julia considered Grant dashing in his uniform and encouraged his daily visits to go horseback riding together. When Grant proposed, however, Julia had just turned eighteen and replied that being engaged would be charming, but marriage would have to wait. Then war was declared with Mexico, and Lieutenant Grant set off for duty as a quartermaster.

Serving under fire with both Zachary Taylor and Winfield Scott, Grant could compare their leadership. He preferred Taylor's style; he said little but wrote out his plans with precision and economy. Scott, as Grant noted later, was not averse to speaking of himself in the third person, which meant he "could praise himself without the least embarrassment."

Grant came to believe that a great advantage to his months in Mexico had been his chance to evaluate many freshly commissioned officers from West Point, as well as the older graduates he would meet in battle again as Confederates. He had learned early that those future rebels, particularly Robert E. Lee, did not possess superhuman powers.

As for the Mexican war itself, Grant considered it "one of the most unjust ever waged by a stronger nation against a weaker nation" and chided himself for not having "the moral courage to resign" his commission. America, he concluded, had been motivated solely by a desire for territory, and he blamed the war for contributing to the aggressive style among Southern politicians that would sweep them toward secession.

By the time General Antonio López de Santa Anna was defeated, the men of Grant's regiment had suffered heavy losses during their sixteen months of battle, and they entered Mexico City in a somber mood. Brevetted twice for bravery, Grant had won his first promotion by replacing a first lieutenant picked off by a Mexican sniper.

As he waited to be sent home, Grant became curious about Mexico's national sport and bought a fifty-cent ticket for a bullfight. He was sickened by what he saw. He could not understand, he said, "how human beings could enjoy the suffering of beasts, and often of men."

On his return to the United States, Grant at last could marry Julia Dent, with Pete Longstreet as his best man. As the bride observed, "I had had four years to prepare for this event." The newlyweds went off to settle in Sackets Harbor, New York, near a battlefield from the War of 1812.

In the peacetime army, Grant was promoted to captain. He was popular with his men. And yet he was increasingly bored by military routine. Assigned next to Detroit and then—without his wife and their two children—to Humboldt Bay in California, the young father foresaw a bleak and lonely future.

To make extra money, Grant invested in a range of schemes—shipping a hundred tons of ice to San Francisco, raising hogs, running a boarding-house. But foul weather thwarted some of his plans, and an absconding partner scuttled another. Given his tendency to lend money freely, Grant began to run up debts and to escape from his worries in alcohol.

According to a story circulating at his post, when Grant did not show up for duty one day, he was given the choice of a court-martial or resigning his commission.

A civilian again, Grant retreated to a farm near St. Louis that Julia had inherited. With no money for livestock, he supported their family by chopping wood and carting it to the city. Julia's father declined to lend him money but offered to put his slaves to work on Grant's property. Grant worked side by side with them and also hired free black laborers at better than the going wage.

When Julia's father gave him a slave outright, Grant set him free. Another slave remembered that Grant "always said that he wanted to give his wife's slaves their freedom as soon as he could."

· · ·

In the spring of 1858, Grant managed at last to plant a full crop—potatoes, corn, wheat. On July 1, a killing freeze destroyed most of it.

At that low point, hearty Pete Longstreet passed through town. After an awkward reunion, they played a few nostalgic hands of brag, their favorite card game.

As Longstreet was leaving, Grant insisted on pressing a five-dollar gold piece into his hand. He had remembered that he had borrowed the money fifteen years before.

Attempting to refuse, Longstreet protested tactlessly that Grant clearly needed the money more than he did.

"You must take it," Grant said. "I cannot live with anything in my possession which is not mine."

Longstreet saw that continuing to refuse would only mortify Grant further. He pocketed the coin, and they shook hands. When they met again, it would be to try to kill each other.

The harsh demands of scratching out a living culminated in Grant's collapse from fever and ague. He gave up farming and entered the real estate business with one of his wife's cousins.

Julia Grant understood her husband's weakness for alcohol. He sometimes went for months entirely sober, then got drunk on less liquor than most men. A few drinks might set off a binge. With Julia at his side, Grant could usually control the impulse, but rumors about his excesses would persist throughout his life.

As a distraction, Grant turned to politics. Since the Whig Party of his boyhood had disappeared, Grant became a Know Nothing for one week before its secrecy and hostility to foreigners caused him to drop out. As for the antislavery movement, even in the North and West Grant had met few out-and-out abolitionists.

In 1856, Grant voted for the first time in his life. Worried that a Republican victory would mean secession by the South, he cast his ballot for James Buchanan and the Democrats. He reasoned that if they won, the South would have no excuse to rebel and Southern extremists would calm down during the four years before the next presidential election.

They were sure to "think before they took the awful leap which they had so vehemently threatened."

"But," Grant concluded, "I was mistaken."

In May 1860, Ulysses Grant, now the father of four, moved his family to Galena, Illinois, to work in his family's leather goods store for six hundred dollars a year. The younger men on staff showed more respect for his age and experience than Grant felt himself. He was unhappy as a billing clerk and more miserable waiting on customers from behind the counter.

Doomed to live out his days in his father's shadow, Grant had substituted cheap cigars for the drinking that had threatened to destroy him. Indulging in that small pleasure, he watched as a once-promising future went up in smoke.

Then rescue came. Within a year, the Confederate governor of South Carolina ordered an attack against the Union camp at Fort Sumter. The town of Galena responded with a town meeting and nominated its one West Point graduate to round up volunteers for the war that was sure to come.

Before the month was out, Grant had borrowed money to buy a spirited horse and was leading volunteers to the station for the train to Springfield. The recruits were togged out in new uniforms. Grant wore his shabby civilian clothes and carried his own carpetbag.

In August, Grant got a promotion before his first battle. President Lincoln recognized his prior service by commissioning him as a brigadier general of volunteers, made retroactive to May 17, 1861.

For the next three years, Grant suffered the randomness of war. A horse was shot from under him in Missouri when he led an unauthorized raid during the Battle of Belmont in November 1861. The rebels saw the outcome as a Confederate victory, but Grant's men felt they had performed well, and they respected their commander's physical courage.

Three months later, Grant won a national reputation during a major Union victory at Fort Donelson, Tennessee, by sending an ultimatum to the beleaguered enemy: "No terms except immediate and unconditional surrender can be accepted." A popular joke turned his initials into "Unconditional Surrender" Grant.

Three of the ranking Confederate generals at the fort agreed to surrender, but Nathan Forrest challenged their decision. He had not come out to fight in order to surrender, Forrest said, and after dark he led five hundred of his men to safety.

Grant knew that he had been lucky in his opposition. From observing Gideon Pillow in Mexico, Grant considered him especially inept. When he learned that Pillow, now a Confederate general, had also slipped away on a small boat, Grant said he was happy to see him go. Pillow would be more useful to the North by fighting for the rebels than he would have been as a prisoner of war.

The following year, Grant learned that he was less surefooted politically than on the battlefield.

By December 1862, he had become frustrated by persistent smuggling and speculation in cotton supplies within his command. He understood that President Lincoln wanted to revive trade in captured areas as a way to win back Southern loyalty. But as a result, merchants were swearing allegiance to the Union, then using their profits to keep the Confederate army from collapse.

Drawing on random examples and hearsay, Grant issued a blunt decree:

"The Jews, as a class violating every regulation of trade established by the Treasury Department and also department orders, are hereby expelled from the department within twenty-four hours from the receipt of this order."

Grant's General Order No. 11 covered the territory from Cairo, Illinois, south to northern Mississippi and from the Mississippi River to the Tennessee River. Grant warned that any Jews returning to the area would be arrested and jailed, then expelled as prisoners.

Grant did not want to listen to appeals. He forbade the issuing of permits to "these people" to visit headquarters for personal applications.

To underscore his determination, Grant had wired to a subordinate: "Refuse all permits to come south of Jackson for the present. The Israelites especially should be kept out."

In protesting their banishment, Jews got assistance from an unexpected quarter. Hours after Grant issued his decree, Nathan Forrest swept down on Grant's rear supply area north of Jackson, Tennessee, cutting telegraph lines and tearing up fifty miles of Mobile & Ohio railroad track.

The attack surprised Grant, and during Forrest's raid his men outfought the far larger Union forces and left behind twenty-five hundred casualties.

By the time Grant's telegram could reach Paducah, Kentucky, one of the Jews marked for expulsion had already ridden to Washington, secured an interview with the president, and informed him of Grant's decree. At once, Lincoln directed General Henry Halleck to rescind it.

Since 1840, the number of Jews in the United States had risen from about 15,000 to 150,000. Now other alarmed Jewish leaders sought their own meeting with Lincoln for guarantees that they were not regarded as aliens.

Lincoln assured them that he accepted "no distinction between Jews and Gentiles." Newspapers denounced Grant's order, Democratic Party leaders in Congress tried unsuccessfully to censure him, and lingering unease persisted among Jews that with the end of slavery they might become the next scapegoat in a divided nation.

Among Grant's fellow officers, his battlefield success had made him a target of envy. At headquarters, General Halleck revived accusations of drunkenness and wrote that Grant had "resumed his former bad habits."

Other charges reached Secretary of War Stanton anonymously—that Grant had vomited during a truce negotiation with the Confederates; that once he had got so drunk that "he had to go upstairs on all fours."

Enough officers came to Grant's defense that Lincoln ordered Halleck either to investigate formally or end the whispering campaign. Halleck backed down, and Grant got his second star. But he neither forgot nor forgave his public humiliation when he felt he had deserved only praise. "I want to whip these rebels once more," Grant wrote to his wife, "and see what all will be said then."

He got more than he wished for—first at Shiloh, then during a siege at Vicksburg, and in March 1864, a third star and appointment as general-in-chief of all U.S. armies.

A month later, on Grant's forty-second birthday, he launched a spring offensive that he expected to end the war. He would fight Lee on the field called the Wilderness, south of the Rapidan River on the road to Fredericksburg, Virginia.

Casualties during the first day were high and, for Grant, intensely personal. Hearing that Brigadier General Alexander Hays, a friend from their cadet days, had been shot in the head, Grant sat on the ground whittling at pine sticks until he could compose himself enough to offer a halting eulogy.

Grant would learn later that the grinding battle had also severely wounded Pete Longstreet, who took a bullet in the neck. That loss forced Robert E. Lee to take over his army's right flank, but he could not prevail against the Union forces.

By the battle's end, the fighting had set new records for ferocity and lives lost. Close to eighteen thousand Union men had been killed, wounded, captured, or missing. Lee's army had suffered equal losses. And General Grant had set a record of his own; in a single day, he had smoked twenty of his pungent cigars.

Soon afterward at Spotsylvania, Lee temporarily blocked Grant, who vowed to frame the terms for their next engagement. "I propose to fight it out on this line," he said, "if it takes all summer."

The result for Grant was a final reversal. At the brutal Battle of Cold Harbor on June 3, 1864, he lost seven thousand Union men in one hour of fighting; Lee lost fifteen hundred. That evening, Grant told his staff, "I regret this assault more than any I have ever ordered."

But Grant had resources to draw upon that Lee did not. As he disengaged his troops, he could pursue his strategy of moving his Army of the Potomac into position and defeating the Confederates at Richmond.

Ten months later, Grant accepted Lee's surrender at Appomattox, and Congress made him the first four-star general in United States history.

Victory guaranteed that the Republicans would nominate Grant unanimously on the first ballot to replace Andrew Johnson. Despite recent evidence that the selection of a vice president was a crucial one, the convention settled on amiable Schuyler Colfax, the Indiana congressman who had once lost Alice Hooper to Charles Sumner.

When news of his nomination reached Washington, Grant was called upon to make his first political speech. He fell back on a standard disclaimer: "Gentlemen," Grant told a rally on Pennsylvania Avenue, "being entirely unaccustomed to public speaking and without the desire to cultivate the power, it is impossible for me to find appropriate language to thank you for the demonstration."

His listeners understood that the next president would be expected to bind up the nation's wounds—not only reconciling North and South but addressing the economic and philosophical divisions that separated factions in both parties, including East Coast merchants from Midwest farmers.

In Grant, the nation seemed poised to hail a latter-day George Washington, and the last sentence of his letter formally accepting the Republican nomination concluded with four words his countrymen longed to hear: "Let us have peace."

Grant did not need to campaign. The *New York Times* reported that when he went to his brother's house in Galena, he did allow a group of tanners to serenade him. And setting off as commanding general to inspect forts on the Western frontier, he found that his stops along the route took on the trappings of a campaign tour. For company, he had invited Philip Sheridan and William Sherman, who stood by while Grant waved to crowds at each train station but made no speeches.

Across the country, Republican surrogates waged the attack in his place. They seized upon Horatio Seymour's response as governor to the

New York City draft riots when he had addressed the rioters as "my friends," and they made certain that Western voters knew about Seymour's close ties to the financiers of Wall Street.

Back home in Galena, Grant turned over his military duties to his chief of staff and told his personal secretary, a former reporter named Adam Badeau, to use his own discretion for any other decisions. Grant wanted no correspondence forwarded unless it absolutely required his personal attention.

But Badeau could not cope with an outcry that erupted over Grant's General Order No. 11. The orders had been issued almost six years earlier, but now that he seemed certain to become president, Jewish communities across the country were sending Grant hundreds of anxious letters.

To reassure them, Grant allowed prominent Jewish leaders to see the answer he sent when a friend, Isaac Morris, forwarded a letter from Adolph Moses, a former captain in the Confederacy. "Our demands," Moses had written, "are simply to be judged like other people and not to have the vices and shortcomings of our bad men illuminated at the expense of the many virtues and excellent qualities of our good men."

Grant replied to Morris that he held "no prejudice against sect or race but want each individual to be judged by his own merit." He added that, without thinking, he had reacted against men who were trading with the enemy, but his blanket order "would never have been issued if it had not been telegraphed the moment penned, without one moment's reflection."

Mollified, Moses wrote a long letter—printed on the *New York Times'* front page—announcing that because Grant had made "a reparation," Moses would not be distracted by a "side issue" and could now follow his political inclinations and vote for him.

Grant's win in November owed more to the 400,000 black voters than to pockets of Jewish support. His margin of 309,584 votes gave him 53 percent of the popular vote and 214 electoral votes to the 80 for Seymour. Grant lost New York by 10,000 votes—Seymour's home state—and even there Republicans were charging fraud. Republicans carried Ohio and Pennsylvania, two states with a significant number of Jewish voters.

Grant received results of the balloting while playing cards at a friend's house in Galena, where a telegraph machine had been set up. At 2 a.m., when the outcome was unmistakable, Grant walked home to his wife, who was waiting impatiently, and told her, "I'm afraid I'm elected."

Grant felt he could now permit his apology to the nation's Jews to be published more widely, and the *New York Times* praised his "frank and manly confession."

As Ulysses Grant, at forty-six, prepared to become the youngest president in his nation's history, Charles Sumner grasped at his last chance to become secretary of state, but Grant was keeping his cabinet selections to himself. As a commander, he had found secrecy a vital element of surprise, and the tactic suited Grant's independent nature. During the four months leading up to his inauguration, Grant enjoyed frustrating his wife's curiosity and claimed to wake up often each night to keep Julia from snatching the list of appointees that he kept under his pillow.

Sumner's hopes rose briefly when Julia Grant asked if he had any inkling of her husband's intentions. She said she was afraid to ask him again because Grant had warned her: "Jule, if you say anything more about it, I'll get a leave of absence, go off west and not come back till the fourth of March."

But long before the election, Sumner's air of superiority, which could amuse Lincoln, had been irking Grant. When told that Sumner did not believe in the Bible, Grant claimed to be unsurprised: "Well, he didn't write it."

Nor did Sumner improve his chances when he insisted on drawling out the new president's name as "Grawnt." Worst of all, Grant resented that he felt compelled to adopt an artificial manner with Sumner to conceal his dislike. Finally, the senator from Massachusetts was simply too effete and self-regarding for the modest soldier.

When Grant chose as secretary of state his friend Elihu Washburne, Galena's congressman since 1852, Sumner retreated to his chairmanship of the Foreign Relations Committee to try to manage foreign policy from the Senate.

Sumner's sole consolation was seeing Henry Seward equally disappointed. After calling on Grant in his private railroad car during a trip to New York, Seward had entertained a distant hope that he would be kept on in the new cabinet.

But it turned out that Seward would have more in common with Sumner than their dashed ambitions. At the age of sixty-eight, Seward had fallen in love with a twenty-eight-year-old woman.

Seward's wife, Frances, had died three years earlier. Following the election, Seward had described to an ambassador's wife "how I accept with thankfulness every expression of feminine respect and affection."

Olive Risley, a good-looking brunette, was the daughter of a New Yorker beholden to Seward for his job in the Treasury Department. Miss Risley declined Seward's invitation to accompany him on an impeccably chaperoned tour of Alaska with his son Fred and his daughter-in-law, but during the trip, Seward wrote to her longingly, "Why did I ever allow myself to become dependent on you so entirely?"

Returning from the Alaska territory—which Seward predicted would become a state one day—Seward's entourage traveled to Los Angeles and on to Mexico. Before he embarked, Seward told the audience at a banquet in his honor that the island of Cuba, being so close, should also become part of the United States.

While Seward was completing his travels in the Caribbean, Olive Risley contracted typhoid fever, then recovered sufficiently to spend a month as Seward's houseguest in Auburn, accompanied by her father.

Later that season, Thurlow Weed arrived and taunted Seward about his prediction in December 1860 that the Southern rebellion would be over in sixty days. The jibe stung, and Seward protested that he had only been trying "to calm the public pulse."

When Seward proposed a round-the-world trip in the autumn of 1870, Olive Risley agreed to go in a party that would include her father, her sister, and Seward's valet. During the voyage, Seward decided that he must find a way to keep Olive at his side—he described her as "noble, impressive, intellectual and attractive"—but not as his wife.

In Shanghai, Seward proposed adopting her, Olive agreed, and Seward redrafted his will to divide his estate evenly among his three sons and his new daughter.

In Grant's final weeks before assuming office, he lived inconspicuously in Washington at his house on I Street, winding up his army duties and naming William Sherman to succeed him as a four-star general.

Grant's business reverses had left him wary about his financial prospects after his presidency, and he was grateful when Alexander Stewart, a department store owner from New York, offered to buy Grant's house for sixty-five thousand dollars and donate it as a residence for General Sherman. Grant had already agreed to sell the house to the mayor of Washington for forty thousand dollars, but he withdrew from their contract, rode out the mayor's accusations of bad faith, and pocketed the difference.

On a cold and overcast March 4, 1869, Grant took the oath of office from Chief Justice Chase on the Capitol's east portico. For the third time in U.S. history, an incoming president's predecessor did not attend.

John Adams had left the capital before dawn to avoid Thomas Jefferson's inaugural. His son, John Quincy Adams, upheld his family's unsporting tradition by refusing to appear with Andrew Jackson. In Grant's case, it was again the president-elect who was snubbed. Stopping at the White House for Andrew Johnson, Grant's entourage was told that Johnson would be too busy to attend the ceremony.

Grant was also rebuffed when he tried to scuttle the traditional inaugural ball. Overruling him, the gala's organizers attracted six thousand guests at ten dollars a ticket to a dance at the new Treasury building.

Julia Grant made an attempt of her own to revise the capital's protocol. During her first reception at the White House, a staff member approached to ask: "Madame, if any colored people call, are they to be admitted?"

Mrs. Grant had taken only a moment to reply: "This is my reception day. Admit all who call."

Her gesture went for nothing. No black guests showed up during the entire time the Grants lived in the White House. Julia Grant took their reluctance as proof that Negroes were "modest and not aggressive." She was sure, though, that "as a race" they had loved her husband "and fully appreciated all he had done for them."

One example of Grant's favor came in his brief inaugural remarks. He called for approaching the next four years "calmly, without prejudice, hate or sectarian pride." Then, along with pledging a new policy toward the nation's Indians, Grant urged passage of the Fifteenth Amendment, which would extend the vote to black men.

No one had expected Grant on the podium to match the eloquence of Lincoln, but his address was warmly received, as were most of his cabinet appointments when he finally revealed them.

An exception was Grant's nomination of Alexander Stewart, his recent benefactor, as secretary of the Treasury. Grant was not alert enough to the Senate's new sensitivity about its powers, and he sent up Stewart's name for confirmation without consulting Roscoe Conkling, the senior senator from Stewart's home state. Nor had Grant considered the ban—initiated by Alexander Hamilton in 1789—against anyone actively engaged in trade or commerce as head of the Treasury Department.

When Charles Sumner objected to an exception being made for Stewart, Grant gratefully accepted Stewart's offer to withdraw his name.

That setback was followed in the same week by the abrupt resignation of Elihu Washburne, who claimed that his health was too frail to allow him to serve as secretary of state. His appointment had been merely a sop from Grant when he could not oblige Washburne with the Treasury post he had already promised to Stewart.

Washburne then asked that he and his French wife be sent to the embassy in Paris. First, though, for the prestige of it, he wanted to be secretary of state for several days. Grant agreed. The day after Washburne resigned that post for health reasons, he was appointed minister to France, where he would serve for eight and a half years.

For other positions, Grant tried to draw upon men with the political shrewdness and social grace he did not claim for himself. He was not alone in his self-deprecation. When Henry Adams was taken to the White House to meet the man who was following his grandfather and great-grandfather in the presidency, the thirty-one-year-old Adams was unimpressed. "The progress of evolution," he wrote, "from President Washington to President Grant was alone evidence enough to upset Darwin."

Adams had sat out the war in London as secretary to his father, the ambassador Charles Francis Adams. But his brother, Charles, Jr., had fought with the First Massachusetts Cavalry, and although he found Grant's appearance "ordinary," he also recognized in him "a man of the most exquisite judgment and tact."

That tact was on display in Grant's handling of the War Department. He held off immediately replacing John Schofield as thanks for Schofield's discreet behavior during the Stanton affair. Then, when he made the change, Grant fulfilled his promise to appoint his chief of staff, John Rawlins, even though he thought Rawlins's history of tuberculosis made him better suited to the climate of the military department in Arizona.

Picking genial Judge Ebenezer Hoar of Massachusetts as attorney general could be expected to gratify Hoar's good friend Senator Sumner. Equally convivial, John Creswell had delivered the Maryland delegation for Grant at the Republican convention and was rewarded with the Post Office Department. Jacob Cox, the former governor of Ohio, became secretary of the interior.

When advisers urged Grant to appoint a Pennsylvanian, he chose Adolph Edward Borie from Philadelphia as secretary of the navy. Enriched by his East Indian trade, Borie, like Stewart, was one of Grant's benefactors and had once given Grant his house on Chestnut Street.

Grant believed that any gifts he received were offered as reward for his military service and not as a down payment on future favors. But some journalists saw the presents differently. In the *New York Sun*, Charles Dana wrote that Grant's appointments were "chiefly distinguished for having conferred on him costly and valuable benefactions."

When Grant selected several of his wife's relatives for positions in his administration, the *New York World* responded as though no president had ever found jobs for his family. The paper warned that civil service examinations would soon ask only two questions: "Are you a member of the Dent family or otherwise connected by marriage with General Grant?"

For the time, Grant could shrug off the attacks.

With Washburne on his way to Paris, Grant was free to name a man better versed in foreign affairs, and he chose Hamilton Fish from New York as secretary of state. Now that Stewart was disqualified for the Treasury, Grant picked George S. Boutwell from Massachusetts.

In those first weeks, Grant also bestowed the two appointments most notorious for potential corruption. As commissioner of Indian affairs, he named Brigadier General Ely S. Parker, a full-blooded Seneca from Galena. Grant had already checked with his new attorney general for reassurance that an Indian—not considered a citizen for tax purposes— was eligible for the appointment. Judge Hoar, finding no precedent to cite, ruled in Parker's favor.

To collect customs taxes at the Port of New Orleans—the office that had enriched Perry Fuller—Grant turned to Pete Longstreet. Besides being one of Grant's oldest friends, Longstreet had been the one Confederate general to urge his fellow Southerners to accept the Reconstruction Acts.

In mid-April 1869, Grant attempted to fill another federal vacancy in Louisiana by appointing Pinckney Pinchback as register of the land office at New Orleans. Pinchback had been rising in Republican ranks from that day eighteen months earlier when he had served as a delegate to the state's constitutional convention.

When he showed up at the Mechanic's Institute, Pinchback's stylish suit and overcoat had distinguished him from many other black delegates who arrived in patched trousers and with holes in their shoes. Pinchback worried that the Democrats would mock the entire enterprise by seizing on the presence of some illiterate delegates and overlooking the many qualified black members.

He argued that the convention officers should not be allotted on the basis of an equal number of whites and blacks but instead chosen for experience and ability, and he carried the day.

During debates over civil rights, Pinchback first leaned toward the conservative position. "Social equality, like water, must be left to find its own level," he said, "and no legislation can affect it."

But when he heard the insulting language from white delegates, he changed his mind and introduced a successful bill that guaranteed equal rights to all citizens in any business that required a municipal or state license.

Pinchback held firm, however, in opposing the stripping of the right to vote from all white men who had joined the Confederacy. He explained that "I firmly believe that two-thirds of the colored men in this state do not desire disenfranchisement to such a great extent."

He lost that argument by a vote of forty-four to thirty and filed a protest, claiming that universal suffrage was "one of the fundamental principles of the Radical Republican Party."

The defeat did not slow his growing influence. Pinchback was one of five men mentioned as potential Republican candidates for governor in April 1868, but he stood instead for a more attainable seat in the state senate.

Pinchback's twenty-six-year-old white patron, Henry Clay Warmoth, went on to take the governorship, and his running mate, a former slave named Oscar James Dunn, became lieutenant governor. In the same election, John Willis Menard, the black publisher of *The Free South* newspaper, was elected to fill a vacancy in the U.S. Congress, but when his opponent challenged the result, the House refused to seat either man.

Pinchback was astounded to lose his own race and charged fraud. It took until the end of August for the state senate—with seven black and twenty-nine white members—to rule on his challenge and find "ballot-box stuffings, fraudulent tallying and the substitutions of Democratic for Republican tickets." Pinchback was seated and awarded back pay from the session's opening.

Three days later—in a repetition of his run-in with his brother-in-law—a mulatto Democrat aimed a pistol at Pinchback, who ducked and fired back. Both men were treated for minor wounds.

The real injury came the next day from the opposition press, which charged that two Negroes firing weapons on a crowded street proved that blacks were unfit to hold public office.

Pinchback was incensed. On the senate floor, he charged that the Democrats had sent the gunman to assassinate him, and he added that if those Democratic "outrages" continued, New Orleans would be reduced "to ashes."

He caught himself immediately and apologized for his tone but not for the sentiment. The New Orleans *Crescent* called his outburst "so despicable as to be beneath contempt." Worse, in Pinchback's view, the newspaper did not even credit his own fury but claimed he had merely "put into words the thoughts which the black arts of our enemies have taught him to think."

The episode left Pinchback subdued throughout the rest of the session, although he spoke out successfully for a law permitting marriage between black couples and for a "social equality" bill to open hotels and other accommodations to black patrons as well as white.

The response from the white community promised trouble ahead. If "any Negro or gang of Negroes" attempted to take advantage of their new rights, the *Commercial Bulletin* warned, "no New Orleans audience will ever permit him to take his seat except in places allotted for colored persons."

Pinchback discovered that Governor Warmoth, despite pledges of equality, was reluctant to alienate the state's wealthy white planters. When he vetoed the social equality bill, Pinchback began to assert his independence. The legislature ratified the Fourteenth Amendment, and Louisiana was readmitted to the Union. Military rule was extended in order to ensure an orderly transition to the new state government.

As the first elections approached, however, angry confrontations with former Confederates left white Republicans roughed up and potential black voters afraid to leave their houses. As brawling increased, Republicans worried about the party losing its hold on the state. Throughout most of the tumult, Pinchback was in Chicago, casting his vote for Grant as the presidential nominee.

On Election Day, the Democrats' intimidation of black voters succeeded. Seven months earlier, more than ten thousand Republicans had voted for governor. Now fewer than three hundred dared to come out.

Despite Grant's epic loss in the state, he had prevailed nationally and could offer Pinchback the federal position in the land office. Pinchback declined. He had business prospects in mind that he could promote better from his senate seat.

In November 1869, Pinchback joined with a natty former barber from their riverboat days and opened a money-lending business. Severing his last ties with Warmoth, he declared he was now a political independent and not "under the lash of any party."

Jay Gould

CHAPTER 14

GOLD AND SANTO DOMINGO
(1869–1870)

ULYSSES GRANT WAS CONTINUING TO LEARN THAT A GENERAL'S ready acceptance of favors from a grateful nation looked less innocent in a sitting president. He was also finding that the involvement of family members in public affairs had consequences beyond a few carping newspaper editorials. And that his respect for successful businessmen was not always reciprocated.

Grant's latest lesson came when he set out to resolve an early challenge with integrity and honor. As president, he was facing the $2.8 billion national debt run up by the war. Bankers in New York and Europe worried that he might listen to those who wanted him to repudiate the obligation.

But Grant considered repayment, with interest, not only the ethical course for the nation but also essential to re-establishing faith in U.S. currency. On March 18, 1869, he received his first bill from Congress, the Act to Strengthen the Public Credit.

The legislation promised that the United States would redeem its paper money and pay off its bonds in gold. When rebel troops had been scoring victories, the Union greenbacks had dropped in value and the price of gold had climbed to new heights. But once Grant signed the new guarantees, gold fell to its prewar level of $130 per ounce.

The conversion was entrusted to the Treasury secretary, George

Boutwell, who enjoyed the confidence of both the president and the nation's business leaders. A former governor of Massachusetts and its first commissioner when the Internal Revenue Service was established in 1862, Boutwell had served more recently in the House of Representatives, where he led the campaign for the Fifteenth Amendment.

Republicans maintained that the Thirteenth Amendment, which had abolished slavery, and the Fourteenth Amendment of 1868, which extended Negro rights under its equal protection clauses, did not go far enough. Now Congress must act again, a year later, to guarantee that the right to vote not be "denied or abridged by the United States or any states on account of race, color or previous condition of servitude."

As first drafted, the amendment also would have granted all citizens the right to hold office. But Southern Republicans wanted to retain the restriction of a loyalty oath in order to keep former rebels out of power, and Republicans in the North and West did not want to risk the election of Irish or Chinese immigrants.

In the Senate, Charles Sumner had derided the entire effort as unnecessary. He claimed that Congress could simply pass a law that enforced voting rights and not stir up new animosity with ratification debates.

But if there was to be an amendment, he argued that the proposal did not go far enough to guard against poll taxes and literacy tests. Bypassing legal niceties, Sumner offered his own expansive interpretation of the U.S. Constitution: "Anything for Human Rights is constitutional."

When the Fifteenth Amendment was put to a vote, Sumner was among the fourteen members who were absent or abstained, but it passed thirty-nine to thirteen in the Senate. The vote in the House also had split along party lines, with no Democrats voting in favor.

At the Treasury, Boutwell was quickly proving his acumen with policies that reduced the national debt by $50 million while keeping the price of gold low. Well pleased, Grant announced that re-establishing of the nation's credit was "policy enough for the present" and went on vacation.

Two tireless speculators would not be taking a summer holiday. At thirty-three, Jay Gould might seem born for speculation. His New

England family traced their roots in America to 1647. Their name had been Gold until it was changed in 1806. And as a young man, Jay had shortened his given name from Jason, ancient pursuer of the golden fleece.

Abstemious, self-effacing, devoted to his wife and children, Gould made a striking contrast with his partner, portly and gregarious James Fisk, Jr. A year older than Gould, Fisk had been born in Vermont on April Fool's Day, 1835. At fifteen, he had run away to join a circus and never shed traces of the midway.

Joining his father as a peddler of pots and pans, Fisk made his first fortune during the war by smuggling Southern cotton to factories of the Jordan Marsh company, which supplied uniforms to the Union army.

Both men had survived early failures. Gould made a bad investment in a tannery business, and even before the war ended Fisk had lost in the stock market what he had not lavished on champagne and diamond stickpins.

They rebounded with a nervy scheme to wrest control of the Erie Railway Company from Cornelius Vanderbilt. Their methods were slippery enough that at one point they had to flee the New York police and hole up in New Jersey.

Along the way, they had courted William Tweed of Tammany Hall. In a showdown, Boss Tweed cast off his past loyalty to Commodore Vanderbilt and, as a reward, accepted a lucrative position on Erie's new board of directors.

By the first month of the Grant administration, Gould had resolved to turn his Midas touch to the financial market. During an evening at the Metropolitan Opera, he put a proposal to Jim Fisk: If the two of them managed to drive up the price of gold during a fall harvest, the result would be cheap money that would stimulate overseas grain sales. But in London, export products were sold in gold. Farmers could charge gold-based prices abroad but earn paper-money profits at home at a better rate.

Gold was measured in double eagle coins, with five weighing a total of 4.838 ounces and quoted against how many greenback dollars they would bring. As Fisk quickly detected, Gould's plan had one flaw: Speculators might buy up the $15 million in gold coins that George Boutwell allowed to circulate, but the Treasury Department's gold reserves approached a hundred million. At any sign of an attempt to corner the market, those reserves could be unloaded to drive the price back down.

As Fisk told a friend, "Gould is a damned fool." The government would never let him get away with it.

Gould saw it differently. Although Grant and Boutwell appeared to be incorruptible, they might be outmaneuvered as Vanderbilt had been. He needed a well-placed ally, and during a trip to New Jersey to buy land, Gould met just the man, a fellow real estate speculator named Abel Rathbone Corbin.

Corbin was both a recent widower and a bridegroom. His wife had died less than a year before Grant's inaugural week in Washington, when Corbin, at sixty-one, charmed Jennie Grant, the new president's unmarried sister.

Julia Grant was generous in praising her thirty-seven-year-old sister-in-law, extolling Jennie's complexion as "exquisitely fair with just a touch of pink" and adding that "this sweet girl was as good as she was beautiful."

Corbin, gray-haired and stoop-shouldered, launched a swift and determined courtship. Within two months, President Grant was giving the bride away to a man he had known and liked from his own scrambling days in prewar Missouri.

For others, however, Corbin's reputation had been compromised in 1856 when he was exposed for trying to extort a fifty-thousand-dollar bribe to guarantee favorable legislation. Leaving Washington, Corbin reinvented himself in New York as a retired diplomat who dabbled in real estate.

When Corbin surfaced again in Washington during Andrew Johnson's stormy term, he strengthened his ties to Grant by selling him his house on I Street. At the same time, he was advising the president not to appoint any of "Grant's men," since they might jeopardize Johnson's re-election.

After their meeting in New Jersey, Corbin sought Gould out at his town house. As Gould recalled, Corbin "came to see me, wanted to make money in some way and asked my opinion, as one gentleman would meet another."

Gould laid out his scheme about gold but not as a way to turn a quick profit. He assured Corbin that their motive would be entirely patriotic. Letting gold prices go up would promote exports, which would raise the income of farmers and workingmen.

By mid-July, Corbin had persuaded Grant to stop over in New York on his way to an appearance in Boston. The president would be sailing on Fisk's steamer *Providence* and dining along the way with Fisk and Gould. Over a three-hour meal, their pitch for a change in policy could not budge Grant from his intention to return to the gold standard.

But the president could still serve their purposes. The partners invited the Grants to a performance of *La Périchole* at a Fifth Avenue theater owned by Fisk. Opera was not an entertainment Grant would have chosen. He had joked about his tin ear and confessed, "I know two songs. One is 'Yankee Doodle,' and the other is not."

All the same, New York society was treated that night to a show of intimacy between the president and the notorious owners of the Erie Railroad.

Meanwhile, Abel Corbin did his part by offering Julia Grant half-interest in the $250,000 bonds he had bought for his wife. Mrs. Grant refused the gift but was said to have appreciated the offer.

With their White House credentials established, Gould and Fisk worked with Corbin to place Daniel Butterfield in Grant's government as assistant U.S. Treasury secretary for the New York Sub-Treasury at an annual salary of eight thousand dollars. Gould assured Butterfield's loyalty with a ten-thousand-dollar personal check "to cover expenses."

Gould also used a half million dollars he collected from Tweed's cronies to buy a controlling interest in the Tenth National Bank of New York. It could provide the certified checks he would need during the pending frenzy.

With the pieces in place on August 12, 1869, Gould bought $375,000 of gold at a rate of $135 for each hundred dollars of gold. Corbin was traveling with Grant and kept pressing Gould's monetary theory. On another steamer ride, Fisk asked the closemouthed president directly for "a little intimation" of his policy.

Grant refused the request but promised to set up a meeting with Treasury Secretary Boutwell. He repeated, however, that Boutwell would be announcing "any changes through the newspapers as usual" to avoid charges of favoritism.

With the price of gold already down four dollars in nine days, Gould rounded up two other investors who joined him in buying up $10 million more. As his contribution, Abel Corbin wrote an anonymous article for the *New York Times* suggesting that Grant now endorsed a soft money policy.

At the Treasury, although Boutwell refused to confirm or deny the speculation, gold prices began to rise. But at Corbin's house, Grant confided to his brother-in-law that he had prevented Boutwell from selling $4 million to $6 million more gold in September than during the previous two months. As Grant was speaking, he did not know that Jay Gould was down the hall, listening and then leaving quietly to take advantage of the tip.

At once, Gould put $1.5 million in gold in Corbin's investment account and gave the same amount to Daniel Butterfield. At his office, Gould began borrowing heavily to buy immense quantities of gold. But without informing him, his new partners decided abruptly to take their profit and start to sell.

Gould was not given to panic. He sent Fisk to call on Corbin for reassurance about Grant's plans, and Corbin brought out Jennie to say that she was "quite positive there will be no gold sold" by the Treasury to depress the price. Fisk was convinced enough to raise his own stake to $7 million.

President Grant was back in New York for one final holiday before returning to Washington. His vacations were becoming a joke to his friends; his critics complained that Grant "recreates excessively."

On a boat ride up the Hudson River to West Point, Grant asked Daniel Butterfield to brief him on the New York financial world. The assistant Treasury secretary could hardly be candid. He had placed a side bet of $1.37 million that Gould's scheme would succeed.

As the president listened to Butterfield and to last-minute arguments from Jay Gould, nothing in his expression betrayed his thinking. Only Julia Grant heard him complain afterward that "Gould was always trying to find something out."

On September 12, 1869, Grant was off on a visit to his wife's family in rural Pennsylvania that would leave him unreachable for a week. He left behind a letter for George Boutwell that showed he understood the stakes in gold speculation. "The fact is," Grant wrote, "a desperate struggle is now taking place, and each party want the government to help them out." He was writing to put Boutwell on his guard, and Grant recommended not changing their policy.

Grant also intervened in a more personal way by dictating a letter for Julia to send to his sister. Frantic, Abel Corbin immediately showed it to Gould. Julia Grant had written that "the general says if you have any influence with your husband, tell him to have nothing to do with Jay Gould and Jim Fisk. If he does, he will be ruined, for come what may, he (your brother) will do his duty to the country and to the trusts in his keeping."

Corbin exclaimed to Gould, "I must get out instantly. Instantly!"

If not, he could forfeit his marriage, his friendship with the president, and his reputation throughout New York society.

Corbin pleaded with Gould to turn over his $100,000 profit on the gold Gould had already bought for him. Then, disencumbered of the stock, Corbin could answer Grant by letter the next morning that he had no stake in the gold speculation.

Gould made no promises, but as he was leaving, he warned Corbin, "If the contents of Mrs. Grant's letter is known, I am a ruined man."

Two days later, on Friday, September 24, 1869, Fisk's brokers began to bid up the price of gold. He and Gould now controlled 5.5 million ounces of gold worth $110 million. Gold fever swept Wall Street as the price continued to rise. Every one-dollar increase promised Gould and Fisk a windfall. As trading became crazed, the price reached $162 in greenback dollars. Gould intended to push the rate to $200.

At the Gold Room where trading was conducted, one investor tried to break the fever. James Brown from the firm Brown Brothers unloaded 250,000 orders at $160. But the allure of quick riches kept the price rising.

Anticipating the madness, Boutwell was poised to act. Before noon, he walked from the Treasury to the White House and proposed to Grant that he break the fever by dumping $3 million in Treasury gold on the market. Boutwell's former commander-in-chief replied, "I think you had better make it five million."

They compromised at $4 million, and Boutwell sent the order by telegram to the highly conflicted David Butterfield.

Minutes after the uncoded message was received in New York, the price of gold fell from $160 to $133. Speculators faced the loss of money they did not have, and the broker who had executed Fisk's instructions to drive up the price now received death threats. Police were summoned to contain the rush of angry merchants and brokers pouring into the streets around the Stock Exchange.

Fisk and Gould had been identified as the ringleaders. Men seeking to confront them were turned away from their offices. Some began to shout, "Lynch! Lynch!"

The two hoped for another getaway as smooth as the one during the uproar over Erie stock. Instead, they found themselves trapped in a small office.

Fisk went to calm the mob. The minute he ventured outside, a furious investor punched him in the face. Fisk hurried back inside until the crowd finally dispersed and Black Friday came to an end.

In the tangled aftermath, Fisk simply disclaimed his debts, accusing his surrogates of running them up without his authorization. He learned that Gould, without telling him, had been selling off gold at the first sign of trouble. As a result, the two of them would net $12 million from their joint investments.

In frustration, Fisk went to the Corbins' house to shout at them for not holding Grant to the scenario they had written for him. Gould went with him, but during the hysteria, he sat quietly and agreed, with little hope, that Corbin must go to Washington and fix what had gone awry.

. . .

At breakfast on Sunday morning, Abel Corbin described to Grant in a detached way the previous Friday's melee on Wall Street. Grant said he had received Corbin's letter with its assurance that he was not involved, "and you can imagine how much relieved I felt," knowing "that you were not engaged in that disgraceful speculation."

When Corbin spoke mournfully of the many men whose fortunes had been wiped out, Grant replied, "I am not at all sorry to hear it. I have no sympathy with gold gamblers."

Momentarily silenced, Corbin waited until later in the day to broach the subject again. He urged Grant to rescind Boutwell's order to sell the gold. Grant's patience was exhausted. He cut Corbin off. "The matter has been concluded," the president said.

Grant was too optimistic. The tumult on Wall Street persisted for months, and the devastation for the nation's farmers lasted for years before wheat, corn, and barley sold again at their prices before Black Friday.

Determined not to be pilloried with Gould as the only villains, Fisk gave the *New York Herald* an interview implicating the president's family in the plot and even Grant himself.

In fact, Fisk said, Corbin had married Jennie Grant only in order to promote the gold scheme. But, he added, "Grant got scared."

The reporter said he would need proof. When Fisk did not produce it, the reporter's article substituted innuendo for direct accusations. In response, Abel Corbin denounced his former partner in the *New York Sun*: "I do not associate with such men as Fisk."

The *Sun* reporter sought out Fisk, who treated Black Friday as "a little innocent fun" set off by a "crazy man" who took him seriously when he joked about buying gold at $160.

Since the *Herald* refused to implicate Corbin by name, Fisk fed his accusations to the *Sun,* professing his "astonishment" that Corbin would denigrate him in the public prints. Fisk and Gould now saw a way to rehabilitate their reputations and went on to give the *Sun* more than twenty interviews, finally blaming Corbin for hatching the scheme in the first place.

Their revelations spurred the New York district attorney to convene a grand jury to investigate. The public did not exonerate Gould and Fisk, but when they offered up Daniel Butterfield as a conspirator, he was forced to resign at the Treasury.

The nation's press rallied around Ulysses Grant, deploring any accusations against him as "preposterous" or "baseless calumny." The taint on his administration, however, would linger.

As the new congressional session opened in December 1869, Grant was taught another harsh lesson when he plunged into the complexities of foreign policy.

The issue dated to Henry Seward and his determination to secure a naval port in the Caribbean that would control the main passages from the Atlantic Ocean. When the Dominican Republic offered to allow the United States to annex its territory, Andrew Johnson had included that proposal in his last message to Congress.

But the members had been in no mood to oblige him. The House decisively defeated both annexation and extending status as protectorates to the Dominican Republic and Haiti.

On taking office, Grant found his admirals still lobbying for the treaty. Remembering the hostile reception that his troops had encountered in Mexico, Grant sent his White House secretary, Brigadier General Orville Babcock, to assess the mood among the Dominican people.

Babcock returned with a favorable report and a treaty that would let the United States either annex or buy the port of Samana Bay for $2 million.

To that point, Grant had kept his own counsel, but he realized that his preference for secrecy might offend the senators who would have to ratify the treaty.

To make amends, the president left the White House on the evening of January 2, 1870, to pay an unannounced call on Charles Sumner at his home. It was not an easy gesture for Grant to make, but he hoped his show of humility in coming in person might win Sumner over.

At first, Grant's ploy seemed to be working. Sumner was clearly surprised by the unprecedented breach of protocol, but he invited the president to join the two journalists who were dining with him. Sumner offered Grant a glass of sherry. Grant refused and launched into the reason for his visit.

After Grant had explained the treaty and was preparing to leave, one of the journalists asked Sumner whether he would support it.

Sumner's response demonstrated why he so regularly infuriated his colleagues. "Mr. President," he began, "I am a Republican and an administration man, and I will do all I can to make your administration a success. I will give the subject my best thought, and will do all I can rightly and consistently to aid you."

Plainspoken Ulysses Grant left the house convinced that he could depend on Sumner's backing for the treaty.

At that moment, the president was neglecting several warning signals: That Sumner had thwarted his nomination of Alexander Stewart at Treasury. That Sumner opposed Grant's early attempt to repeal the Tenure of Office Act. That Sumner had expressed a marked preference for overseas expansion only to the north and his hope that one day Canada would be annexed.

In the Senate, Sumner fell back on a tactic as habitual to him as secrecy was to Grant. He held up the treaty in his committee for more than two months.

During that period, the president and Sumner had reason for more friction. The Fifteenth Amendment had been working its way through the states, but a dispute in Virginia had split the Republican ranks.

When the state held the election mandated by Congress for readmission, voters had chosen a governor hostile to the Radicals and the "unprincipled carpetbaggers" allied with them.

Grant and most members of the Senate judiciary committee held that Virginia had complied with the rules and, although the outcome at the polls had been disappointing, the state should be readmitted.

Enlisting Radical support, Sumner insisted on new requirements. Now Virginia must ratify the Fifteenth Amendment, make blacks as eligible as whites to hold office, and set up integrated public schools.

That revision of the accepted criteria alienated fifteen Republicans, whose less uncompromising spirit had labeled them New Radicals. But Sumner controlled a slightly larger bloc and overcame the challenge.

When the decision arose over Mississippi, Sumner was able to impose the Virginia terms again. The result was an irony impossible to imagine ten years earlier: Hiram Revels, a black graduate of Knox College, took his place in the Senate where Jefferson Davis had once sat.

As his committee hashed over the Santo Domingo treaty, several aspects troubled Sumner—some minor, some not. Under the law, General Babcock should have resigned from the army before going on a civilian diplomatic mission. And the dictatorship controlling the Dominican Republic was not only bankrupt but closely allied with two American generals known to be profiteers.

When Sumner marshaled his arguments against the treaty, however, he trod a delicate line on its racial implications. The United States, according to Sumner, was "an Anglo-Saxon Republic and would ever remain so by the preponderance of that race."

While other senators might see the possibility of the Dominican Republic absorbing much of America's former slave population, Sumner preferred that the "integrity" of the existing "colored community" on the island be preserved to "try for themselves to make the experiment of self-government."

Sumner seemed to persuade fellow Radicals to join with the Democrats, who were determined to block any of Grant's initiatives. The president's anger grew when the Senate debate was allowed to lapse without a vote.

Grant was concluding, like Andrew Johnson before him, that Sumner and his old-style Radicals were the enemy. He would turn instead to the younger New Radicals, with their more tractable convictions.

But by the showdown vote, Sumner had corralled enough support to defeat Grant's treaty with a twenty-eight–twenty-eight tie.

Stung, the president struck back by threatening to recall Sumner's good friend, a Harvard history professor named John Lothrop Motley, from his post as ambassador to Great Britain.

When he had made the Motley appointment, Grant had agreed with Sumner that Britain should be punished for aiding the Confederacy. Sumner set the cost to the Union of that assistance at $2 billion and urged that Britain sign over Canada to the United States as a partial payment.

More recently, however, Hamilton Fish and George Boutwell had changed the president's mind. Grant now favored a compromise on such specific grievances as the damage done by the Confederacy's *Alabama* and other ships built in English shipyards.

Out for revenge, Grant could both punish Sumner and improve relations with Britain by removing the ambassador who had pressed the more extensive claims. Motley's monocle and manners already had provoked contempt at the White House, where General Babcock was also sneering at Charles Sumner as "a poor *sexless* fool."

Hamilton Fish had hoped to ease relations with the Senate by shipping off Sumner to London as Motley's replacement. But when he called on the senator at home, he found Sumner sunk in despair: His expenses were ruinous, Sumner complained. His house was making him a pauper, and the publishing of his collected works required fifteen hundred dollars a year.

"You can't understand my situation," Sumner said sadly. "Your family relations are all pleasant. Why, many and many a night when I go to bed I almost wish that I may never awaken."

But Sumner would not agree to displace Motley, "who is my friend." In fact, when word of his friend's removal reached him, Sumner wanted the world to know that Motley, "an ultra-American," was being punished only for Sumner's vote against the Santo Domingo treaty. In the Senate, he asked the clerk to read the relevant dates: the rejection of annexation—June 30. The president's demand for Motley's resignation—July 1.

For Sumner, the treatment of Motley was "the most atrocious crime" in diplomatic history. In that fevered state, he set off on a speaking tour almost as disastrous as Andrew Johnson's Squaring the Circle. Financially, the seven thousand dollars he earned were a godsend, but his thirty-eight lectures, almost one a day throughout the Midwest, were not always well received.

At the University of Michigan, Sumner spoke for two and a half hours. When he finally said, "In conclusion," the hall erupted with such enthusiasm that Sumner felt obliged to decline his fee.

To a reporter along his route, Sumner termed Grant "simple-minded" and, although honest himself, a man lured into a corrupt deal in Santo Domingo by Babcock and other young military aides.

Returning to Washington, Sumner could do no better than to claim that the report was "a mixture of truth, of falsehood, and of exaggeration, producing in the main the effect of falsehood."

But in the new session of Congress, the New Radicals attempted to strip Sumner of his chairmanship of the Foreign Relations Committee.

By now, Sumner was imagining parallels between the debate over the treaty and the raucous battle over Kansas that had nearly cost him his life. On the Senate floor, he gave a rousing speech that he later published as "Naboth's Vineyard," an allusion to King Ahab's greed for the grapes of a poor neighbor.

Hitting back, the New Radicals, too young to remember the battles of yesteryear, called into question Sumner's loyalty, judgment, even his sanity.

Sumner decided that Hamilton Fish's behavior had been so outrageous that he must cut the secretary of state dead and refused to speak to him on anything but official business. Given Fish's position, Sumner's vow of silence became intolerable. And when Sumner again insisted on the British withdrawing from Canada as the price for settling the war claims, the stress on him proved too much for a man turned sixty.

On February 15, 1871, Sumner was awakened by a crushing pain in his chest and left arm, but he forced himself to report to the Senate, where a doctor ordered two weeks of absolute rest.

Sumner's disability gave opponents their opening. When the Forty-second Congress convened on March 4, Charles Sumner was dropped from the Senate's Foreign Relations Committee.

He retreated to his house to read the hundreds of letters that came praising him and indignant over his ouster. At the White House, visitors

found President Grant relieved and happy, as convinced as his predecessor that it been necessary "to teach these men that they cannot assail an
administration with impunity."

When two congressmen tried to effect a reconciliation, Grant proved
more unyielding than he had been at Appomattox. He told them "that
whenever Sumner should retract and apologize for the slanders he had
uttered against me, in the Senate, in his own house, in streetcars and
other public conveyances, at dinners and other public entertainments
and elsewhere, as publicly, openly and in the same manner in which he
has uttered these slanders, I will listen to proposals for a reconciliation."

From Sumner's letters to friends, Grant would not be getting an
apology soon. He was describing the president as "without moral sense,
without ideas, without knowledge." And for good measure, "the lowest
President, whether intellectually or morally, we have ever had."

A PROSPECTIVE SCENE IN THE CITY OF OAKS, 4TH OF MARCH, 1869

CHAPTER 15

KU KLUX KLAN (1870–1872)

DESPITE WHAT ULYSSES GRANT HAD ONCE THOUGHT ABOUT POLITI-
cal bias within the Freedmen's Bureau, Oliver Howard believed he had
kept his agency free from partisanship. After the Reconstruction Act of
1867 granted the vote to freedmen, Howard ordered his staff to avoid
overt politicking.

By the end of that year, Howard had sounded hopeful. He reported
that the freedmen now had "all the rights of citizenship," but he asked
that his bureau be continued in order to guide former slaves through
their first election. Howard ruled that his agents could instruct the
freedmen on their rights but could not recommend a particular party.

That claim of neutrality did not persuade the South's disgruntled
whites. Howard's field offices reported that those former Confederates
who were already bitter over being banned from voting were convinced
that the bureau was indoctrinating blacks with Republican propaganda.

Southerners watched the many military men from Howard's staff
moving into state jobs as civilians and considered them tarred by their
association with Northern carpetbaggers. The bureau's critics also
claimed—with some justification—that a bureau agent was more likely
to be reprimanded for trying to influence Negroes to vote for the Democrats than to vote for the Republicans.

Howard's recent policies were dismaying the bureau's clients, as well.

After trying to give former slaves their forty acres, Howard had been stymied by Andrew Johnson's rapid restoration of their property to white Southern landowners.

With the president demanding that he conform to Washington's approach, Howard fell back on allocating only abandoned land, but he understood that any more ambitious program of compensation was doomed.

Nor was homesteading a realistic possibility since Southern and Western legislators were conniving to keep black families out of their territories. Of the 67,609 homestead applications filed throughout the South, only four thousand came from former slaves.

Caught between the president and his own black constituency, Howard recommended that the freedmen accept cash payment for their labor. But when they returned to their former plantations as sharecroppers, the terms of their agreement tethered them to a white man's plantation as securely as slavery had done.

Before the presidential election of 1868, Congress had already scaled back the bureau's activities to education and to paying Negro soldiers who had never collected their enlistment bonuses. Then Congress cut $100,000 from Howard's $187,500 budget for the fiscal year ending in June 1871, and he accepted that the end had come to his efforts.

Since his agents would now report directly to the army's district commanders under the Military Reconstruction Act, Howard recommended that the War Department assume his bureau's final duties after it officially went out of existence in June 1872.

By now, Howard regretted his earlier optimism about racial healing in the South. Privately, he had come to endorse—with charitable regret—the attempt to remove Andrew Johnson from the White House. "I do not wish him ill," Howard said, "but I do wish my country well."

Throughout his failure to distribute land, Howard had never lost faith in education as the best tool for guaranteeing former slaves their place in the postwar South.

Despite the continual shortage of money, Howard had presided over nearly three thousand schools serving 150,000 pupils. Most of them had been funded by missionary societies and local black communities.

Teachers were often Northern white women who had graduated from normal schools. Life for those volunteers meant giving up familiar comforts and either living alone or boarding with a black family. These white women were passed over for jobs as principals or superintendents in favor of their male colleagues, and they stayed in Southern schools for an average of two years.

Meantime, the Freedmen's Bureau was also recruiting black teachers as it moved to fulfill Howard's vision—first, the spread of elementary and trade schools and then the South's first black colleges: Atlanta, Fisk, and Tugaloo.

As the capstone, Howard saw a university that would offer degrees in law, medicine, and theology, with enrollment not limited to black students.

Such a university was approved by Washington's First Congregational Church and opened in 1867 as a theological seminary in the District of Columbia. With the range of courses expanding, the institution was named, over his protest, for the man who had inspired it.

When General Howard resigned officially from the Freedmen's Bureau, he accepted the presidency of Howard University.

Once in the job, Howard described his new position to John Forney, the former Senate secretary, who himself had taken up new duties: After backing Grant for the presidency, Forney had been appointed collector at the port of Philadelphia.

With evident satisfaction, Howard wrote that his institution was proving daily "that the dark color of the skin does not of itself unfavorably affect the intellect."

At the time when Howard was recoiling from an increase in violence against Southern blacks, members of Congress were also being forced to pay attention. Benjamin Butler got an anonymous warning as early as the spring of 1868:

"Butler, prepare to meet your God! The avenger is upon your track! Hell is your portion! KKK."

Ben Wade and other Republican leaders had received similar threats as the Freedmen's Bureau support for public schools was setting off increasingly bloody retaliation. Schools and black churches were being destroyed, white teachers whipped and sometimes killed.

It was a town in South Carolina that provoked a showdown between the Klan and Washington, D.C. Residents of Yorkville were informed by Klan members that a group of former slaves was threatening to burn down the town. The Klan posted notices that if any fires were set, Klansmen would kill ten local black men as revenge, along with two white carpetbaggers.

They underscored the threat by shooting a Negro named Tim Black from nearby Rock Hill eighteen times before they cut his throat.

More violence flared throughout the state. A black county commissioner was murdered, a house filled with former slaves attacked, two black men lynched—all Republicans.

Compelled finally to act, Congress launched a bruising debate and, over the objection of Democrats, passed the first of three measures on May 31, 1870, to stem the racial crimes throughout the South. Called the Enforcement Acts, they made any attempt to deprive a citizen of his civil or political rights a federal crime.

To empower the legislation, Congress added a Department of Justice to the president's cabinet. As his new attorney general, Grant reached deep into Georgia for an obscure and unlikely champion of Negro rights named Amos T. Akerman.

A former Confederate army officer, Akerman had come to Grant's attention by campaigning for him in 1868 and had been repaid with an appointment as his state's U.S. attorney.

That honor alone would have gratified a modest small-town lawyer, but when Grant resolved to remove Ebenezer Hoar, another of Charles Sumner's cronies, from his cabinet, he settled on Akerman as Hoar's replacement.

Because Akerman lived thirty miles from the nearest telegraph office, he had not yet learned of his appointment when senators were already wondering just who he might be.

• • •

On arriving in Washington, Akerman soon demonstrated unique qualifications for his assignment. Born in New Hampshire and graduating
from Philips Exeter Academy and Dartmouth College, he had moved
south to practice law in a town northeast of Atlanta. For the next twenty
years, he deplored the drumbeat leading to war, but when war came,
Akerman, at age forty, signed on with the Georgia home guard.

After Lee's surrender, Akerman had accepted the peace terms, spoken freely on behalf of the rights of former slaves, and joined the 1868
campaign that restored Georgia's delegates to Congress.

To assist Akerman in his crusade, Grant created the new position of
solicitor general and appointed another Southerner, Benjamin Bristow,
who had proved himself as U.S. attorney in Kentucky.

Neither man underestimated the growing strength of their adversary.
Akerman announced that to crush the Klan would "amount to war," and
he and Bristow authorized federal troops throughout the South to make
massive arrests.

The Carolinas were an early target. An estimated forty thousand
Klan members in North Carolina had contributed to the terror that
elected five Democrats of the state's seven congressmen. The state legislature was equally out of balance, with thirty-six conservative senators and only three Negroes and two Northerners. In the lower house,
seventy-five conservatives outnumbered the nineteen Negroes and two
carpetbaggers.

Akerman found conditions in South Carolina even worse. He announced that "from the beginning of the world until now" no community "nominally civilized has been so fully under the domination of
systematic and organized depravity."

Grant agreed that the Klan had become an invisible empire throughout the South and appealed to the Forty-second Congress for even
broader powers to combat it.

Butler of Massachusetts and Representative Samuel Shellabarger of
Ohio were quick to respond with legislation that would make a federal
crime of conspiring "to overthrow or destroy by force the government of
the United States."

Butler had lost his prosecution of Andrew Johnson, but he intended
to prevail now. He read aloud to his colleagues a hasty note sent to the

wife of a missionary just before the Alabama Klan lynched him. "Let each member of the House read the letter," he said when he had finished. "Then let them vote against a bill to repress such outrages, if he dare, and then reckon with the people of his country and afterward with his God."

Grant was seeking the kind of emergency powers that Lincoln had assumed with the outbreak of war, including new authority to suspend habeas corpus wherever the president declared a state of insurrection.

That venerable writ required that suspects not be held in secret but be brought before a judge to determine whether they had been legally detained.

To enforce the new legislation—called the Ku Klux Klan Act of 1871 or simply the Force Bill—the president could call out the army, and the scope of the measure united conservative Republicans like Lyman Trumbull of Illinois with Democrats who saw the bill as an intolerable intrusion on states' rights. Trumbull, never comfortable with the Radicals in his party, had sided with them only after Andrew Johnson made compromise impossible.

In recent months, Trumbull had bridled at Grant's role in deposing Charles Sumner from his chairmanship. He wanted justice for Sumner, Trumbull said, although "I am not a special friend of the Senator from Massachusetts" and often had differed with him—"I am sorry to say, unpleasantly."

Grant had won out then. Confronted now with the Ku Klux Klan legislation, Trumbull was torn. He deplored the beatings and lynchings of Negroes, but he considered the Republican governments throughout the South to be both corrupt and inept. The KKK bill was "a great humbug got up by Butler" and other Radicals to perpetuate the rule "of the carpetbaggers and scalawags in the South."

His judiciary committee ignored Trumbull's objections and passed the bill, but he refused to participate in the ritual of presenting it to the full Senate. During the debate, Trumbull drew a distinction between civil rights and other political rights that were not protected by the U.S. Constitution.

"Individual rights," he concluded, "are safest, as a general rule, when left to the protection of the locality."

As the debate came to a climax, Trumbull announced that denying the vote to white rebels had been a fatal error because it had transferred power to "corrupt and dishonest persons" who had plundered their state governments. At least, the Confederates "whatever may be said of their guilt as rebels, were neither robbers nor thieves."

Trumbull ignored testimony that showed a new crisis throughout the South. Carpetbaggers were sometimes attacked for offering Negro workers higher wages than Southern employers were willing to match. When the cotton yield in Georgia proved to be larger in 1870 than any produced under slavery, it became more difficult to argue that black men and women would not work as hard now that they had their freedom.

As for corruption, when a railroad owner like Hannibal I. Kimball spread large bribes throughout the legislatures to obtain rights of way and easements, his money was colorblind. Most of it ended up with the local white officials who still controlled their governments.

Rebuttal to Trumbull from his own party came swift and angry. Oliver Morton of Indiana countered the charge of corruption in Southern Republican governments by pointing to Trumbull's own embrace of the spoils system: He had extorted from the Grant administration 103 jobs for his friends.

When objections from the Democrats and men like Trumbull seemed about to sink the bill, Grant responded with a personal appeal. Taking his cabinet officers along, he went to the Capitol on March 23, 1871, to rally the Republican legislators.

They explained to the president that their Northern constituents were losing interest in further punitive measures. Unless he was willing to lead the crusade and risk his popularity, the legislation would fail.

Grant cut off the discussion and began to write out a statement:

"A condition of affairs now exists in some of the States of the Union rendering life and property insecure, and the carrying of the mails and the collection of the revenues dangerous."

Grant was giving congressmen an excuse for federal intervention. He concluded with a pledge that underscored the urgency he felt: He would not recommend legislation on any other subject during the current congressional session.

The bill passed one month later.

Congress then appointed a joint committee of seven senators and nine representatives to investigate what its members called the "Ku Klux conspiracy," and during the congressional recess its members traveled south to hear testimony.

They intended to verify the widespread rumors of murder and cruelty with eyewitness accounts. Besides South Carolina, the committee would also hear evidence from as many as a hundred witnesses each in Alabama, Florida, Georgia, Mississippi, and North Carolina.

South Carolina's governor was appealing to Grant for emergency aid since his limited force could not stand up to the Klan and its sympathizers. In Unionville, forty Klan members had stormed a jail where two dozen black militia were being held in connection with the murder of a Confederate veteran. The Klan seized five prisoners from their cells and shot them.

When the sheriff tried to protect the remaining Negroes, hundreds of armed white men cordoned off the town and brought the sheriff's wife to the jail with a gun to her head. Yielding, he gave up ten more blacks to the mob for execution.

General William Sherman had already responded to the savagery in South Carolina by sending the Seventh U.S. Cavalry in March 1871 to restore order, transferring a thousand soldiers from the Western plains, where they had been contending against the Cheyenne, Comanche, and other tribes as the nation pushed westward.

Six months later, Attorney General Akerman went personally to Yorkville, South Carolina, to sift through the evidence being collected. His arrival spurred the federal marshal to join with Sherman's troops and begin to make arrests.

Grant agreed to suspend the writ of habeas corpus in the most virulent South Carolina counties. That crackdown led to a flight of Klan leaders from the state, with James W. Avery, a planter and owner of a large general store, among those who vanished.

Since 1868, Major Avery had headed the local Klan, whose members were devoted to political intimidation and had little interest in petty crime. Avery had tried to curtail the abuses that would lead to federal intervention, but his rank and file proved impossible to control.

Elias Hill, a black Baptist minister with legs misshapen from childhood, had opened a local school for Negro children. One midnight, six shrouded Klansmen burst in on him, carried him out of his house, denounced him as an agitator, and whipped and beat him.

When he recovered, Hill concluded that he could never again live peaceably in the white South. Organizing a group of 136 Negroes at the end of 1871, he sailed for the black settlement in Liberia. Writing home from the capital at Monrovia, Hill reported that his companions had been received warmly and promised good land for their fresh start.

To protect those blacks who chose to remain in Yorkville, Akerman sent four hundred soldiers throughout the area to round up those Klansmen who had not disappeared with Major Avery. Hoping for milder punishment, many Klansmen were confessing their membership, and their numbers became too great for the jail cells. They were allowed to remain free on their personal parole until their cases could be heard.

By the beginning of 1882, 195 persons in York County had been imprisoned; another hundred had fled the county. At least five hundred more surrendered and were deported or released.

Those locked up in the three-story county jail received daily visitors bringing food and flowers. A reporter for the *New York Tribune* detected no shame among townsfolk over the Klan's behavior. They were outraged instead by Grant's suspension of habeas corpus.

The Democrats accused the government of inhuman treatment, but the prisoners themselves did not make that charge. In fact, a town's more prosperous citizens welcomed the disbanding of a Klan that had turned thuggish and lawless.

Moving through Alabama, the congressional panel heard from men like Augustus Blair of Huntsville, Alabama, an elderly former slave. During the war, he had been a trusted guardian of white children, but in the new South, Blair had seen his grown son dragged from their house and kicked to death for an offense never explained.

When Blair went into town to file a complaint against the Klan members he recognized, white officials warned him to go back to his farm. He did as he was told and found that while he had been away, his thirty hogs, milk cow, and four bales of hay had been stolen.

At another hearing, this one in Atlanta, Maria Carter, a twenty-eight-year-old former slave, testified about the night the Klan came hunting for her next-door neighbor, John Walthall.

At the sight of the masked intruders, Walthall's wife started to scream. Mrs. Carter said, "I heard some of them say, 'God damn her, shoot her.'"

Maria Carter cowered in her bed with her newborn infant and listened as Walthall was forced to wrap his arms around his wife so they could be whipped together.

When three of the men came back to her cabin and caught Mrs. Carter's husband and her elderly uncle returning home, they beat them bloody in front of her. One man in "a sort of gown" put his gun to her face, but another of them said, "Don't you shoot her."

When they had left, her husband tried to shield her from his pain, but she saw his clothes sticking to his raw wounds "and his shoulder was almost like jelly." Venturing out the next morning, Maria Carter found blood everywhere. The Walthall house "looked like somebody had been killing hogs there."

The investigator asked, "Did you know this man who drew his gun on you?"

"Yes, sir."

"Who was he?"

"Mr. Much."

"Where does he live?"

"I reckon about three miles off. I was satisfied I knew him and Mr. Hooker."

"Were they considered men of standing and property in that country?"

"Yes, sir."

The hearings established that Southern women were often targets for the Klan. White prostitutes in South Carolina who were rumored to have Negro clients were covered with tar and driven from their town. One black father was killed because his daughter "had caused embarrassment" to a white family by giving birth to a child by the family's son.

Wanting to limit the number of federal troops, President Grant had also authorized a fleet of plainclothes detectives to gather evidence by posing as businessmen or workers looking for a job.

As the congressional hearings moved to Washington in May, the Republicans called the detectives as witnesses. Democrats dismissed their testimony as nothing more than lies concocted to influence the 1872 presidential election.

With the proceedings open to the public, the nation could follow the testimony in the press. Some Democratic newspapers challenged the reports of Klan terror by claiming that black witnesses were testifying in order to receive the two-dollar per diem and mileage allowance that Congress had authorized.

Since Southern Democrats could no longer persuade Northern readers that the Klan was merely a band of high-spirited youths, they turned to other defenses. A novel published anonymously called *The Masked Lady of the White House* implied that any racial crimes had been committed by the Radical Republicans to discredit their opponents.

Reporting from Spartanburg, South Carolina, the *New York World* claimed that "many a vagabond negro" had displayed welts from a beating "which in many cases no doubt was done years ago at the pillory for crimes."

The *Atlanta Constitution* compared the congressional investigation to the Spanish Inquisition.

When the investigators called their most celebrated witness on June 27, 1871, Nathan Bedford Forrest was confronted with a dilemma. He preferred to deny his involvement with the Klan entirely. If that was impossible, he wanted to take credit for curtailing its abuses once he realized that it was no longer attracting only "the best men."

Forrest could point to a general order issued two years earlier that directed all Klan members to destroy their masks and end their activities: "The order of the K.K.K. is in some localities being perverted from its original honorable and patriotic purposes."

But Forrest still received enough letters on Klan business to keep his private secretary busy, even as he devoted his efforts to building a new fortune by capitalizing on the rapid expansion of the nation's railroads.

The Central Pacific, built with laborers from China, and the Union Pacific, built by Irish immigrants, had expanded until a network of railways now ran through the territories of the Louisiana Purchase all the way to California. Men like Leland Stanford, Collis Huntington, and Mark Hopkins had become rich by moving passengers and freight along their transcontinental rails.

Forrest's goal was more modest. He bought a controlling interest in a local line that became the Selma, Marion, and Memphis Railroad. As he raised funds through subscription and solicited government favors, his Klan connection became a liability.

When a reporter asked about expanding his line, Forrest said he intended to depend on former slaves: "Negroes are the best laborers we have ever had in the South."

In the months before Forrest was called to testify, four dozen Klansmen had surrounded the house of a Republican judge in Greensboro, Tennessee. When the judge appealed to Forrest for protection, Forrest kept him safe for a week, then persuaded him to leave the county.

To Klan members, Forrest explained that, although the judge had "given bad advice to the Negroes" that kept them from returning to work on the nearby plantations, his offenses were due to his being "a drinking man" but one without "any harm to him."

Nathan Forrest showed up before the congressional panel as a proud soldier and a legitimate businessman, and that was how, despite a few sharp questions, he was treated.

He had enhanced his reputation the previous month by joining with twenty-one other Confederate officers in urging assistance for Washington College in Lexington, Virginia. Robert E. Lee had served as its president until his death in the fall of 1870, and Lee's former comrades were petitioning "our friends in the United States" to give money to the renamed Washington and Lee University.

As the final congressional report on Klan activities would note, "Our design is not to connect General Forrest" with the Klan, although, it continued, "(the reader may form his own conclusion upon the question)."

In his testimony, Forrest admitted nothing but tried to explain for the committee the atmosphere at home that might justify Southerners protecting themselves.

"When the war was over," Forrest said, "our servants began to mix with the Republicans, and they broke off from the Southern people and were sulky and insolent. There was a general fear throughout the country that there would be an uprising."

He added that agitators from the North were adding to that fear by forming their Union Leagues, that the Negroes were holding night meetings, and that "ladies were ravished by some of those Negroes." The Klan "was got up to protect the weak, with no political intention at all."

But committee members had resurrected an imprudent interview Forrest had given in August 1868 to a reporter for the *Cincinnati Commercial*. Forrest had denied being a Klansman but said he was "in sympathy and will cooperate with them."

Forrest claimed now that the reporter had caught him at a moment when he was "suffering from a sick headache" and had "misrepresented me almost entirely." They had talked for only "three or four minutes," Forrest insisted, perhaps only "twenty words." He soon had to backtrack: "I should have said twenty minutes, I reckon."

To ward off further incrimination, Forrest took refuge in a faulty memory. As congressmen pressed for details about the Klan's organization, Forrest responded with "I heard," "I do not recollect," "I do not know."

When all else failed, Forrest appealed to the constitutional safeguard of the Fifth Amendment: "I do not think I am compelled to answer any questions that would implicate me in anything."

After his appearance, a friend asked Forrest how it had gone and quoted Forrest's reply: "I have been lying like a gentleman."

Horace Greeley

CHAPTER 16

HORACE GREELEY (1872)

Amos Akerman never said publicly why he resigned from President Grant's cabinet at the end of 1871. His vigorous prosecution had broken the Klan in South Carolina, but rumors in Washington suggested that Akerman deplored the sporadic nature of the prosecutions elsewhere.

Although the Klan seemed to be a spent force throughout the South, congressional Republicans criticized Grant for not bringing the full weight of the Force laws on the Klan in Florida, Mississippi, and Alabama.

Grant's defenders blamed the Congress for not allocating money for an expanded judiciary system to handle the backlog of cases. But since the Klan's terrorism no longer seemed to threaten the 1872 elections, support for the funding had diminished. Akerman's replacement, George H. Williams, a former Oregon senator, had begun to limit federal prosecution to murder charges.

With federal agents standing guard at the polls, black Americans were ready to vote in unprecedented numbers. There was no doubt that Grant would be their choice, and Republicans hoped his popularity would carry them in state and local elections, even in South Carolina.

Frederick Douglass, the nation's most celebrated former slave, endorsed Grant as the reformers' best hope. Henry Ward Beecher, whose daughter had written *Uncle Tom's Cabin*, assured a Brooklyn audience that there "had never been a president more sensitive to the wants of the people."

Carl Schurz disagreed. Like Charles Sumner and other disaffected Republicans, Schurz found the Grant administration uninspiring and corrupt, with the president himself personally compromised by the Gold Ring. Then in 1870, Grant had appointed a fellow general, John A. McDonald, to the sprawling St. Louis federal revenue district. Allegations soon reached Washington of a Whiskey Ring—government appointees who were conspiring to defraud the Treasury of millions in tax revenue from the liquor industry.

Since Grant was certain to be the Republican nominee, Schurz combined with three disillusioned newspaper editors in Chicago; Springfield, Illinois; and Louisville, Kentucky, to stage a rival convention in Cincinnati.

Old-line politicians who felt pushed aside in the postwar era were drawn to this Liberal Republican Party. Lyman Trumbull was on board, along with Sumner's Massachusetts friends indignant at the way he had been treated. The movement also attracted Eastern men of letters like James Russell Lowell and William Cullen Bryant, who had never been comfortable with Grant.

The Liberal Republicans promised to reform the civil service, lower taxes, and end the land grants to railroads, but they would need votes from Democrats. To court them, Schurz put aside his former commitment to black suffrage and committed his party to states' rights and "property and enterprise," which Southerners understood to mean white property and white enterprise.

Schurz and his allies planned to offer a presidential candidate who would provide the sharpest contrast with Grant—Charles Francis Adams, urbane son of John Quincy Adams, the nation's sixth president.

Before he left on a prolonged trip, Adams acknowledged his interest in the nomination, and his absence would not necessarily be a liability. Even his allies had found his father difficult to like, and Charles himself had been described as "the greatest iceberg in the northern hemisphere."

Schurz's intention was upended by the arrival in Cincinnati of Whitelaw Reid, a brash newspaperman from the *New York Tribune*, who was determined to nominate the paper's owner, Horace Greeley.

Reid had challenged Ulysses Grant before. As a reporter for a Cincinnati paper at the Battle of Shiloh, Reid had filed sensational stories about Grant's poor performance. He got most details wrong, but he set off excoriating editorials in other newspapers, including the *Tribune*. Greeley wrote that Grant had made no more preparation for battle "than if he had been on a Fourth of July frolic."

The abuse stung, but Grant had kept his head down and launched a successful counterattack the following day. Mildly, he remarked to a *Tribune* reporter, "Your paper is very unjust to me, but time will make it all right. I want to be judged only by my acts."

At the convention, Whitelaw Reid went to work after the first ballot to reduce Adams's lead. After six ballots over five hours, Greeley was nominated, with former Missouri senator B. Gratz Brown as his running mate.

To build support for that moment, Greeley had been running a stealthy campaign for months. After he had received Charles Sumner's assurance that he would not be a Liberal Republican candidate, Greeley published a magazine article to spell out his own bland political platform. He advised young men to study a trade, maintain healthy habits, renounce liquor, avoid debt, and never despair.

Greeley was approaching sixty, but exhorting the young had always come easily. As early as 1838, when Greeley was twenty-seven himself, he had written, "If any young man is about to commence in the world, we say to him, publicly and privately, Go to the West."

By 1865, that advice had been distilled into "Go West, young man. Go West and grow up with the country."

Greeley's own life had taken improbable turns since Thurlow Weed first picked him to edit a publication supporting William Henry Harrison. Chafing under Weed's partisan demands, Greeley broke the bond in the spring of 1841 and went to New York to launch his *Tribune*.

The paper had dozens of competitors, but Greeley was determined to lift the *Tribune* above the ruck of murders, scandal, and society chit-chat. One fellow publisher, Phineas Taylor Barnum, became a close friend. He described Greeley fondly as a "gangling, wispy-haired, pastycheeked man, high-domed and myopic, with the face of somebody's favorite grandmother."

To that catalogue, Barnum might have added grit. When the four-story *Tribune* building was destroyed by fire in 1845, Greeley lost his supplies of paper and every manuscript. He rented an office nearby and the next morning published his paper on schedule.

Critics and competitors took a bemused view of Greeley's eccentric enthusiasms. He became enamored of the utopian communities promoted by William Henry Channing and the French socialist Charles Fourier. Investing in them, he lost heavily. And their collective ethic finally could not withstand Greeley's need for untrammeled freedom.

Greeley's relations with women could seem conflicted. He had met Molly Cheney when they were living in a New York City boardinghouse committed to vegetarian meals with no coffee or alcohol. But their marriage was blighted by the death of an infant son. After a miscarriage five months later, Molly, who had been a lively Connecticut schoolteacher, fell into a depression from which she never fully recovered.

While his wife retreated to her bed, Greeley submerged himself in work. Following another miscarriage, Molly seemed to be going blind. Greeley tried without success to find a cure at Brook Farm, the community outside Boston run by a cousin of Ralph Waldo Emerson.

When they returned to New York, it was to live in a barren house with no furniture, rugs, or curtains. Greeley complained to friends that waiting on his wife's every need had become hard for him. Then Molly delivered a son they called "Pickie," and the family moved to a wooden farmhouse on the East River. To live with them, Greeley invited his new book review editor, Margaret Fuller.

An intrepid young member of Emerson's Transcendental Club, Miss Fuller published three articles a week in the *Tribune* during the next two years. Greeley took pains to assure the world that his protégée was his wife's friend, not his. But their guest was finding Molly Greeley increasingly demanding and Pickie a neglected and willful child.

Traveling to Europe to be Greeley's foreign correspondent, Margaret Fuller took as her lover a young Italian aristocrat. As they were returning to America, the couple and their infant son were drowned during a storm off the coast of Fire Island.

When Pickie died of cholera at the age of seven, his father worried that Molly would not survive another loss. As for himself, Greeley wrote that he now understood at thirty-eight "that the summer of my life was over" and "that my future course must be along the downhill of life."

Work remained his reliable salvation. Greeley opposed the war with Mexico. He alienated abolitionists by holding aloof from their increasingly urgent debates, arguing that the low wages paid in the North to both white and black workers were the equivalent of the actual slavery of the South.

Rather than spout more "angry vituperation against slaveholders," Greeley wrote, abolitionists should improve the black schools and churches and the living conditions in the North.

In 1848, Greeley got his one exposure to political office in Washington when a New York congressman was removed for election fraud and the Whig Party bosses turned to him as a three-month interim appointment.

During that time, Greeley delighted in becoming the House scourge. He assailed fellow congressmen in his newspaper for missing votes and for padding their expense accounts. He exposed their wrongdoing by contrasting the shortest routes to each district with the mileage that representatives were claiming for reimbursement.

Among Greeley's examples was freshman congressman Abraham Lincoln, accused of pocketing $630 by overcharging for the 780 miles from Springfield.

The one result of Greeley's crusade was to outrage his colleagues. They retaliated with scant support for his land-reform measure, which would have allowed homesteaders to buy forty acres at $1.25 an acre. He had no better luck in trying to redraw the boundary between New Mexico and Texas.

Despite Greeley's criticism of Lincoln, the two men became friendly. They disagreed, however, about a bill to end the slave trade in the District of Columbia; Lincoln voted against the bill.

• • •

Out of Congress once more, Greeley promoted the cause of the political revolutions raging across Europe. And in London, he was dazzled by the Crystal Palace, a vast structure of steel and glass dedicated to human achievement.

Eager to duplicate the spectacle on Sixth Avenue in New York, Greeley formed a corporation and appointed his friend P. T. Barnum as director of an exhibition between Fortieth and Forty-second Streets. Well satisfied with the result, Greeley promoted his homegrown palace as a "beauty and a wonder," a celebration of American ingenuity. Both he and Barnum lost their investments.

By the time the debate erupted over slavery in Kansas, Greeley had become committed to abolition and sent his paper to the forefront of the battle. He remained personally cautious, however, instructing his editor, Charles Dana, to avoid anything that was "impelled by hatred of the South" or a desire to humiliate the region.

Greeley had joined with other editors in establishing the Associated Press to share the cost of gathering news, but his weekly edition of the *Tribune* now blanketed the nation and dominated the conversation in literate households throughout the American West. Readers gladly overlooked Greeley's crotchets to embrace what one Lincoln secretary called "The Gospel according to St. Horace."

When war came, Greeley lined up with the Radical Republicans and their impatience with the president. In August 1862, he published a letter to Lincoln, "Prayers of Twenty Millions," that urged the immediate emancipation of America's slaves.

Lincoln responded with a telegram to the *Tribune*, pledging himself to save the Union either "without freeing any slaves" or "by freeing all the slaves" or by "freeing some and leaving others alone." Lincoln wrote that his personal wish was that "all men everywhere could be free."

When Lincoln issued his emancipation order a month later, Greeley responded in print with "God Bless Abraham Lincoln."

But Thurlow Weed, who resisted tying emancipation to the struggle to preserve the Union, warned Lincoln that his former protégé now "possesses the power to ruin our country."

• • •

By 1864, however, it was Greeley who faced ruin, or worse. He had predicted to Secretary of War Stanton that the draft lottery would be unpopular. Military pay was too low, and rich men should not be able to pay poor men to take their place. "The burdens of society," Greeley wrote, "must be made to fall upon property where they justly belong."

Greeley's foresight did not protect him from the riots that Southerners would cite later to justify the violence in New Orleans and Memphis. In Chappaqua, Molly Greeley was threatened by a drunken mob until Quaker neighbors took her in, and protesters in Manhattan damned Greeley for endorsing emancipation. Between their looting and burning down draft offices, rioters massed in front of the *Tribune* building. To the tune of "John Brown's Body," they sang impromptu choruses of "Hang Horace Greeley to a Sour Apple Tree."

As his workers protected the *Tribune* office with rifles and hand grenades, Greeley went about publishing the next day's edition.

When the rioting ended, more than a thousand lives had been lost, but Greeley exulted, "I was in no wise harmed by the mobs, though they must have hurt their throats howling at me."

The Union army's victory at Gettysburg calmed Northern spirits. Thanks to a *Tribune* reporter at the battlefield who checked his story against Lincoln's notes, Greeley could print the text of the president's brief address at the battle site.

As war came to an end, Greeley agreed to write a popular history of its battles. By 1867, his popular first volume had sold a remarkable 125,000 copies.

During Lincoln's campaign for re-election, Greeley entertained the idea of dropping him to run instead John C. Frémont, with his sweeping vow to end slavery throughout the country, not only behind Confederate lines.

Greeley made a desultory gesture at convening a third-party convention but in the end did not attend it. Frémont withdrew his candidacy in September and endorsed Lincoln. Then, after Sherman took Atlanta, Greeley wrote an editorial urging a vote for Lincoln over George McClellan, after all.

• • •

During the aftermath of the assassination, Greeley had been steadfast in backing the Freedmen's Bureau, and he endorsed both the Fourteenth and Fifteenth amendments. But his thinking about race illustrated an ambivalence common in the North. Speaking to a friend in 1870, Greeley blamed the blacks themselves for the dependence fostered by slavery. He described Negroes as an "easy, worthless race, taking no thought for the morrow" and deplored a tendency to "look to others to calculate and provide for them."

Greeley tried to hasten the transformation to self-sufficiency by investing six thousand dollars to buy land for freed slaves in North Carolina. But because of an inept white partner, he wound up owning 150 acres of the Great Dismal Swamp.

When Greeley joined in the unpopular move to stand bail for Jefferson Davis, Andrew Johnson's summation of Greeley was not unkind. "Angelic child," the president called him. "All heart and no head . . . like a whale ashore."

Greeley's eye for talent had brought him not only journalists such as Whitelaw Reid and Charles Dana, but also a young Missouri writer he hired as a foreign correspondent. In 1867, the *Tribune* paid Samuel Clemens forty dollars each for reports from Paris, Jerusalem, and Cairo. Clemens collected the columns and published them as *Innocents Abroad* under the name Mark Twain.

With Greeley nominated by the Liberal Republicans, prominent women would be speaking out during the campaign, even though they were denied a vote of their own, but Greeley's halting conversion to the cause of women's rights had left Elizabeth Cady Stanton preferring to "see Beelzebub President over Greeley."

Other women forgave his ambiguity. They saw that Greeley was clearly torn: He knew, he said, that women had "a natural right" to vote, but he remained convinced that demanding that right was "unwise or unnatural."

That tepid backing was enough for Anna E. Dickinson to leave the Republican Party and work to defeat Grant. A graduate of DePauw University in Indiana and a popular speaker at political rallies, Miss Dickinson laced into the president, claiming that he had shown a "greater fondness for the smoke of a cigar and the aroma of a wine glass" than for carrying out his duties.

An abolitionist from her earliest years, she accepted the judgment of the Liberal Republicans that Reconstruction had succeeded and called for an end to "special legislation" for blacks. Instead, the nation should allow "the democratic process to work its magic in the South."

During their convention in Baltimore, the Democrats responded to the overtures from Liberal Republicans by adopting their entire platform. As the campaign progressed and Grant played no part, a Philadelphia editor worried that the president was not taking the challenge seriously. He went to the White House to voice his concern in person.

Grant did not argue with him. He sent for a map, spread it out across his desk, and pointed one by one to the states his Republicans would carry.

On September 4, 1872, a headline in the *New York Sun* threatened to shatter Grant's complacency. "The King of Frauds," it proclaimed. "How the Crédit Mobilier Bought Its Way Through Congress."

The paper charged that Union Pacific had bribed members of Congress for favors with railroad stock in its construction company, Crédit Mobilier. One of the largest corporations in the nation's history, Union Pacific depended on the government at every level—federal land grants for right of ways as well as state and county investments in its stock.

As Union Pacific was prospering, Grant had still been at war with the Confederacy. A Massachusetts congressman named Oakes Ames had been summoned to the Lincoln White House. As Ames told the story, the president turned over to him the stewardship of Union Pacific and a sense of urgency about its completion. "If the subsidies provided are not enough to build the road," Ames quoted Lincoln as saying, "ask double and you shall have it."

By completing this essential railroad line, Lincoln assured Ames, he would "become the remembered man of your generation."

Inspired, Ames and his brother Oliver bought a controlling million dollars of the line's Crédit Mobilier stock. On December 12, 1867, the company declared its first dividend, a profit on investment of 76 percent. Oakes Ames saw a way to use the earnings to influence legislators and promote ever-greater investment. He persuaded two U.S. senators and nine representatives to buy stock.

Union Pacific continued to flourish. A golden spike driven on May 10, 1869, at Promontory, Utah, joined Union Pacific's lines with those of the Central Pacific, and overnight the exhausting journey from New York to San Francisco with its thousand-dollar ticket became drastically shortened. Travelers could now make the same trip in a Pullman sleeping car for $150.

When the *Sun* published names of public officials with stock in Crédit Mobilier, their investment was seen as an obvious conflict of interest. President Grant was not on the list, but his vice president, Schuyler Colfax, appeared prominently.

Other compromised investors included two Republican representatives, Speaker of the House James G. Blaine from Maine and James A. Garfield from Ohio. As the *Sun*'s competitors undertook their own investigations, Oakes Ames claimed to see no scandal. He said he had simply wanted to place the Crédit Mobilier stock "where it would do the most good."

But the firm's business practices could not withstand the new scrutiny. It had provided swollen profits by delaying payment to its subcontractors and to its low-paid workers, in some cases refusing to pay them altogether.

To readers of the *North American Review*, the accusations were nothing new. Crédit Mobilier had been able to ride out the bad publicity three years earlier from a denunciation in the journal by Charles Francis Adams, but the *Sun* exposé jolted Congress into action.

Although hearings were already under way while the presidential voting was being held, the scandal had not yet caught the public's imagination. Horace Greeley, who might have exploited the issue, had been singed by earlier accusations that he had been allowed to buy Northern Pacific stock at bargain rates in exchange for favorable coverage in his *Tribune*.

The investigation would exonerate Blaine, Treasury Secretary Boutwell, and Roscoe Conkling of New York, all of whom were found to have refused Ames's bribes. The evidence against Garfield and Schuyler Colfax was deemed inconclusive.

James W. Patterson of New Hampshire was expelled from the Senate. Oakes Ames and New York congressman James Brooks were censured; Brooks died in May 1873, and when Ames died a week later, friends claimed it was from shame.

President Grant, however blameless, was once more tainted by his associations. Yet when the votes were counted on November 5, 1872, his resulting landside confirmed every one of Grant's state-by-state predictions. He won 55.6 percent of the popular vote, the highest number in the forty-four years since Andrew Jackson beat John Quincy Adams.

Backing from the Democrats allowed Greeley to take six Southern and border states—Georgia, Tennessee, Texas, Kentucky, Missouri, and Maryland. But the president's popularity carried over to the Congress, with Grant Republicans winning two-thirds majorities in both Houses.

For Grant, the personal attacks had been hurtful. In a rare burst of self-pity, he lamented, "I have been the subject of abuse and slander scarcely equaled in political history."

During the month of November, Horace Greeley lost not only the election but almost everything else he valued. Like Grant, he saw himself as a target for viciousness: "I have been assailed so bitterly that I hardly knew whether I was running for President or for the Penitentiary."

Several days before the election, Molly Greeley died. Within weeks, Greeley lost control of the *Tribune* to shareholders unhappy with its declining circulation. On Thursday, November 20, feverish and unable to sleep, Greeley went to bed and waited for the end.

Nine days later, as his daughters and Whitelaw Reid kept vigil, Horace Greeley died at the age of sixty-one.

President Grant led the funeral procession in an open carriage through the streets of Manhattan to the Greenwood Cemetery in Brooklyn. Grant's cabinet accompanied him, as did General Sherman and Chief Justice Chase.

Looking over the mourners, Henry Ward Beecher pronounced his eulogy: "The government itself stands still on his demise."

Hiram Revels

CHAPTER 17

HIRAM REVELS (1872–1873)

As PRESIDENT GRANT's RE-ELECTION CAMPAIGN WAS ENDING, Pinckney Pinchback's alliance with Governor Henry Clay Warmoth had become further frayed but not entirely over. To Pinchback's disgust, the governor had opposed the Civil Rights Bill of 1870. More unforgivably, he blocked Pinchback's bid for an open U.S. Senate seat a year later.

Like many white Republicans throughout the country, Warmoth was aggressively courting his state's Democrats, which led to a reluctance to endorse Negro candidates. Following his lead, white Republicans in Louisiana sent to Washington a white Union veteran; Pinchback's seven votes came entirely from fellow black legislators.

For the moment, Pinchback submerged his bitterness and joined with his state senate colleagues, whatever their race, in devising new schemes for pocketing public money.

Rumors about the bribes to Pinchback had become routine. In one instance, he was said to have demanded a thousand dollars to vote for legislation that would enrich the Jackson Railroad.

A more flagrant offense came to light when Pinchback was appointed as a New Orleans park commissioner. He and his four colleagues bought city land along the Metairie Ridge for sixty-five thousand dollars. Four months later, they sold half of the property for eighty thousand.

Even that transaction might have escaped notice if Pinchback's former partner, state senator Caesar Carpetier Antoine, had not complained loudly about being cheated out of his share of the spoils.

When Louisiana's graft could no longer go unchallenged, Congress sent a committee of five members to investigate. Pinchback did not deign to appear at their hearings. Instead, he sent a letter calling the accusations against him "unqualifiedly false" and attributing them to lobbyists for the Jackson Railroad seeking revenge because he had spurned their overtures.

Pinchback assured his senate colleagues, "I do not claim to possess all the honesty in the state. Yet I venture to say that my character would appear as the driven snow" in comparison with that of his accusers.

Unwilling to get involved, the congressmen recommended against federal intervention.

Rifts within the Republican ranks were forcing Pinchback to forgive Warmoth, at least long enough to combat a rival faction led by Oscar James Dunn, the black housepainter who had defeated Pinchback for lieutenant governor.

Animosity ran so high between the camps by August 1871 that the courthouse had been ringed by deputy marshals; two of them were armed with the new, rapid-fire Gatling guns.

Warmoth chose to move his convention to nearby Turner Hall, where delegates elected Pinchback as their presiding officer. Accepting the position required him to acknowledge his personal differences with the governor but claim he had always supported his administration.

With that, Warmoth sent Pinchback to Washington to resolve a patronage dispute with President Grant. The issue was sensitive because the man Warmoth wanted fired was Grant's brother-in-law, James F. Casey. But en route, Pinchback saw no need for diplomacy.

Casey "hadn't a handful of brains," he told a reporter from the *Cincinnati Commercial*, "and no will of his own."

They met at Grant's summer cottage in New Jersey, and the president heard out the charges against Casey. But when he said nothing and took no action, Lieutenant Governor Dunn seemed to have emerged as the dominant black voice in Louisiana politics.

Then, as Pinchback was evaluating his future, Oscar Dunn contracted pneumonia and died.

Now it was Warmoth who had to forget that he had once called Pinchback "restless, ambitious," even dangerous. He overrode protests from his new white Democratic allies and nominated Pinckney Pinchback as Louisiana's lieutenant governor.

In the state senate, C. C. Antoine, by now entirely estranged from Pinchback, voted against him. So did—given the etiquette of the day—Pinchback himself. With the result headed toward a tie, a Customs House worker named J. B. Lewis put his vote on the market.

The Republicans promised Lewis fifteen thousand dollars cash to cast the deciding ballot. They also extorted his pledge to vote with the Warmoth faction through the end of the legislative session, when he would receive his payoff.

Learning of the deal, Pinchback protested that the bribe had been too high until he saw a note from the opposition offering Lewis five thousand dollars. The Republicans said they had no choice but to improve on Lewis's inflated price.

When the vote was called, Pinchback was confirmed, eighteen to sixteen.

His term was troubled from the start. To prevent a quorum, opposition senators hid aboard a U.S. revenue cutter supplied by James Casey and sailed down the Mississippi. As tension rose, Warmoth secretly deputized 250 new policemen to stop the House from acting without the Senate's being in session.

The governor's enemies struck back by invoking the 1871 Enforcement Act, intended to protect against the Klan. Now Warmoth and Pinchback were accused under the act of depriving a class of citizens of their rights; they were arrested and released on bail.

When the legislative session finally opened, Pinchback was challenged again as presiding officer. This time, he ignored tradition, voted for himself, and took his seat.

For all its drama, the session accomplished little. Pinchback did use his position, however, to place his nine-year-old son, Pinckney Napoleon, in an all-white school. Pinchback anticipated the hostility the child would face. But he was determined that his son get the education he had been deprived of.

From his earliest speeches in Alabama, Pinchback had reminded black audiences of the effects of that deprivation:

"Take any race, keep them in the most miserable condition possible, enslave them for two hundred and forty-odd years as the colored race has been, and compare them with the colored race. I do not think that you will find much difference."

His speech concluded with a plea to give the former slaves "as many years in freedom and opportunity as they have been in slavery, and if they do not compare favorably with any other race on earth, then I say let them be branded an inferior race."

Until then, if he ever failed to speak out for black equality "may my right hand forget its cunning and my tongue cleave to the roof of my mouth."

In March 1872, Pinckney Pinchback became the first black governor in the history of the United States, but there was an asterisk next to his achievement: He was only acting governor, because Henry Warmoth had gone to New York to endorse Horace Greeley and the Liberal Republicans.

Across the South, other black candidates were also reaching high rank, but were often denied their victories. When John W. Menard had been elected to the U.S. Congress from Louisiana four years earlier, white congressmen blocked his being seated. Menard made history all the same. Permitted fifteen minutes to argue his case, Menard became the first black man to speak on the House floor.

With Democrats holding firm as the white man's party, the black candidates who won offices throughout the former Confederacy were always Republicans. In South Carolina, Jonathan Jasper Wright was elected to the state's supreme court. Another black South Carolinian, Joseph H. Rainey, won his seat when Representative Benjamin F. Whittemore, a white Republican, was forced to resign for selling appointments to the military academies.

Rainey achieved what John Menard had been denied. On December 12, 1870, he became the first black member of the House. A month later, Jefferson Long of Georgia followed him, and Robert Brown Elliott, also from South Carolina, was seated in that Forty-first Congress.

In the next House, their number increased by three: Robert Carlos DeLarge from South Carolina; Benjamin S. Turner from Alabama; and Josiah T. Walls from Florida.

And in 1870, Mississippi sent Hiram Rhodes Revels to the U.S. Senate as its first black member. An elated Charles Sumner welcomed him warmly: "Today," he said, "we make the Declaration a reality."

Hiram Revels had never been a slave. His parents, a free couple in Fayetteville, North Carolina, had managed to evade the state's law against educating black children before they shipped their adolescent son north to seminaries in Indiana and Ohio.

In his early twenties, Hiram married Phoeba Bass, a free black Ohio woman; they would have six daughters. He followed his father into the pulpit as a Baptist preacher and tried to avoid incendiary topics. Yet Revels was arrested in St. Louis for his mild sermons to a black congregation.

To support his family, Revels cut hair in a barbershop while he continued his academic studies at Knox College in Galesburg, Illinois.

When war came, Revels volunteered as a chaplain to Maryland's first black regiment.

With the peace, he went to Kansas to organize black schools for the Freedmen's Bureau and then to Mississippi and a new role in politics. In 1868, Revels was a compromise selection for the state senate. When Congress approved the Fifteenth Amendment the following year, Mississippi was eligible to send its two senators back to Washington, and Revels became a popular choice. Although he would be taking the second seat, not the one held by Jefferson Davis, the symbolism reverberated throughout the nation.

The political cartoonist Thomas Nast portrayed Jeff Davis exiting a theater stage as Iago and muttering, "For that I do suspect the lusty Moor hath leap'd into my seat, the thought whereof doth like a poisonous mineral gnaw my innards."

. . .

To the state's Republicans, Revels was a godsend. A free man without the resentments or ingrained deference of a former slave, he was devoted to his family and had been exposed to higher education. Heavy-set, light-skinned, well-dressed, Revels greeted the world with a ready smile.

But he had entered politics sharing his party's distrust of the Democrats. If they have the chance, Revels assured audiences, they would rescind black rights "as certainly as the sun shines in the heavens."

Despite strong support from Sumner and his fellow Radicals, Democratic cartoonists were drawing Revels as a wild-eyed Zulu, and opponents quibbled over seating him on the grounds of Chief Justice Taney's ruling that he could not be a citizen.

That mention of the Dred Scott decision stoked Sumner's oratorical fire. He called the decision "a putrid corpse . . . a stench in the nostrils and a scandal to the Court itself."

Sumner predicted that seating Hiram Revels would have repercussions far beyond the Capitol. "Doors will open, exclusions will give way, intolerance will cease, and the great truth will manifest in a thousand examples: Liberty and Equality are the two express promises of our fathers. Both are now assured."

When Revels was confirmed by a comfortable margin, he rose unflustered from his place on a sofa behind Sumner's desk and at 4:40 p.m. on Friday, February 25, 1870, took the oath of office.

From Philadelphia, the *Inquirer* mocked the prevailing hysteria among the Democrats. "The colored United States Senator from Mississippi has been awarded his seat, and we have not had an earthquake, our free institutions have not been shaken to their foundations, nor have the streets of our large cities been converted to blood."

Revels was canny in choosing the subject of his maiden speech. The state of Georgia had been devising inventive subterfuges for refusing to send elected black delegates to Congress. White Democrats endorsed the strategy, which they called "masterly inactivity." One approach admitted that Georgia's new state constitution gave black citizens the right to vote but not the right to hold office.

The Senate galleries were packed with black faces eager to hear Revels make history. He began hesitantly. Then, shifting into his pulpit cadences, he reminded the chamber that when the Confederate army conscripted white soldiers, their mothers, wives, sisters, and daughters had been left at home to be protected by their black slaves.

"And now, sir, I ask how did that race act? Did they evince the malignity of which we hear so much? They waited, and they waited patiently. In the absence of their masters, they protected the virtue and chastity of defenseless women.

"Mr. President, I maintain that the past record of my race is a true index of the feelings which today animate them."

Revels built upon the acclaim for that speech with an appeal for a general amnesty for his state's former Confederates. Like other Republicans, he wanted to disprove the accusation that they favored continuing the ban against whites voting in order to perpetuate themselves in office. In fact, white Republicans were courting Democrats across the nation as Warmoth had done, usually at the expense of their black constituents.

Given that development, Revels could assure the Senate that "the people now are getting along as quietly, pleasantly, harmoniously, and prosperously as the people are in any of the formerly free states."

He concluded, "I am in favor of amnesty in Mississippi. The state is fit for it."

As Republicans formed alliances with Democrats, the former rebels made accommodation easier for them by avoiding their rabid oratory. Less than a month after Lincoln had been elected in 1860, Mississippi's governor had called for secession to avoid the menace of "Black Republican politics and free negro morals." A colleague from his state had argued that "our fathers made this a government for the white man, rejecting the negro as an ignorant, inferior, barbarian race, incapable of self-government, and not, therefore, entitled to be associated with the white man upon terms of civil, political or social equality."

These days, Democrats preferred to frame their motive in seceding not as racism but entirely as a defense of states' rights. Everywhere but in the Klan, their language had been toned and polished, much in the way that the vitriol against Lincoln had abated. Rather than denounce the martyred president, Democrats now assailed his successor.

Republican leaders themselves granted that their white candidates in the South seldom reflected the business or professional background of their constituents. Coming from the North made them vulnerable to the charge of being carpetbaggers.

Since few of them, black or white, had an independent political base like Pinchback's, they depended on federal patronage, and to survive, they sometimes alienated voters by inflating their government salaries.

But Pinchback's temporary perch in the governor's chair was not translating into either money or new powers. His chief duty that year was to preside over Mardi Gras, which had been declared a legal holiday for the first time. Pinchback looked on as white men impersonating the mythic Comus and Circe used the celebration to mock Warmoth and the other leading carpetbaggers.

Reporting to the governor, Pinchback boasted about the size of the bribes he was turning down. He could not be bought, he said, for a hundred thousand dollars these days.

Throughout the presidential campaign, Pinchback stood aloof from the Liberal Republicans and assured reporters that his "relations with President Grant are at present most friendly" and that he knew "that the leading colored men" felt the same.

To satisfy himself that Grant remained committed to black equality, Pinchback went twice to Washington for interviews with the president. Once more, Grant's vague assurances disappointed him; Pinchback was already impatient with the slow progress that was still forcing Louisiana Negroes to eat in separate restaurants and attend segregated theaters.

To hurry the pace, Pinchback joined with other prominent blacks— including Antoine—in inviting black officeholders from across the country to Louisville, Kentucky, for a National Colored Convention.

The event was guaranteed national attention when Frederick Douglass agreed to serve as its chairman.

As delegates arrived from as far away as Ohio and Massachusetts, conservative newspapers took alarm and charged organizers with trying to recruit "a negro party," an accusation the convention immediately voted to deny.

And sharp divisions within the black ranks were soon on public display. When a firebrand from Kansas invoked the spirit of Nat Turner, he was rebuked by an Alabaman, who warned that such rash talk could lead to his death at the hands of white supremacists.

Pinchback was contemptuous of that timidity, and Douglass won unanimous passage of a platform calling for "just rights and privileges" in public places and on public transport.

Pinchback chose the convention for announcing that if Charles Sumner were running for president, he would support him "even if there were forty thousand Grants." Instead, he was backing the Republican nominee.

General Grant "has done a good deal for me," Pinchback said. "He has, by the iron hand, stayed bloodshed in this Southern country. He has kept thousands of my race from being assassinated. He has in every way showed his appreciation."

Pinchback concluded lightly that Grant "may be a little crotchety, but many of those crochets are influenced by his wife, Mrs. Grant."

With Warmoth committed to the Liberals, Pinchback could congratulate himself on choosing the winning side. The future seemed to present no obstacle to his becoming governor in his own right. Or a member of the House of Representatives. Or a U.S. senator. Or, given his talent, nerve, and connections, all of them.

Morrison Waite

CHAPTER 18

GRANT'S SECOND TERM
(1873–1876)

ULYSSES GRANT HAD FOUND HIS FIRST TERM AS PRESIDENT LESS onerous than he feared and expected the second to unroll as smoothly. Before it ended, however, the next four years of peace would test him as harshly as war had done. Grant would learn that a military commander's steadfast loyalty to his officers became less admired in a civilian president.

The travail began the day before Grant's second inaugural when Ben Butler succeeded in passing a bill to repair long-standing inequities in the federal payroll. Butler's proposal doubled the size of the president's salary from the annual $25,000 that dated from George Washington's day. His bill would also raise the pay of cabinet officers and Supreme Court justices.

Even the increase for congressmen from $5,000 to $7,500 might have provoked no outcry; their salary had not gone up since 1852.

But the bill made the raise retroactive for the two years from the start of the current Congress. Members might call that extra $5,000 a "bonus." An infuriated public labeled it a "salary grab."

The bill included the same back pay for Grant. Either he signed it or the government would be left without funding until Congress met again at the end of the year. Grant signed, and then watched anger build until the first business taken up by the Forty-third Congress in December was repealing the pay raise for the Forty-second.

. . .

Only a fluke linked Grant's administration to the name of the next crisis. Republicans had dropped his first vice president, Schuyler Colfax, from their ticket because of the Crédit Mobilier investigation and replaced him with Henry Wilson, even though Wilson was also tainted by scandal. And he was still trailed by suspicions that, early in the war, he had inadvertently revealed military secrets about the pending Battle of Bull Run to a Washington hostess who turned out to be a Southern spy. But in facing the Greeley challenge, Wilson was a dependable Massachusetts Radical.

Vice President Colfax, so genial that colleagues called him "Smiley," had been popular among Louisiana Republicans, who named a new voting district in his honor. Three hundred and fifty miles north of New Orleans, bordered by the Red River and composed of only a few hundred white and black voters, Colfax was one more nondescript Southern hamlet. Until Easter Sunday, 1873, when Colfax became notorious.

The Grant administration had recently certified the election of a Republican governor, William Kellogg. Democrats in Colfax refused to recognize him, and both parties claimed control of the town's two-story courthouse.

William Ward, along with another black Republican and a white friend named Daniel Shaw, occupied the building and underscored their determination by marching their small number of recruits through the town square. As weapons, the men shouldered antiquated rifles or, lacking those, pitchforks and hoes.

The confrontation seemed headed toward a meaningless standoff until rumors spread among the white community that this black militia intended to seize the entire town. Ward's face had been badly scarred during the war, which lent menace to his past threats to confiscate the neighboring white plantations.

The stories grew wilder. A black ally of Ward's from Pennsylvania was accused of breaking into the house of a white Democratic judge and defiling the coffin of his young daughter.

When the judge rode to New Orleans to demand protection, Republicans accused his fellow white Democrats of inventing the charge to whip up resentment against blacks, and Governor Kellogg refused to send troops.

By Easter Sunday, Christopher Columbus Nash, the Democratic sheriff, had brought together 150 white men from neighboring hamlets. After shouting threats in front of the courthouse, Nash called for a thirty-minute truce to allow black women and children to withdraw to safety.

When they had scattered, Nash's men opened fire. The black men under siege returned the barrage with their shotguns. After three hours of bloodless volleying, the white attackers took time off for dinner and a game of cards.

During that time, Ward and his defenders had concocted two jerry-built cannon by drilling holes in stovepipe that would let them fire a hail of bolts and nails. At the first shot from that improvised artillery, Nash's men dragged up an old cannon and launched a cannonball.

The courthouse caught fire. Overcome by smoke, black men appeared at the upstairs windows, waving scraps of white cloth and yelling, "Don't shoot! We are whipped!"

A few stray shots from the courthouse wounded two white leaders on the street, however, and convinced Nash that the surrender had been a trick. His men surrounded the burning building and shot or bayoneted the blacks as they fled. Some who tried to escape through a cypress pond were shot in the back.

A witness reported that "one could have walked on dead Negroes almost an acre big."

White revenge then moved to a cotton field where black prisoners were working. Told that they were being moved to a neighboring town, they were led two by two out of sight of the others and shot. A witness said that the gunfire "was like popcorn in a skillet," as forty-eight blacks were executed.

As reports of the massacre reached New Orleans, Governor Kellogg was stymied in sending federal troops because white steamboat owners refused to ferry them. They said that cooperating with Kellogg would destroy their business.

New Orleans police reached Colfax within days, however, and federal forces a week later. Because some victims had sunk in the river, no accurate count of the dead was possible, but more than a hundred men had been gunned down. Even compared with Nathan Forrest's wartime bloodbath at Fort Pillow, Colfax became known as the worst atrocity of Reconstruction.

With midterm elections approaching, racial violence spread across Louisiana. Although Grant's crackdown had disbanded the Klan, its spirit survived in a network called the White Leagues. Armed members began rampaging through black parishes, seizing power by murdering black Republican officeholders.

In New Orleans, Grant's old friend James Longstreet led a rally of local police and black militia to repel the thirty-five hundred White Leaguers who were determined to take over the hotel that was serving as the statehouse.

The league lost twenty-five dead and nineteen wounded, but members occupied the building and seated their own Democratic state officials. News of their coup set off widespread white rejoicing across the state, and the conciliatory Democrat they named as governor promised peace and protection for the state's blacks.

The next midterm elections reflected a historic shift in the national mood. For the first time since 1856, Democrats won control of the House of Representatives nationally and picked up ten seats in the Senate.

To end the Democrats' revolt in Louisiana, Grant sent General Sheridan to the scene with three gunboats and five thousand troops. When they surrounded the statehouse, white resistance evaporated.

Sheridan asked Grant for authorization to arrest leaders of the White League and try them by courts-martial. When his proposal was leaked to the press, not only did the South erupt in fury, but Northerners joined in protesting the infringement on the Constitution. Grant sent Sheridan back an encouraging telegram but did not issue the proclamation.

Instead, he released a report deploring that "the spirit of hatred and violence is stronger than law" in Louisiana. But with Sheridan's threat still hanging over them, White League members stayed at home, and Sheridan could exult to Washington that "the dog is dead."

The opposition press was unforgiving. The *New York Tribune* called the president's actions outrageous: "General Grant has vanquished the people of Louisiana again." But at a memorial for the dead in New Orleans, Pinckney Pinchback spoke for grateful Republicans as he mourned the black victims by quoting from Shakespeare's *Richard III*: "Give me no help in lamentation."

In court, the outcome of the murders proved damaging to Pinchback's cause. The federal government indicted ninety-eight white men under the Enforcement Acts. Nine were brought to trial; a hung jury freed eight. A second trial convicted three, including a man named William Cruikshank.

When the Supreme Court ruled later in *United States* v. *Cruikshank*, members found unanimously that the right of the black victims at Colfax to assemble had not been guaranteed because they were neither petitioning Congress nor protesting a federal law. Assembling for any other cause was not protected.

The Supreme Court ruling was another blow to Grant's attempt to keep Reconstruction alive through the executive branch. By then, he had learned not to depend on rulings from Salmon Chase, whose health had been a concern for years.

When Chase's daughter Kate put the Chief Justice on display to prove him still fit for his duties, Carl Schurz found Chase's "futile effort to appear youthfully vigorous and agile" merely pathetic.

Two strokes had left his speech halting and slurred. Chase seemed to accept his decline, although he continued to say that, as president, "I would have been useful to my country." During Court testimony, on May 5, 1873, Chase remarked, "I feel as though I were dead, though alive." Two days later, he was gone.

Grant's attempts to fill Chase's position frustrated a military commander proud of being decisive. Once again, he refused to announce his nomination before the Senate reconvened to ratify it. "I thought a chief justice should never be subjected to the mortification of a rejection," Grant said.

But his first choice, the leader of Senate Republicans, Roscoe Conkling from New York, was forty-four and afflicted with the same ambition as Salmon Chase. Preparing for a presidential campaign, Conkling turned Grant down.

After that unexpected refusal, the president flailed about. He offered the post to Secretary of State Fish and was refused again. With the Court about to convene, the president turned to George Williams, his current attorney general, but he was thwarted by public opinion, which held that Williams had botched the Crédit Mobilier prosecution, losing the government's case despite overwhelming evidence.

Those false starts left Grant with Morrison Remick Waite, who was popular with the Ohio bar but largely unknown outside his state. *The Nation* praised Grant sardonically for "the remarkable skill with which he evaded choosing any first-rate man."

By April 1874, support for Negro rights was diminishing as the country turned toward the future and the promise of riches along an expanding frontier. As he pursued policies to redeem his earlier promises, Grant was charting a course that sometimes put him at odds with his political advisers. With his 1874 veto, for example, he freed the country from its wartime reliance on greenbacks, despite warnings that he would jeopardize Republican candidates in the midterm election.

But Grant judged hard money to be the only sound and stable monetary policy, and Congress sustained his veto.

As he was combating inflation, however, the president was hit by scandals that were harder to explain away than Crédit Mobilier.

In one instance, Congress had turned over a lucrative tax collector's post to an ally of Benjamin Butler. An investigation suggested—but could not definitely prove—that the appointee had split illegal profits with Grant's secretary of the Treasury, William Richardson, and had paid out $156,000 in bribes.

Although Grant refused to ask for Richardson's resignation, he left the cabinet one step ahead of a censure vote by the House. The country seemed willing to trust Grant's integrity, but a drumroll of accusations had begun that would outlast his presidency.

Benjamin Bristow, the forty-year-old solicitor general who served Grant well in his showdown with the Klan, was making enemies with his unrelenting prosecution of the Whiskey Ring. Bristow had seen the Treasury Department's chief clerk convicted of corruption, along with a collector and his deputy in St. Louis. Now Bristow turned up evidence that implicated Grant's personal secretary, Brigadier General Orville Babcock.

Grant's friends were convinced that the president would favor principle over personal loyalty, but they knew that any decision would be wrenching for him.

To Bristow, Grant urged a full investigation: "Let no guilty man escape if it can be avoided." He assured his attorney general that "if Babcock is guilty, there is no man who wants him so proven guilty as I do, for it is the greatest piece of traitorism to me that a man could possibly practice."

To Grant's relief, the evidence against his closest aide was flimsy— two telegrams from Babcock that might be interpreted as referring to a matter unrelated to the Whiskey Ring. Grant pronounced himself satisfied. Then, early in December 1875, Babcock demanded that a military court be convened to clear his name.

His gamble backfired. Instead, a federal grand jury in St. Louis indicted Babcock for conspiring to defraud the Treasury. Grant was convinced the charge was a political attempt to embarrass him, and it took strenuous protests from his cabinet members to dissuade him from traveling to Missouri to rebut the charges.

Grant settled on drafting a disposition addressed to Chief Justice Waite that upheld Babcock's honor. Coming from a general venerated for his truth-telling, Grant's affidavit resolved the matter in the public mind. Babcock was acquitted. But Grant's faith in his discretion had been shaken, and Babcock was shunted off to become inspector of lighthouses. Grant's sons took over his secretarial duties.

Bristow added to the president's discomfort by trying to avoid a congressional hearing and invoking executive privilege. Grant wanted to avoid any further cloud over the White House, and he opened all relevant records and directed Bristow to testify.

Those accusations were playing out against the background of a spoils system first introduced to Washington by Andrew Jackson. His newly victorious Democrats had boasted openly in 1828 that they intended to use government appointments to reward their party's friends.

It offered little consolation to Grant now that he had detected rot in the process and had worked to change it. He had seen the aftermath of the war leave hundreds of positions for his party to fill, and yet the country expected him to wring out partisan corruption. Grant called the spoils system "an abuse of long standing," and early in his second term he had proposed rigid new criteria.

All applications and promotions were to be awarded on the basis of examinations overseen by experts from the specific department. "A true reform," Grant said, "will let the office seek the man," rather than have party loyalists scratching for jobs.

Congress did not share the president's vision, and the crusade lapsed. Four years later, the need for reform had become clearer than ever when Grant's secretary of war, William Belknap, and his free-spending wife, Carrie, were accused of extorting money from a lucrative Oklahoma trading post.

Carrie Belknap died soon after the payoffs were arranged, but quarterly payments of fifteen hundred dollars continued to pass to Belknap's new wife, a sister-in-law of Carrie's whom he married late in 1873. By the time the bribes were uncovered, the Belknaps had collected twenty thousand dollars.

Barely one step ahead of his congressional critics, Belknap rushed to the White House and begged Grant to accept his resignation. Unaware of the urgency, Grant said, "Certainly, if you wish it." Only afterward did the president learn that the House of Representatives had voted unanimously to impeach his secretary.

His frantic resignation served its purpose, however, when Congress could not establish that it had control over a private citizen.

To his cabinet, Grant spoke of the sorrow the scandal had caused him, given his affection for Belknap's family. Other times, however, the president was harder to read.

What motive had influenced him, for example, when West Point expelled the academy's first black cadet? James W. Smith, a graduate of a South Carolina Freedmen's Bureau school, had been admitted to the class of 1870 but was harassed for three years before being dismissed on trumped-up charges. Critics suggested that Grant had refused to intervene because his son was a member of Smith's class.

Black leaders also deplored Grant's inaction after the economic depression of 1874 wiped out the Freedmen's Saving and Trust Company. The deposits of sixty-one thousand blacks were lost, including ten thousand dollars from Frederick Douglass.

Looking for reasons to praise Grant's second term, his defenders pointed to his endorsement of Charles Sumner's final crusade for Negro rights. But the history of Grant's support told a different story.

By the time of the re-election campaign, the two men had become irreparably estranged, and yet Sumner held back from joining the Liberal Republicans. He disapproved of their strategy of currying favor with Democrats by offering a general amnesty throughout the South.

Sumner recognized that the issue was all but moot. After Andrew Johnson pardoned white rebels in the mid-1860s, no federal law prevented them from voting once their states had been readmitted to the Union.

The exception was a handful of prominent Confederates—a few thousand throughout the South—who were still barred by the Fourteenth Amendment from holding public office. They had to be specifically pardoned by a two-thirds vote in both houses of Congress.

Much as he longed for Grant's defeat, Sumner was sure that former slave owners, once returned to power, would deprive blacks of their rights. His instinct was confirmed by reports from the South that no whites were being convicted for violations of their states' civil rights acts.

Flouting of the law could be flagrant. In 1874, Virginia would promise to end school segregation just long enough to seat its congressional delegation. Soon afterward, the state imposed mandatory segregation in its schools.

Given his limited influence in the Senate, Sumner chose not to challenge the amnesty bill as it passed in the House. Instead, he proposed a broad amendment to the Senate version. Sumner included federal guarantees of "equal and impartial enjoyment" of all public transportation on land or water, of inns and theaters, of schools and churches. His amendment challenged racism to the grave: Cemetery associations were forbidden to discriminate.

Sumner had introduced variations of this—his "crowning work"—since May 1870 and had fought colleagues who tried to soften them. He was particularly infuriating to anyone who raised constitutional objections. Sumner declared that the Sermon on the Mount was a higher authority, and so was the Declaration of Independence—"earlier in time, loftier, more majestic, more sublime in character and principle."

Although Sumner's amendment did not provide for enforcement, it would test the sincerity of those arguing for amnesty. Did they want true equality? Or were they conniving to let white Southerners rule over second-class blacks? Sumner was setting a trap for Grant, who favored amnesty but without Sumner's amendment.

The battle revived Sumner's passion. He said, "A measure that seeks to benefit only the former rebels and neglects the colored race does not deserve success."

But neither Democrats nor Liberal Republicans responded to his call. And even most former Radical Republicans remained loyal to the president.

When Democrats denied the bill the necessary two-thirds vote, Grant was the winner. He had survived the showdown without alienating either whites or blacks.

As the election neared, a mild movement arose to nominate Sumner for the presidency. But black leaders, including Frederick Douglass, worried that Sumner's candidacy would ensure a Democratic victory.

Their apprehension turned out to be needless, since Sumner did not run. From his enforced retirement, Andrew Johnson spoke for much of the nation:

"The idea of the Democracy supporting Charles Sumner is too utterly preposterous to talk about."

Brooding over his options, Sumner waited until late July 1872 to endorse Horace Greeley. By then, all he had accomplished was to alienate

his steadfast Republican allies. Henry Longfellow berated Sumner for believing promises from Democrats that they were prepared to protect the rights of black Southerners. And a *Harper's Weekly* cartoonist, Thomas Nast, drew Sumner as Robinson Crusoe, deserting the Negro people as he sailed off with the Democrats and their new Liberal allies.

The tensions further strained Sumner's ailing body and troubled mind. Reluctantly, he accepted his doctor's insistence that he must abstain from politics to avoid a complete breakdown. Friends tried to smuggle him out of the country on a ship bound for Europe, but Grant heard of his departure and predicted contentedly that Sumner would never be healthy enough to return to the Senate.

For the second time, his enemies counted him out too soon. After ten weeks of enforced leisure, Sumner came home to learn that he would have to fight to remain within the Republican Party. Clashing with party leaders, he was even censured at one point by the Massachusetts legislature.

Influential friends tried to get the insult revoked, but equally imposing witnesses denounced Sumner for his history of egotism and for his fulsome praise of his new allies. Julia Ward Howe singled out Greeley Republicans for their "high-handed and overbearing man-worship" of Sumner.

All the while, angina attacks and digestive woes often had Sumner out of bed twenty times a night. The doctor who had guided him back to health after the assault by Preston Brooks was now sending advice from New York, but Sumner's Washington doctors missed the severity of his arterial stoppage. To permit him moments of rest, a local physician came by every evening at ten-thirty to administer a shot of morphine.

Over the next months, Sumner's condition improved enough that he could endure the fifteen-minute hearing that ended his marriage on grounds of desertion, and he could show up when the Senate opened a special session on March 4, 1873.

At the beginning of the Senate's regular session that December, Sumner once again introduced his comprehensive civil rights bill. At first, Republicans loyal to Grant were ready to mock Sumner for expecting Liberals and Democrats to keep the promises they had been making.

But while his ebbing strength kept Sumner all but housebound, he received two consolations: The Massachusetts legislature did rescind its condemnation, and in the Senate Sumner's bill was showing surprising vigor.

Even those favorable omens took their toll. The man who handed him the legislature's vindication recalled that after Sumner read the document, "He turned his head and wept as I never saw a man weep before." Collecting himself, Sumner said, "I knew Massachusetts would do me justice."

The same newspaper that carried the story from the legislature included an item about his ex-wife: Alice Sumner was considering marriage again, news that contributed to Sumner's angina. He required ever larger injections of morphine and described his pain as like "a toothache in my heart."

One evening in mid-March 1874, Sumner said good night to his dinner guests at nine o'clock and retired to his study. At eleven, his servants heard a thud and discovered his body on the floor.

Morphine revived him and allowed him to sleep. He murmured that he was weary but worried about the volume of his writings that he was editing. "I should not regret this," Sumner said, "if my book were finished."

One obligation was even more urgent. When Rockwood Hoar arrived the next morning, Sumner awoke long enough to say, "You must take care of the civil rights bill—my bill, the civil-rights bill. Don't let it fail."

He repeated that plea an hour later when Frederick Douglass came to call: "Don't let the bill fail."

His doctor refused him another injection of morphine as too risky, and Sumner grew quiet. Just before 3 p.m. on March 11, his exhausted body rose up in convulsions. He vomited, gasped to breathe, and fell back dead.

• • •

In death, Charles Sumner achieved a harmony that had eluded him in life. When the Massachusetts legislature invited a prominent Mississippi politician to deliver his official eulogy, Lucius Quintus Cincinnatus Lamar rose in the House of Representatives and praised Sumner and his "instinctive love of freedom."

Lamar was the white Southerner who had drafted Mississippi's call to secede from the Union. Now newspapers across the United States printed his eloquent call for the hearts of North and South to "grow toward each other once more."

During the subsequent debate over Sumner's civil rights bill, Ben Butler acted as its Senate manager. Butler extolled the gallantry of the black soldiers whom he had once commanded. He forgot the missteps in Louisiana to remember instead that he had once sworn to himself a solemn oath. He would "defend the rights of these men who have given their blood for me and my country."

Butler had been defeated in the last Massachusetts election, and his short time left in office made him anxious to protect the remnants of Reconstruction. He tied Sumner's bill to other legislation that would broaden its appeal, including an expansion of the Enforcement Acts and the federal courts. He also added a subsidy for the Texas and Pacific Railroad.

But Butler jettisoned specifics. The bill would no longer integrate Southern cemeteries. That was a minor concession. He also agreed, however, to strike out the provision most valued by Sumner, Oliver Howard, and other crusaders for equality: The civil rights bill would no longer require public schools to be integrated.

In fact, the legislation that Butler managed to get passed was even weaker than it seemed since there was still no provision for its enforcement. Individual black plaintiffs would have to go to court to sue for their rights.

All the same, some white Northerners joined the Southern opposition. Fearing the powers that Grant had assumed to quell the insurrection in Louisiana, they were more concerned for their own rights than for those of the blacks.

Wendell Phillips was shouted down at Faneuil Hall in Boston as he reminded the audience of past injustices to blacks. Even the revered abolitionist had to confront the rapid shifting in the nation's mood.

The *New York Times* observed that Phillips and his fellow crusader William Lloyd Garrison were "not exactly extinct from American politics, but they represent ideas in regard to the South which the majority of the Republican Party have outgrown."

As speculation grew about whether Grant would stand for re-election, corruption in Washington was becoming impossible to ignore. And yet when Congressman James Garfield of Ohio encountered the president, he was awed by Grant's public composure:

"His imperturbability is amazing," Garfield wrote in his diary. "I am in doubt whether to call it greatness or stupidity."

Grant's equanimity could be explained in part by an announcement he issued on May 29, 1875, two days after the Pennsylvania Republican Party had endorsed him for a third term. Grant called his cabinet to the White House after Sunday dinner to hear his reaction to the endorsement. Once again, he had not discussed his intentions with his wife, and Hamilton Fish had to assure her that it was mere coincidence that the cabinet officers had all come to call at the same time.

When the president entered the room, Julia Grant knew the men were about to light up their cigars and she withdrew. She waited impatiently until they left and then returned to announce to her husband, "I want to know what is happening. I feel sure there is something, and I must know."

Grant was not done with teasing her. "I will explain as soon as I light my cigar." Out of her sight, he handed an envelope to a messenger at the door. Coming back to her, he reminded Julia about the speculation over his future. "Well, until now," he said, "I have never had the opportunity to answer."

Grant had felt it was improper to address an issue that had not been formally raised, but now the Pennsylvania vote had given him "the opportunity of announcing that I do not wish a third term, and I have written a letter to that effect."

Julia asked why he had not read the letter to her.

"Oh, I know you too well," Grant said, chuckling. "It would never have gone if I had read it to you." Knowing she would be disappointed with his decision, he had "lingered in the hall to light my cigar" while he gave the letter to be posted. Now his future was beyond his wife's power to reshape it.

Rutherford B. Hayes

CHAPTER 19

RUTHERFORD BIRCHARD HAYES (1876)

From his tentative entrance to the world, Rutherford B. Hayes was considered diffident. His father had uprooted the family from New England to seek his fortune in a rustic town on a branch of the Ohio River, and within a few years, he had become partner in a distillery and a stalwart of the Presbyterian Church. But when the noxious fevers of an 1822 epidemic struck Ohio, Hayes was carried off three months before his namesake was born.

The infant looked destined to follow. Neighbors asked regularly whether Mrs. Hayes's baby had survived the night.

But Sophia Birchard Hayes had recently also lost a daughter, and she dedicated herself to sustaining this son, with his large head and enormous, watchful eyes. Her mission became more urgent when her older son went larking on a river with friends, crashed through its ice, and froze to death.

In time, Rutherford was robust enough to go off to Kenyon College, although any form of sport was beyond him. On graduation, he returned home to study with a local lawyer. But the townspeople who found the young man unassuming missed his strong instinct for self-improvement.

He traveled to Massachusetts to enroll in Harvard Law School and applied himself to his courses. In later years, though, classmates remembered little about him but his good nature.

During that period, his mother's brother had become the wealthiest businessman in the state, and Hayes seemed likely to set up a desultory law practice and spend his days reading for pleasure while he awaited his inheritance.

Instead, he married Lucy Ware Webb, a doctor's daughter who channeled his talents into becoming an advocate for local workingmen. While Rud Hayes still indulged his bookish interests at the Cincinnati Literary Club, he also took on and won celebrated cases that furthered his reputation. In politics, he was a Whig—opposed to slavery but no abolitionist. Yet his practice expanded to include the defense of runaway slaves, and he once found himself on a legal team with Salmon Chase.

At home, the city council named Hayes to his first public office, as Cincinnati's solicitor. By then, he had joined the group of political strays who called themselves Republicans. As the new decade opened in 1860, Hayes could survey his prospects contentedly.

But the success of his presidential candidate that year upended Hayes's comfortable life. When the new Confederacy struck at Fort Sumter, his literary society immediately organized its own military company with Hayes in its front rank. He wrote that he feared disunion less than compromise. Unencumbered by the slave states, the North "if we must go on alone, will make a glorious nation."

After the Union loss in Baltimore, Hayes was commissioned as an army major and resigned himself to "a just and necessary war." As uneventful months passed with no action, it was only a routine vacancy that led to his promotion to colonel.

And yet, army service turned out to be a revelation for this man whose early hold on life had been tenuous. Hayes had developed into a sturdy five-foot-eight-inch young man with a fledgling beard and his early moderation still intact. Assessing candidates in his new Republican alliance, Hayes valued Abraham Lincoln for the same coolness toward abolition that troubled the party's Radical wing.

Hayes's first taste of battle left him, he said, no more fazed than he felt at the beginning of any major lawsuit. During a series of minor skirmishes, Hayes was nicked by a rifle ball while Lucy was at home giving birth to their second son.

During the battle leading to Antietam, Hayes was wounded more severely. His men lost track of him in the confusion of battle, and Hayes, nearly dead, had to overcome his native reticence to shout, "Hallo, Twenty-third men! Are you going to leave your colonel here for the enemy?" At a lull in the shooting, a lieutenant carried him to safety.

In September 1862, when the president issued his preliminary proclamation freeing Confederacy slaves, Hayes still doubted its wisdom. But he had come to trust Lincoln—and he wished that he would take a firmer hand in running the war.

His own modest renown on the battlefield was thrusting Hayes further into politics, replacing the amiable attorney with an intense commander, who had been wounded five times and promoted to brigadier general in the last months of the conflict. Still bogged down in a military skirmish, Hayes learned that he had been elected to Congress in Ohio with a twenty-four-hundred-vote margin.

Lincoln's assassination shook Hayes, and he was not at all sure about this new career. He considered serving one term and then retiring to his congenial law practice in Cincinnati. As he told Lucy, one phrase often ran through his head: "Politics is a bad trade."

Once in Washington, however, Hayes was agreeably surprised to find the House of Representatives "more orderly and respectable" than he had expected. He reveled in his luck at being appointed to the Joint Committee on the Library, and from that unlikely watchtower, he tried to promote unity among the postwar Republicans. He soon realized, however, that Andrew Johnson had thrown in with the former rebels.

All the same, his innate moderation made Hayes uncomfortable around Charles Sumner and Thaddeus Stevens, and he was inclined to believe the rumors of corruption within the Freedmen's Bureau.

Hayes left his first session to bury a young son, dead of scarlet fever, but he returned in time to vote for the Fourteenth Amendment, with its guidelines for readmitting the rebel states into the Union.

By the time that his district's Republican convention nominated Hayes for a second term, he confessed to finding the job "pleasant." The one drawback was his separation from Lucy, who stayed at home with their ailing family.

His hopeful nature let Hayes detect encouraging signs of racial progress. "The Negro prejudice is rapidly wearing away," he assured his uncle, although he conceded that it was still very strong among "the ignorant and unthinking generally." When other Republicans wanted to soften the provisions of Thaddeus Stevens's Reconstruction bill, Hayes was deeply moved by Stevens's rebuttal and stood with him.

But Hayes was no crusader. Instead, he had acquired a reputation as "the most patient listener in the Capitol." Hayes said that was because he knew his own limitations. And, besides, he added, congressmen talked too much.

When Ohio Republicans nominated Hayes as their candidate for governor, he resigned from Congress and based his campaign on voting rights for Negroes.

"They are not aliens or strangers," Hayes repeated in his stump speech. "They are here by the misfortune of their fathers and the crime of ours."

In September 1867, Lucy Hayes gave birth to a baby girl to join her surviving sons. When Ohio senator Ben Wade lost his seat in a Democratic sweep, Hayes surprisingly prevailed and took the governorship by slightly less than three thousand of the 484,603 votes cast.

Lucy and their children moved with Hayes to Columbus, where he took pride in giving the shortest inaugural address in Ohio history. As governor, he continued to press for Negro voting rights, even as the Democratic legislature launched its failed attempt to repeal the Fourteenth Amendment.

Ohio governors had no veto power, which insulated Hayes from many policy debates. All in all, he found the job of being governor "the pleasantest I've ever had—not too much hard work, plenty of time to read, good society, etc."

When the state's delegation wired from Washington for guidance on the verdict in Andrew Johnson's impeachment trial, Hayes sent back an economical one word: "Conviction."

Although he worried that Grant's 1862 edict restricting Jews might cost his party votes, Hayes was otherwise enthusiastic about Grant's presidential candidacy. He also pushed for Ben Wade as vice president, but the nomination went to Schuyler Colfax of Indiana.

Two years later, Hayes's margin for re-election was larger than before, helping carry Republicans in the legislature to a majority. His annual message for 1870 called for ratifying the Fifteenth Amendment.

With Lucy's prompting, Hayes backed a variety of social measures, including better care for the state's orphans. He took up civil service reform and an end to electing judges by a popular vote, which he claimed encouraged corruption. Although Hayes carried the vote on the Fifteenth Amendment, his zeal for voting rights did not extend to women.

"The proper discharge of the function of maternity," Hayes wrote, "is inconsistent with the political duties of citizenship." He got no argument from Lucy, despite her having relatives in the suffragette movement.

During a trip to Washington, Hayes enjoyed an evening with Grant on the White House portico with the Washington Monument, almost completed, rising before them. The president was incensed that the Senate had opposed the Santo Domingo treaty and lashed out against Charles Sumner as "puffed-up" and Carl Schurz as "an infidel and an atheist." Hayes listened politely.

In September 1870, Hayes took his son, Birch, to enter his freshman year at Cornell. Lucy fretted over the temptations ahead, but Hayes's only mild suggestion was that the boy avoid tobacco, liquor, billiards, and card playing.

As governor, Hayes had to confront an increase in Ohio taxes over the past ten years. State taxes had risen 37 percent, and local taxes had gone up nearly 170 percent. Hayes defended the past expenditures because they had been for public works that stimulated trade. But he warned state employees that his rule would now be "pay as you go." Hayes resolved, however, not to cripple his social programs, which included more humane treatment within the state prison system.

Yet for Rud Hayes, there had become one towering issue—the treatment of Negroes in the American South. Now the Fourteenth and Fifteenth amendments had put the nation on the right track, and Hayes felt he could refuse a third term and retire from politics.

Leaving office early in 1872, Hayes pronounced himself "a free man and jolly as a beggar."

Moving his family back to Cincinnati, Hayes went merely as an observer of the Liberal Republicans when they met there to nominate

Horace Greeley to oppose Grant. The prospect of a coalition with the Democrats that could defeat the president alarmed Hayes enough for him to stand once again for Congress.

Over the course of a grueling campaign, Ohio voters taught Hayes that they no longer responded to his impassioned plea for Negro suffrage, or for hard currency or for civil service reform. When Hayes was defeated, his relief outweighed his chagrin.

Leaving Lucy at home, Hayes stayed in Fremont to tend his ailing uncle's banking and real estate portfolios. He was pleased that his financial prospects allowed him to reject Grant's offer of a job as assistant U.S. treasurer, which Hayes dismissed as "small potatoes." He turned instead to buying up property around Toledo and rejoiced during the Crédit Mobilier scandal that he was free of politics.

At fifty-one, Hayes might be heavier and shorter of breath, but he admired his own "elastic spirit" and his "fondness for all young people and their employments and amusements."

Then, amid his rounds of army reunions and public ceremonials, Hayes was hit hard, grieving at his uncle's bedside when he died in 1873 and shaken by that year's financial panic that swept Ohio Democrats back into power. In August 1874, he and Lucy lost their youngest son, Manning, the third of their six children not to survive.

As a private citizen but a popular one, Hayes launched a campaign tour for the Republicans that ended, for the first time since the war, with the national Democrats taking control of the House of Representatives.

Hayes felt he could not refuse when his party turned to him to stop its decline. He would run again for governor. Privately, Hayes agreed that Ben Butler and his fellow Radicals had been lax about corruption in their ranks. But he traveled energetically throughout September and was returned to the governorship, along with Republican majorities in both Ohio chambers. His victory was narrow—five thousand votes out of almost six hundred thousand cast. But it made Rutherford Hayes a plausible candidate for president in 1876.

• • •

Samuel Tilden

In New York, Governor Samuel Jones Tilden was being hailed as the Democrat who could cleanse government of the scandals of the Grant administration.

Sallow, short, and balding, Tilden had not matched Hayes in outgrowing his frail constitution. With a sagging left eyelid and racked by other physical complaints, Tilden struck voters as at least a decade older than his sixty-two years. He blamed his bad digestion on powerful doses of laudanum that had been administered to him as a three-year-old.

Tilden's father was as devoted as Hayes's mother to strengthening his sickly child. At his general store in New Lebanon, New York, Elan Tilden drew the boy into the political life of a town at the gateway to the Hudson Valley. From an early age, Samuel read widely. At the store he learned to listen.

Poor health had kept Samuel at home until the age of eight. Sent off to Williams Academy in Massachusetts, he could tolerate only three months, and in 1834, he dropped out of Yale after one term because of the indigestible meals.

By the time he transferred the following year to New York University, Tilden was already speaking publicly on behalf of Andrew Jackson and a fellow New Yorker, Martin Van Buren. As he studied law at NYU, Tilden became a spokesman for the Democrats, but the financial panic of 1837 destroyed President Van Buren's chance for re-election.

Despite his party's reverses, Tilden's hard work was propelling him forward—first as corporate counsel for New York City, then as a state assemblyman. Even when a vote went against him, Tilden was establishing himself as a man of principle. But when he was offered backing to run for Congress, Tilden declined and returned to the law to lay the foundation for a personal fortune.

He knew he was too demanding to take a partner. Even friends admitted that Tilden was too quick to say "I told you so." Instead, he set up his own practice, recruiting clients from the nation's expanding railroad companies. A highly eligible bachelor of thirty-six, Tilden joined the boards of the New-York Historical Society and the Metropolitan Museum of Art.

Although he kept company with a number of young women who, he said, made his "heart thump," Tilden explained to a sympathetic dowager that he had "never been accustomed to surrender to my inner life."

Instead, he was torn between his detestation of slavery and his allegiance to the concept of states' rights. He resisted joining the new Republican Party, even though he admitted that Republicans were more likely to be "men of culture, wealth and force." But theirs was "a party of self-seekers." He would stick with the Democrats, a party whose members could be more easily shaped "by the mere force of ideas."

Enough New York Democrats were put off by one of Tilden's ideas—his strenuous opposition to slavery—that he lost elections in the late 1850s for state attorney general and even for his former job as the city's corporate counsel. Tilden responded by declaring that he was "out of politics."

The rise of Abraham Lincoln drew him back in. Worried that a split within Democratic ranks would elect Lincoln, Tilden spoke at Cooper Union for Stephen Douglas and followed up with a manifesto warning that a Republican victory would mean civil war. In despair, he wrote, "It is too late!"

When he was proved right, Tilden overcame his misgivings and lined up behind President Lincoln, a man he was coming to see as warmhearted but too inexperienced to lead the nation. Tilden advised Secretary of War Edwin Stanton that their one hope rested in the Union having far greater industrial strength than the South, and three times the number of recruits to draw upon.

Being more loyal to the Union than to its president, Tilden denounced Lincoln's wartime curbs on constitutional rights, and in 1864 he backed George McClellan and his call for an immediate cease-fire.

After the North achieved victory, Tilden became party chairman in the nation's leading Democratic state. When Salmon Chase lost the presidential nomination in 1868, his daughter Kate blamed Tilden personally, adding, "I fear that when the South seceded, the brains of the party went with it."

Even though the Democrats lost twice to Grant, Tilden scored a victory of his own when he took on William M. Tweed and his powerful machine, the "Society of Saint Tammany"—a divinity not found in the traditional Catholic hierarchy.

Boss Tweed, a former bookkeeper, had amassed power through his unabashed combination of bribes and street-corner bullying. Tammany's slogan was "Something for everyone," and it was Tweed who introduced the Irish immigrants flooding into New York to the wisdom of "vote early and vote often."

From the humble position of deputy street commissioner, Tweed could appoint state supreme court justices and rake in exorbitant kickbacks from city contracts. His masterstroke was the New York County Courthouse, where construction began in 1862 and was completed only a full ten years later.

Tweed carpenters were paid $2.1 million for work worth $30,000, and his plasterer received $1.9 million. Critics charged that all New York City could have been carpeted for the nearly $5 million spent to cover the courthouse floors. The total original budget had been $250,000. Tammany ran up the bill until estimates of the final cost went from $4 million to—not improbably—$14 million.

THE "BRAINS"

Boss Tweed

Politicians and Tweed's contractors were not the only ones offered a share. Thomas Nast's many cartoons for *Harper's Weekly* featured stereotypes of ignorant and drunken Irish immigrants. But when Nast drew blood at Tammany Hall, Tweed sent an agent to offer him a personal art scholarship—five hundred thousand dollars, for study in Europe.

At the time, Nast was being paid an annual five thousand dollars for his Tweed cartoons, but his other drawings paid handsomely enough that he could refuse the offer. Nast explained that he had no time for travel since he was busy putting a gang of thieves behind bars.

As the Democratic Party chairman, Tilden had his own regular dealings with Tammany Hall, and yet when the *New York Times* revealed the orgy of corruption in 1872, he claimed to have had no knowledge or suspicion. Quietly, however, Tilden had already taken modest steps toward reform, and Tweed had mocked his upstate values:

Tilden, he said, "wants to stop the pickup, starve out the boys, and run the city as if it was a damned little country store in New Lebanon."

Despite his recent dismal losses at the polls, Tilden was now edging back into the fray. As a candidate for the state assembly, he devoted ten days with accountants to going over Tammany's bank records. The result was evidence that Tweed had pocketed more than $1 million of public money.

In a Cooper Union speech, Tilden attacked the "cabal of corrupt men" who had seized local government for their "personal plunder."

New York governor John Hoffman was deeply indebted to Tweed, but he was forced to investigate the charges. As a special agent, Hoffman chose Charles O'Connor, famous for successfully defending Jefferson Davis against charges of treason.

On Election Day, Tilden and his reformers carried every contest. Tweed himself was not up for re-election, but he never again showed up in the state senate seat he had paid for.

One confrontation between the two men had left Tilden trembling with anger, and he predicted that Tweed would "close his career in jail or in exile."

So it proved. The *Times* exposé resulted in Tweed's being indicted on 120 charges ranging from forgery to grand larceny. After he was sentenced to twelve years in prison, Tweed escaped with his henchmen to California and had moved on to Spain before being extradited to New York. He would die in prison in 1878, shortly after his fifty-fifth birthday.

New Yorkers rewarded Tilden for his role in vanquishing Tammany Hall by electing him their governor in 1874. He carried his reformer's zeal to Albany, where he thwarted a scheme to bilk millions from the state's canal system.

As the next presidential election approached, a friendly editor wrote that he was praying for a Hercules who would clean out Grant's Augean stables as thoroughly as Tilden was ridding the muck from New York.

Almost a thousand Democratic convention delegates concluded that Samuel Tilden was that man. Tilden might seem haughty and cold, but hard times had slashed the price of Southern cotton nearly in half and contributed to the Democrats' regaining the House in 1874. Two years later, personality should matter less than party label.

Tilden's support among the nation's bankers seemed to guarantee him ample funds for the coming campaign. Since voters were less attracted by the idealism of the radical Republicans, it did not matter that no blacks were in the convention hall on the day that Tilden was nominated.

On the Republican side, even Julia Grant could not ignore the sentiment in the House of Representatives against a third term for her husband. By a vote of 233 to 18, members approved a resolution praising the two-term limit that George Washington had imposed upon himself. A third term "would be unwise, unpatriotic and fraught with peril for our free institutions."

With Grant out of the competition, the Democrats also would not face the undeniable appeal of former House Speaker James G. Blaine. Clean government would be a potent campaign issue, and Blaine had been tarnished by a dubious railroad deal in Arkansas.

Instead Republicans turned to Governor Hayes. As his vice president, they chose William A. Wheeler, a New York congressman who had not only voted against the retroactive pay raise of 1873 but returned his share to the U.S. Treasury. Without enthusiasm, *The Nation* magazine described the ticket as "eminently respectable men—the most respectable men, in the strict sense of the word, the Republican Party has ever nominated."

Summing up Rud Hayes, Henry Adams was more succinct: "A third-rate nonentity."

Hayes would not be attacking Tilden on matters of race. His own ardor for black rights had cooled along with that throughout the country, especially after the recent Supreme Court ruling in *U.S.* v. *Cruikshank* that overturned the only three convictions from the Colfax massacre. The charges, brought under the Enforcement Act of 1870, had alleged a conspiracy to deny the victims their civil rights.

The justices, five to four, held that the prosecution had not specified race as being the motive for the riot. More broadly, the Court limited the federal government's role in punishing violations of Negro rights. It reserved to state and local authorities the penalties for crimes by individuals. When those officials refused to act, blacks were left unprotected.

• • •

Given the venerable anniversary, 1876 was being hailed as the Centennial Election. To honor the nation's founding, nearly ten million visitors—20 percent of the population—journeyed to Philadelphia for an exposition called "the Progress of the Age."

The celebratory mood was marred only briefly by news that George Armstrong Custer and two hundred of his Seventh Cavalry had been cut down in Montana at the Battle of Little Big Horn. Led by chiefs Sitting Bull and Crazy Horse, Sioux and Cheyenne warriors had been protecting the land deeded them under an 1868 treaty.

For Grant, Custer's loss marked a more serious defeat: the failure of the president's attempt to preserve peace with the native peoples of the Great Plains. Throughout his career, Grant's sympathies had gone to the tribes, not to the white settlers encroaching on their land. As a young officer in California, he had written to reassure his wife, who worried about the danger of living among Indians:

The neighboring tribes, Grant wrote, "are the most harmless people you ever saw. It really is my opinion that the whole race would be harmless and peaceable if they were not put upon by whites."

To his brother, Grant attributed the condition of "this poor remnant of a once powerful tribe" to "those blessings of 'civilization,' whiskey and smallpox."

Over the years, Grant had never trusted George Custer's judgment and regarded the battle of Little Big Horn as "wholly unnecessary." As president, he had tried to end corruption within the Indian Bureau and promote fair dealings with the tribes. It galled him now that his countrymen were hailing Custer as a fallen hero.

During the presidential campaign, a third candidate had emerged from an upstart Greenback Party. At age eighty-five and firmly committed to the workingman, Peter Cooper was demanding an end to the entrenched oligarchy of rich men who ran the country. According to Cooper, they were enslaving the mass of Americans as ruthlessly as slavery had ever done.

But that message was not resonating within the Republican Party, where the pliant approach of its Liberal faction on racial justice had won many converts. Northerners might still deplore the lack of education among former slaves. But—unlike General Howard and other Radicals—they now often tended to blame the slaves themselves.

"The truth is, the Negroes are ignorant, many of them not more than half civilized," one Northerner wrote, and "no match for the whites." He concluded that the Republican policy toward the South had been "wrong."

As Hayes campaigned, he saw that only one issue could galvanize a Republican like that man, and it was not racial equality. Nor, despite Democratic strategy, was it civil service reform. Republicans feared most that the election could deliver the White House to their same wartime enemies who had just taken the House again.

Hayes saw the bad economy as his "deadliest foe, and our strong ground is the dread of the solid South, rebel rule, etc., etc."

But to press for that change in emphasis, Hayes risked alienating the reformers who were demanding his commitment to erasing the stigma of the Grant years. From Harvard Yard, college president Charles Eliot spoke for them when he reported "less & less faith that Hayes & reform are synonymous."

Hayes had evidence for his new priority. From the U.S. attorney general, Alphonso Taft, he learned that sustaining several Southern governments would require more federal troops. Such troops were vital for retaining Republican electoral votes, but Democrats in the House of Representatives "had crippled us very much" by refusing to appropriate funds for the army.

Democrats were acting on the choice set out starkly at Charles Sumner's funeral by Mississippi congressman Lucius Lamar when he warned that the South "must be part of the government or held in duress under it."

If Republicans could retain power in a state only with soldiers at their side, Democrats argued that the time had come to let that state revert to its natural leaders—even though they were the Confederate rebels, wealthy planters, and former slave owners. Southern Republicans worried that Northerners might soothe their conscience by accepting the same assurances of racial harmony that had lulled Liberals during the last presidential election. Those Republicans knew the South, and they knew better.

Alphonso Taft agreed that Southern Republicans had suffered "incredible" wrongs from a Democratic Party that had adopted murder or "a common threat of intimidation" to keep blacks from voting or testifying in court.

The attorney general said he had written off Mississippi, where the Democrats had scared off every black man from registering to vote. But he vowed to keep trying to enforce the Fifteenth Amendment in Louisiana, Florida, and South Carolina.

To Hayes, Taft's warning was irrefutable proof that Republicans had to embrace "the bloody shirt campaign," familiar shorthand for the choice that Hayes wanted his party to hammer home: "Are you for the Rebellion, or are you for the Union?"

Indications suggested that Hayes would carry his home state of Ohio but that Indiana would fall to the Democrats, since the state's governor, Thomas Hendricks, was Tilden's running mate. To win, Hayes would need to peel off electoral votes from the Southern states where some 2,800 federal troops remained stationed.

Even at that, New York could be crucial. Republicans hoped to offset the appeal of Governor Tilden with campaigning by their New York senator, Roscoe Conkling. But Conkling had ridden to Congress on his iron control of the New York Customs House. He detested reformers and had not forgiven Hayes for a tepid early pledge to overhaul the civil service.

Carl Schurz, who was campaigning for Hayes in New York's German communities, was angered by the apathy of the Conkling political machine. "If the Republicans do not carry New York," he complained to Hayes, "it will be their own fault."

Schurz urged Hayes to announce his own plan for reforming campaign financing. Since Republican presidents had held the White House for the past sixteen years, thousands of officeholders owed their jobs to the Republican Party. So far, at each election they had been called on to prove their gratitude.

Any employee making more than a thousand dollars a year was expected to contribute 2 percent of his salary to the Republican campaign fund. If he refused, he was labeled uncooperative and his name given to his superiors.

Before Schurz broke away with the Liberals, he had failed to persuade the Grant administration to end that extortion. Now he had no more success with Hayes. If what Schurz was advocating "so earnestly were carried into effect," Hayes explained, "it would be a surrender of the campaign."

As a sop, Hayes sent party officials a letter calling the payments a "plain departure from correct principles." But he did not require them to stop, and federal employees ended up contributing substantially to his campaign.

Among the Democrats, Tilden was annoying his backers by contributing very little of his own fortune, which was estimated at $5 million, and probably more.

Not knowing of Tilden's tight fist, Republicans continued to worry about being outspent. Alphonso Taft tried to reassure Hayes by noting that the Enforcement Act of five years earlier had contained specific safeguards against Democratic fraud. Taft said he could guarantee "a reasonably honest election in New York."

But Hayes was not to be comforted. He predicted that if he lost, it would be because of bribery and stuffed ballot boxes in the North and "violence and intimidation" in the South.

Methodical Samuel Tilden was working to correct his own party's weaknesses. First, he had to smooth over a division on monetary policy with his vice presidential candidate. Thomas Hendricks was a leading advocate of soft money, unlike Tilden and his New York financiers. Hendricks believed in helping farmers through the economic depression by printing greenbacks, since the resulting inflation would ease the repayment of debts. Tilden, to the contrary, was being vilified as "the Great Forecloser."

As a distraction, the Democratic platform in St. Louis had sought to

prove that Grant might remain personally popular but that his administration was impossible to defend. Their litany was unsparing:

"When the annals of this Republic show the disgrace and censure of
a Vice President; a late Speaker of the House of Representatives marketing his rulings as a presiding officer; three Senators profiting secretly by
their votes as law-makers; five chairmen of the leading committees of
the late House of Representatives exposed in jobbery; a late Secretary
of the Treasury forcing balances in the public accounts; a late Attorney-
General misappropriating public funds; a Secretary of the Navy enriched
or enriching friends by percentages levied off the profits of contracts
with his departments; an Ambassador to England censured in a dishonorable speculation; the President's private secretary barely escaping
conviction upon trial for guilty complicity in frauds upon the revenue;
a Secretary of War impeached for high crimes and misdemeanor—the
demonstration is complete" that only men from the opposition party can
restore honesty to government.

The *New York Times* was trying to boost Republican chances by questioning the effect of Tilden's lucrative law practice on benefits to the nation's railroads, and a campaign song had taken up that theme: "Sly Sam,
the Railroad Thief."

More seriously, Tilden would be asking Southerners to overlook his
years of outspoken opposition to slavery. To make amends, Tilden sent
emissaries South to explain away as "youthful indiscretions" the statements he had made in his midforties.

Tilden's aides also saw to it that prominent former Confederates who
visited New York were escorted to his residence at 15 Gramercy Park.
There, according to the editor of the *Louisville Courier-Journal*, they
could satisfy themselves that Governor Tilden, while undeniably a Yankee, "measured to the Southern standard of the gentleman in politics."

For all of his own bias, President Grant was determined to bring
rigorous impartiality to the election of his successor. He faced an early
test on the Fourth of July in Hamburg, South Carolina, when two white
men rode up to a band of black militia parading down a public street.

After curses and threats, the black troops parted to let the two pass. But the next day, the father of one of them filed a suit against the militia commander for obstruction. Saying that he feared violence in open court, the commander took refuge with other blacks in the town's armory.

The white attorney for the prosecution, a former Confederate general named Matthew C. Butler, demanded that the blacks turn over the armory's weapons to the local white authorities.

In the shootout that followed, the black town marshal was killed and five black troopers were murdered after being captured. During the next week, the Democrats threatened further violence and announced they would not hire or rent land to any black Republicans. Black Democrats were caught in the cross fire, sometimes stripped and beaten for their allegiance to the white man's party.

As violence spread, Grant declared a state of insurrection and sent more than three companies of federal troops to Columbia.

The uncontrolled bloodshed had convinced even many Democrats that Grant's action was justified. On the scene, the army commander won over other white citizens by promising an impartial monitoring of their vote.

In Washington, Election Day passed without alarm. An early tally showed that Tilden could count on 184 of the required 185 electoral votes. Hayes, trailing with 166, would need every one of the votes being disputed in South Carolina, Florida, and Louisiana.

Before he set off for bed, the president told his guests, "Gentlemen, it looks as if Mr. Tilden is elected."

Hosting his own evening party, Rutherford Hayes heard that Tilden was expected to take New York City by fifty thousand votes, and he had reached Grant's conclusion. As he and Lucy sent their guests home after midnight, however, Hayes seemed composed, almost cheerful. Only to himself did he confess that the future looked grim: The equality amend-

Daniel Sickles

ments would be nullified, chaos would still reign, and better economic times, for whites and blacks, would be "pushed off for years."

But at least the tension had ended, and Hayes "fell into a refreshing sleep."

As Hayes slept, retired general Daniel E. Sickles in New York was heading home after a Broadway show and a late supper. On the way, he decided to stop by the Republican Party headquarters at the Fifth Avenue Hotel.

Most of the dejected staff was gone. Scanning the telegraph wires, however, Sickles saw a reason for hope that more despairing men had missed. Although many years had passed, Sickles remained notorious for his headstrong temperament, as well as for the unique plea that once saved his life.

Thirty-nine years old at the time, Sickles had been on trial for shooting to death Philip Barton Key, who was having an affair with his wife. It was in that case that Edwin Stanton had persuaded a jury—for the first time in the United States—that his client was not guilty by reason of temporary insanity.

During the war, Sickles repaired his reputation. He was awarded the Medal of Honor for gallantry at the Battle of Gettysburg, which had cost him a leg. After Sickles joined the Radical Republican attempt to remove Andrew Johnson, Grant as president overlooked the blemish in his civilian résumé and appointed him ambassador to Spain.

From the U.S. embassy, Sickles publicly romanced deposed queen Isabella II. To his nickname of "Devil Dan," he added the more respectful "Yankee King of Spain."

Sickles had resigned his post and was touring Europe when he learned that Samuel Tilden—whose Democratic policies he despised—was likely to win the 1876 election. Hurrying home as a volunteer, he found New York Republicans cool to his offer of aid, but Hayes appreciated his advice about how to exploit memories of the late war.

Alone now at Republican headquarters, Sickles tallied up the electors for himself: If Hayes held Oregon and then South Carolina, Florida, and Louisiana, he would edge out Tilden in the electoral college, 185 to 184.

At once, Sickles drafted telegrams to the Republican officials in those four states with the same instructions: "With your state sure for Hayes, he is elected. Hold your state."

Sickles had no standing in the campaign, however, and the hotel's night clerk refused to forge the name of Zachariah Chandler, the Republican Party's national chairman. Earlier in the evening, Chandler had retired to his room upstairs with a bottle of whiskey and instructions not to be disturbed.

Sickles was stymied until he ran into Chester A. Arthur in the lobby. As tax collector for the Port of New York, Arthur readily signed off on the wires and Sickles settled in to wait for the replies.

At the offices of the *New York Times*, editors were picking up the same faint hints that had spurred Sickles to action. Managing editor

John C. Reid, a bitter-end Republican, rushed to the Fifth Avenue Hotel intent on preventing his party from issuing a premature concession.

Reid pushed his way through a crowd that was gathering to hear election news. Thirty minutes had passed since Sickles had received positive responses from Oregon and South Carolina and gone home.

Reid encountered William Chandler, a Republican lobbyist for the railroad interests, and demonstrated to him how Hayes could still win. Chandler tried to take him to Zachariah Chandler, who was no relation. But without the chairman's room number, their random knocking alarmed female guests in two other rooms. Finally, Zachariah Chandler came to the door in his nightshirt.

The chairman was in no condition for an arithmetic lesson. After several futile minutes, Chandler told Reid to do whatever was necessary and went back to bed.

Reid drafted a telegram much like those sent by Sickles and took a carriage to the central office of Western Union. When the clerk said that the Republicans had no account at his branch, Reid told him to bill the charges to the *New York Times.*

Zachariah Chandler was himself again by the time he received answers to Reid's wires, and he sent out his own telegram: "Hayes has 185 electoral votes and is elected."

Until that moment, Democratic newspapers had been jubilant. Only in Chicago did the Republican *Tribune* lament, "The Country Given Over to Democratic Greed and Plunder."

In Ohio, Rutherford Hayes had appeared as usual at his office, showing no sign that losing had devastated him. He told a reporter for the *Cincinnati Times* that the Republicans and the country would all survive the Democrats' victory, but he did care for the poor colored men of the South. Hayes predicted that white Southerners would ignore the recent constitutional amendments and then the colored man's fate would be worse than when he was in slavery, with a humane master to look after his interests.

At the White House, Grant shared Hayes's misgivings. He issued an order that army commanders in Florida and Louisiana be vigilant to preserve peace and good order. The nation's newspapers reported Grant's demand that any suspicion of ballot tampering must be reported and denounced at once.

The president added, "No man worthy of the office of the presidency should be willing to hold it if counted in or placed there by fraud. Either party can afford to be disappointed in the results, but the country cannot afford to have the result tainted by the suspicion of illegal or false returns."

Grant's idealism had not been shared by either party at the polls. In Florida, the Republican board of state canvassers converted Tilden's win of 86 votes into a loss to Hayes by 922 votes. Republicans in South Carolina worked the same legerdemain, certifying as winners not only Hayes but their party's governor and state legislators.

Once again, the country turned to Louisiana, since Tilden needed only one elector and was running ahead in the state by 6,400 votes. But in the past, the state's certifying board had been censured after two different congressional investigations.

When Grant raised the question of fraud with his cabinet, Alphonso Taft was among those who urged him to send troops, challenge the Louisiana verdict, and announce victory for Hayes. Secretary of State Fish's approach was more to Grant's liking, and he appointed a bipartisan panel of senators to travel to New Orleans and assure the nation that the final tally was as honest as possible.

The group's predictable findings were no help. Democrats insisted that their initial count had been accurate. Republicans stressed the intimidation of black voters. A Louisiana parish that had recorded 1,688 Republican votes in the last election showed only one this year. Republicans estimated that throughout the South at least a quarter of a million blacks had been frightened away from the polls. They told of songs that the white rifle clubs sang as they rode through the countryside at midnight:

"A charge to keep I have, a God to glorify.

"If a nigger don't vote with us, he shall forever die."

Northern congressmen came away shaken by testimony of the violence against blacks. Eliza Pinkston from Ouachita Parish was carried into the proceedings, where she displayed deep gashes on her thigh and breast and serious wounds to her head. She described events on the Saturday night before the election:

An enforcement party of Democrats had ridden up to her cabin, kicked in the door, slashed her husband with knives, shot him seven times, killed the baby she was holding, raped her, shot and stabbed her, and left her for dead.

Senator John Sherman wrote to assure Hayes that he would have carried Louisiana handsomely in a fair election. He called the state's parishes "more like the history of hell than of civilized and Christian communities."

On December 6, 1876, the legal date for the meeting of the electoral college, Louisiana's canvassing board announced that Hayes had won the state by 4,807 votes. That verdict gave him a sweep of the three disputed Southern states.

Democratic slates in South Carolina, Florida, and Louisiana convened separately, however, hoping to eke out one more electoral vote for Tilden. Intricate legal maneuvering had failed. Attempted bribery had failed. Even a plot to lock up Republican electors in South Carolina until after the vote had come to nothing.

Discouraged but undaunted, the Democrats' national chairman announced on December 13 the election of Tilden and Hendricks. Deploring the claim as an incitement to violence, the *New York Herald* compared it to "a gentleman in Utica, the inmate of a public institution, who regards himself as the emperor of China."

The memory of the horrific casualties only a dozen years earlier tempered the nation's response now. Partisan threats of violence were ignored, even laughed away. Yet without a compromise, the Democratic majority in the House might declare Democrat Samuel Tilden the president of the United States. Because the Constitution provided for the Senate to name the vice president, that position might go to Republican William Wheeler.

The turbulent state of American politics made a solution even harder to achieve. After the Crédit Mobilier scandal disqualified Schuyler Colfax for Grant's re-election ticket, the president turned to Henry Wilson. But last year, Wilson had died in office, and Senator Thomas W. Ferry of Michigan had become acting president of the U.S. Senate.

As set out by the Twelfth Amendment in 1803, the limits of that position were hazy. Republicans held that the Senate president was empowered both to count the votes and to announce the new president. Democrats claimed that he could only report the tally before sending the ballots to the House. Under that interpretation, Tilden would be declared the winner.

The impasse was broken when Iowa congressman George McCrary persuaded the House to let the Speaker appoint five members to meet with the same number of senators and justices of the Supreme Court. They would then come up with a solution—either a law or a constitutional amendment.

Democrats knew that Samuel Tilden, sure he had won, opposed any compromise. But in Washington the frosty governor had no reserves of popularity to enforce his wishes.

Hayes was also watching from the sidelines. He disapproved of the tactics of men like William Chandler and said he wanted "no taint of dishonesty" on the Republican side.

Roscoe Conkling sent word that his continued support hinged on Hayes's repudiating his promise of reform. Hayes refused. But tacitly he was agreeing to other conditions so long as they were kept sufficiently vague. He stressed that he would promote honest and capable local government throughout the South, while his agents gave a guarantee to "the better class of white men" that Hayes would recall federal troops from everywhere in the former Confederacy.

Hayes was annoyed that Tom Ferry had not made the call on his own, and some of the nominations for the new commission alarmed him. But when the Supreme Court settled as its fifth member on Joseph P. Bradley, a Republican from New Jersey, Hayes began to feel confident. "The committee seems to be a good one," he said.

Deliberations began on February 1, 1877, with the first questions being raised about the count in Florida. The previous month, the state's supreme court had upheld the Democrats' victory. But on February 9, the new Washington commission awarded Florida to Hayes. The vote, thanks to Justice Bradley, was eight to seven.

As the eight–seven decisions continued, Democrats on the committee did not listen to their outraged constituents, who called on them to resign or filibuster. Instead, the members dug in to extract concessions from the Hayes camp. They wanted nothing less than complete Democratic control over Louisiana and South Carolina. To get it, they bypassed public hearings and began to meet in secret behind locked doors.

The third and final such session was held at Wormley's Hotel on the corner of Fifteenth and H streets, NW, and it would become notorious. Gathering there for a final agreement were Hayes's trusted Ohio coterie, including former attorney general William Evarts and Senator Sherman. Southern congressmen and wealthy civic leaders had come to represent Louisiana and South Carolina.

James Garfield, attending for the first time, was appalled to learn that Hayes's men had already committed him to very specific terms, including a Democrat in the cabinet, a Southern railroad contract, and, crucially, a promise to withdraw all federal troops from the former Confederacy.

Trying belatedly to protect his candidate, Garfield spoke up: "The entire nation would honor these Southern men who are resisting anarchy and thus preventing civil war," he said. "But neither they nor we could afford to do anything that would be, or appear to be, a political bargain."

With that, Garfield picked up his hat and left the hotel.

That the fate of four million black Americans was sealed at a hotel owned by James Wormley, a wealthy black businessman, was an irony too rich to ignore, and the meeting quickly took its place in Washington lore. Yet both parties were simply acknowledging ways in which the past dozen years had not changed the American South.

JIM CROW,

Pub. by Hodgson 111 Fleet Street & Turner & Fisher New York & Philadelphia

US762-13935

CHAPTER 20

JIM CROW (1877)

On Monday, March 5, 1877, relieved to see the impasse ending, thirty thousand Americans gathered at the East Portico of the Capitol for the inauguration of Rutherford B. Hayes as the nation's nineteenth president.

Three days earlier, bitter Democrats had yielded only after prolonging the congressional session to 4:10 a.m. on March 2 before they would allow Thomas Ferry to announce 185 electoral votes for the Republican ticket.

The *New York Sun* protested in its headline, "The Fraud Consummated," and, later, "Mr. Hayes Is Not President." When outrage had inspired threats of assassination and renewed violence, President Grant and Secretary of State Fish had arranged as a precaution for Hayes to take the oath of office on Sunday evening in a secret White House ceremony.

Although Grant had agreed to withdraw army troops from Louisiana, he was now delaying the order to maintain calm. But Stephen Packard, the Republican governor, had been warned that he could expect to be replaced soon by his Democratic challenger. As realists in the North saw it, both Packard and Republican Daniel H. Chamberlain in South Carolina were governors in name only. They controlled no more than a square mile around their statehouses, and that much only because of troops sent by Washington.

The entire U.S. Army was down to twenty-five thousand soldiers, however, and Democrats in the House were threatening to cut the military appropriation still further. Add that to a growing sentiment across the nation that Radical Reconstruction had been a failure, and neither the outgoing Grant nor the incoming Hayes was willing to go on propping up those last two Southern regimes.

Even Hayes's waving the bloody shirt had not traumatized voters in New York and Indiana enough that they feared a return to Democratic rule. The country's attention was focused instead on the lagging economy and the allure of Western expansion. Congressional appropriations were available for new railroad lines, not for funding black schools.

Even as Hayes bowed to that reality, he hoped to guarantee a secure future for the black citizens of the South and, not incidentally, for the Republican Party there.

Within weeks of his inaugural address, Hayes acted on its most widely quoted phrase—"he serves his party best who serves his country best." By withdrawing the last Northern troops, however, he was ending the careers of the two Southern governors whose party loyalty had made him president.

Daniel Chamberlain was enraged by the betrayal and vowed to leave South Carolina along with the troops and go north to practice law in New York City. Stephen Packard tried to keep control of the few square blocks of New Orleans, but his Democratic opponent, Francis Nicholls, was undercutting his efforts with demonstrations of goodwill. Nicholls appointed twenty-one blacks to state offices and ratified the election of another 240.

Andrew Kellar, who had represented Hayes at Wormley's Hotel, arrived in New Orleans to buy off members of an arbitration commission set up to resolve the impasse in Nicholls's favor. Kellar assured the president's son, Webb Rutherford, that responsible white men of the city's Cotton Exchange and the hardworking local blacks "will unite and support the administration."

Pinckney Pinchback had been offstage during the wrangling. For three frustrating years, he had waited for Congress to grant him the seats he had won, first in the House, then in the Senate. Pinchback had watched as the Mississippi legislature sent to Washington thirty-four-year-old Blanche Kelso Bruce, a former slave who had become a successful cotton farmer.

Without Pinchback's formidable enemies, Bruce was promptly seated, while Pinckney Pinchback was finally rejected and entered into a political eclipse that lasted until his death in 1921.

On April 17, 1877, the U.S. Senate adjourned, silencing the last voices critical of Hayes's Southern strategy. Two days later, Chamberlain wired the president from Columbia that he was removing the last federal troops from the American South.

The news came as Hayes was hosting his first state dinner, honoring two visiting sons of the Russian tsar. But when toasting with strong wine punch created unseemly hilarity, the president banned all liquor from future White House dinners, and Hayes himself became a teetotaler.

Ulysses and Julia Grant soon left the United States on a trip to London and then on to Paris, Rome, Berlin, Moscow, the Middle East, and Asia. Grant was traveling when the Democrats at home took control of the U.S. Senate for the first time in twenty years. Republicans began to pressure him to return and ensure that they did not lose the White House as well. Hayes had always said he would not run for re-election.

Urged on by his wife, Grant agreed to be a candidate when the Republican convention opened in Chicago in June 1879. But Grant's surrogates, men like Roscoe Conkling, turned out to be tone-deaf in courting delegates. His cause looked lost by the time of the vote, and Grant spurned Julia's suggestion that he appear at the convention to stampede the hall into nominating him. "I would rather," Grant told her, "cut off my right arm."

On its thirty-sixth ballot, by a vote of 399 to 306, the convention turned to James G. Blaine of Maine.

Because former presidents received no pension, the Grants retired to New York, dependent on $250,000 raised from Republicans on Wall Street. Another $100,000 from J. Pierpont Morgan and his friends allowed them to buy a large new house in Manhattan at 3 East Sixty-sixth Street.

Grant's investments quickly indicated that he would have no better luck in the dawning Gilded Age than in the drab decades that had preceded it. Unscrupulous partners fleeced him of paper profits of $16 million and threatened to leave him destitute.

Grant's personal distress distracted him from the nation's problems, including a worrisome resurgence of white supremacy throughout the South. Even if some Radicals had never overcome their misgivings about Grant, he had been a staunch ally in the White House through his first term. Early in his second term, however, an erosion of black rights had been detected.

One portent was the resistance from Salmon Chase's Supreme Court to further expansions of federal power. In *Blyew* v. *United States*, the first challenge to the legality of the 1866 Civil Rights Act, a federal court found two white men in Kentucky guilty of murdering a black family. But a six-to-two decision from the Supreme Court reversed that verdict and thwarted further congressional interference in state affairs.

The Court underscored its determination in the Louisiana slaughter-house rulings of 1873. Four hundred butchers, most of them white, sued, claiming they had been put out of work by a state law intended to keep offal and dung out of the water supply. When their lawyer argued that the Fourteenth Amendment of 1868 protected their rights, a majority of justices ruled again for a narrower reading of the amendment that limited federal intervention.

In replacing Chase, Morrison R. Waite of Ohio may have been Grant's fifth choice, at best. But in his home state, Waite was being hailed as a hero. The negotiating team he headed had returned from London with a $15.5 million settlement after proving that England had violated its neutrality by outfitting Confederate warships.

A Yale graduate from Lyme, Connecticut, Waite had gone west to study law in Ohio, south of Toledo. He married Amelia Warner of Lyme and they began a family that would include three sons and a daughter. As a politician, however, Waite failed regularly. He ran for Congress as a Whig, lost, then ran unsuccessfully as a Republican. Although he had backed Lincoln, Waite drew a distinction that might have troubled President Grant: Waite was strongly against the institution of slavery, but he felt no particular sympathy for the slaves themselves.

At the time of his appointment, critics noted that Waite had never argued a case before the Court he would now be leading. And Stephen J. Field, Lincoln's last Supreme Court appointment, saw a more serious shortcoming. "We have a Chief Justice," Field wrote to a friend, "that would never have been thought of for the position by any person except President Grant."

But at fifty-eight, Mott Waite came to Washington still basking in the bipartisan acclaim for his British negotiations. He was resolved to impose his will, and usually he carried his associates with him. By the time of *United States* v. *Cruikshank* in 1876, Waite was ruling that indictments brought under the Enforcement Law against the eight white defendants were invalid. As a consequence, blacks now found it harder—and often impossible—to secure their right to vote.

Waite's approach was no more favorable to women. In previous years, he had ruled that since women had never had the right to vote, the recent constitutional amendments did not protect them against infringement of that right.

Those harbingers would be confirmed several times over as Waite ruled regularly against the federal government and in favor of state control. It was in that spirit that his Court would put an end to Charles Sumner's most cherished legacy.

In a sweeping negation in 1883, Joseph Bradley, the justice whose vote had installed Hayes as president, refuted the specifics of Sumner's original language. Writing for the Court, Bradley asked, "Can the act of a mere individual, the owner of the inn, the public conveyance or place of amusement, refusing accommodations, be justly regarded as imposing an ordinary civil injury, properly cognizable by the laws of the state, and presumably subject to redress by those laws until the contrary appears?"

Bradley answered his question: "Individual invasion of individual rights" was not the subject of the Equal Protection Clause. For the government to involve itself in private transactions was unconstitutional.

Bradley's ruling was assailed by advocates of black rights, including Frederick Douglass, who called it "a concession to prejudice." But the sole dissent from within the Court itself came from fifty-year-old John Marshall Harlan, Rutherford Hayes's first appointment to the bench.

A rangy and pugnacious redhead, Harlan fought for the Union in the Tenth Kentucky Volunteers, even though he had owned slaves and denounced the Emancipation Proclamation. By the war's end, however, he had become a Grant Republican.

Harlan's own political aspirations had come to nothing, but his skillful maneuvering at the 1876 convention helped deliver the nomination for Hayes, and the Court was his reward.

During his thirty-three years as an associate justice, John Harlan would prove his commitment to racial justice and to the spirit of the Reconstruction amendments. In his decisions, he warned that the rights of black citizens were threatened not only by state governments but by "the hostile actions of corporations and individuals."

Some twenty years after his appointment, Harlan was again in the minority in 1896 when he chastised his colleagues in *Plessy* v. *Ferguson* for upholding segregation on railroad trains. He reminded them that the United States had no ruling class or caste system, and he predicted that their majority opinion "will, in time, prove to be quite as pernicious as the decision made by this tribunal in the Dred Scott case."

In his first months as president, Rutherford Hayes had no persuasive answer for the flood of angry letters from Southern Republicans about the way he had betrayed them, and he was distracted as well by new accusations from Louisiana that his victory had been fraudulent. Congress put the charges to rest, but only after months of further uncertainty.

In the interim, Hayes pushed forward with a commission to study civil service reform. Its reputation for integrity was enhanced when he named as chairman John Jay, a grandson of the first U.S. Chief Justice.

But when the Jay report called for removing all customs-house revenue from political appointees, Roscoe Conkling rose up with other Republican leaders to block the change.

About the same time, Hayes was confronted by the largest labor strike in the nation's history. Railroad workers were protesting a 10 percent cut in their wages, and miners across the West were also walking off their jobs. With one hundred thousand men on strike, riots raged from Baltimore to Chicago.

Hayes issued proclamations, sent troops, and restored peace with a minimum of bloodshed. But he understood that his actions had provided no lasting remedy. "Can't something be done," he wondered, "by education of the strikers, by judicious control of the capitalists, by wise general policy, to end or diminish the evil?"

Whatever his problems, Hayes's sanguine nature prevailed. He was enjoying the presidency because he felt that his election had finally healed ruptures throughout the South. When he toured Kentucky, Georgia, Tennessee, and Virginia, respectful audiences did not challenge that view. They could have held up opposition newspapers that were still running Hayes's photograph with the word "Fraud" printed across it.

Hayes encountered an equally well-mannered response when he assured former slaves in Alabama that by leaving white communities alone, he was serving black interests better than federal intervention had ever done. He buttressed that argument by claiming there had been fewer outrages against blacks during the six months of his presidency than at any other time since the war ended.

As James Garfield complained to fellow Republicans, "It seems to be impossible for the president to see through the atmosphere of praise in which he lives."

President Hayes had not been entirely wrong in detecting a new mood throughout the South, but he misjudged its scope and duration. For years, the Southern businessmen who watched the retreat of the Northern carpetbaggers had styled themselves Redeemers, set on redeeming their state governments. What they called Redemption meant a commitment to white supremacy but also to repressing labor—black and white—as the alliance between Northern Democrats and conservative Republicans was shifting the emphasis from race to economics.

The Redeemers' goal became industrial development with a focus on expanding trade and completing the nation's rail system. Since the last federal troops had been removed, Northerners could persuade themselves that a truce had been called in the South's race wars.

But as unreconstructed Democrats asserted themselves in their state legislatures, their means of dealing with the black population varied from border states and the Upper South to the Deep South of Mississippi and Alabama. The result was a patchwork of laws, codes, and constitutional provisions that revived the doctrine of white supremacy and imposed segregation in public and private life.

First, legislators had to resolve the question of who was black. Alabama reverted to its prewar definition of a Negro—anyone with a black great-grandparent. Kentucky's miscegenation law dealt instead in percentages. Before 1893, no white person could marry anyone who was more than 12 percent black; after that, Kentucky banned mixed marriages altogether.

Florida was among the first states to rule that schools for white children and schools for Negro students should be conducted separately. Georgia segregated restaurants and playing fields.

In 1894, Kentucky fined railway agents up to fifty dollars for allowing black or white travelers to use an inappropriate waiting room.

Louisiana made two races' sharing a house a misdemeanor, while Mississippi banned the printing of written material that promoted social equality between whites and Negroes; infractions could be punished with a five-hundred-dollar fine, six months in prison, or both.

North Carolina decreed that schoolbooks must not be interchanged between white and black schools. South Carolina banned the adoption of white children by Negroes, and Texas expanded its segregation laws to include "persons of Mexican descent."

Virginia demanded that "any public hall, theater, opera house"—and later, movie theaters—must separate "the white race and the colored race."

Northern states had experimented with similar laws. The Washington Territory outlawed miscegenation from 1866 until the law was repealed eleven years later, two years before Washington became a state.

Wyoming expanded its miscegenation law beyond Negroes and mulattoes to include "Mongolians and Malaya," and from 1889 required potential voters to be able to read its state constitution.

In 1905, Kansas was allowing separate schools by race but outlawed discrimination in the state's existing high schools. Oklahoma segregated public baths and lockers in 1903 but permitted the facilities for both races to share the same building.

Ohio enacted its miscegenation law in 1877, the year that the state sent Governor Hayes to Washington as president. A school segregation law followed a year later.

The jumble of legislation that outlawed racial offenses became known as Jim Crow laws. The term was an unwitting legacy from a Yankee actor whose success came long before the Civil War.

Growing up on Manhattan's Lower East Side, Thomas Dartmouth Rice had mingled every day with his free black neighbors. It was only when he toured Kentucky in the early 1830s, however, that he hit upon the act that would make him famous.

Looking out at the livery stable next to the Louisville theater where he was performing, Rice was captivated by a lame old slave who passed the time by singing to himself as he did a little dance. Rice studied his routine and wrote comic verses with a livelier tempo.

When Rice returned to New York for a music-hall turn at the Park Theater, he blackened his face and dressed in ragged clothes with a battered hat. As an old black field hand, he sang:

> *Turn about, and wheel about, and do just so,*
> *And every time I turn about, I jump Jim Crow.*

Selling out theaters at home and in London, the entertainer became beloved as "Daddy Rice," and he wrote several popular plays that featured his creation. A London critic found "something in his chuckle which is not to be described, but which is equally rich, voracious and inimitable."

Sometimes Rice called the slave "Cuff," sometimes "Bone Squash." But he was always recognizable as Jim Crow.

Rice's portrayal of the illiterate but cunning slave made him rich enough to afford vests with gold guineas as their buttons and a diamond embedded in each coin.

With the passing years, however, the rise of minstrel shows made Rice's act seem stale. When he died an alcoholic at fifty-two, three months before South Carolina seceded from the Union, a public collection was taken up to bury him. But for many years a carved wooden statue of Rice in his celebrated role survived in front of a bar on Broadway.

For many poor whites throughout the South, Jim Crow laws alone could not ease their most persistent fear. In regions like northern Louisiana, with little but pine trees rising from its barren soil, white men found themselves competing with emancipated blacks, and during the dozen years of Reconstruction they had not known which race would prevail.

Such men had dropped away from the Ku Klux Klan after President Grant's crackdown, but their simmering resentments had grown. With control of the South passing again to the Democrats, powerless whites were joining plantation owners to ensure that black workers remained without their basic rights.

Lucius Lamar's praise for Charles Sumner at his funeral had helped lull Northerners who wanted to believe that the nation's most shameful chapter was now closed. A truer sentiment was expressed by the sheriff of Warren County, Georgia, who said that calling a man a Radical who believed in racial equality "was worse than to call a man a horse thief."

Before Jim Crow took hold, some former slaves might have agreed with the black Virginia legislator who announced in 1877 that he relied for protection of his rights on "the well-raised gentlemen" of the white South rather than on "poor white trash."

But in South Carolina, those gentlemen had already passed a law requiring voters to put their ballots in a box with their candidate's name on it. That "Eight-Box Ballot Act" was designed to screen out illiterate voters, and by 1895, white officials had turned to poll taxes and literacy tests to suppress the black vote. Those requirements had been upheld by the U.S. Supreme Court as being within the legitimate powers of the states, not the federal government.

Occasional reminders of violence in the South could penetrate the North's indifference to Jim Crow, but those brief explosions died away like summer lightning. An exception was the response to D. W. Griffith's *The Birth of a Nation.*

The director's technical skill won praise from critics who responded to the film's "thrills piled upon thrills." Rare dissenting views came from the National Association for the Advancement of Colored People, which had been formed in 1906, and from the chairman of the National Board of Censorship, who deplored its effect on "ten million citizens who are degraded by this product."

The sitting U.S. Chief Justice, seventy year-old Edward D. White, agreed to attend its Washington premiere—the first motion picture he had ever seen. White confided to Thomas Dixon, author of the novel the film was based on, that he had once been a member of the Ku Klux Klan himself and had walked his beat through the ugliest streets of New Orleans with a rifle on his shoulder.

After seeing the film, however, the justice hurried to disassociate himself from its racist message. It was the year that White voted to strike down Southern "grandfather laws" aimed at keeping from the polls poor and illiterate blacks, but not poor and illiterate whites.

At the White House, where Woodrow Wilson was host for a screening, the president seemed unconcerned. Raised in Virginia, Wilson had never objected to the Jim Crow laws in the nation's capital. In fact, until rioting against the film broke out in Boston, the president seemed to endorse Griffith's version of history. He was joined by enthusiastic Northern audiences who were identifying with Southern whites and with Wilson's Democratic Party.

· · ·

Griffith's polemic against Reconstruction also renewed national interest in the Ku Klux Klan, whose leadership had fallen to a heavy-drinking Methodist preacher, William Joseph Simmons of Harpersville, Alabama. The Klan was only one in an era rife with fraternal orders in the nation's expanding cities—Masons, Odd Fellows, Moose. Laid up for three months by an accident, Joe Simmons got hold of an 1867 Klan document and mapped out his vision for the new century.

His opening came in 1915, when Leo Frank, a Jew from New York, was convicted on false evidence of murdering fourteen-year-old Mary Phagan in Marietta, Georgia. Simmons's revitalized Klan sprang into action. Twenty-five white men kidnapped Frank from a prison farm and lynched him.

A week later, Simmons, calling himself the Imperial Wizard, carried a wooden cross eighteen miles outside Atlanta. At the top of Stone Mountain, he set it on fire.

He intended the fiery cross to become the symbol of the Twentieth Century Klan, which, Simmons stipulated, would be "a classy order of the highest class." There would be "no 'rough necks,' no 'rowdies,' no 'yellow streaks' admitted."

Recent waves of immigration spurred his recruitment drive. Fourteen and a half million new citizens had come to the United States in recent decades and were no longer readily absorbed into the prevailing culture. With Europe racked by war, suspicion of foreigners—German-Americans, Irish-Americans—had spread. To Woodrow Wilson, mistrust was only prudent.

"Anyone who carries a hyphen about with him," the president warned, "carries a dagger that he is ready to plunge into the vitals of this Republic whenever he gets ready."

Along with the new immigrants and isolated cases like Leo Frank, America's black population remained the Klan's dependable target. World War I had drawn 750,000 black workers to Northern jobs, which evaporated with the armistice of 1918. Competition became as venomous as in the poorest Southern districts.

Simmons joined forces with Edward Young Clarke, an energetic public relations man in Atlanta, and their Klan expanded within a year to eleven hundred Imperial Kleagles. Those men headed local chapters and supported themselves by selling Klan memberships for ten dollars and keeping four dollars for themselves. They also poached for members on the rival fraternal organizations, especially the Masons. Griffith's film became a useful recruiting tool. In little more than a year, Clarke could claim an increase in nationwide membership from three thousand to a hundred thousand.

One emerging Klan leader boasted a high pedigree. Nathan Bedford Forrest III, the general's grandson, said he was getting twenty letters a week urging the Klan to start punishing minor offenses with threats or flogging. According to Forrest, some women were requesting the Klan to stage lynchings to avenge their honor.

By late 1921, that demand for threats and flogging was being obliged. Klansmen had surfaced before the election of Warren G. Harding to warn Southern blacks away from the polls, and reports reached the North of a black dentist in Houston "mutilated" by hooded Klansmen for his affair with a white woman. Another victim in Texas was kidnapped from jail, where he was charged with insulting a white woman, and released with a sign on his back, "Whipped by the K.K.K."

Offenses could be more abstract. An Episcopal archdeacon in Mississippi was whipped for preaching racial equality. In Birmingham, Alabama, a black butcher was whipped for his "friendly relations" with white customers.

From his perch in the ambivalent city of Baltimore, H. L. Mencken offered his distinctive defense of the Klan:

"If the Klan is against the Jews, so are half of the good hotels of the Republic and three-quarters of the good clubs. If the Klan is against the foreign-born or the hyphenated citizens, so is the National Institute of Arts and Letters. If the Klan is against the Negro, so are all of the States south of the Mason-Dixon Line. If the Klan is for damnation and persecution, so is the Methodist Church."

But Klan membership was not always mocked. After President Harding backed anti-lynching legislation—which failed—his enemies retaliated with a story that he had accepted Klan membership in a secret White House ceremony in the Green Room.

The public's ambivalence about the Klan was reflected in the unexpected result of a 1921 exposé by the *New York World*. It turned out that not all Americans were appalled to read about the 152 crimes recently committed by Klansmen. Instead, a rush to join raised Klan membership for the first time above one million.

Simmons's background as a preacher served the Klan well during the 1920s, an era of religious fundamentalism. Protestant ministers—estimates put their number as high as forty thousand—joined the Klan, and some became Exalted Cyclops. In Pennsylvania, Texas, Colorado, and North Dakota, clergymen were elevated by their state to the rank of Grand Dragon.

And yet fissures were erupting. One high-level Klan officer quit, publicly claiming that Clarke kept Simmons constantly drunk so that he could loot the Klan Treasury. New voices emerged that urged the Klan to become more political and less religious, and Simmons was cast aside into the newly created office of Emperor. By the presidential conventions of 1924, the Democrats confronted an anti-Klan plank in their platform and defeated it by a mere four-fifths of a single vote.

During the 1930s, as rifts between Northern and Southern Methodists and other denominations began to heal, the ideal of universal brotherhood slowly asserted itself. Klan influence gave way to the combined national presence of twenty million American Catholics, three million Jews, twenty million immigrants, and twelve million blacks.

Looking on from the sidelines, one critic assessed the Klan as having "all of the defects of clandestine and reactionary organizations without the strength." He was a Vietnamese journalist living in exile under several aliases, the last of them "Ho Chi Minh."

With the Klan declining, the number of blacks who cast a ballot rose from 2 percent of the eligible number in 1940 to an estimated 1.2 million voters twelve years later. In the upper tier of Southern states, black candidates were being seated on city councils and school boards.

But the exclusively white Southern juries ensured that a black defendant would be found guilty. A publicized example was the case of the Scottsboro Boys, nine black Tennessee teenagers imprisoned for decades on perjured testimony from two white women who claimed rape.

• • •

During World War II, the number of blacks living outside the South nearly doubled to 4.6 million. Since Franklin Roosevelt and his wife, Eleanor, were seen as sympathetic, there was a shift in allegiance among blacks, particularly those who had moved to the North, to the Democratic Party, despite its powerful and unrepentant Southern wing.

It was Roosevelt's successor, however, who issued the most sweeping racial decree since Emancipation. On July 26, 1948, Harry S. Truman ended by executive order all legal discrimination within America's armed forces.

Slowly and grudgingly, branches of the service obeyed. By 1950, the army, which had been the last to comply, was sending mixed companies of white and black soldiers to fight in Korea. On military bases at home and abroad, the bars and messes, athletic teams and swimming pools, were all integrated with little of the resistance that had been predicted.

At the same time, the U.S. Supreme Court was reversing its decades of tolerance for Jim Crow. Starting with *Morgan* v. *Virginia* in 1946, the justices struck down segregation on trains crossing state lines. Dwight Eisenhower, who followed Truman in the White House, declined to call for federal legislation, and local trains continued to segregate the races.

But Eisenhower struck a far more lethal blow to Jim Crow than he knew by appointing as Chief Justice his Republican political rival, former governor Earl Warren of California.

In 1954, segregating students in public schools was required by law in seventeen states and the District of Columbia. But there were politicians who anticipated the trend of court decisions. South Carolina governor James F. Byrnes said his state would soon be "forced to do now what we should have been doing for the last fifty years."

On May 17, 1954, Chief Justice Warren spoke for his unanimous Court when he wrote that the nation "could not turn the clock back" to the time when *Plessy* v. *Ferguson* had been written. In present-day America, he continued, "segregation of white and colored children has a detrimental effect on the colored children."

Warren's ruling added, "We conclude that in the field of public edu-

cation the doctrine of 'separate but equal' has no place. Separate educa-
tional facilities are inherently unequal."

How fast would Jim Crow disappear? Not fast enough to save Emmett
Till. A black fourteen-year-old visiting Money, Mississippi, in August
1955, Till assumed that a cheeky flirtation with a white cashier in town
would be as harmless as it would have been back home in Chicago. Instead, the woman complained to her husband, who enlisted a friend to
help him kidnap and murder the boy. The men were brought to trial, but
an all-white jury acquitted them after deliberating for just over an hour.

From its formation in Indianola, Mississippi, a white movement of
so-called Citizens Councils spread rapidly. Council members were less
clandestine than the Klan but as firmly pledged to segregation forever.

After a year's deliberation, the Supreme Court allowed school boards
to set the tempo for their own integration so long as they acted in "reasonable time." Georgia's jubilant lieutenant governor pointed out that
the phrase "could be construed as one year or two hundred."

But racial change in America again was moving outside the courts.
In 1956, the admission of a black student, Autherine Lucy, to the University of Alabama set off rioting, and Virginia senator Harry Byrd
called on the South to mount "massive resistance" to integration.

When the university suspended Lucy "for her own safety," Eisenhower proved to be more like Hayes than Grant. He refused to send
federal troops, and the Alabama campus remained segregated for the
next seven years.

That pattern seemed destined to repeat in Arkansas the following
year when Governor Orval E. Faubus called up his state's National
Guard to prevent nine black children from attending all-white Central
High School in Little Rock. This time, however, Eisenhower sent a
thousand paratroopers to uphold the law and put the state Guard under
federal control.

As Arkansas children returned to school, the Supreme Court ruled
against further delays of desegregation. To retaliate, Faubus closed all of
Arkansas' public high schools for the 1958 year.

On February 1, 1960, four black college students in Greensville,

North Carolina, took seats at a Woolworth's lunch counter and ordered coffee. The local Jim Crow law required that they be ignored, but they went on sitting at the counter.

By the end of the month, that passive approach—labeled a "sit-in"—had spread to seven more Southern states. A founder of the Southern Christian Leadership Conference, the Dr. Martin Luther King, Jr., explained the nonviolent tactic: "We will wear you down by our capacity to suffer."

Within a year, more than a hundred Southern lunch counters were serving black customers.

The movement, persistent but peaceful, attracted Northern sympathy and Southern resistance. John F. Kennedy, the winning presidential candidate in 1960, placed a well-publicized call to King's wife after the minister was arrested in Birmingham, Alabama. Political analysts agreed that the call had inspired black voters and contributed to the narrow Democratic victory.

In September 1962, James Meredith, a black student, was turned away from the University of Mississippi in Oxford. But six years had passed since the drama of Autherine Lucy. Kennedy sent federal marshals to escort Meredith onto the campus.

Mississippi governor Ross Barnett had told Kennedy he would maintain order. When he did not, the riot that broke out rivaled those of the Reconstruction era. Two people were killed and 375 injured, including 66 federal marshals.

During the next years, the Klan looked to the racial strife as its one last recruiting appeal. After a Birmingham rally, dynamite exploded at the home of Dr. King's brother and at a black political headquarters. With television cameras now on the scene, the world could watch as peaceful demonstrations and racist crimes competed to define the nation's future.

On June 12, 1963, in Jackson, Mississippi, Medgar Evers, thirty-seven years old, World War II veteran, father of three, and a field agent for the NAACP, was shot and killed in an ambush by a member of the local White Citizens Council. Three months later, a bomb killed four black girls at Birmingham's Sixteenth Street Baptist Church.

• • •

President Kennedy called that year for civil rights legislation to end segregation in public schools and public accommodations. His critics within the civil rights movement complained that his proposals were too mild and that they lacked rigorous enforcement.

On August 25, 1963, an outpouring of two hundred thousand men, women, and children, black and white, gathered in front of the Lincoln Memorial in Washington. Robert Kennedy, the attorney general, had offended prominent black leaders by asking that they delay their rally until after his brother was re-elected in 1964. They refused.

The audience that afternoon heard Martin Luther King call for racial harmony and justice and assure the nation, "I have a dream" that the day would come.

When Kennedy invited congressmen to the White House in October to press for the civil rights bill, it was Southern members of his own party who resisted most adamantly. The Democratic chairman of the House Rules Committee let the president know that his bill would remain locked up in committee.

The following month, on November 22, Kennedy was assassinated in Dallas. His vice president, Lyndon Johnson from Stonewall, Texas, flew back to Washington with Kennedy's widow, Jacqueline, still wearing her bloodstained suit.

Johnson was a tactical master of the Senate, which he had dominated for years as majority leader. Five days after the assassination, he used his first congressional address to assure a grieving nation that no tribute "could more eloquently honor President Kennedy's memory than the earliest passage of the civil rights bill for which he fought so long."

Johnson's former colleagues were unmoved. A close Senate ally, Richard Russell of Georgia, vowed to "resist to the bitter end" any attempt to achieve social equality. Privately, Russell warned Johnson that advocating civil rights would ensure Johnson's defeat in 1964 if he ran for president in his own right. As it turned out, Johnson won that election against Republican senator Barry Goldwater of Arizona by a margin of 27.6 percent.

Senator Strom Thurmond of South Carolina had challenged Truman for the presidency in 1948, in part because Truman integrated the armed forces. Now he denounced the civil rights bill as "reminiscent of Reconstruction proposals and activities of the Radical Republican Congress."

During a filibuster that tied up the Senate for weeks, three young civil rights volunteers disappeared on the night of June 21, 1964, near Philadelphia, Mississippi. Forty-four days later, the bodies of James Chaney, Andrew Goodman, and Michael Schwerner were found. They had been shot at close range by Mississippi law officers who belonged to the local White Knights chapter.

As the filibuster ground on, Robert Byrd of West Virginia spoke for fourteen hours and thirteen minutes. When the bill's manager, Senator Hubert Humphrey of Minnesota, concluded that he finally had more than the 67 votes he needed, he cut off debate and brought the bill to success on the Senate floor. On July 2, 1964, the House passed it, 289 to 125.

Five hours later, the president went on television to speak to the nation. He wanted to assure his countrymen, he said, that the new law would in no way restrict their freedoms.

"It does say," Johnson continued, "that those who are equal before God shall now also be equal in the polling booths, in the classrooms, in the factories and in hotels and restaurants, and movie theaters, and other places that provide service to the public."

He concluded, "Let us close the springs of racial poison. Let us pray for wise and understanding hearts. Let us lay aside irrelevant differences and make our nation whole."

With that, President Lyndon Johnson picked up a pen and signed the Civil Rights Act of 1964, ninety-nine years after the end of the Civil War.

President Lyndon Johnson, July 2, 1964

ACKNOWLEDGMENTS

Alice Mayhew's writers agree about her extraordinary gifts, but I want to thank another editor as well—Sue Horton, to whom this book is dedicated.

For more than a year, Sue drove from her office as opinion editor of the *Los Angeles Times* to manage the logistics of transmitting my manuscript to New York. My time in a hospital bed, followed by months shut in at home, made her assistance essential, and it came with an unfailing sense of optimism and fun. As I completed my fourscore years, I have thought often about my luck in friendships and how richly rewarded I've been by knowing Sue.

Because this will be the final installment in my telling of the American story, I also want to mention other friends who have brightened my life since the series began in 1988, and often long before that: Charles Fleming and Julie Singer, Angel Cruz, Carl Byker, and Joe and Barbara Saltzman.

Also Joe Domanick and Judy Tanka; Natalie Narvid; Donald and Patty Freed; Joan Dew; Ben Donenberg; Marilyn Burns; Marshall and Sue Blumenfeld; Richard and Peggy Houdek; Tom Waldman; Qidong Zhang, Jackson Wen, and Alexandra Lu; Frank Snepp; Andrew and Caelia Bingham; Sarah Bingham; Julia Halberstam; Miles Beller and Laurette Hayden; Gene Lichtenstein and Jocelyn Gibbs; Steve Randall; Lore Segal; Gordon and Anne Goldstein; Tom and Marilyn Clagett; Clancy Sigal; Frances Ring; Anne Taylor Fleming; Robert Schoenberg; Marcia Brandwynne; Rose Marie Tuohy; Bunny Svatos; JoAnn Menzies, Gordon Menzies, and Bonnie Summers; Seymour and Audrey Topping.

And Rosa Bolaños; Jessica Saenz; Jerome Sutherland; Benigno Robles; Phillip Griggs; Martin DeKarver; Richard Sharpe; Helen Sklar; Leo Rhodes. In Rio de Janeiro, Nesio, Mirtes, and Gabriela de Oliveira;

Helga Vargas; Jorge Bomfim; Julio Cesar Oliveira de Fernandez. In London, Peter Craske; Sally Taylor and Colin Franey; Caroline Moorhead. In Tuscany, Rennie Airth.

For the first time, I also have occasion to thank three skilled and dedicated doctors: Dr. Thomas Y. Tom, Dr. Thomas G. Mahrer, and Dr. David S. Marlin of Kaiser Permanente, Los Angeles.

My friend Lynn Nesbit, now of Janklow and Nesbit, has represented me adroitly since 1965. Lynn steered me to Simon & Schuster, which has been a supportive home for my last seven books.

In 2014, the publishing company's highly talented roster includes Jonathan Karp, publisher; Jackie Seow, cover design; Akasha Archer, interior design; Al Madocs, production editor, and Lisa Erwin, production manager; Stephen Bedford, online marketing; and two editors during the course of writing this book: first Roger Labrie, now Jonathan Cox. Thank you to Sean Devlin for his meticulous copyediting. Not surprisingly, Alice Mayhew attracts first-rate colleagues. To conclude: again and always, Alice.

I have also incurred a different sort of obligation. My own histories have been possible only because of the labor of hundreds of scholars and writers who preceded me. I have hoped that my end notes and bibliographies would lead readers to books that offer a fuller study of individuals and events than my broad surveys could accommodate.

This time, my debt is especially strong to Professor Eric Foner of Columbia University. Until he published *Reconstruction* in 1988, many scholars, in the North as well as in the South, tended to absolve the former Confederates of failing to guarantee full civil rights for the freed slaves. They blamed instead the corruption of the carpetbaggers and the misdeeds and ineptitude of the Negroes themselves.

There were such notable exceptions as W. E. B. DuBois and his *Black Reconstruction in America*, but Professor Foner denounced much of the scholarship from the Jim Crow era as academia's "everlasting shame."

Now a great number of exemplary works exist, and I was particularly grateful for the insights and impressive work of David Herbert Donald, Jean Edward Smith, Hans L. Trefousse, Ari Hoogenboom, and many others.

Almost every day in recent years, I have come upon an incident or detail that increased my appreciation of our legacy. It has been especially rewarding to scrape away the worshipful patina from George Washington and find fallibility and compromise but also a true hero who ranks with the greatest men of any age.

Some chapters could be painful to relive—slavery, the abuse of native tribes, Jim Crow. But at the worst of times, the spirit from our heritage shone through and sustained the nation's promise.

NOTES

APRIL 14, 1865

1 Lt. General Ulysses S. Grant begged off: U. S. Grant, *Memoirs*, 640.

1 Julia Grant felt she had been snubbed: Chamlee, 4.

1 "Is anything the matter?" Julia Grant, 156. Some early details wired to Grant were mistaken. Seward was stabbed with a bowie knife, not shot, and his son was struck with the butt of a revolver. A later, more accurate account of events appears on page 51.

1 President Lincoln had been assassinated: J. E. Smith, 410.

1 Like most of his relatives: Farina, 26.

2 Where there had been joy: U. S. Grant, *Memoirs*, 641.

3 Grant remembered that Lincoln had set: U. S. Grant, *Memoirs*, 644.

3 He allowed Lee's officers to retain: Waugh, 99.

3 "He thought," Grant recalled: U. S. Grant, *Memoirs*, 648.

3 And the rebellious Southerners "surely": U. S. Grant, *Memoirs*, 642.

CHAPTER 1. CHARLES SUMNER (1865)

5 Sumner's grandfather had fought: Benson, 11.

5 A lifelong crusader, the elder Sumner: A. M. Taylor, 6.

5 He developed a loathing for the theatrical: A. M. Taylor, 58.

5 Calling on Chief Justice Roger Taney: A. M. Taylor, 63.

6 Sumner dined at the Garrick Club: Sumner, *Memoir*, 2, 21.

6 At Windsor Castle, he toured: Sumner, *Memoir*, 2, 16.

6 The familiar ritual at Tremont Temple: Sumner, *Memoir*, 2, 339.

6 Sumner began by denouncing: Sumner, *Memoir*, 2, 343.

7 "In our age there can be no peace": Sumner, *Memoir*, 2, 348.

7 In contrast, the warship *Ohio* docked in Boston Harbor: Sumner, *Memoir*, 2, 350.

7 "War is known as the last reason": Sumner, *Memoir*, 2, 354.

7 To restore a semblance of good humor: Sumner, *Memoir*, 2, 357.

7 But at least one Boston general admired: Sumner, *Memoir*, 2, 357.

7 He worried that taking the position would mean: A. M. Taylor, 193.

7 Over the next two years, Sumner became: Benson, 16.

8 To heighten the insult: A. M. Taylor, 306.

8 "Nothing but politics now": A. M. Taylor, 280.

8 One friend observed that at any gathering: Donald, *Sumner . . . Civil War*, 30.

8 Even so, Brooks was expelled before: Benson, 26.

9 As a Democrat who did not favor: Benson, 26.

9 Sumner had already annoyed fellow senators: Donald, *Sumner . . . Civil War*, 198.

10 Back home, Sumner's speeches berated the Know Nothings: Donald, *Sumner . . . Civil War*, 228.

10 Once he had asked Sumner, as a personal favor: J. M. Taylor, 91.

10 But even she had advised Sumner: Goodwin, 184.

11 If only Butler had been born: Donald, *Sumner . . . Civil War*, 176.

11 Now Sumner claimed that there was nothing: Benson, 117.

11 The first Democrat to respond: Donald, *Sumner . . . Civil War*, 240.

11 Speaking next, Stephen Douglas: Benson, 122.

11 Douglas asked, "Is it his object": Donald, *Sumner . . . Civil War*, 242.

11 Answering Douglas, Sumner referred to him: Benson, 130.

11 When newspapers published extracts: Donald, *Sumner . . . Civil War*, 241.

12 Brooks realized that his cousin was expected: Benson, 131–32.

12 But when he confided that plan: Donald, *Sumner . . . Civil War*, 245.

12 Edmundson saw that Brooks had taken a seat: Benson, 140.

12 "Mr. Sumner," Brooks began: Benson, 132.

13 As the beating continued, however: Donald, *Sumner . . . Civil War*, 246.

13 The unrelenting blows had splintered: Donald, *Sumner . . . Civil War*, 247; Benson, 132.

13 One of Brooks's friends, Representative Laurence Keitt: Benson, 139.

13 But the two reached the scene: Donald, *Sumner . . . Civil War*, 247.

13 Awakening from his frenzy, Brooks mumbled: Donald, *Sumner . . . Civil War*, 247.

13 A doctor arrived to stanch: Benson, 206.

13 As he drifted off to sleep: Donald, *Sumner . . . Civil War*, 249.

13 The doctor was optimistic: Donald, *Sumner . . . Civil War*, 262.

14 When Sumner finally returned to the Capitol: Donald, *Sumner . . . Civil War*, 273.

14 In Paris, the young novelist Henry James: Donald, *Sumner . . . Civil War*, 274.

14 From the time of the attack, crowds throughout: Donald, *Sumner . . . Civil War*, 251.

14 At an Indignation Meeting, Emerson spelled out: Benson, 176.

14 The *Herald* of Laurensville, South Carolina: Benson 164.

14 The merchants of Charleston: Donald, *Sumner . . . Civil War*, 255.

14 That theme was taken up by the *Richmond Whig*: Goodwin, 185.

15 But North Carolina's *Wilmington Herald*: Benson, 170.

15 At that, Butler shouted, "You are a liar!": Donald, *Sumner . . . Civil War*, 257.

15 After he declined to appear: Donald, *Sumner . . . Civil War*, 250.

15 *"But he quickly answered, No"*: Donald, *Sumner . . . Civil War*, 260.

15 In New York State, Frances Seward was resigned: J. M. Taylor, 102.

16 When he died from a throat infection early in 1857: Benson, 203.

16 To another friend, Sumner said: Donald, *Sumner . . . Civil War*, 284.

16 Sumner said he dreaded being again: Donald, *Sumner . . . Civil War*, 289.

16 On their side, Southerners had forgiven: Donald, *Sumner . . . Civil War*, 292.

16 Brown did not speak but held it: Donald, *Sumner . . . Civil War*, 293.

16 Yes, he condemned Brown's actions: Donald, *Sumner . . . Civil War*, 293.

17 Sumner heard Buchanan out: Donald, *Sumner . . . Civil War*, 309.

17 Sumner began mildly: Donald, *Sumner . . . Civil War*, 295.

18 "I have not yet found time": Donald, *Sumner . . . Civil War*, 299.

18 The young women were described as "laughing": Holzer, 50.

18 "A poet has said that the shot": Holzer, 51.

18 "Much as I desire the extinction": Benson, 219.

18 *"They will all go"*: Donald, *Sumner . . . Civil War*, 313.

19 Sumner declined with a reproach: Donald, *Sumner . . . Civil War*, 319.

19 He told the story afterward: Holzer, 417.

19 "When with the Romans": Eaton, 309.

19 But, Sumner added, Lincoln might not recognize: Donald, *Sumner . . . Civil War*, 319.

20 Mary Lincoln reported that: Donald, *Lincoln Men*, 214.

21 Before reading his proclamation aloud: Goodwin, 464.

21 Then, when "the eagle of victory": Goodwin, 468.

22 The Union army responded by publishing: John Fabian Witt, "Lincoln's Code: The Laws of War in American History," *New York Times*, September 22, 2012, A21.

23 Lincoln lamented, "If there is a worse place than hell": Goolrick, 92–93.

23 Further Union losses served to test the alliance: Donald, *Lincoln Men*, 186.

24 "Remember that I am President of the United States": Goodwin, 687.

25 One of his friends, a Polish translator in the Senate: Donald, *Sumner . . . Rights*, 152.

CHAPTER 2. WILLIAM HENRY SEWARD (1865)

27 "Assassination is not an American habit": J. M. Taylor, 240.

27 Seward had already dislocated a shoulder: J. M. Taylor, 62.

28 She wrote to her sister that, seeing him: J. M. Taylor, 241.

28 At fifteen, he entered Union College: Stahr, 13.

28 Eight weeks later, Henry's father read: J. M. Taylor, 17.

28 Graduating from Union College at nineteen: J. M. Taylor, 18.

29 During that campaign, Seward denounced: Hale, 47.

29 Sixteen at the time of the War of 1812: Van Deusen, 11.

30 Jury members did not leave their seats: Weed, 36.

30 Very soon, however, politics proved irresistible: Van Deusen, 16.

31 By 1830, however, Weed was confessing: Weed, 209.

31 Seward's move to Albany set a pattern: Hale, 83.

31 But he had also found it "easy to enlist": Weed, 317.

31 If Jackson's Democrats were so afraid: Hale, 94.

31 They came away feeling, in the words: Hale, 95.

32 Thurlow Weed granted that his "disappointment": Weed, 431.

32 While he had been traveling in Europe: J. M. Taylor, 34.

32 Seward burned the letters without reading them: Stahr, 39.

32 "My heart turns to you": J. M. Taylor, 36.

33 He wrote to his former friend, pointing out: J. M. Taylor, 37, cites WHS to Albert Tracy, December 29, 1834, Seward Papers, University of Rochester.

33 Weed had calculated that Seward was the best: Weed, 452.

33 He took care not to offend: Weed, 452.

33 Pressed by abolitionists to spell out: Stahr, 57.

33 He courted the growing Irish vote: Hale, 165.

33 "God bless Thurlow Weed!" Stahr, 57.

34 Very soon, Weed established such sway: Van Deusen, 107.

34 To pursue that line of attack: J. M. Taylor, 51.

34 Promoting the catchy "Tippecanoe and Tyler, too": Williams, 53.

34 To pay off their bets, he wrote, "please call": Van Deusen, 113.

35 "My principles are too liberal": J. M. Taylor, 53.

35 Frances's father had moved his bed: J. M. Taylor, 53.

35 "You will say that Henry Clay is a slave owner": J. M. Taylor, 60.

35 When their son, Augustus, graduated: Stahr, 106.

36 For his efforts, Taylor's brother had promised: Stahr, 109.

36 But Seward granted that Lincoln: J. M. Taylor, 73.

37 Finally, in Seward's telling, Lincoln "admitted": J. M. Taylor, 74; Stahr, 110–11, questions the anecdote.

37 Looking on, Thurlow Weed fretted that the ensuing outcry: Hale, 192.

37 "All is dark for him and for the country": Hale, 195.

37 Although Weed was urging caution: Weed, 428.

38 "Come on, then, gentlemen of the slave states": Hale, 218.

38 He said, "The heart of the country is fixed": Hale, 235.

38 "She is too noble a woman": J. M. Taylor, 102.

38 But by the time the Republicans convened: Stahr, 163–64.

39 after Mississippi's second senator, Henry "Hangman": Denton, 59.

39 Mrs. Davis later praised his genuine: Denton, 58.

39 Carl Schurz, a young German-born journalist: Schurz, 2, 34.

39 As for renown, Seward's speeches: Denton, 57.

39 "I am not," Lincoln had said, "nor ever have been": Guelzo, xxv.

40 One of them warned the Republicans, "You may elect": Hale, 256.

40 "Let us have faith that right makes might": Denton, 31.

40 But Seward's delegate count still fell: Stahr, 192.

40 Despite his aching disappointment: Hale, 259.

41 He wrote back to one sympathizer: J. M. Taylor, 119.

41 His retinue had picked up Charles Francis Adams, Jr.: J. M. Taylor, 120.

41 "I sat and watched the old fellow": Denton, 64.

41 To a Detroit audience, he described Negroes: J. M. Taylor, 122.

41 "Loyalty to the Union will be treason to the South": W. Davis, *Deep Waters*, 33.

41 When they said good-bye, Lincoln asked playfully: Weed, 623.

42 Weed had been furious since 1854: J. M. Taylor, 120.

42 She wrote to her husband, about to turn sixty: J. M. Taylor, 120.

42 In formally tendering the offer: J. M. Taylor, 127.

43 For the first time, Washington began to censor: Goodwin, 353.

43 He also urged Lincoln to act when a secessionist mob: Goodwin, 354–55.

44 Recent evidence of military incompetence: J. M. Taylor, 207.

44 They already viewed Seward with suspicion: J. M. Taylor, 205; Goodwin, 489.

44 Led by Salmon Chase, the Radicals called: Goodwin, 487.

44 In the *Chicago Tribune*, Joseph Medill: J. M. Taylor, 205.

44 Informed on December 16, 1862, of an impending vote: Donald, *Lincoln Men*, 167.

44 Seward by then had the run of the White House: J. M. Taylor, 189, cites Frederick W. Seward, "Lincoln and Seward," in *Obediah Seward of Long Island and His Descendents*, printed privately, 1948.

45 But in fact, Mary Lincoln harbored misgivings: Goodwin, 495.

45 As for the secretary of state's role: Goodwin, 494.

46 Charles Sumner declined a dinner invitation: J. M. Taylor, 211.

46 Seward had also adroitly resolved the *Trent*: J. M. Taylor, 185.

46 he read and admired a draft of brief remarks: J. M. Taylor, 222.

47 When a celebration in Washington erupted: J. M. Taylor, 234.

48 Powell knocked her to the floor: Weichmann, 82–83.

48 Powell was arrested, taken before a military court: Chamlee, 163.

49 Booth replied curtly that it would be: Weichmann, 83.

49 In Booth's view, "the country was formed for the white man": Weichmann, 50–51.

49 Powell learned that Surratt had been carrying messages: Weichmann, 30.

50 Damning every victory by the Northern: Weichmann, 21.

50 Most of Mrs. Surratt's borders were family: Weichmann, 97–98.

51 "I must go up, must see him": Chamlee, 1.

51 Terrified, William Bell ran out the front door: Weichmann, 161.

51 Seward's daughter Fanny had been keeping a vigil: Chamlee, 2.

51 When he grabbed at a figure: Chamlee, 2.

51 Frederick was left behind with a fractured skull: Weichmann, 162.

CHAPTER 3. JEFFERSON DAVIS (1865)

53 Although he soon learned of General Lee's surrender: W. Davis, *Jefferson Davis*, 619–20.

54 Alone with his aides inside the house: Dodd, 259, cites Stephen R. Mallory, "Last Days of the Confederate Government," Parts 1 & 2, *McClure's Magazine*, December 1900 and January 1901.

54 Growing up in Kentucky, "Little Jeff": W. Davis, *Jefferson Davis*, 7.

54 Davis's father, Samuel, an ambitious farmer: Cooper, 13–14.

54 She and her husband indicated their determination: W. Davis, *Jefferson Davis*, 6.

54 At age eight, Little Jeff was sent: Cooper, 16.

54 Back home as a teenager, he tried to rebel: Cooper, 28.

55 Edgar Allan Poe, who arrived at West Point: Cooper, 34.

55 He explained that he always called Pemberton: W. Davis, *Jefferson Davis*, 80.

55 The tedium of army life was relieved: W. Davis, *Jefferson Davis*, 52.

55 He was talked out of challenging Taylor: W. Davis, *Jefferson Davis*, 53.

56 To a friend, Taylor lamented: Cooper, 66.

56 Knoxie wrote to reassure her parents: Cooper, 72.

56 Men meeting the twenty-seven-year-old: W. Davis, *Jefferson Davis*, 85.

56 With the outbreak of war with Mexico: Cooper, 128.

56 Davis seldom won the affection of his men: W. Davis, *Jefferson Davis*, 137.

56 He stayed in the saddle, stanched his wound: W. Davis, *Jefferson Davis*, 138.

57 In his official report, Taylor praised Davis: Cooper, 155.

57 When the general came by to visit: Allen, 155.

57 In an overtly political letter: W. Davis, *Jefferson Davis*, 162.

57 Davis wrote to let her know: Cooper, 163.

58 He accused Davis of trying "to crush": W. Davis, *Jefferson Davis*, 229–30.

59 By withdrawing from the Union, the South had "merely": Dew, 13.

59 Thomas Jefferson and other Founders had believed: Dew, 14.

59 He was sure that Anderson, as a Kentucky slave owner: J. Davis, I, 184.

59 A showdown had been averted then only because the ship: Allen, 251.

60 At 3:20 on the morning of April 12, 1861: J. Davis, I, 248.

60 "We have the honor to inform you": J. Davis, I, 248.

61 As Confederate hopes spiraled downward: Dodd, 346.

62 When Davis caught up with his wife's party: W. Davis, *Jefferson Davis*, 635.

62 Then, before dawn, a former slave: J. Davis, II, 594.

62 He would put his hand under the man's boot: J. Davis, II, 595.

62 Watching them slip off, Davis endorsed their decision: J. Davis, II, 596.

CHAPTER 4. PINCKNEY BENTON STEWART PINCHBACK (1865)

65 When the speaker finished, the white commander: Beatty, 73.

65 And in Washington, a fugitive slave: Foner, *Reconstruction*, 1.

66 The *New York Times* joined in the rejoicing: Foner, *Reconstruction*, 2.

66 First, though, Pinchback took Eliza to Philadelphia: Haskins, 3.

66 Lighter even than his mother: Haskins, 6.

66 For different reasons, neither of them took to formal: Haskins, 7.

67 Eliza Stewart learned from the major's executor: Haskins, 9.

67 Landing a job on a riverboat: Haskins, 12.

67 Stories circulated later about the risks: Haskins, 16.

67 But after many affairs, he fell in love: Haskins, 17.

68 "I nearly fainted in court": Haskins, 22.

69 His stand provoked the wrath: Nolan, 31.

69 "Whoever employed by this corporation": Nolan, 34.

70 "As God lives and I live": Nolan, 34.

70 "I think no man has won more": Nolan, 76.

71 "That is frank, that is fair," Lincoln answered: Nolan, 92.

71 Light-skinned, often wealthy, more at ease: Foner, *Reconstruction* 47.

71 He ordered a reeking canal cleansed: Nolan, 163.

71 When a group of city matrons ostentatiously: Nolan 178.

72 "When any female shall, by word, gesture": Nolan, 177.

72 Southerners next accused him of confiscating: Allen, 342.

72 Butler admitted later that he had been frightened: Nolan, 159.

72 With that hanging, Butler became detested: J. Davis, II, 242.

72 He followed up his flouting of the Fugitive Slave Law: Nolan, 192.

73 The other officers were "inimical to me": Haskins, 25.

73 He appealed to a basic sense of fairness: Haskins, 27.

73 In speeches, he praised Benjamin Butler: Haskins, 30.

75 As long ago as 1861, Wade had written to a friend: Hendrick, 277–78.

75 Lincoln described to a friend: Trefousse, *Wade*, 204–5.

75 the Wade-Davis manifesto, which appeared: Document, *From Revolution to Reconstruction*, University of Groninger, The Netherlands, 1994.

76 That night, to Butler's great surprise: Nolan, 223.

76 Butler, however, could point to the fact: Nolan, 272.

77 "If this temporary failure succeeds": Nolan, 320.

77 "General Butler certainly gave his very earnest": U. S. Grant, *Memoirs*, 426.

77 "Butler's greater intellect overshadowed Grant": Nolan, 326.

78 But he also made clear that it was "only": Foner, *Reconstruction*, 49.

78 He calculated that since the Emancipation Proclamation: Goodwin, 548.

78 Before he could apply for an interview: Haskins, 32.

78 By autumn, however, Pinchback's impatience: Haskins, 38.

79 On March 3, 1865, President Lincoln signed: Du Bois, *Black Reconstruction*, 1998, 221.

79 "I do not believe it is necessary to secure": Du Bois, *Black Reconstruction*, 1998, 222.

CHAPTER 5. ANDREW JOHNSON (1865)

81 Right up to Election Day, he had been apprehensive: Goodwin, 664.

82 "Damn the Negroes," Johnson said: Andrew Johnson, *Encyclopedia Brittanica*.

82 "Whenever you hear a man prating": Harris, 430.

82 "A loyal Negro," Johnson said: Patton, 126.

82 "I'm not well," Johnson complained: Stewart, 8.

83 As a boy named for Andrew Jackson: McKitrick, 86.

83 "Some day," he vowed, "I will show": McKitrick, 87.

84 Gideon Welles was nearly spared: Means, 90.

84 "I kiss this book in the face": Means, 91.

85 "Both read the same Bible": Goodwin, 698.

85 Mary Lincoln, not always the most obliging: Goodwin, 700.

86 "O, was it not a glorious sight": Means, 94.

86 Charles Sumner lamented the "frightful": Sumner, *Letters*, II, 272, n.4.

86 Johnson's letter to the Senate's recorder: Means, 95.

86 To the comptroller of the currency, the president said: Means, 95.

86 When she died on June 21: J. M. Taylor, 247.

87 In Washington, however, the earlier protests: J. M. Taylor, 251.

87 The Yankees had left him "one inestimable": Trowbridge, 577.

87 Johnson issued a sweeping amnesty: Johnson, *Papers*, vol. 8, 129–30.

88 But when Johnson appointed William Holden: McKitrick, 7.

88 For Charles Sumner, the question of voting: Donald, *Sumner*, II, 219.

88 "There is no difference between us": Donald, *Sumner*, II, 220.

88 Asking for full restoration of his rights: Johnson, *Papers*, 8, 232.

91 In Washington, a young actress named Ella Starr: Guttridge, 153.

91 "He told me that his name was Boyd": Guttridge, 177.

92 They also uncovered a letter from Samuel Arnold: Weichmann, 181.

92 "Before God, I do not know this man": Weichmann, 186.

93 "I know you," Bell exclaimed: Weichmann, 187.

93 New York senator Edwin Morgan: Johnson, *Papers*, 8, 135.

93 He and Andrew Johnson had been personal and political foes: Dodd, 362.

94 Since Secretary of War Stanton had left Davis's treatment: W. Davis, *Jefferson Davis*, 643.

94 As one newspaper put it, "a peal of inextinguishable": W. Davis, *Jefferson Davis*, 646.

94 By August, the prisoner's health had improved: W. Davis, *Jefferson Davis*, 647.

95 If he were released eventually, he was determined: W. Davis, *Jefferson Davis*, 649.

95 "You should be governed by the opinions": Chamlee, 232.

96 Powell was also the male defendant: Steers, 30.

96 Samuel Arnold and Michael O'Laughlen came off better: Steers, 30.

96 George Atzerodt, as a German foreigner: Steers, 30.

97 Observers were puzzled by Dr.Samuel Mudd: Steers, 30.

97 None of the men in the courtroom: Steers, 30.

97 As the trial proceeded, a grand jury in the District: Chamlee, 353.

97 During the forty-eight days of testimony: Steers, 35.

98 David Herold was the first to be sentenced: Chamlee, 436–38.

99 The prospect of hanging a women: Chamlee, 441.

99 In any case, the new president might have balked : Chamlee, 444.

100 One heavily veiled woman: Chamlee, 461.

100 John Surratt, unwilling to jeopardize his sanctuary: Chamlee, 467–68.

100 Powell said, "You know best, Captain": Chamlee, 471.

101 With the spectacle ended, the crowd moved out: Chamlee, 474.

CHAPTER 6. OLIVER OTIS HOWARD (1865)

103 Custis Lee—whose father, Robert E. Lee: Carpenter, 8.

104 He described them as "full of gas": Carpenter, 9.

104 When the preacher called for sinners: Carpenter, 17.

104 When Major General Phil Kearny, who had lost: Carpenter, 33.

105 Then, in an unexpected reversal, Howard's name: Carpenter, 63–64.

105 "I anticipated a real pleasure in serving": Carpenter, 81.

105 The *New York Times* praised the selection: McFeely, 9.

106 Now her father described Howard as "of all men": McFeely, 9.

106 Beecher envisioned Howard carrying: McFeely, 87.

106 Sherman had already warned Howard: McFeely, 18.

106 Given the expectations for the bureau: Foner, *Reconstruction*, 143.

106 In the war's earliest days, when Ulysses Grant: Bentley, 21.

106 As thousands of former slaves followed Sherman: Bentley, 45.

106 To his wife, Howard wrote that "the negroes": Carpenter, 93.

107 He expected enlightened Southerners: Du Bois, *Black Reconstruction*, 1998, 224.

107 Howard expected his assistant commissioners: Farmer-Kaiser, 25.

107 Saxton decreed that a wife who left her husband: Farmer-Kaiser, 25.

107 In appointing his first ten assistants: Carpenter, 97.

107 Major General George Hartsuff had been a cadet: Bentley, 57.

108 Eaton had commandeered the estate of Jefferson Davis: Bentley, 55.

108 They would be working out of a Washington townhouse: McFeely, 65.

108 hordes of black men roamed the desolate landscape: Stewart, 27–28.

108 White lawmakers in South Carolina decreed: Du Bois, *Black Reconstruction*, 1998, 168.

109 In North Carolina, orphans were sent to work: Fitzgerald, 33.

109 Florida law made either disobedience or "impudence": Du Bois, *Black Reconstruction*, 1998, 167–68.

109 For months, some slaves had gone on: Peirce, 133, cites Report of the Joint Committee on Reconstruction (Washington, 1866), 186.

109 One South Carolinian predicted that they would perish: Stewart, 30.

109 But Grant said that conversations with bureau: Peirce, 57.

110 "Arson is a crime, robbery is a crime": Schurz, *Autobiography*, III, ch. vi.

110 He had struck up a conversation with a well-spoken: Schurz, *Autobiography*, III, ch. vi.

111 "Dead Negroes were found in considerable numbers": Stewart, 31.

112 Its language had been kept deliberately cloudy: Du Bois, *Black Reconstruction*, 1998, 158.

112 Oliver Howard considered education to be the major answer: Bentley, 63.

113 "What? For niggers?" he demanded: Du Bois, *Black Reconstruction*, 1998, 637.

113 At the war's end, fewer than 150,000: Du Bois, *Black Reconstruction*, 1998, 638.

113 He noted that the races were still segregated: Du Bois, *Black Reconstruction*, 1998, 643.

113 But in Mississippi, black men who donated money: Du Bois, *Black Reconstruction*, 1998, 647.

113 One white teacher arriving in Adams County: Du Bois, *Black Reconstruction*, 1998, 647.

113 Thomas Conway, Oliver Howard's appointee in Louisiana, warned: Du Bois, *Black Reconstruction*, 1998, 647.

114 As the bureau's assistant for South Carolina: McFeely, 97.

114 The plantations on those Atlantic islands: McFeely, 40.

115 Saxton wrote to Howard that the former slaves were owed: Cimbala, 52.

115 "The pardon of the President will not be understood": McFeely, 105.

CHAPTER 7. THADDEUS STEVENS (1865–1866)

117 At the core of their dispute, Lincoln had seemed: Donald, *Sumner . . . Rights*, 207.

117 When Sumner heard of Lincoln's assassination: Donald, *Sumner . . . Rights*, 216.

118 But the meeting went well: Donald, *Sumner . . . Rights*, 220.

118 The president had appointed as governor: Means, 202.

118 This was "inconsistent with what he said to me": Donald, *Sumner . . . Rights*, 223.

118 To meet the demand, Johnson was at work: Means, 224.

119 McLean pronounced his white neighbors "well satisfied": Johnson, *Papers*, vol. 8, 316.

120 "I write," he confided to a friend: Trefousse, *Stevens*, 164.

120 "I am sure you will pardon me": Meltzer, 168.

120 At the war's end, prominent Confederates could hope: Brodie, 220, quotes *The Nation* on the Southern mood.

121 Once seated, Stephens would be joined in Congress by four Confederate generals: Meltzer, 169; released from prison in Boston Harbor, Means, 224.

121 For two and a half hours, the president sidestepped: Donald, *Sumner . . . Rights*, 238.

122 Lately, Stevens had asked Sumner to recommend: Trefousse, *Stevens*, 170.

123 Their father, a failed farmer and part-time shoemaker: Brodie, 23–24.

123 "Manifest contempt, Your Honor?": Meltzer, 17.

124 Stevens was approached by a slave owner: Hoch, 20.

124 "The next president," Stevens said: Trefousse, *Stevens*, 14; Brodie, 33.

124 Neighbors in Gettysburg heard that Stevens took a hatchet: Meltzer, 21.

125 "He is a happy man who has one true friend": Hoch, 27.

125 "I never stand aside for a skunk": Brodie, 95.

125 The infant died at nine weeks: Brodie, 96.

125 Whatever their relationship became: Brodie, 88.

126 One scandal had arisen: Brodie, 33–41.

126 He was not so lewd as Henry Clay: Brodie, 91.

126 Hearing those words, Stevens said: Brodie, 112–13.

127 "Preach the Gospel," he said, "but don't attempt": Brodie, 55.

127 Four years later, Stevens stood for Congress: Trefousse, *Stevens*, 77.

127 He contrasted New York and Pennsylvania with Virginia: Trefousse, *Stevens*, 80.

127 He offered only tepid support to the presidential nominee: Trefousse, *Stevens*, 94.

128 When Stevens was nominated for Congress: Trefousse, *Stevens*, 96.

128 With secession looming, Stevens attacked: Trefousse, *Stevens*, 107.

128 Better, he added, to let the entire region: Trefousse, *Stevens*, 112.

128 Stevens had kept a straight face: Brodie, 145.

129 And when Lincoln asked Stevens whether: Brodie, 148.

129 When the president announced that emancipation: Brodie, 159.

129 But the president backed away from supporting Stevens: Brodie, 166.

130 "Treason must be made infamous": Means, 117.

130 He considered *The Nation*, a fledgling New York weekly: Donald, *Sumner . . . Rights*, 228.

130 If "the colored people of the South": Donald, *Sumner . . . Rights*, 231.

131 "The infernal laws of slavery": Korngold, 303.

132 Because he was reading Darwin's *Origin*: Trefousse, *Stevens*, 190.

132 As he read the roll, McPherson omitted the Southerners': Stewart, 43.

133 Looking ahead twelve days to the expected ratification: Johnson, *Papers*, vol. 9, 474.

133 But on this day, Johnson's target: McKitrick, 146.

133 Now at last, he predicted, the Confederate South: Johnson, *Papers*, vol. 9, 475.

134 "In less than twenty days": Johnson, *Papers*, vol. 9, 600 note.

134 "The moment the insurrection was terminated": Korngold, 301.

134 Lulled by their sense of relief: Du Bois, *Black Reconstruction*, 1998, 272.

134 "Freedom is not simply the principle to live": Brodie, 260.

134 Now Johnson, facing the first test: Du Bois, *Black Reconstruction*, 1998, 274.

135 One Delaware senator used the debate: Du Bois, *Black Reconstruction*, 1998, 274.

135 "The talk about his health is ridiculous": J. M. Taylor, 257, cites Welles, *Diaries*, vol. 3, 4–5.

135 Seward wrote a veto message: Du Bois, *Black Reconstruction*, 1998, 272.

136 The president wrote the final salvo himself: Stewart, 50.

136 Back then, Stevens said, he had waited them out: Brodie, 253.

137 The most unlikely tribute used bookbinding as a metaphor: Du Bois, *Black Reconstruction*, 1998, 277.

137 Speaking at Cooper Union, Seward dismissed: Du Bois, *Black Reconstruction*, 1998, 277.

137 Instead, the president listed several of his Confederate: Du Bois, *Black Reconstruction*, 1998, 279.

138 Grieving prematurely over his own martyrdom: Stewart, 52.

138 Senator William Fessenden of Maine had been able to work: Donald, *Sumner . . . Rights*, 248.

138 His detestation became so great: Donald, *Sumner . . . Rights*, 253.

139 *"No more states with inequality of rights!"*: Donald, *Sumner . . . Rights*, 259.

CHAPTER 8. THE FOURTEENTH AMENDMENT (1866)

143 A friend of Thaddeus Stevens had sent him an item: Brodie, 262.

144 Witnesses quoted him as calling, "Boys": Brodie, 266.

144 "I said we were not that sort of women" D. Sterling, 161.

145 Two weeks after the bloodshed, the Tennessee: Du Bois, *Black Reconstruction*, 1998, 574.

145 In an early version, the amendment would forbid: Trefousse, *Stevens*, 184.

145 "I must do my duty, without looking": Donald, *Sumner . . . Rights*, 262.

145 Since he had introduced very similar legislation: Stewart, 37.

146 "Show me a creature, with lifted countenance": Donald, *Sumner . . . Rights*, 246.

146 Stevens took consolation in reminding himself: Trefousse, *Stevens*, 186.

146 Glib, charming, and only twenty-three, Warmouth: Du Bois, *Black Reconstruction*, 1998, 461–63.

147 In disguises and carrying brass knuckles: Brodie, 273; Du Bois, *Black Reconstruction*, 1998, 465.

148 Anthony Dostie, a dentist from New York: Sterling, 93.

148 "Gentlemen!" he cried, "I beseech you to stop": Du Bois, *Black Reconstruction*, 1998, 465.

148 "God damn you! Not one of you will escape": Brodie, 278.

148 A white spectator told later of a young white man: Brodie, 279.

149 "There is little doubt," he wrote in his diary: Brodie, 280.

149 But the massacre had horrified the country: Brodie, 280.

149 "My experience," he wrote, trying to buck up: Donald, *Sumner . . . Rights*, 265.

150 He gave a hint in a letter to Henry Longfellow: Sumner, *Letters*, II, 373.

150 Encountering a Boston man who favored: Donald, *Sumner . . . Rights*, 270.

151 The day that the Thirteenth Amendment: Brodie, 204.

151 Senator Fessenden watched with disbelief: Donald, *Sumner . . . Rights*, 271.

151 He inherited sixty-five thousand dollars: Donald, *Sumner . . . Rights*, 272.

151 After they married and she had come to deplore: *Dictionary of Unitarian and Universalist Biography*.

152 Sumner did, however, warn his fiancée: Donald, *Sumner . . . Rights*, 274.

152 He added, "I write this gaily, & yet": Sumner, *Letters*, II, 382.

152 By October 17, 1866, Sumner had thrown off his doubts: Donald, *Sumner . . . Rights*, 274.

153 Fifty-two postmasters and more than sixteen hundred: Stewart, 62.

153 "It does not become radicals like us": Trefousse, *Stevens*, 198.

153 The president announced that he did not want the South: Brodie, 287.

154 Privately, he said that he expected to see: J. M. Taylor, 260.

154 These days, Seward saw himself as a man: Brodie, 285.

154 In St. Louis, Johnson assured the crowd: Brodie, 281.

155 "The President of the United States cannot enter upon an exchange": McKitrick, 438.

155 Appealing for "your attention for five minutes": McKitrick, 431.

155 What Grant had said privately to General John Rawlins: McKitrick, 428 note.

156 Accompanying the tour was Sylvanus Cadwallader: Cadwallader, 350.

156 When subordinates refused to intervene: Cadwallader, 104.

156 Rawlins made it clear to junior officers: Cadwallader, 119.

156 Whenever she turned up in camp: Cadwallader, 118.

156 At last, Rawlins advised her to engage a reputable: Cadwallader, 120.

156 On this tour with Andrew Johnson, Grant was confirming: Cadwallader, 116.

157 There, Gideon Welles's son, Edgar: Niven, *Welles*, 552.

157 Seward owed his impassive expression: Stewart, 60.

157 When Seward fulfilled the obligation: J. M. Taylor, 263.

158 But when Johnson also arrived: J. M. Taylor, 266.

158 Losing Fanny, he said, he felt "a sorrow": J. M. Taylor, 266.

158 " 'The Radicals would thrust the Negro into your parlors' ": Brodie, 288.

159 The scourge of Radical Republicans, Bennett: McKitrick, 441.

159 Since Raymond enjoyed an agreement with the *Times* owner: McKitrick, 442.

159 "Yes, yes, they are ready to impeach": McKitrick, 435.

CHAPTER 9. EDWIN STANTON (1867–1868)

161 When Edwin McMasters Stanton first met Abraham Lincoln: Goodwin, 174.

161 Ten years later, as Lincoln's secretary of war: Goodwin, 743; Thomas, 399.

162 During campaigns, he was free with insults: Thomas, 25.

162 Stanton wrote to a friend that the "calamity: Thomas, 35.

162 "Events of the past summer," Stanton began one letter: Thomas, 41.

163 "There are not many pretty faces on the avenue": Thomas, 51.

164 Stanton not only got Sickles acquitted, but in the process: Thomas, 84.

164 With the onset of the war: Goodwin, 383.

165 He anticipated the anger it would arouse: Goodwin, 401.

165 To a friend, the president said that Stanton's: Pratt, 469.

165 He granted to his niece that Stanton was: Pratt, 470.

165 "He gets wrought to so high a pitch": Thomas, 151.

166 The president called it, "Going to see Old Mars": Pratt, 143.

166 "You have done your best to sacrifice this army": Pratt, 211.

167 "Stanton is the most unmitigated scoundrel": Thomas, 209.

167 "I am tired of the sickening sight of the battlefield": Pratt, 206.

167 To which, the president said mildly, "Mr. Secretary": Pratt, 321.

167 "Couldn't let go his basket to unbutton": Thomas, 383.

168 He had come to appreciate the fact: Niven, *Welles*, 525.

168 When he was forced to state his position: Niven, *Welles*, 572.

168 "Reconstruction is more difficult": Pratt, 443.

169 Speaking to officials from Alabama, the president called: Trefousse, *Johnson*, 270.

169 Johnson learned just how outraged congressmen were: *Yale Law*, Impeachment, iv, 1.

170 As a result, Southern courthouses could punish: Thomas, 516.

170 Their test was a bill to extend voting rights in the District: Trefousse, *Johnson*, 273.

171 Meeting in private with Charles Nordhoff: Trefousse, *Johnson*, 279. Nordhoff's

grandson, Charles Bernard Nordhoff, was the coauthor of *Mutiny on the Bounty.*

172 In the House, Thaddeus Stevens's version not only included cabinet appointees: Brodie, 297.

173 But for less easily identifiable offenses, George Mason: Stewart, 78.

173 Thaddeus Stevens then attached that language: Brodie, 296.

173 General Philip Sheridan, who was now commanding Texas and Louisiana: Pratt, 449.

175 Pinchback accused the Southern aristocracy: Haskins, 52–54.

175 Pinchback attacked a measure to strip several categories: Haskins, 60.

176 General Lafayette Baker from the War Department: *Yale Law*, Impeachment, iv, 2–3.

177 The *New York World* called Alaska a "sucked-dry orange": J. M. Taylor, 278.

177 He would change his mind if "the Secretary of State": Donald, *Sumner . . . Rights*, 307.

178 Kate considered Alice Sumner a "flutterfly": *Deseret News*, Salt Lake City, Utah, October 14, 1898.

178 One midnight at a dance, guests heard: Donald, *Sumner . . . Rights*, 290.

178 One shrewd Washington matron thought: Donald, *Sumner . . . Rights*, 291 note.

179 He asked, "Where are you going": Donald, *Sumner . . . Rights*, 292.

179 As Sumner protested in vain, she cursed: Donald, *Sumner . . . Rights*, 294.

179 She let it be known that she had left: Donald, *Sumner . . . Rights*, 314.

179 Charles Sumner became "The Great Impotent": Donald, *Sumner . . . Rights*, 314.

179 Varina Davis overcame her contempt: Dodd, 368.

180 his critics suggested that his chief concern: Cooper, 560.

180 As attorneys for Davis wrangled over his case: Cooper, 563.

180 Lee assured his former president that Davis's release: Cooper, 568.

181 He had already decided to remove Edwin Stanton: Niven, *Welles*, 549.

181 The president had worked himself up to a white heat: J. Grant, 165.

182 "I thought, Mr. Stanton, it was but just": J. Grant, 165.

182 The president told the faithful Gideon Welles, "If Congress can bring": Pratt, 450.

182 He railed against the prospect of "negro domination": J. E. Smith, 443.

183 Wilson asked, "Are we to impeach the President": *Yale Law*, Impeachment, iv, 2.

CHAPTER 10. SALMON PORTLAND CHASE (1868)

185 The day after their embarrassing defeat: Stewart, 112.

185 He wrote to William Sherman, "All the": Grant, *Papers*, 17, 343.

186 The angry correspondence ended: J. E. Smith, 451.

186 "He is a bolder man than I thought him": Brodie, 332.

186 William Fessenden, despite his regular clashes: Brodie, 333.

186 But, Stevens concluded, "Grant isn't on trial": Brodie, 334.

186 His first choice was John Potts: Thomas, 580.

187 Put in charge of abandoned plantations: Blue, 199.

187 Stanton felt only contempt: Thomas, 163.

187 Describing Thomas as "only fit": Stewart, 132.

187 For his part, Thomas was either more forgiving: Thomas, 379.

187 And Johnson expected that "the nation": Thomas, 582.

187 Inadvertently, however, Thomas had deprived: Thomas, 583.

187 Formally, Thomas said, "I am directed": Thomas, 584.

188 Johnson went to report to his cabinet: Thomas, 584.

188 Senators were sending their own: Thomas, 585.

189 the weekend commemorating George Washington's: Thomas, 587.

189 Judge Carter had accepted Stanton's affidavit: Stewart, 139.

190 The two men exchanged good mornings: Ross, 118.

190 "Thomas: I am Secretary of War *ad interim*": *New York Times*, February 22, 1868; Ross, 118.

190 Thomas reported later that he told Stanton: Stewart, 139.

191 The *New York Times* reporter was convinced: *New York Times*, February 22, 1868.

192 Brooks called Stanton's refusal to resign: Brodie, 335.

192 He claimed that "Robespierre, Marat and Danton": Stewart, 144.

192 Johnson sent to the Senate the name of Thomas Ewing: Stewart, 145.

193 Now he advised Johnson to begin: Stewart, 147.

193 Fuller had already bribed enough clerks: Stewart, 147.

193 Stevens assured his listeners unconvincingly: *Congressional Globe*, 40 Congress, 2 session, February 24, 1865, 1399–1400; Brodie, 336.

193 The Republicans chose Stevens and Ohio representative: Korngold, 419.

194 Finding limited support: Schuckers, 76.

194 Lincoln explained privately: Goodwin, 635.

194 Chase had been attracted to: Blue, 10.

195 He found "her features large": Blue, 23.

195 Since early in the century: Blue, 28.

195 Yet as a lawyer, Chase took up: Schuckers, 52.

195 It would do more to show "the true character": Blue, 107.

195 But when a political bulletin listed: Beatty, 45.

196 At the Baltimore convention: Beatty, 52.

196 He overcame his own antipathy to paper money: Blue, 151.

196 When Chase was chosen, Frank Blair told his brother: Blue, 245.

197 Lincoln concluded that he "would despise myself": Goodwin, 679.

197 In the Senate, Charles Sumner called: Blue, 242.

197 When a jubilant Charles Sumner hurried to tell: Blue, 245.

CHAPTER 11. BENJAMIN FRANKLIN WADE (1868)

199 observing him later in life: Trefousse, *Wade,* 18–19.

200 "Until the laws of nature and of nature's God": Trefousse, *Wade,* 36.

201 "As the world goes," he wrote to his wife: Trefousse, *Wade,* 53.

201 As he explained, "I cannot and will not": Trefousse, *Wade,* 63.

202 In Washington, Wade enjoyed being a senator: Trefousse, *Wade,* 73.

202 At the theater, the former cattle driver: Trefousse, *Wade,* 93–94. It is possible that Wade was playing to his uncouth reputation.

202 Despite his earlier rejection of dueling: Trefousse, *Wade,* 103.

202 "I know it isn't so bad to have no religion": Trefousse, *Wade,* 125.

203 Wade pulled his carriage across the route: Trefousse, *Wade,* 150.

203 He had summed up Henry Seward: Trefousse, *Wade,* 154.

203 "If any of them come back": Trefousse, *Wade,* 167.

203 "Are the President and Mrs. Lincoln aware": Trefousse, *Wade,* 167.

204 Already in his midsixties, Wade threw himself: Trefousse, *Wade,* 268.

204 Writing to Susan B. Anthony in November 1866: Trefousse, *Wade,* 288.

205 Congress "cannot quietly regard the terrible distinction": Trefousse, *Wade,* 287.

205 Kate's anger with his vacillation alarmed her doting father: Niven, *Chase,* 424.

206 "I'll see you damned first": Bumgardner, 72.

206 Since throwing in his lot with the Radicals: Nolan, 329.

207 Butler had wanted to see Andrew Johnson: Stewart, 194.

207 When the subject turned to heavy drinking: Stewart, 208.

208 They were bound only: Stewart, 195.

208 At one point, he praised the Constitution: Martinez, 49.

208 Butler's theatrics could not substitute: Stewart, 199.

208 He was replaced by William Evarts: Niven, *Welles,* 562.

209 But Seward joined with Thurlow Weed in raising: J. M. Taylor, 284.

209 And when Seward happened to encounter William Fessenden: J. M. Taylor, 285.

209 Defense lawyers wanted to buttress that argument: Blue, 279.

209 Sherman was permitted to report: Ross, 129.

209 A Philadelphia journalist reported that Stevens: Korngold, 421.

210 But when his turn came: Ross, 214.

210 Yet he concluded by demanding: Korngold, 423.

211 the politics of Weed's latest paper: Van Deusen, 325.

211 With no apparent irony, Butler also was offering: Stewart, 246.

212 As Salmon Chase put on his robe: Blue, 280.

213 But like other conservatives: Kennedy, 136.

213 Born so tiny that his mother could cover: Bumgardner, 15.

214 by 1859, the lure of expanding opportunities: Bumgardner, 39.

214 Major Ross survived but only after two horses had been shot: Harrington, 44.

214 Senator James Lane had voted against: McKitrick, 323.

214 "We need a man with backbone": Harrington, 49.

215 "There is a bushel of money!": Harrington, 72.

215 As another point of attack: Stewart, 266.

215 General Daniel Sickles, removed by Johnson: Harrington, 73; Stewart, 270.

216 The second time, firmly and audibly: Bumgardner, 95.

216 "Your motives were Indian contracts": Harrington, 76.

216 If Congress did not remove Johnson: Brodie, 350.

216 Now bitterness and frustration gave Stevens: Trefousee, *Stevens*, 234.

216 Former Tennessee representative Thomas Nelson: Stewart, 278.

216 To a *New York Times* reporter: Stewart, 278.

217 On May 26, the second and third articles: Trefousse, *Wade*, 328.

217 the *New York Sun* was describing Johnson: Brodie, 329.

217 Publicly, Chase claimed that "the subject": Blue, 282.

217 "Bribery and personal vindictiveness": Sumner, *Letters*, II, 427.

217 Pliant senators were offered: Stewart, 186.

218 But Pomeroy was among the most Radical: Kennedy, 122.

218 witnesses, who included Thurlow Weed: Stewart, 286.

218 When an enterprising reporter: Stewart, 297.

218 A thirty-seven-year-old West Point graduate: Stewart, 223.

219 Ross wrote that the appointment was "vital": Stewart, 298.

CHAPTER 12. NATHAN BEDFORD FORREST (1868)

221 the president would now be free to proclaim: Trefousse, *Johnson*, 333.

221 One such man, condemned by his neighbors as a scalawag: Trefousse, *Johnson*, 333.

221 Half a dozen young Confederate officers: Hurst, *Forrest*, 278.

221 Their town had been named for Casimir Pulaski: Chalmers, 8.

222 As an oath, candidates were only required: Wade, 34.

222 One of the six founders pointed out: Wade, 37.

222 A Klan member might carry a skeleton's arm: Wade, 35.

223 Captain George Judd, the Freedmen's Bureau agent: Chalmers, 9.

223 In April 1867, men from various supremacist: Chalmers, 9.

224 The South became the Empire: Trelease, 14–15.

224 The official pennant featured a flying dragon: Wade, 39.

224 "This is an institution of Chivalry": Trelease, 16.

225 Forrest set up his own regiment: Wills, 45.

225 "If we are whipped," Forrest told them: Hurst, *Forrest*, 5.

225 "Come on, boys, if you want a heap of fun": Wills, 71.

225 Forrest brushed aside a doctor: Hurst, *Forrest*, 129.

226 A Confederate soldier wrote to his sister: Hurst, *Forrest*, 173.

226 When Fitch requested the protection: Hurst, *Forrest*, 176–77.

227 In his official report to Jefferson Davis: Wyeth, 333.

227 In its account of the battle, the *Chicago Tribune:* Hurst, *Forrest*, 179.

227 When the scandal reached the White House: Hurst, *Forrest*, 180.

227 At the war's end, Forrest won praise: Foote, 1002.

228 Testimony developed that Forrest had become outraged: Wills, 327.

228 Forrest acknowledged that "I am": Wills, 334.

228 When Johnson approved his pardon: Wade, 17.

228 witnesses claimed that during the 1867: Hurst, *Forrest*, 285; Wills, 336.

229 Police had told a group of parading Negroes: Trelease, 26.

229 "This is no joke either. This is cold, hard": Trelease, 22–23.

229 A *Citizen* reporter wrote that the leader: Trelease, 23.

229 Dens were being set up in small towns: Chalmers, 10.

229 In South Carolina, where Negroes constituted a majority: Chalmers, 11.

229 Captain Judd of the Freedmen's Bureau: Trelease, 24–25.

230 "Unless something is done immediately": Wade, 45.

230 Captain Judd was accused of running the League: Trelease, 25.

230 "Speak in whispers and we hear you": Wade, 42.

230 In later testimony, General Forrest estimated: Tourgee, 29.

230 "That they would never submit": Tourgee, 31.

231 He believed that the people would ultimately: Trefousse, *Johnson*, 335.

231 At the Democratic convention in July: Trefousse, *Johnson*, 339.

231 "I have experienced ingratitude": Trefousse, *Johnson*, 339.

231 "Have a care," he instructed: Niven, *Chase*, 432.

232 In William Fessenden's view, "Andy": Trefousse, *Johnson*, 340.

232 In his final message to Congress: Trefousse, *Johnson*, 341.

232 To Stevens, that safeguard was the only way: Brodie, 361.

232 The convention backed away: Brodie, 360.

233 And yet, Stevens was confident: Brodie, 363.

233 "My life has been a failure": Brodie, 363.

233 "Especially present my compliments": Brodie, 365.

233 Stevens's will left five hundred dollars a year: Brodie, 365.

233 As a final note of respect, his local Republican: Brodie, 366.

234 New York newspapers acknowledged the sweep: *New York Times,* August 13, 1868; *New York Tribune*, August 12, 1868.

234 In 1905, an evangelist and writer named Thomas Dixon, Jr.: Dixon, xi.

234 Dixon gave Stoneman a heavy brown wig: Dixon, 39.

234 "We must assimilate or expel": Dixon, 46.

CHAPTER 13. ULYSSES S. GRANT (1869)

237 She sympathized with those who thought: J. Grant, 170.

237 Now, as the Republicans departed: J. Grant, 171.

238 "Mrs. Grant, you must now be prepared": J. Grant, 172.

238 A loud and ornery voice at town meetings: Perry, 3–4; Wilentz, in Isaacson, 63.

239 Getting ready to leave for New York: Wilson, 133.

239 In a letter to a cousin, Grant showed: U. S. Grant, *Memoirs*, 878.

239 His good friend James "Pete" Longstreet: J. E. Smith, 26.

239 Somewhat shy, Grant could not match: Farina, 3.

239 At graduation in 1843, Granted ranked twenty-first: Waugh, 24.

239 Given a family history of consumption: U. S. Grant, *Memoirs*, 34.

240 A merchant's daughter pampered by four indulgent: Waugh, 25.

240 When Grant proposed, however: J. Grant, 52.

240 Scott, as Grant noted later: U. S. Grant, *Memoirs*, 95.

240 As for the Mexican war itself: Waugh, 31; Wilson, 133.

241 He could not understand, he said, "how human beings": U. S. Grant, *Memoirs*, 119.

241 with Pete Longstreet as his best man: Waugh, 33.

241 As the bride observed, "I had had four years": J. Grant, 55.

241 According to a story circulating at his post: Waugh, 38.

241 When Julia's father gave him a slave: Waugh, 42; Wilentz in Isaacson, 64.

242 With Julia at his side, Grant could usually control: Waugh, 39.

242 Worried that a Republican victory: U. S. Grant, *Memoirs*, 144.

242 Southern extremists would calm down: U. S. Grant, *Memoirs*, 145.

244 "No terms except immediate and unconditional": Farina, 88.

244 He had not come out to fight: Kastler, 53.

244 Pillow would be more useful: Farina, 87.

244 But as a result, merchants were swearing allegiance: Sarna, 38–39.

245 "Refuse all permits to come south of Jackson": U. S. Grant, *Memoirs*, 1015.

245 Hours after Grant issued his decree: J. E. Smith, 227.

245 At headquarters, General Halleck revived accusations: Farina, 92–93.

246 "I want to whip these rebels once more": Farina, 94.

246 Hearing that Brigadier General Alexander Hays: J. E. Smith, 323.

246 And General Grant had set a record of his own: J. E. Smith, 333.

246 "I propose to fight it out on this line": J. E. Smith, 349.

246 That evening, Grant told his staff: J. E. Smith, 364.

247 "Gentlemen," Grant told a rally: J. E. Smith, 456.

247 "Let us have peace": Waugh, 120.

247 They seized upon Horatio Seymour's response: J. E. Smith, 458.

248 "Our demands," Moses had written: J. E. Smith, 460 note.

248 Grant replied to Morris that he held "no prejudice": J. E. Smith, 460.

249 Grant received results of the balloting: J. E. Smith, 461.

249 "I'm afraid I'm elected": Waugh, 122, cites Ross, *The General's Wife*, 202.

249 Grant felt he could now permit: Sarna, 78.

249 During the four months leading up to his inauguration: J. E. Smith, 465.

249 She said she was afraid to ask him again: Donald, *Sumner . . . Rights*, 370.

249 "Well, he didn't write it": J. E. Smith, 502.

249 Nor did Sumner improve his chances: Donald, *Sumner . . . Rights*, 369.

250 Following the election, Seward had described: J. M. Taylor, 288.

250 Miss Risley declined Seward's invitation: J. M. Taylor, 290.

250 The jibe stung, and Seward protested: J. M. Taylor, 292.

250 During the voyage, Seward decided that he must: J. M. Taylor, 293.

251 Grant had already agreed to sell: J. E. Smith, 462–63.

251 Stopping at the White House: J. E. Smith, 466.

251 "Madame, if any colored people call": J. Grant, 175.

252 One example of Grant's favor came: Waugh, 124.

252 Nor had Grant considered the ban: J. E. Smith, 470.

253 "The progress of evolution," he wrote: J. E. Smith, 475.

253 In the *New York Sun*, Charles Dana: *New York Sun*, 1869.

253 The paper warned that civil service: *New York World*, March 1869.

254 Judge Hoar, finding no precedent to cite: J. E. Smith, 472 note.

254 Pinchback worried that the Democrats: Haskins, 57.

255 "Social equality, like water, must be left": Haskins, 59.

255 He lost that argument: Haskins, 60.

255 with seven black and twenty-nine white: Haskins, 62.

256 if those Democratic "outrages" continued: Haskins, 64.

256 The New Orleans *Crescent* called his outburst: *New Orleans Crescent*, September 4, 1868.

256 If "any Negro or gang of Negroes": Haskins, 66.

256 more than ten thousand Republicans had voted: Haskins, 69.

257 Severing his last ties with Warmoth: Haskins, 75.

CHAPTER 14. GOLD AND SANTO DOMINGO (1869–1870)

260 "Anything for Human Rights is constitutional": Donald, *Sumner . . . Rights*, 353.

260 At the Treasury, Boutwell was quickly proving: J. E. Smith, 481.

260 Well pleased, Grant announced that re-establishing: Grant to Badeau, July 14, 1869, 19 Grant Papers, 212–13.

260 His New England family traced their roots: Ackerman, *Gold Ring*, 47.

261 They rebounded with a nervy scheme: Ackerman, *Gold Ring*, 16.

262 As Fisk told a friend, "Gould is a damned fool": Ackerman, *Gold Ring*, 49.

262 As Gould recalled, Corbin: Ackerman, *Gold Ring*, 58.

263 He had joked about his tin ear and confessed: Waugh, 22.

263 Abel Corbin did his part by offering Julia Grant: "Gold Panic Investigation," House of Representatives, Report No. 31, 44th Congress, 2nd session, 1870, 270–71.

263 Gould assured Butterfield's loyalty: J. E. Smith, 483.

263 Corbin was traveling with Grant, and kept pressing: Ackerman, *Gold Ring*, 83.

264 At once, Gould put $1.5 million in gold: Ackerman, *Gold Ring*, 88.

264 to say she was "quite positive there will be no": Ackerman, *Gold Ring*, 100.

264 His vacations were becoming a joke: Ackerman, *Gold Ring*, 119.

265 Only Julia Grant heard him complain: Ackerman, *Gold Ring*, 122.

265 "The fact is," Grant wrote, "a desperate struggle": J. E. Smith, 483.

265 Julia Grant had written that "the general says if you have": J. Grant, 182.

265 Gould made no promises, but as he was leaving: Ackerman, *Gold Ring*, 157.

266 "I think you had better make it five million": J. E. Smith, 489.

266 Fisk and Gould had been identified: Ackerman, *Gold Ring*, 198.

267 Grant said he had received Corbin's letter: Ackerman, *Gold Ring*, 225.

267 "The matter has been concluded": J. E. Smith, 490.

267 In fact, Fisk said, Corbin had only married: Ackerman, *Gold Ring*, 248.

267 When the *Sun* reporter sought out Fisk: Ackerman, *Gold Ring*, 252.

268 The nation's press rallied around Ulysses Grant: Ackerman, *Gold Ring*, 257.

268 When the Dominican Republic offered to allow the United States: J. E. Smith, 500.

269 "Mr. President," he began, "I am a Republican": J. E. Smith, 503; Donald, *Sumner . . . Rights*, 436.

269 At that moment, the president was neglecting: Donald, *Sumner . . . Rights*, 370.

269 Enlisting Radical support, Sumner insisted: Donald, *Sumner . . . Rights*, 425.

270 And the dictatorship controlling the Dominican: Donald, *Sumner . . . Rights*, 440.

270 The United States, according to Sumner: Donald, *Sumner . . . Rights*, 442–43.

271 urged that Britain sign over: J. E. Smith, 508.

271 Out for revenge, Grant could both punish Sumner: Babcock to Adam Badeau, June 18, 1870; U. S. Grant, *Papers*, 20, 164.

271 "You can't understand my situation," Sumner said: Donald, *Sumner . . . Rights*, 455–56.

271 For Sumner, the treatment of Motley: Donald, *Sumner . . . Rights*, 461.

272 At the University of Michigan, Sumner spoke: Donald, *Sumner . . . Rights*, 461.

272 Returning to Washington, Sumner could do no better: Donald, *Sumner . . . Rights*, 461 note.

272 At the White House, visitors found President Grant: Donald, *Sumner . . . Rights*, 498.

273 He told them "that whenever Sumner should retract": Nevins, 408.

273 He was describing the president as "without": Nevins, 408.

CHAPTER 15. KU KLUX KLAN (1870–1872)

275 He reported that the freedmen now had: McFeely, 301.

275 Howard ruled that his agents could instruct: Carpenter, 139.

276 Southern and Western legislators were conniving: McFeely, 163.

276 Then Congress cut $100,000: Carpenter, 224.

276 "I do not wish him ill," Howard said: Carpenter, 239.

276 Despite the continual shortage of money: Foner, *Reconstruction*, 1998, 144–45.

277 Such a university was approved: Carpenter, 170.

277 Once in the job, Howard described: Carpenter, 181.

277 "Butler, prepare to meet your God!": Trelease, 65.

278 Ben Wade and other Republican leaders: Trelease, 294.

278 Because Akerman lived thirty miles from the nearest: Nevins, 367.

279 Born in New Hampshire and graduating: J. E. Smith, 542.

279 Neither man underestimated the growing strength: J. E. Smith, 545.

279 He announced that "from the beginning of the world": Martinez, 67.

280 "Let each member of the House read the letter": Martinez, 69

280 He wanted justice for Sumner, Trumbull said, although: Krug, 297.

280 He deplored the beatings and lynchings: Krug, 297–98.

281 "Individual rights," he concluded, "are safest": Krug, 299.

281 As the debate came to a climax: Krug, 302.

281 As for corruption, when a railroad owner like Hannibal I. Kimball: Du Bois, *Black Reconstruction*, 1998, 509–10.

281 He had extorted from the Grant administration: Krug, 302.

281 "A condition of affairs now exists": J. E. Smith, 546.

282 In Unionville, forty Klan members: Martinez, 73–74.

282 General William Sherman had already responded: Martinez, 75.

283 Elias Hill, a black Baptist minister: Trelease, 372.

283 By the beginning of 1882, 195 persons: Trelease 404–5.

284 in the new South, Blair had seen his grown son: Du Bois, *Black Reconstruction*, 1998, cites *KKK Report, Alabama*, part 2, p. 676.

284 At another hearing this one in Atlanta: *Testimony, Select Committee, Georgia*, vol. 1, 4-11-412.

285 President Grant had also authorized: Trelease, 392.

285 A novel published anonymously called *The Masked Lady*: Wade, 52.

285 Reporting from Spartanburg, South Carolina: Trelease, 395.

285 He preferred to deny his involvement: Wills, 359.

286 The Central Pacific, built with laborers from China: Ambrose, 19.

286 "Negroes are the best laborers": Wills, 359.

286 When the judge appealed to Forrest for protection: Wills, 362.

286 He had enhanced his reputation the previous month: Hurst, *Forrest*, 337.

287 As the final congressional report on Klan activities would note: U.S. Congress, *Report of the Joint Select Committee*, 463.

287 "When the war was over," Forrest said: Wills, 253.

287 But committee members had resurrected an imprudent interview: Wade, 51; Wills, 365.

287 When all else failed, Forrest appealed: Wills, 364.

287 "I have been lying like a gentleman": Chalmers, 21.

CHAPTER 16. HORACE GREELEY (1872)

289 Although the Klan seemed to be a spent force: Trelease, 411.

289 But since the Klan's terrorism no longer seemed to threaten: Trelease, 415.

289 Frederick Douglass, the nation's most celebrated: J. E. Smith, 548.

290 with the president himself personally compromised: J. E. Smith, 583–84.

290 were drawn to this Liberal Republican Party: J. E. Smith, 548.

290 Lyman Trumbull was on board: Foner, *Reconstruction*, 500.

290 his absence would not necessarily be: Foner, *Reconstruction*, 502.

291 Greeley wrote that Grant had made no more preparation: Maihafer, 121.

291 At the convention, Whitelaw Reid went to work: Maihafer, 237.

291 He described Greeley fondly as a "gangling": Williams, 60.

293 As for himself, Greeley wrote that he now understood: Williams, 117.

293 Rather than spout more "angry vituperation against slaveholders": Williams, 104.

293 He exposed their wrongdoing: Williams, 115.

294 Well satisfied with the result: Williams, 181.

294 He remained personally cautious, however: Williams, 191.

294 Readers gladly overlooked Greeley's crotchets: Williams, 62.

294 Lincoln responded with a telegram to the *Tribune:* Williams, 234.

294 But Thurlow Weed, who resisted: Williams, 235.

295 "The burdens of society," Greeley wrote: Williams, 240.

295 When the rioting ended, more than: Williams, 241.

296 Speaking to a friend in 1870, Greeley blamed: Williams, 261.

296 "Angelic child," the president called him: Williams, 273.

296 In 1867, the *Tribune* paid Samuel Clemens forty dollars: Williams, 265.

296 Greeley's halting conversion to the cause of women's rights: Williams, 305.

296 A graduate of DePauw University in Indiana: Waugh, 143.

297 "The King of Frauds," it proclaimed: Ambrose, 373.

297 "If the subsidies provided are not enough": Ambrose, 132.

298 He said he simply wanted to place the Crédit Mobilier: Ambrose, 374.

298 Horace Greeley, who might have exploited the issue: Williams, 304.

298 In a rare burst of self-pity, he lamented: J. E. Smith, 551.

298 "I have been assailed so bitterly that I hardly knew": Williams, 306.

299 Looking over the mourners Henry Ward Beecher pronounced: J. E. Smith, 551 note.

CHAPTER 17. HIRAM REVELS (1872–1873)

301 He and his four colleagues bought: Haskins, 86.

302 Instead, he sent a letter: Haskins, 126.

302 "I do not claim to possess": Haskins, 129.

302 Animosity ran so high between the camps: Haskins, 92.

302 Casey "hadn't a handful of brains": Haskins, 96.

303 Now it was Warmoth who had to forget: Haskins, 100.

303 Learning of the deal, Pinchback protested: Haskins, 109.

304 Pinchback anticipated the hostility: Haskins, 117.

304 "Take any race, keep them in the most miserable": Haskins, 118.

305 "For that I do suspect the lusty Moor": Dray, 69.

306 "as certainly as the sun shines in the heavens": Dray, 61.

306 He called the decision "a putrid corpse": Donald, *Sumner . . . Rights*, 427.

306 "The colored United States Senator from Mississippi": Dray, 73.

307 "And now, sir, I ask how did that race act?": Dray, 75.

307 "the people now are getting along as quietly": Dray, 75.

307 Less than a month after Lincoln had been elected: Dew, 22.

307 A colleague from his state had argued: Dew, 29.

308 Since few of them, black or white: Foner, *Reconstruction*, 350.

308 Pinchback stood aloof from the Liberal Republicans: Haskins, 133.

309 When a firebrand from Kansas invoked the spirit: Haskins, 134.

309 Pinchback chose the convention for announcing: Haskins, 135.

309 Pinchback concluded lightly that Grant "may be a little crotchety": Haskins, 135.

CHAPTER 18. GRANT'S SECOND TERM (1873–1876)

312 As weapons, the men shouldered antiquated rifles: Dray, 142.

312 The stories grew wilder: Dray, 143.

313 After shouting threats in front of the courthouse: Dray, 145.

313 A witness reported that "one could have walked on": Dray, 146.

313 A witness said that the gunfire "was like popcorn in a skillet": Dray, 146.

315 "General Grant has vanquished the people": J. E. Smith, 564–65.

315 "Give me no help in lamentation": Dray, 148.

315 "I thought a chief justice should never be subjected": J. E. Smith, 559.

316 *The Nation* praised Grant sardonically: J. E. Smith, 562.

317 "Let no guilty man escape": J. E. Smith, 590.

318 Grant called the spoils system "an abuse": J. E. Smith, 589.

318 "A true reform," Grant said, "will let the office": J. E. Smith, 589.

318 "Certainly, if you wish it": J. E. Smith, 594.

319 reports from the South that no whites were being convicted: Donald, *Sumner . . . Rights*, 530.

319 Instead, he proposed a broad amendment: Donald, *Sumner . . . Rights* 531.

320 the Sermon on the Mount was a higher authority: Donald, *Sumner . . . Rights*, 532.

320 "A measure that seeks to benefit only the former rebels": Donald, *Sumner . . . Rights*, 535.

320 "The idea of the Democracy supporting Charles Sumner": Donald, *Sumner . . . Rights*, 541.

321 And a *Harper's Weekly* cartoonist, Thomas Nast: Donald, *Sumner . . . Rights*, 553.

321 Julia Ward Howe singled out Greeley Republicans: Donald, *Sumner . . . Rights*, 570.

322 The man who handed him the legislature's vindication: Donald, *Sumner . . . Rights*, 584.

322 described his pain as having "a toothache": Donald, *Sumner . . . Rights*, 585.

322 "I should not regret this," Sumner said, "if my book": Donald, *Sumner . . . Rights*, 586.

322 He vomited, gasped to breathe, and fell back dead: Donald, *Sumner . . . Rights*, 587.

323 When the Massachusetts legislature invited a prominent: Foner, *Reconstruction*, 524.

323 He forgot the missteps in Louisiana: Foner, *Reconstruction*, 533.

323 He tied Sumner's bill to other legislation: Foner, *Reconstruction*, 553.

324 The *New York Times* observed that Phillips: Foner, *Reconstruction*, 559.

324 And yet when Congressman James Garfield of Ohio encountered: J. E. Smith, 595.

324 "His imperturbability is amazing": J. E. Smith, 595.

324 "I want to know what is happening": J. E. Smith, 585.

CHAPTER 19. RUTHERFORD BIRCHARD HAYES (1876)

327 His father had uprooted the family from New England: Conwell, 31.

327 In later years, though, classmates remembered: Conwell, 59.

328 Yet his practice expanded to include the defense: Trefousse, *Hayes*, 15.

328 He wrote that he feared disunion less: Conwell, 70.

328 After the Union loss in Baltimore: Conwell, 71.

329 As he told Lucy, one phrase: Hoogenboom, 189.

329 the House of Representatives "more orderly": Hoogenboom, 193.

329 By the time that his district's Republican convention: Hoogenboom, 201.

329 "The Negro prejudice is rapidly wearing away": Hoogenboom, 203.

330 Instead, he had acquired: Hoogenboom, 208.

330 "They are not aliens or strangers": Hoogenboom, 212.

330 Ohio governors had no veto power: Hoogenboom, 215.

331 "The proper discharge of the function of maternity": Hoogenboom, 228.

331 The president was incensed that the Senate: Hoogenboom, 230.

331 Leaving office early in 1872, Hayes pronounced himself: Hoogenboom, 239.

332 At fifty-one, he might be heavier and shorter of breath: Hoogenboom, 249.

333 He blamed his bad digestion: Morris, 83.

334 Tilden's hard work was propelling him forward: Morris, 92.

334 Even friends admitted that Tilden was too quick; Tilden, *Letters*, I, xxvii.

334 Although he kept company with a number: Morris, 93.

334 He resisted joining to the new Republican Party: Tilden, *Letters*, I, xxv.

335 In despair, he wrote, "It is too late!": Morris, 96.

335 When Salmon Chase lost the presidential nomination: Morris, 98.

335 Boss Tweed, a former bookkeeper: Morris, 100.

335 His masterstroke was the New York County Courthouse: Morris, 100.

336 But when Nast drew blood: Morris, 101.

336 "wants to stop the pickup, starve out the boys": Morris, 102.

337 In a Cooper's Union speech, Tilden attacked the "cabal": Akerman, *Tweed*, 230.

337 governor John Hoffman was deeply indebted: Akerman, *Tweed*, 240.

337 One confrontation between the two men: Morris, 103.

337 Tweed escaped with his henchmen: Akerman, *Tweed*, 234–35.

337 a friendly editor wrote that he was praying: Morris, 105.

338 By a vote of 233 to 18, members approved: Haworth, 11.

338 A third term "would be unwise, unpatriotic": Haworth, 11.

338 Instead Republicans turned to Governor Hayes: Foner, *Reconstruction*, 567.

338 *The Nation* magazine described the ticket: Foner, *Reconstruction*, 567.

338 Summing up Rud Hayes, Henry Adams: Foner, *Reconstruction*, 567.

339 The neighboring tribes, Grant wrote, "are the most harmless": J. E. Smith, 520 and 692, note 26.

339 Over the years, Grant had never trusted George Custer's: J. E. Smith, 539.

339 they were enslaving the mass of Americans: Foner, *Reconstruction*, 568.

340 "The truth is, the Negroes are ignorant, many of them": Foner, *Reconstruction*, 569.

340 Hayes saw the bad economy: Hoogenboom, 269.

340 From Harvard Yard, college president Charles Eliot spoke for them: Hoogenboom, 269.

340 but Democrats in the House of Representatives: Hoogenboom, 270.

340 Democrats were acting on the choice set out: Morris, 119.

341 "Are you for the Rebellion, or are you for the Union?": Hoogenboom, 270.

341 "If the Republicans do not carry New York": Hoogenboom, 272.

342 If what Schurz was advocating "so earnestly": Morris, 120.

342 the Enforcement Act of five years earlier had contained: Hoogenboom, 272.

342 He predicted that if he lost: Hoogenboom, 272.

343 "When the annals of this Republic show the disgrace": Haworth, 32.

343 "Sly Sam, the Railroad Thief": Haworth, 42, note 1.

343 To make amends, Tilden sent emissaries South: Morris, 107.
343 There, according to the editor of the *Louisville Courier-Journal*: Morris, 108.
343 He faced an early test on the Fourth: Haworth, 131–40.
344 Before he set off for bed, the president told his guests: J. E. Smith, 598.
344 The equality amendments would be nullified: Morris, 167.
346 From the embassy, Sickles publicly romanced deposed queen Isabella II: Morris, 11.
346 "With your state sure for Hayes": Tilden, *Letters*, II, 483.
347 But without the chairman's room number: Morris, 16.
347 "Hayes has 185 electoral votes and is elected": Haworth, 52.
347 He told a reporter for the *Cincinnati Times* that the Republicans: Morris, 167.
347 He issued an order that army commanders: J. E. Smith, 598.
348 When Grant raised the question of fraud: J. E. Smith, 598.
348 "A charge to keep I have, a God to glorify": Quarles, 51.
348 Eliza Pinkston from Ouachita Parish: *New York Times*, December 30, 1876.
349 Senator John Sherman wrote to assure Hayes: J. E. Smith, 599.
349 Even a plot to lock up Republican electors: Haworth, 154–55.
349 Deploring the claim as an incitement to violence: Haworth, 189.
350 Democrats claimed that he could only report: Morris, 201.
350 But in Washington the frosty governor had no reserves: Haworth, 191.
350 He disapproved of the tactics of men like William Chandler: Hoogenboom, 276.
350 "The committee seems to be a good one": Hoogenboom, 286.
351 "The entire nation would honor these Southern men": Morris, 233.

CHAPTER 20. JIM CROW (1877)
353 bitter Democrats had yielded only after prolonging: Trefousse, *Hayes*, 81.
354 Within weeks of his inaugural address, Hayes acted: Hoogenboom, 310.
354 Kellar assured the president's son, Webb: Hoogenboom, 312.
355 "I would rather," Grant told her: J. E. Smith, 616.
356 The negotiating team he headed had returned from London: Grier, 106.
357 "We have a Chief Justice," Field wrote to a friend: Grier, 107.
357 Waite's approach was no more favorable to women: Grier, 109.
357 Writing for the Court, Bradley asked, "Can the act of a mere individual": Schwartz, 166.
358 In his decisions, he warned that the rights of black citizens: Grier, 114.
358 He reminded them that the United States had no ruling class: Grier, 114.
359 "Can't something be done," he wondered: Trefousse, *Hayes*, 95.
359 As James Garfield complained to fellow Republicans: Trefousse, *Hayes*, 96–97.

361 A London critic found "something in his chuckle": (London) *Times*, November 8, 1836, 5.
362 Lucius Lamar's praise for Charles Sumner: Du Bois, *Black Reconstruction*, 1998, 124.
362 A truer sentiment was expressed: Tourgee, 121.
362 Before Jim Crow took hold, some former slaves: Woodward, 51.
362 But in South Carolina, those gentlemen had already passed: Packard, 69.
363 Rare dissenting views came from the National Association: Wade, 134.
363 White confided to Thomas Dixon: Wade, 127.
364 A week later, Simmons, calling himself the Imperial Wizard: Wade, 147.
364 "Anyone who carries a hyphen about with him": Wade, 148.
364 In little more than a year, Clarke could claim: Wade, 157.
365 "If the Klan is against the Jews": Wade, 165.
366 assessed the Klan as having "all of the defects": Wade, 204.
367 South Carolina governor James F. Byrnes said his state: Woodward, 145.
367 On May 17, 1954, Chief Justice Warren spoke: Woodward, 146.
368 Georgia's jubilant lieutenant governor pointed out: Woodward, 153.
368 In 1956, the admission of a black student, Autherine Lucy: Woodward, 156.
368 "We will wear you down by our capacity": Woodward, 170.
370 Now he denounced the civil rights bill as "reminiscent": United Press International (UPI), *Year in Review*, 1963.
371 "It docs say," Johnson continued, "that those who are equal": *New York Times*, July 3, 1964, 9.

BIBLIOGRAPHY

Ackerman, Kenneth D. *Boss Tweed*. Falls Church, Virginia, 2011.

———. *The Gold Ring: Jim Fisk, Jay Gould, and Black Friday, 1869*. New York, 1988.

Adams, Russell L. *Great Negroes Past and Present*. Chicago, 1963.

Allen, Felicity. *Jefferson Davis: Unconquerable Heart*. Columbia, Missouri, 1999.

Ambrose, Stephen E. *Nothing Like It in the World*. New York, 2000.

Appendix to Diplomatic Correspondence of 1865: *The Assassination of Abraham Lincoln, Late President of the United States of America*. Washington, D.C., 1866.

Ash, Stephen V. *When the Yankees Came: Conflict & Chaos in the Occupied South, 1861–1865*. Chapel Hill, North Carolina, 1995.

Baggett, James Alex. *The Scalawags: Southern Dissenters in the Civil War and Reconstruction*. Baton Rouge, Louisiana, 2003.

Baker, Bruce E. *What Reconstruction Meant: Historical Memory in the American South*. Charlottesville, Virginia, 2007.

Bay, Mia. *To Tell the Truth Freely: The Life of Ida B. Wells*. New York, 2009.

Beale, Howard K. *The Critical Year: A Study of Andrew Johnson and Reconstruction*. New York, 1958.

Beatty, Jack. *Age of Betrayal: The Triumph of Money in America, 1865–1900*. New York, 2007.

Belz, Herman. *Emancipation and Equal Rights: Politics and Constitutionalism in the Civil War Era*. New York, 1978.

Benson, T. Lloyd. *The Caning of Senator Sumner*. Belmont, California, 2004.

Bentley, George R. *A History of the Freedman's Bureau*. Philadelphia, 1955.

Beth, Loren P. *John Marshall Harlan: The Last Whig Justice*. Lexington, Kentucky, 1992

Bigelow, John. *The Life of Samuel J. Tilden*. New York, 1895.

Blackmon, Douglas A. *Slavery by Another Name*. New York, 2009.

Blount, Roy, Jr. *Robert E. Lee*. New York, 2003.

Blue, Frederick J. *Salmon P. Chase: A Life in Politics*. Kent, Ohio, 1987.

Boatner, Mark M., III. *The Civil War Dictionary.* New York, 1991.

Bolden, Tonya. *W. E. B. DuBois.* New York, 2008.

Boles, John B. *Black Southerners 1619–1869.* Lexington, Kentucky, 1983.

Bonekemper, Edward H., III. *McClellan and Failure.* Jefferson, North Carolina, 2007.

Brands, H. W. *The Man Who Saved the Union: Ulysses Grant in War and Peace.* New York, 2012.

Brodie, Fawn M. *Thaddeus Stevens: Scourge of the South.* New York, 1959.

Brown, Thomas J., ed. *Reconstructions: New Perspectives on the Postbellum United States.* New York, 2006.

Buckmaster, Henrietta. *The Fighting Congressmen.* New York, 1971.

Bumgardner, Edward. *The Life of Edmund G. Ross: The Man Whose Vote Saved a President.* Kansas City, Missouri, 1949.

Burt, John. *Lincoln's Tragic Pragmatism: Lincoln, Douglas and Moral Conflict.* Cambridge, Massachusetts, 2013.

Cadwallader, Sylvanus. *Three Years With Grant.* Lincoln, Nebraska, 1996.

Carpenter, John A. *Sword and Olive Branch: Oliver Otis Howard.* Pittsburgh, Pennsylvania, 1964.

Carter, Dan T. *When the War Was Over: The Failure of Self-Reconstruction in the South: 1865–1867.* Baton Rouge, Louisiana, 1985.

Chadwick, Bruce. *1858: Abraham Lincoln, Jefferson Davis, Robert E. Lee, Ulysses S. Grant and the War They Failed to See.* Naperville, Illinois, 2008.

———. *Lincoln For President.* Naperville, Illinois, 2009.

Chalmers, David M. *Hooded Americanism: The History of the Ku Klux Klan.* Durham, North Carolina, 1987.

Chamlee, Roy Z., Jr. *Lincoln's Assassins.* Jefferson, North Carolina, 1990.

Chase, Salmon P. *Inside Lincoln's Cabinet: The Civil War Diaries of Salmon P. Chase.* New York, 1954.

Cimbala, Paul A. *The Freedmen's Bureau.* Malabar, Florida, 2005.

Cooper, William J., Jr. *Jefferson Davis, American.* New York, 2000.

Davis, Jefferson. *The Rise and Fall of the Confederate Government,* 2 vols. New York, 1990.

Davis, William C. *The Deep Waters of the Proud.* New York, 1982.

———. *Jefferson Davis: The Man and His Hour.* New York, 1991.

Denton, Lawrence M. *William Henry Seward and the Secession Crisis.* Jefferson, North Carolina, 2009.

Dew, Charles B. *Apostles of Disunion.* Charlottesville, Virginia, 2001.

Dickerson, Donna L. *The Reconstruction Era: Primary Documents on Events from 1865 to 1877.* Westport, Connecticut, 2003.

Dixon, Thomas, Jr. *The Clansman.* Lexington, Kentucky, 1970.

Dodd, William E. *Jefferson Davis.* Lincoln, Nebraska, 1997.

Dodge, Grenville M. *Personal Recollections.* Council Bluffs, Iowa, 1914.

Donald, David Herbert. *Charles Sumner and the Coming of the Civil War.* Naperville, Illinois, 2009.

———. *Charles Sumner & The Rights of Man.* New York, 1970.

———. *"We Are Lincoln Men."* New York, 2004.

Douglass, Frederick. *Narrative of the Life of Frederick Douglass, an American Slave.* New York, 2004.

Downs, Gregory P. *Declarations of Dependence.* Chapel Hill, North Carolina, 2011.

Downs, Jim. *Sick From Freedom: African-American Illness and Suffering During the Civil War and Reconstruction.* New York, 2012.

Drabelle, Dennis. *The Great American Railroad War.* New York, 2012.

Dray, Philip. *Capitol Men: The Epic Story of Reconstruction Through the Lives of the First Black Congressmen.* Boston, 2008.

Du Bois, W. E. B. *Black Reconstruction in America: An Essay Toward a History of the Part Which Black Folk Played in the Attempt to Reconstruct Democracy in America, 1860–1880.* New York, 2007.

———. *Black Reconstruction in America 1860–1880,* New York, 1998.

Dunning, William Archibald. *Essays on the Civil War and Reconstruction.* Gloucester, Massachusetts, 1969.

Eaton, John. *Grant, Lincoln and the Freedmen: Reminiscences of the Civil War.* With Ethel Osgood Mason. New York, 1907.

Farina, William. *Ulysses S. Grant, 1861–1864: His Rise from Obscurity to Military Greatness.* Jefferson, North Carolina, 2007.

Farmer-Kaiser, Mary. *Freedwomen and the Freedmen's Bureau.* New York, 2010.

Faust, Drew Gilpin. *This Republic of Suffering: Death and the American Civil War.* New York, 2009.

Fellman, Michael. *Citizen Sherman: A Life of William Tecumseh Sherman.* New York, 1995.

———. *The Making of Robert E. Lee.* New York, 2000.

Fitzgerald, Michael W. *Splendid Failure: Postwar Reconstruction in the American South.* Chicago, 2007.

Flagel, Thomas R. *History Buff's Guide to the Civil War.* Naperville, Illinois, 2010.

Flood, Charles Bracelen. *1864 Lincoln at the Gates of History.* New York, 2009.

Foner, Eric. *The Fiery Trial: Abraham Lincoln and American Slavery*. New York, 2010

———. *Forever Free: The Story of Emancipation and Reconstruction*. New York, 2006.

———. *Politics and Ideology in the Age of Civil War*. New York, 1980.

———. *Reconstruction: America's Unfinished Revolution 1863–1877*. New York, 2002.

———. *A Short History of Reconstruction*. New York, 1990.

Foreman, Amanda. *A World on Fire: Britain's Crucial Role in the American Civil War*. New York, 2010.

Frankel, Noralee. *Break Those Chains at Last: African Americans 1860–1880*. New York, 1996.

Franklin, John Hope. *Reconstruction After the Civil War*. Chicago, Illinois, 1961.

Freehling, William W. *The Road to Disunion, vol. 1, Secessionists at Bay 1776–1854*. New York, 1990.

Freeman, Douglas Southall. *R. E. Lee: A Biography*. 4 vols. New York, 1934–35.

Fremon, David K. *The Jim Crow Laws and Racism in American History*. Berkeley Heights, New Jersey, 2000.

Giddings, Paula J. *Ida: A Sword Among Lions*. New York, 2008.

Ginzberg, Eli, and Alfred S. Eichner. *The Troublesome Presence: American Democracy and the Negro*. New York, 1966.

Goldman, Robert M. *Reconstruction & Black Suffrage: Losing the Vote in Reese & Cruikshank*. Lawrence, Kansas, 2001.

Goodwin, Doris Kearns. *Team of Rivals: The Political Genius of Abraham Lincoln*. New York, 2005.

Goolrick, William K. *Rebels Resurgent*. Alexandria, Virginia, 1985.

Gordon-Reed, Annette. *Andrew Johnson*. New York, 2011.

Graham, Lawrence Otis. *The Senator and the Socialite*. New York, 2006.

Grant, Julia. *The Personal Memoirs of Julia Dent Grant*. New York, 1975.

Grant, Ulysses S. *Papers*, John Y. Simon, ed. Carbondale, Illinois, 1967– .

———. *Personal Memoirs of U.S. Grant*, Lincoln, Nebraska, 1996.

———. *Personal Memoirs of U.S. Grant/Selected Letters 1839–1865*. New York, 1990.

Guelzo, Allen C. *Lincoln and Douglas: The Debates that Defined America*. New York, 2008.

Guttridge, Leonard F., and Ray A. Neff. *Dark Union: The Secret Web of Profiteers, Politicians and Booth Conspirators that Led to Lincoln's Death*. Hoboken, New Jersey, 2003.

Hale, Edward Everett, Jr. *William H. Seward*. Philadelphia, 1910.

Hamilton, Holman. *Jefferson Davis Before His Presidency*. Lexington, Kentucky, 1978.

Harrington, Arthur Elliot. *Edmund G. Ross: A Man of Courage*. Franklin, Tennessee, 1997.

Harris, Alexander. *A Review of the Political Conflict in America*. New York, 1876.

Hartranft, John Frederick. *The Lincoln Assassination Conspirators*. Edward Steers, Jr., and Harold Holzer, editors, Baton Rouge, Louisiana, 2009.

Haskins, James. *Pinckney Benton Steward Pinchback*. New York, 1973.

Haworth, Paul Leland. *The Hayes-Tilden Disputed Presidential Election of 1876*. Ithaca, New York, 2012.

Hendrick, Burton J. *Lincoln's War Cabinet*. New York, 1946.

Hoch, Bradley R. *Thaddeus Stevens in Gettysburg: The Making of an Abolitionist*. Gettysburg, Pennsylvania, 2005.

Hodes, Martha. *White Women, Black Men: Illicit Sex in the 19th-Century South*. New Haven, Connecticut, 1997.

Holzer, Harold. *Lincoln, President-Elect*. New York, 2008.

Hoogenboom, Ari. *Rutherford B. Hayes: Warrior & President*. Lawrence, Kansas, 1995.

Horowitz, Robert F. *The Great Impeacher: A Political Biography of James M. Ashley*. New York, 1979.

Howard, Oliver Otis. *Autobiography of Oliver Otis Howard, Major-General, United States Army: Pt. 1. Preparation for Life. Pt. 2. The Civil War*. Nabu Public Domain Reprints, 1907.

Hurst, Jack. *Born to Battle: Grant and Forrest—Shiloh, Vicksburg, and Chattanooga*. New York, 2012.

———. *Men of Fire: Grant, Forrest, and the Campaign that Decided the Civil War*. New York, 2007.

———. *Nathan Bedford Forrest: A Biography*. New York, 1993.

Isaacson, Walter. *Profiles in Leadership: Historians on the Elusive Quality of Greatness*. New York, 2010.

Jacobs, Harriet. *Incidents in the Life of a Slave Girl*. New York, 2004.

Johnson, Andrew. *Papers*. Vols. 8, 9. Knoxville, Tennessee, 1989, 1991.

Kastler, Shane E. *Nathan Bedford Forrest's Redemption*. Gretna, Louisiana, 2010.

Kennedy, John F. *Profiles in Courage*. New York, 2003.

Klarman, Michael J. *From Jim Crow to Civil Rights*. New York, 2004.

Korngold, Ralph. *Thaddeus Stevens: A Being Darkly Wise and Rudely Great*. New York, 1955.

Kremer, Gary R. *James Milton Turner and the Promise of America*. Columbia, Missouri, 1991.

Krug, Mark M. *Lyman Trumbull: Conservative Radical*. New York, 1965.

Latham, Frank. *The Great Dissenter: Supreme Court Justice John Marshall Harlan*. New York, 1970.

Lawson, Elizabeth. *The Gentleman from Mississippi*. New York, 1960.

Lemann, Nicholas. *Redemption: The Last Battle of the Civil War*. New York, 2006.

Maihafer, Harry J. *The General and the Journalists: Ulysses S. Grant, Horace Greeley, and Charles Dana*. Washington, D.C., 2001.

Mantell, Martin E. *Johnson, Grant, and the Politics of Reconstruction*. New York, 1973.

Martinez, J. Michael. *Carpetbaggers, Cavalry and the Ku Klux Klan*. Lanham, Maryland, 2007.

McFeely, William S. *Yankee Stepfather: General O. O. Howard and the Freedmen*. New Haven, Connecticut, 1968.

McKitrick, Eric L. *Andrew Johnson and Reconstruction*. New York, 1960.

McPherson, James M. *Battle Cry of Freedom*. New York, 1988.

———. *Crossroads of Freedom*. New York, 2002.

McVeigh, Rory. *The Rise of the Ku Klux Klan: Right-Wing Movements and National Politics*. Minneapolis, Minnesota, 2009.

Means, Howard. *The Avenger Takes His Place: Andrew Johnson and the 45 Days That Changed the Nation*. New York, 2006.

Meltzer, Milton. *Thaddeus Stevens and the Fight for Negro Rights*. New York, 1967.

Morris, Roy, Jr. *Fraud of the Century*. New York, 2003.

Muller, John. *Frederick Douglass in Washington, D.C.* Charleston, South Carolina, 2012.

Nevins, Allan. *Hamilton Fish: The Inner History of the Grant Administration*. New York, 1937.

Niven, John. *Gideon Welles: Lincoln's Secretary of the Navy*. Baton Rouge, Louisiana, 1973.

———. *Salmon P. Chase*. New York, 1995.

Nolan, Dick. *Benjamin Franklin Butler: The Damnedest Yankee*. Novato, California, 1991.

Oldaker, Nikki, with John Bigelow. *Samuel Tilden: The Real 19th President Elected by the People's Vote*. 2006.

Packard, Jerrold M. *American Nightmare: The History of Jim Crow*. New York, 2002

Packwood, Cyril Outerbridge. *Detour—Bermuda. Destination—U.S. House of Representatives: The Life of Joseph Rainey.* Hamilton, Bermuda, 1977.

Paolino, Ernest N. *The Foundations of the American Empire: William Henry Seward and U.S. Foreign Policy.* Ithaca, New York, 1973.

Parton, James. *The Life of Horace Greeley.* New York, 1970.

Patton, James Welch. *Unionism and Reconstruction in Tennessee, 1860–1869.* New York, 1934.

Peirce, Paul Skeels. *A Chapter in the History of Reconstruction.* New York, 1971.

Perry, Mark. *Grant and Twain: The Story of a Friendship that Changed America.* New York, 2004.

Peskin, Allan. *Garfield.* Kent, Ohio, 1978.

Pratt, Fletcher. *Stanton: Lincoln's Secretary of War.* New York, 1953.

Quarles, Benjamin. *Lincoln and the Negro.* New York, 1991.

Rafuse, Ethan S. *McClellan's War: The Failure of Moderation in the Struggle for the Union.* Bloomington, Indiana, 2005.

Randall, J. G., and David Donald. *The Civil War and Reconstruction.* Boston, 1961.

Riddle, A. G. *The Life of Benjamin Wade.* Cleveland, Ohio, 1886.

Riddleberger, Patrick W. *1866: The Critical Year Revisited.* Lanham, Maryland, 1884.

Ross, Edmund G. *History of the Impeachment of Andrew Johnson, President of the United States.* Teddington, England, 2007.

Russell, Sharman Apt. *Frederick Douglass.* New York, 1988.

Sarna, Jonathan D. *When General Grant Expelled the Jews.* New York, 2012.

Schuckers, J. W. *The Life and Public Service of Salmon Portland Chase.* New York, 1874.

Schurz, Carl. *The Reminiscences of Carl Schurz.* 3 vols. New York, 1907–8.

Schwartz, Bernard. *A History of the Supreme Court.* New York, 1993.

Simmons, William J. *Men of Mark: Eminent, Progressive and Rising.* New York, 1968.

Smith, Elbert B. *The Presidency of James Buchanan.* Lawrence, Kansas, 1975.

Smith, Jean Edward. *Grant.* New York, 2001.

Stahr, Walter. *Seward: Lincoln's Indispensable Man.* New York, 2012.

Stampp, Kenneth M. *The Era of Reconstruction: 1865–1877.* New York, 1965.

Steers, Edward, Jr. *Blood on the Moon: The Assassination of Abraham Lincoln.* Lexington, Kentucky, 2001.

Sterling, Dorothy, ed. *The Trouble They Seen: The Story of Reconstruction in the Words of African Americans.* New York, 1994.

Sterling, Philip, and Rayford Logan. *Four Took Freedom.* New York, 1967.

Stewart, David O. *Impeached: The Trial of President Andrew Johnson and the Fight for Lincoln's Legacy.* New York, 2009.

Stokes, Melvin. *D. W. Griffith's The Birth of a Nation.* New York, 2007.

Sumner, Charles. *Memoir and Letters.* Vol. II. Edward L. Pierce, ed. Boston, 1877.

———. *The Selected Letters of Charles Sumner.* Vol. II. Beverly Wilson Palmer, ed. Boston, 1990.

Swanson, James. *Bloody Crimes: The Chase for Jefferson Davis and the Death Pageant for Lincoln's Corpse.* New York, 2010.

———. *Lincoln's Assassins: Their Trial and Execution.* And Daniel R. Weinberg. New York, 2001.

Taylor, Anne-Marie. *Young Charles Sumner and the Legacy of the American Enlightenment, 1811–1851.* Amherst, Massachusetts, 2001.

Taylor, John M. *William Henry Seward: Lincoln's Right Hand.* New York, 1991.

Thomas, Benjamin P., and Harold M. Hyman. *Stanton: The Life and Times of Lincoln's Secretary of War.* New York, 1962.

Thompson, Julius E. *Lynchings in Mississippi: A History, 1865–1965.* Jefferson, North Carolina, 2000.

Tilden, Samuel J. *Letters and Literary Memorials.* Vols. I and II. John Bigelow, ed. New York, 1908.

Tischauser, Leslie V. *Jim Crow Laws.* Santa Barbara, California, 2012.

Tourgee, Albion Winegar. *The Invisible Empire.* Baton Rouge, Louisiana, 1989.

Trefousse, Hans L. *Andrew Johnson.* New York, 1989.

———. *Benjamin Franklin Wade.* New York, 1963.

———. *Rutherford B. Hayes.* New York, 2002.

———. *Thaddeus Stevens: Nineteenth-Century Egalitarian.* Chapel Hill, North Carolina, 1997.

Trelease, Allen W. *White Terror: The Ku Klux Klan Conspiracy and Southern Reconstruction.* New York, 1971.

Trowbridge, John T. *The South: A Tour of the Battle-fields and Ruined Cities.* Hartford, Connecticut, 1866.

United Press International. *Year in Review, 1963.*

United States Congress. *The Impeachment and Trial of Andrew Johnson, President of the United States.* New York, 1974.

United States Congress. *Report of the Joint Select Committee Appointed to Inquire into the Condition of Affairs in the Late Insurrectionary States.* Washington, D.C., 1872.

Van Deusen, Glyndon G. *Thurlow Weed: Wizard of the Lobby.* Boston, 1947.

Wade, Wyn Craig. *The Fiery Cross: The Ku Klux Klan in America*. New York, 1987.

Warmoth, Henry C. *War, Politics, and Reconstruction* (1930). New York, 2006.

Waugh, Joan. *U. S. Grant: American Hero, American Myth*. Chapel Hill, North Carolina, 2009.

Weaver, Willis. *Meet Edwin M. Stanton: Patriot Preeminent for a Quarter of an Hour*. Chicago, 1922.

Weed, Thurlow. *Autobiography*. Boston, 1884.

Weichmann, Louis J. *A True History of the Assassination of Abraham Lincoln and of the Conspiracy of 1865*. Floyd E. Risvold, ed. New York, 1975.

Wells, Ida B. *Crusade for Justice*. Afreda M. Duster, ed. Chicago, 1970.

———. *Southern Horrors and Other Writings*. Boston, 1997.

Wheelan, Joseph. *Terrible Swift Sword: The Life of General Philip H. Sheridan*. New York, 2012.

Wilentz, Sean. "President Ulysses S. Grant," in Isaacson, *Profiles in Leadership*.

Wilkerson, Isabel. *The Warmth of Other Suns*. New York, 2011.

Williams, Robert C. *Horace Greeley: Champion of American Fredom*. New York, 2006.

Wills, Brian Steel. *A Battle From the Start: The Life of Nathan Bedford Forrest*. New York, 1993.

Wilson, Edmund. *Patriotic Gore*. New York, 1962.

Woodward., C. Vann. *The Strange Career of Jim Crow*. New York, 2002.

Woodworth, Steven E. *Davis and Lee at War*. Lawrence, Kansas, 1995.

———. *Jefferson Davis and His Generals: The Failure of the Confederate Command in the West*. Lawrence, Kansas, 1990.

Wyeth, John Allan. *That Devil Forrest: Life of General Nathan Bedford Forrest*. Baton Rouge, Louisiana, 1959.

Yale Law School, The Avalon Project, History of the Impeachment of Andrew Johnson. avalon.law.yale.edu/19th_century/john_chap_04.asp.

INDEX

NOTE: Bold page numbers refer to photographs

PHOTO CREDITS

ABOUT THE AUTHOR

A. J. Langguth is the author of eight books of nonfiction and three novels. *After Lincoln* marks his fourth book in a series that began in 1988 with *Patriots: The Men Who Started the American Revolution*. He served as a Saigon bureau chief for the *New York Times*, after covering the Civil Rights movement for the newspaper. Langguth taught for three decades at the University of Southern California and retired in 2003 as emeritus professor in the Annenberg School for Communication and Journalism. He lives in Los Angeles.